CASE
The Potential and the Pitfalls

Books and Training Products From QED

DATABASE

Data Analysis: The Key to Data Base Design
Diagnostic Techniques for IMS Data Bases
The Data Dictionary: Concepts and Uses
DB2: The Complete Guide to Implementation
and Use
Logical Data Base Design
DB2 Design Review Guidelines
DB2: Maximizing Performance of Online
Production Systems
Entity-Relationship Approach to Logical Data
Base Design

SYSTEMS DEVELOPMENT

Effective Methods of EDP Quality Assurance
Handbook of Screen Format Design
The Complete Guide to Software Testing
A User's Guide for Defining Software
Requirements
A Structured Approach to Systems Testing
Practical Applications of Expert Systems
Expert Systems Development: Building
PC-Based Applications
Storyboard Prototyping: A New Approach to
User Requirements Analysis
The Software Factory: Mananging Software
Development and Maintenance
Data Architecture: The Information Paradigm
Advanced Topics in Information Engineering

MANAGEMENT

Planning Techniques for Systems
Management
Strategic and Operational Planning for
Information Services
The State of the Art in Decision Support
Systems
The Management Handbook for Information
Center and End-User Computing
Disaster Recovery: Contingency Planning
and Program Analysis
Techniques of Program and System
Maintenance

MANAGEMENT (cont'd)

The Data Processing Training Manager's
Trail Guide
Winning the Change Game
Information Systems Planning for
Competitive Advantage
Critical Issues in Information Processing
Management and Technology
Developing World Class Information
Systems Organization

TECHNOLOGY

Handbook of COBOL Techniques and
Programming Standards
1001 Questions and Answers to Help You
Prepare for the CDP Exam
1001 Questions and Answers to Help You
Prepare for the CSP Exam
VSAM Techniques: Systems Concepts and
Programming Procedures
The Library of Structured COBOL Programs:
Concepts, Definitions, Structure Charts,
Logic, Code
How to Use CICS to Create On-Line
Applications: Methods and Solutions
CICS/VS Command Level Reference Guide
for COBOL Programmers
Data Communications: Concepts and
Systems
Designing and Implementing Ethernet
Networks
C Language for Programmers
Data Network Concepts and Architectures
SQL Spoken Here for DB2: A Tutorial
SQL for dBASE IV
Systems Programmer's Problem Solver
CASE: The Potentials and the Pitfalls

THE QED INDEPENDENT STUDY SERIES

Managing Software Development (Video)
SQL as a Second Language
DB2: Building Online Production Systems
for Maximum Performance (Video)

For Additional Information or a Free Catalog contact

QED INFORMATION SCIENCES, INC. • P. O. Box 82-181 • Wellesley, MA 02181
Telephone: 800-343-4848 or 617-237-5656

CASE
The Potential and the Pitfalls

QED Information Sciences, Inc.
Wellesley, Massachusetts

Library of Congress Catalog Number: 88-35085
International Standard Book Number: 0-89435-285-7

Printed in the United States of America
89 90 91 10 9 8 7 6 5 4 3 2

Library of Congress Cataloging-in-Publication Data

CASE : the potential and the pitfalls / Chantico.
    p. cm.
  ISBN 0-89435-285-7
  1. Computer-aided software engineering. I. Chantico Press.
QA76.758.C37 1989
005.1—dc19

This material was developed by the Chantico Publishing Company, Carrollton,
Texas, in association with the Profit Oriented Systems Planning program.

CONTENTS

PREFACE

Ask anyone involved with information services (IS) what the acronym CASE stands for and you will get a number of different answers. The "A" may stand for aided, assisted or automated. The "S" may stand for systems or software. Not only is there little agreement on what it stands for, there is even less agreement on what constitutes a CASE tool, how it should be used, the potential productivity gain, the costs involved, the training needed or the impact on an organization. This is the natural reaction to any new technology. Touch it, feel it, squeeze it. . . . what will it do for me? . . . will it work? . . . Oh, woe is me!

As more companies are reporting in about their research and experience with CASE, a base of experience seems to support the fact that companies that plan and manage the use of CASE are usually successful. Those that neglect the management and force fit the technology invariably fail. This is not surprising when we consider that lack of good management is the primary reason IS has failed to meet the expectations of senior corporate management. CASE has the potential, in my opinion, to force standardization, structure, interaction and possibly good management practice. Today's complex technology and systems require new approaches. This is what CASE is all about.

The value of this book is that it goes beyond the CASE technology and gives a clear and practical description of the management processes that help IS managers use the technology effectively. It puts the management concerns of systems development in perspective and provides the advice and counsel needed to make the transition from the individual specialist approach to software development to the disciplined, structured world of CASE where there is interaction, consistency and structure.

The authors define CASE as a discipline and structured engineering approach to software and systems development. Modern CASE includes analysis and design tools, coding and programming support tools, and management and project support tools. Learning the technology is the easiest task faced by IS professionals. We are good at learning technology, but we are not good at applying it effectively. Part of this problem is caused by inertia and resistance to change. We saw this in the early days of COBOL. Like COBOL, CASE is here to stay because it does help with systems development. However, it too, brings its share of problems.

One thing is clear. CASE tools are altering the way systems are specified, designed, implemented and maintained. The future will bring more advanced and complex tools that will not only impact the life cycle process but will alter the way that all those involved with systems development will interact with the process. It will do no good to resist this change. The only unanswered question now is, how long will it take this to happen? This book goes a long way toward providing what you need to know so you can answer that question as it applies to you and your organization.

Edwin F. Kerr
Executive Vice President
and Publisher

QED Information Sciences, Inc.

CHAPTER 1

What Is CASE?

Overview

*I*nformation services managers have long been aware of both the potential and the problems of various application systems development methods. They have been alert to the fact that application system development is now much too complex to be attempted without disciplined, standardized methods for managing it. Enter Computer-Aided Systems Engineering (CASE). Commercial software developers and other vendors have also been alert to the fact that development improvements are needed. They have offered a sometimes unrelated profusion of methodologies, systems, and tools intended to enable information services to effectively exploit the vast capabilities of the available technology, both hardware and software. This book is an excellent tool to make the necessary decisions between those various commercial offerings.

CASE can be defined as the disciplined and structured engineering approach to software and systems development. It emphasizes structured methods, with defined and standardized procedures. There is a trend to a convergence of many hardware and software technologies to give the presently available CASE approaches. Modern CASE includes analysis and design tools, coding and programming support tools, and management and project support tools.

CASE is not limited to any particular set of tools available from vendors today. There is a continuum of methods in the CASE arena that stretches from their use on PCs to central computers to cooperative networks. CASE is a concept that application systems can be "engineered," and more and more management and systems approaches will come under this umbrella, spanning the full systems development life cycle.

CASE is most effective when the change to it in the organization is managed well. Methodology is next in importance, followed by an understanding of the techniques and the technology. CASE can provide across-the-board staff productivity improvement. In doing so, it can also substantially increase systems quality, which can alleviate later maintenance. CASE is an important part of the overall problem of application development and maintenance. It helps meet the current challenges of productivity improvement and timely support of executive management.

1.1   THE VALUE OF THIS BOOK TO YOU

Key elements of CASE have been proven and are a practical reality. There is considerable momentum towards the greater use of effective and efficient CASE methods. Many corporations have successfully used a wide variety of CASE tools and techniques to improve their system development productivity and the quality of their systems. Others have been less successful in the implementation of CASE methods, however. What is the difference? The former have managed the change to CASE effectively; the latter have concentrated on the methodology and techniques, and have neglected the overall management control. CASE is advertised by vendors as a variety of technology-oriented packages—the "tool kit" of CASE. This is a smoke screen that obscures the vision of strategic CASE implementation. The "tools" that are being sold are only useful if management insists that CASE be planned and managed, step by step. CASE succeeds when it is approached by users as a philosophy of developing application systems, with an associated body of knowledge and a number of tested techniques. Always remember that the order of importance in the management of CASE projects is:

- Managing the change in the organization in thought and method.
- Developing a coordinated methodology in which all participate.
- Understanding the available techniques and their usefulness.
- Reviewing the technology and selecting appropriate systems tools.

This book has been written, first, to give a clear and practical description of the management processes that are available to help both information services managers and the developers of application systems to decide on the optimum methods and approaches to use for their specific problems. Secondly, it has been written to clarify the uses of the various new methodologies and tools. Some specific tools are addressed and their uses described, but there is no attempt to list all the available tools and their vendors. Such lists are frequently published and updated in a variety of technical journals. But such lists are of much greater value when the concerned manager initially makes a careful decision on the functional requirements that are desired, and then makes an objective, weighted selection of the best tool to employ, considering the various factors that are described in this book.

This book puts the management concerns of application systems development in perspective. It emphasizes the new systems development improvements that can be acquired, developed, or otherwise realized, and it describes how to define, compare, and decide on the key points of differentiation between the useful variety of development methodologies that are available on the market. There is a concentration on the obvious need for the enhancement of application development productivity. The different perceptions of what is needed in application system development management, automation, and organization are clarified. It shows where the various approaches that are being called "CASE" methods actually fit in the overall picture, and outlines the relationship of the great variety of viewpoints that have sprung up.

This book gives practical, how-to advice on the many problems of system development project management and on the comparison and selection of commercial offerings. It reminds the reader of numerous, important management considerations in the related areas of systems planning, staff organization, data administration, internal control, security, and disaster recovery. In short, the Computer-Aided Software Engineering book is a valuable compendium of clearly explained management methods and procedures for the design, production, and maintenance of effective, efficient, and profitable computerized application systems.

The development of useful and controllable applications software for computers is clearly the most difficult and complex task facing information services management. There is much more computer power available in the hardware of the average organization than is ever used for profit and competitive advantage. There are many excellent ideas simply waiting to be implemented, but many of them simply tend to be relegated to the "backlog," which has grown steadily and consistently over the years. But the backlog sits there not because there are no people to handle it, but because those necessary people are engaged elsewhere, on the ever-present and omnivorous maintenance tasks. We are spending our time patching older systems instead of designing newer and more effective systems that may well have strategic advantages to the corporation. CASE methods do not suddenly wave a magic wand over this dilemma and solve it, but they help us to build new systems or to reengineer older systems today that will reduce the future maintenance effort. We must continue to solve today's problems, laboriously and one at a time. The use of CASE, however, will allow us to solve tomorrow's problems much more expeditiously than we solve today's problems.

This book points out that the use of CASE is *not* a way of greatly increasing systems development productivity immediately. In fact, the initial CASE systems development efforts may take longer to accomplish than development of less formal methods. But the use of CASE *is* a way of greatly increasing future systems productivity through the introduction of more efficient methods, the improvement of systems quality, and the marked reduction of the subsequent maintenance work that will be needed on the developed systems. It is clear that in the long-term, adopting CASE approaches will greatly decrease the cost of maintaining systems.

This point is emphasized several times in this book because present experience is that anywhere from 50 to 90 percent of the systems staff effort in a typical information services organization is being devoted to maintenance of older systems. Therefore, if we can learn from the experiences of others and start using a systems development methodology that will substantially reduce this major maintenance effort in the near future, it will be attractively profitable to do so. How does one do this? By following the management approaches that are detailed in the following pages.

1.2 APPLICATION DEVELOPMENT AND MAINTENANCE

CASE is at the heart of systems development work, but it is only one particular area in the overall corporate problem of application development and maintenance. It is currently the area with much attention in the literature, and with the most tools being developed by vendors, but it is only part of the overall systems development efforts. In America, CASE is becoming more inclusive and is incorporating many management and control methods. It is moving toward the concept that is already popular in Europe, Integrated Programming Support Environments (IPSE), which groups management and planning tools with the application development tools. There is every reason to believe that the boundaries described for CASE in this book will be constantly enlarging in the next several years. This is one reason why this book is part of a planned series covering several areas of overall management interest in application development and maintenance. Suffice to say, CASE is positioned centrally in all the areas of management concern in systems development.

Information services management has a problem, and CASE is positioned to solve it. The concerns of management spring from the growth in demand that is illustrated in Figure 1. There has been a steady increase in the purchase of both hardware and software over the years, and this increase is expected to accelerate rather than slow down. The demands for personnel to run the hardware and to develop the software or to adapt purchased software are stretching the capabilities of nearly all corporations, particularly in light of the common management insistence on flat

FIGURE 1. The information services problem.

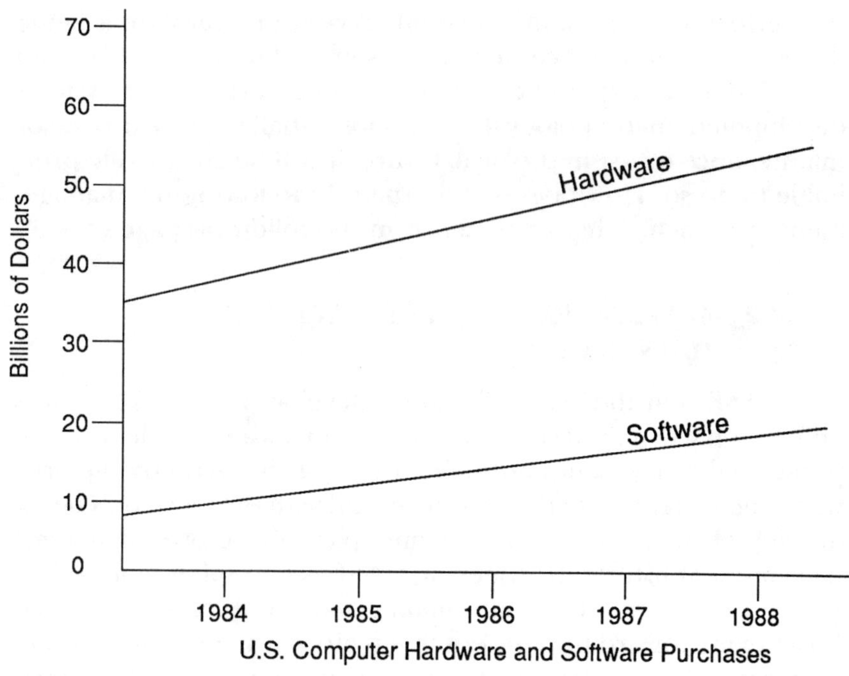

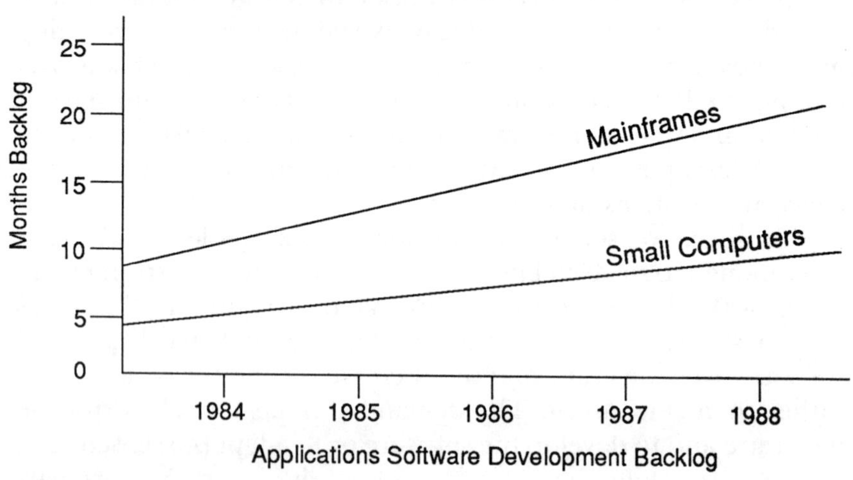

budgets. This results in the continuing increase of applications software development backlog, principally because of the proliferation of small computers: personal computers, departmental minicomputers, micros as terminals, and control computers. The "PC revolution" was touted as cutting the application backlog and as doing away with central, large computers. Instead, the PCs have become so powerful that there is a new, large demand for complex application software for them, and there is a tremendous demand put on the central computers to turn out greater volumes of usable data from the corporate files.

There are two major challenges facing information services managers today in the area of application development and maintenance. The number-one issue in larger organizations is productivity. Any way of improving the productivity of the costly staff working on the development and maintenance of application systems is always welcomed. Productivity in the development process is difficult to measure on a comparative basis, however, as will be discussed, and the reported results of experimental approaches have hàd mixed success. To management, productivity is frequently simply equated with beating promised delivery dates and planned costs. Thus, they often view traditional computer systems development work as unproductive, since there are frequent time overruns.

The second issue is supplying adequate support to executive management, gaining credibility with executive management, and becoming more aligned with the business functions. This is a challenge that every group faces—trying to get more in touch with the business side and providing services that will be supportive. Management will generally believe that they are being properly supported by information services if there is responsiveness to requests for computer systems solutions. They expect answers in the time frame that will do the business some good. They also expect good control over the time estimation, effort expended, and product delivery of systems.

These two challenges cannot be met when the applications development people are mired down in older approaches and methodologies that set them apart from mainline company personnel and thwarted communications with management in the past. When management is concerned with such things as the global nature of competition and the economy and the shifting values of the dollar, they are little inclined to be patient with systems development groups that are using the same old excuses for never meeting their deadlines and for being unable to keep up with system requests and maintenance. There is a clear and compelling need for information services people to learn and adopt new approaches to applications development and new methods for managing their work, so that they can be responsive to management and can talk in terms of plan-vs-actual, budget variances, and time-phased staff assignments. Recognized professionalism is a necessity.

Information services often plays a central role in an organization, whether or not the computer management people are considered truly professional. The computer systems tie together and support all of the major functional areas of the business. More and more, developers of computer systems are being driven towards understanding both the outside forces and the internal factors that influence the business so that they can clearly recognize the business necessities and priorities. Business factors must drive the applications development efforts, even with the complexity of increasing business change and uncertainty. The implications of this situation are that computer-driven applications must be tied more closely to the constantly moving business targets, and that systems must be professionally developed, under control, and on time.

There are also clear enterprise demands being forced on the information services function. The critical ones are:

- More strategic applications in order to maintain competitive advantages.

- More flexible and more rapidly constructed executive decision support systems to aid the management decision process.

- More effective methods for delivering application systems, in a time frame that is of interest to management.

- More responsiveness to requests for application systems, so that they can be of rapid advantage to the business.

- Greater flexibility in adapting systems to business change and uncertainty.

These enterprise demands may be met in a variety of ways by the information services function, but the area that has the most room for improvement is the development, installation, and maintenance of application systems. Application systems are the core issue in meeting management demands. Information services groups exist to deliver operational application systems. There should be management emphasis on improving this delivery for several reasons:

- Application systems provide the fundamental operating controls for the enterprise.
- Application systems provide the foundation data for specialized analysis and decision support systems.
- Application systems are increasingly providing the key competitive advantage for the successful enterprise.
- Application development and maintenance efforts account for an important part of information services expenditures.

In the face of these imperatives, information services (IS) truly has a dilemma facing their management. The predicament that IS is finding itself in over time is that the complexity of the environment is changing extremely rapidly, as illustrated in Figure 2. The rate of change is accelerating in all areas. Products such as CASE packages are proliferating. New methodologies are changing the old tried-and-true methods. New technologies in hardware, software, and communications are introducing new approaches and demands for newly trained people. The biggest part of the dilemma still comes from the ever-growing backlog of required maintenance. The central issue within the average IS department today is the maintenance of their large number of existing systems that are crucial to the operation of the organization. Typically, surveys find that 50 percent to 80 percent of the applications development resources are dedicated to maintenance. That problem will not soon go away, and new ways are needed for addressing it. Some of these ways will be discussed.

Effective and efficient applications development and maintenance is clearly a critical success factor for the enterprise of the 1990s. The role of information systems is growing in importance,

FIGURE 2. The information services dilemma.

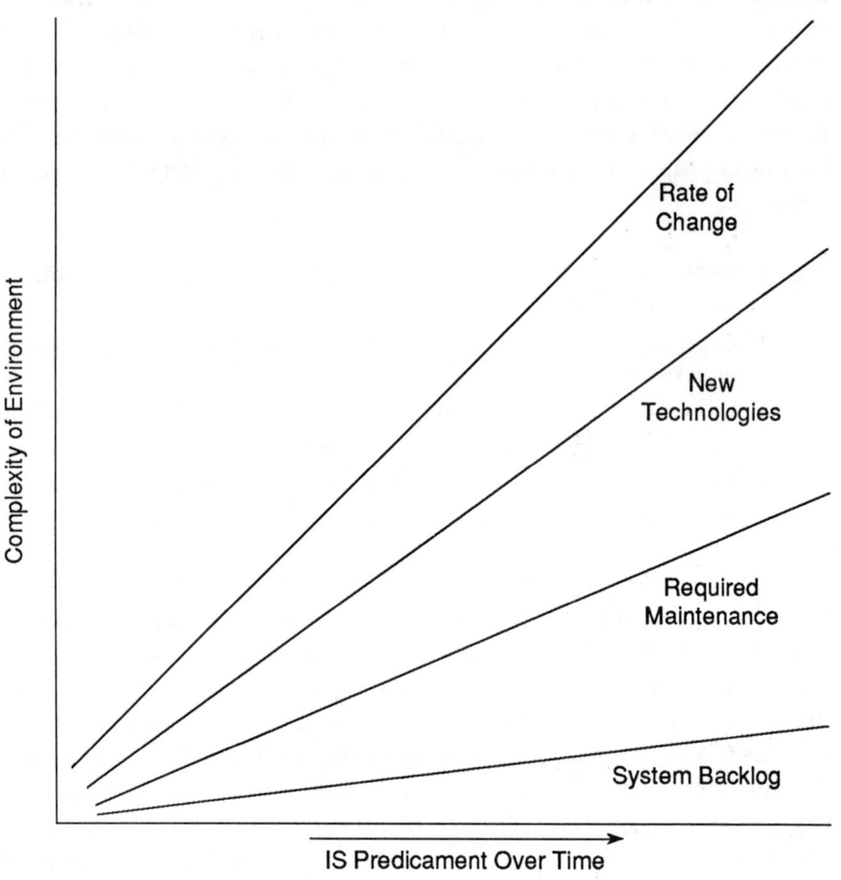

and applications development is a central part of information systems.

- We need to develop quality systems, and we need to be able to do it quickly and effectively.
- We need to help management capitalize on business opportunities by giving them strategic systems in the time frame they request.
- We need to enhance critical business decisions by developing effective executive support systems.

Applications development and maintenance is a broad subject within the broader area of information services, and CASE is only one critical part of it. This book will extend the normally too narrow boundaries of CASE, however, by touching on such subjects as:

- Transitional methodologies for nonautomated systems.
- Productivity across the whole range of information services, from planning to operations.
- The decision whether to use reverse engineering on existing systems, or to continue with maintenance.
- The management of technological change for the benefit of the enterprise, including the change review process.
- The process of application portfolio assessment and selection.
- The search for business priorities and strategic initiatives.
- Structured approaches imposed on the traditional system development life cycle.
- Code generators and shell codes for improving productivity and quality.
- The use of fourth-generation languages.
- The advantages of embedding knowledge-based systems within other systems.

Even though the computer technology is changing rapidly, a large amount of what is done to develop applications is oriented to people rather than technology. This means that, although descriptions are given of technologies, processes, and methodologies, it is often not easy to get your hands around the real problems. But for those in charge of applications development in organizations, it is obvious that many functions have a level of commonality. And for those who understand the new possibilities, it is possible to become a catalyst for change. Ideas can often generate the momentum and support needed to break the bonds of inertia. Possibly productivity improvement can be the rallying cry. Whether your company is rapidly expanding, rapidly contracting, or trying to remain level, "more results from fewer resources" is the current requirement. The concepts in this book follow the threads of productivity and quality improvement through many different avenues. They are intended to help you:

- Look at the current and emerging technologies.
- Explore a variety of organizational concepts.
- Examine different paths of communication.

The fundamental principles of technology management are simple:

- Stick to the basics. Know who your customers are. Deliver a quality product that meets the customer's needs on time and within budget.
- Focus on the accomplishments, the plan-vs-actual, within your own organization. Ignore the folklore published by the technical press that says that everyone else is getting 150 percent improvements with this technique or that. Relax, as it is not likely that you or your professional colleagues could have missed a trick that would instantly boost productivity.
- In all cases, measure. A crude measurement is better than none at all. As time goes on, the measurement process can be refined and the ambiguity reduced. Ambiguity does not always mean lack of direction. People respond to being treated as intelligent.

Within the broad spectrum of building and maintaining computer-based applications, this book is written to explore the reality of CASE, the way that some companies have implemented the concepts, and the possible future opportunities as seen by companies, academic institutions, and vendors. The procedures, worksheets, checklists, and other suggestions are starting points for you that should be freely tailored to make them fit your own environments.

1.3 CASE TECHNOLOGIES

Computer-Aided Software Engineering, or CASE, is the disciplined and structured engineering approach to systems development. It is in no sense limited by any given set of systems development "tools" or procedures. It is not a prescribed methodology. It simply takes the classical engineering approach that there is a commonality of data structures and computer processes such that the mathematical and computer science assumptions and processes may be applied uniformly to the system of concern. There are numerous CASE "technologies." A number of different vendor-supplied tools, user-prepared routines, and database files may be linked and used conjointly to yield a desired result, which can be determined analytically in advance.

Software engineering is an emerging discipline with a goal of producing reliable software products cost-effectively. It does this with a number of technologies, including structured techniques and automated development systems. Its various elements have been developed independently for the past 25 years, and have been brought together as a cohesive approach in the last few years. In the past, it has been experimental. It has now been proven and is changing the way information services works.

CASE makes the transition from the world of individual, unique approaches in software development to a disciplined, structured, standardized world of software engineering. The production of software is in the process of growing up from a world of individual specialists, or artists, to an engineering world where a group of technologists can freely interrelate their information and interconnect their programs.

A software system can be defined as an organized collection of data, machines, procedures, documents, and other entities that interact with each other and their environment to attain a desired goal. That is why software engineering is only part of the whole picture. Software engineering obviously handles the automated procedures, but it must also consider the manual procedures, the data, the human interface, and the organization of the network of machines to support the whole. Mechanical engineers do not design a factory without considering the flow of materials and goods and the activities of the factory personnel. Thus the overall thrust of software engineering includes all aspects of the system that will be run, centered on the computers. CASE technologies are of greatest use when they are integrated into a whole system rather than standing alone.

It has become much clearer in recent years that the users— the clients—are really only interested in a complete operational system that performs the procedures they need. For 20 to 30 years, information system professionals, on the other hand, have been working out how to apply technology to bring organized automation to the central aspects of the systems desired by users. Users have been asked to "fit in" to the realistic bounds of the available technology, and often to change their requirements to adapt to the operation that can be made available. CASE technologies are allowing us to systematically rethink the "system" from one with specific program limits to one that approaches the users' desires.

CASE technologies are engineering technologies. Engineering is defined by *Webster's* as "the application of science and mathematics by which the properties of matter and the sources of energy in nature are made useful to man in structures, machines, products, systems, and processes." This is exactly analagous to CASE in information systems. Science and mathematics are obviously applied. For "the properties of matter and the sources of energy in nature," simply read "the properties of data and the sources of computational energy." For what we are producing are data structures, computing machines, information products, application systems, and system processes.

But what do we really mean when we call the application development process "engineering"? We mean that we are agreeing:

- To accept a common set of assumptions, and ways of describing those assumptions.

- To use provable structures and proven, reusable sets of code.

- To describe all facets of the description and calculations in a standardized, well-understood manner.

- To display the information, processes, and resultant outputs in standardized, well-understood formats.

- To use the system itself to produce clear and common documentation.

Whether an engineer is in America, Germany, or China, there are common graphic symbols that are used for communication and well understood by all. For example, the symbol *Si* would be immediately recognized in France, Canada, and Japan as the symbol for Silicon, and would carry with it all the common understanding of the properties, structure, and chemical reactions of Silicon. There are few direct analogies of such clear and information-intensive symbols in systems engineering, but we are now developing many structured techniques, diagrams, and graphical methods that will readily cross language barriers. The interesting thing is that many of the language barriers between countries have been no more difficult in the past than those between the system development professionals and the end user, such as an accountant. CASE technologies are offering the future opportunity of considerable commonality of language in the computer area.

The essence of all CASE technologies is that they have a structured approach. This means that they consist of a way of attacking systems development that has well-defined methods and standardized procedures. These methods and procedures are used because they have a sound theoretical basis. They also call for meaningful, standardized documentation. Thus the results of a structured approach are that:

- The system has a well-defined structure.
- Parts of the system have reusability characteristics at many levels.
- The system and its components are well documented.

An important aspect of a structured approach that is always present in good CASE applications is that any element, module, or section of it can be readily understood by someone other than its writer who is trained in that method. This means that groups of systems analysts and programmers can work more closely together, follow what is being done, and interface easily with any part of it. Users can state their requirements in a formal way, and there can be easy translation of those requirements into the pool of information that is being used by the group. Structured input yields structured output in a uniformly understood path and pattern. This is the engineering approach in action.

Within this fairly broad definition of CASE, then, what are the technologies? The subject is complex, because different vendors draw their own circles within which to place CASE, and claim to limit it. This introduction has simply established the field in which the game of CASE is played. The rules will vary, but they should all be considered as subsets of the whole CASE arena.

Figure 3 is the classical representation of the interlocking of areas that may be completely separate in individual software packages. Management methods, CASE development techniques, and CASE tools are separate technology areas, but are interdependent and are all needed for CASE efforts.

- First, if there are CASE tools and CASE development techniques in place, but no management methods, there will be no management support and no standards. This will result in no consistency in the application products and no way of integrating multiple efforts.

- Second, if there are management methods and CASE tools in place, but no CASE development techniques, the result will be no training in methodology and little acceptance of the multiple CASE tools with no coherent driving technique.

- Third, if there are management methods and CASE development techniques in place, the result will be an expensive, uncoordinated mixture of CASE tools that is quite impractical to use to develop a full system.

All three types of CASE technologies are required. They are like the legs of a three-legged stool. If any are missing, the effort will collapse. As shown in Figure 3, they are interlocking, inter-

FIGURE 3. CASE technologies.

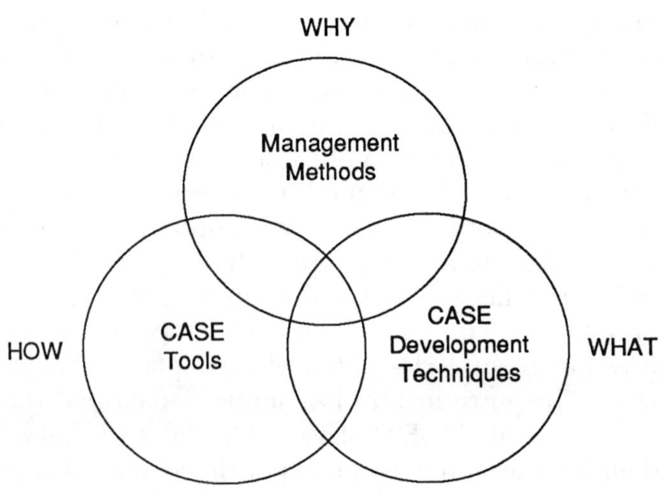

dependent, and indispensable. The relationship between methodology, technique, and tool in CASE offerings is hierarchical. Management methods should control the CASE development techniques, and the development techniques should control the use of the CASE tools.

A CASE management method is the overview of the use of CASE. It covers WHY the work is to be done and how it will be controlled. It sets the plan and the objectives to be reached. A CASE development technique covers WHAT should be done to implement and use CASE tools. It is the logical and coordinated approach to the use of CASE tools. CASE tools indicate HOW CASE efforts are physically accomplished. They are the computer application systems that aid in the delivery of CASE applications.

Figure 4 elaborates on these three areas of CASE technologies.

- MANAGEMENT METHODS establish the CONTROL that is necessary to set plans and objectives, to ascertain that the plans are being followed, and to determine when the objectives have been met. Examples of management methods are: systems planning and the setting of objectives, fixing and measuring metrics to ascertain accomplishment, the estimation and management of projects, and the management of a set of structured postulates employed by a discipline, such as CASE.

- CASE DEVELOPMENT TECHNIQUES are the PROCESSES by which the CASE work is carried out and the CASE tools are used. They are usually structured development methodologies. A methodology is a system of methods, rules, and the set of procedural steps to be followed in order to achieve a desired end. It is a systematic way of doing things. These are the structured development methodologies. For example, information engineering can be classed as a methodology. It is a philosophical approach that looks first at the business area, then at the opportunities for automation, then the procedures to be followed and the steps to be taken. Other processes or techniques include dataflow diagramming and the use of relational databases. Reverse engineering can be classed as a process, since it includes the use of a number of tools. Expert systems and prototyping are approaches, or processes, rather than tools. Another technique is IBM's JAD (Joint Application Design), which is an approach to bringing user and developer together. CASE techniques are an essential part of the implementation of specific CASE tools.

FIGURE 4. CASE technologies (Cont.)

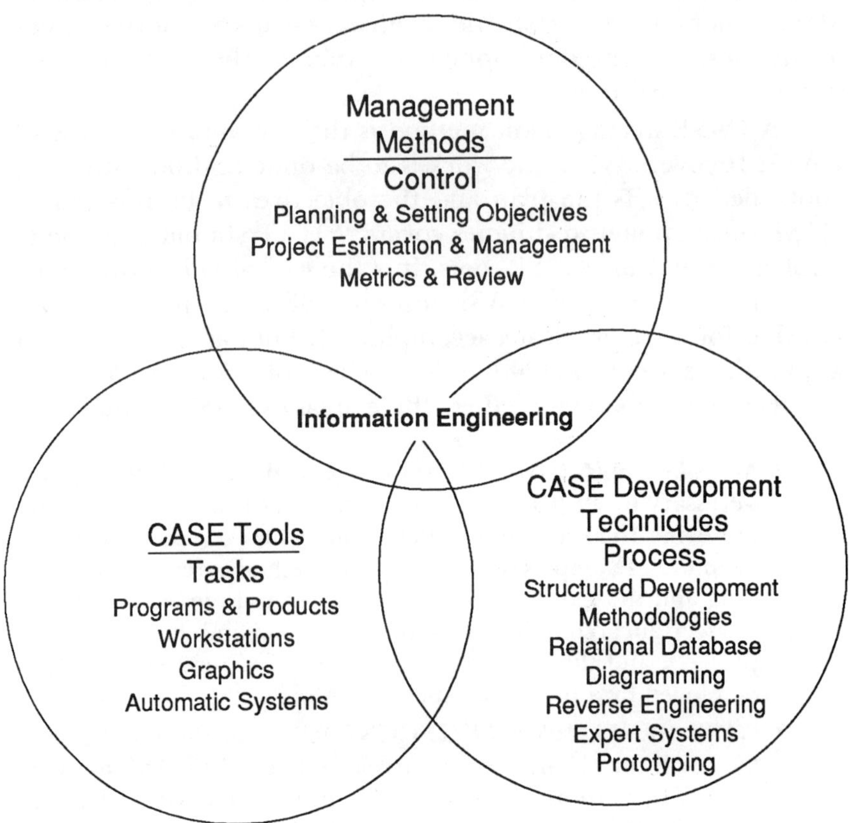

- CASE TOOLS perform the TASKS necessary in CASE development processes. They provide the capabilities of performing steps in the methodologies. They are objects that make a technique easier, or possible, to apply. Tools are physical things which support the application of the technique. The CASE programs and products that are advertised are principally CASE tools. They include graphics systems, for example, and numerous other automatic design and programming products. Workstations designed for CASE work may also be considered as CASE hardware tools.

The degree of coupling between method, technique, and tool is important to understand. On the opposite end of this spectrum are two popular CASE products, Index Technology's *Excelerator* and Texas Instrument's *Information Engineering Facility*. The product *Excelerator* is the most widely used and has the largest market share today. It is a product that contains a number of tools. It has a tool for drawing dataflow diagrams, a tool for drawing inter-relationship diagrams, and a dictionary for capturing the descriptions of the data that appear in these diagrams. It is easy to use, and can be used as a presentation aid. It does not enforce any sequence for doing things, so any part may be used at any time. It is neutral towards any methodology.

The *Information Engineering Facility*, at the other extreme, has been specifically designed to support the methodology of information engineering in a rigorous way. You must begin by doing an interrelationship analysis. You then have to do a process analysis and bring the two together and refine them. There is a specific set of tools that have to be used together in a specific way. If you do that, things come together. You get through the life cycle, press a button, and out comes a generated application.

Just as CASE tools alone do not make up a CASE effort but are completely intertwined with CASE development techniques and management methods, neither do the three CASE areas shown in Figures 3 and 4 make up a successful CASE effort that is completely integrated with the organization and with other information services activities. Management cannot run CASE by a set of structured and objective methods that give them some control. It is imperative that a full CASE environment be established for optimum results. This is illustrated in Figure 5. Setting up such an environment requires leadership from the director of information services, cooperation between all the groups involved, and the direct interest of senior management. All groups that are interested in, or can contribute to, the success of the CASE effort should participate. Some of the key elements of an optimum CASE environment are:

- *Management commitment* at all levels, indicated by continuing participation and an adequate budget. It is insufficient for management to simply express their interest in CASE and sign off a set of objectives. There must be enough detailed interest shown as the work progresses so that all who are involved understand that

FIGURE 5. CASE environment.

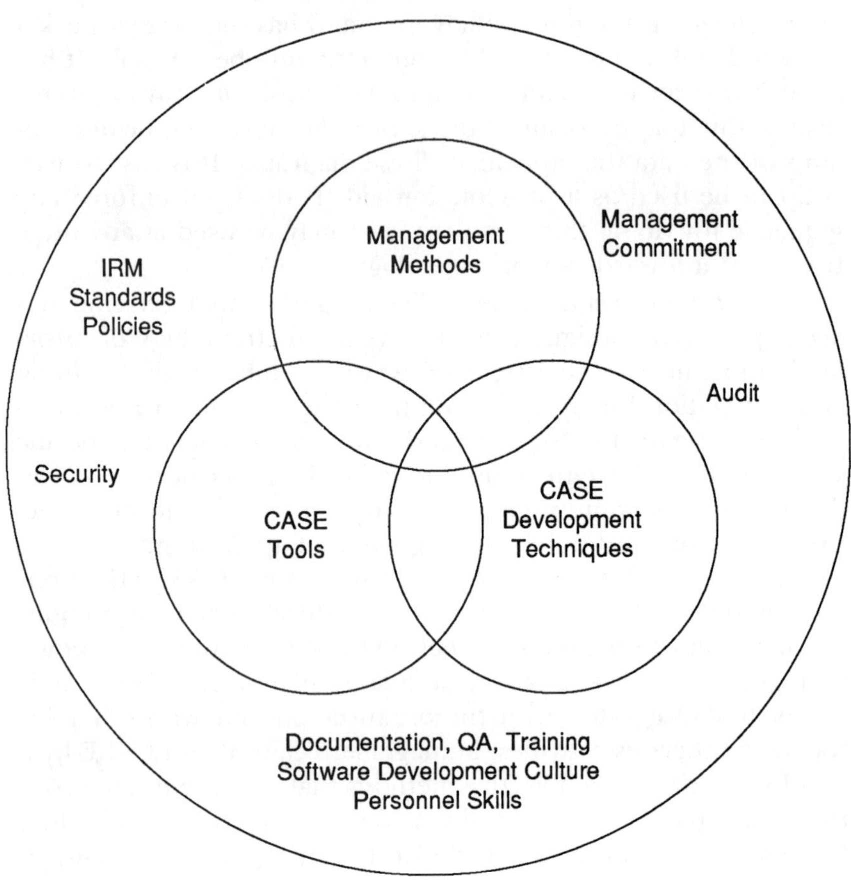

they have backing for the full time it takes to produce results. There must be understanding that CASE is not simply a one-year project that succeeds and fails on the products at the end of that year, but that it is a new philosophy that takes time to reach fruition. Management commitment is proven at budget time during the second and third years of the effort.

- *Information Resource Management* as an umbrella over all the Information Services efforts that brings CASE into the mainstream of the development efforts and supplies the information and tools that are necessary to fit CASE-developed products with other systems. IRM is a philosophy of unity and single control over all development and operational areas around the computers. This is the type of environment that CASE efforts require.

- *Policies and standards* flow naturally from IRM and an attempt to establish a cooperative CASE environment. They set the boundaries and the rules, and indicate territory. They are a necessary part of attaining objectives.

- *Audit* plays a key role that is seldom appreciated by professional system developers. Not only does audit reveal whether policies and standards are being adhered to and whether the objectives are being reached, but it also presents such information in terms that demand the attention of senior management. Favorable audits can go a long way toward maintaining management commitment at higher levels.

- *Security and disaster recovery* concerns must be an integral part of a CASE environment that is accepted by users and management alike. One of the great advantages of CASE is that it states objectively what is happening in the systems development work, and operational management feel that they have some control over it. CASE helps to explain to them the actual operation of highly technical systems. As soon as they grasp such information, they will be equally concerned with the audit controls, the security controls, and the disaster recovery preparations that have been designed.

- *Documentation and library management* are fundamental to CASE. CASE development moves from document to document automatically. Those parts of documentation and library management that are not automatic in the systems used must be carefully coordinated with the whole body of documentation and kept up to date and available.

- *Quality Assurance (QA)* brings together and reports many of the points that have been noted above. QA checks on the following of policies, standards, procedures, audit controls, and security controls. It reviews whether the activities are leading to the objectives in a recognized way. Like audit reports, QA reports find their way to management desks and can solidify management interest in the work.

- *Training and the selection and development of personnel skills* has new demands as CASE is used, and there must be a complete understanding of what is being attempted in CASE with the staff groups involved. There may be a need to change or scrap time-honored courses. There may be a need for new considerations in hiring. In many companies already, CASE has lead to a restructuring of position titles and a rewriting of position descriptions. The personnel involved must understand the reason for, and the direction of, such changes.

- A new *software development culture* starts developing under CASE, which may not easily fit into the thinking of many of the experienced staff. Management commitment and the clear statement of management policies can start changing the culture, but, basically, it can only be changed by the supervisors of the work teams. In their routine activities they must embrace the CASE concepts and not struggle against them. They may not like the "hype" and the enthusiastic articles written about CASE, but they must be prepared for a new outlook on systems development, new relationships with the users, and new staff functions in the work groups. It is obviously imperative that management attention and training classes be directed more toward the experienced development staff that will be crucial to the CASE tasks than to new staff and the lower levels.

Thus CASE is not just a set of new, highly advertised tools and the methodologies that pull them together and coordinate them. There are many highly technical and complex elements in the systems and programs that drive the automation of the tasks within CASE and produce the results and their documentation. Such "high-tech" approaches do *not* operate successfully untouched by human hands. They must be organized by people and controlled by people. Those people must be trained and managed. The managers must know what is going on. CASE is *not* just a set of tools. CASE is a philosophy of systems development that requires the establishment of an environment where all efforts are coordinated and everyone knows what is happening. A functional, well-managed CASE environment is essential to the success of CASE efforts.

1.4   A CONTINUUM OF CASE METHODS

No CASE tools stand alone as a unique and separate set of system development tools to be used only by a select group, such as professional systems analysts on the central computer. CASE is definitely not limited to the tools and methods mentioned in this book, or to any particular vendor's integrated set of CASE tools. There is a continuum of methods in the CASE arena that stretches from productivity aids for users developing systems on PCs, to the familiar CASE tool sets on mixed configurations of large and mini- and microcomputers, to the advanced networked systems of the future developed with cooperative application development and operated under cooperative processing. All these methods are spanned by management control systems, quality assurance, and training systems, among others. The CASE approach will develop and expand rapidly in the future, with such features as:

- Full coverage of the whole system life cycle.
- Coordination of CASE systems from various vendors.
- Reverse engineering of massive amounts of code that is embedded in production systems.
- The detailed capture of physical usage information, even in complex networks.
- The ready simulation of advanced production systems.
- Technology selection during the modeling phase.
- User specifications leading directly to system design and development.

The key feature of CASE work in the future will be the tight linking of tools, systems, and management controls, starting with the design phase, to yield the optimum group of CASE tools for a particular application design. Also, the problem space will extend far beyond the types of applications that are now being handled, to complex configurations and mixtures of new development and reverse engineering.

CASE is *not* just a certain set of tools. *CASE is a concept that application systems can be "engineered."* CASE can include any approach where science and mathematics are applied (engineered) in tested and recognizable ways to use the properties of computers and computer languages to develop computer systems in a way that can be anticipated, validated, and reproduced. This means that:

- In any organization, there exists a common set of data with properties that can be described.

- The wide and growing range of CASE tools is essentially standard analytical and design methods, and can be cataloged, used when needed, and strung together in different combinations.

- A number of trained professionals, who understand the data sets and the use of the tools, can be involved in the development process interchangeably and cooperatively.

- Those who are not systems professionals but who will be using the final, engineered products, have a key role to play throughout the development cycle, in the analysis, design, code generation, and testing phases. They will gain systems expertise as they participate, and will eventually take over more and more of the process.

- As an engineered system is developed, it will be thoroughly documented in a coordinated manner at every step of the way. This documentation will continue to be available, and be updated, throughout the modification and maintenance phase.

- There is no "final" CASE software product with a fixed and rigid design, but CASE products will continue to be developed in an evolutionary way. Every further maintenance or development effort will be able to draw on all that has been learned in the previous efforts with that system.

This means that systems development under the CASE approach can be handled with varying tools and methods, so long as they all integrate with the data files and the documentation system. They do not have to all be labeled as "CASE" tools, but can be a variety of systems and methodologies that fit together and can be managed. The intent is to span the full system development cycle with automated tools. Different companies will link their own selection of a group of systems packages to develop unique system combinations that provide their own new, effective, controlled environment for application development.

Do *not* put CASE tools in a labeled box to distinguish them from all other tools. There is no reason, for example, that the many high-productivity applications development systems on microcomputers, such as screen generators, cross-tabulation systems, fourth-generation languages, and so on, cannot be included in the range of CASE tools as long as they can be integrated with the existing CASE tools and are controlled in this own use in an engineering sense.

IPSE.

In Europe, the continuum of CASE methods is recognized by the acceptance of *Integrated Project Support Environment (IPSE)*. IPSE is a term that includes the full life-cycle impact of new tools on all aspects of systems development. Many CASE tools have been developed as standalone applications and are intended to aid the early phases of systems development. They are most useful in the preliminary and detailed design of systems, and some are useful for code generation and debugging. IPSE includes all the phases of systems development, from planning and project selection through the requirements definition and the full structured development methodology to the installation and control of the application system. IPSE is a logical extension of the wide variety of CASE tools to coordinate their use and to impose management control over the whole development process.

IPSE was developed in Europe by a consortium of large firms. The European Commission hopes to develop a comprehensive "environment" that provides automated, integrated tools for all aspects of software development. In the past several years, the "Esprit" project has developed sweeping standards for the approach. This group involves Bull in France, GEC and ICL in Britain, Nixdorf and Siemens in West Germany, and Olivetti in Italy. The goal of the work is to develop a "software factory" with automated tools for every facet of programming and development. Similar approaches are being followed by firms in Japan and by Microelectronics & Computer Technology Corp. (MCC) in Austin, Texas.

IPSE is an "environmental" approach that provides a framework for all the CASE tools that may be used. It has proven a realistic way to introduce standardization to the systems development process in Europe. IPSE offers the possibility of looking at all development efforts together and making a reasonable estimate of the productivity of the parts and of the use of all CASE tools that interact.

The way many CASE tools are now marketed, they may be looked upon as project-oriented. Their virtues are described in terms of particular phases or steps in the overall process. They may be risk-prone because their interaction with other methods is not known. IPSE thinking is less risky because it is less project-oriented and more method-oriented. It has been attractive in Europe because it has been looked on as an architectural solution that helps systems design approach classical engineering. It is an approach that builds the conceptual framework for the system, its budgeting, and its management first, after which specific applications are derived.

This thinking in the whole continuum of CASE methods is particularly attractive to planners because it supports the notion of developing applications in the context of a company's overall business strategy and plans. It helps to bring together the thinking of those planning strategic systems development with those planning particular systems designs, and with those concerned with controlling the systems development and increasing the overall productivity of the development, the operations, and the systems maintenance and control groups all at the same time.

Many CASE tools are quite technical in their description, and when they are described to management to obtain funds for purchasing them, they look like another piece of obscure technical equipment that must be acquired simply because information services says it is needed. The relationship to business advantage is not clear. The use of an overall framework puts the CASE tools and other purchases in perspective to management. It not only emphasizes planning and relationship to business needs, but it also emphasizes integration of techniques and commitment to a methodology that should maximize the investments that have already been made. This gives a more attractive message to management and a very clear message to those who are responsible for screening new techniques and products.

If company management sends conflicting signals about developing excellent applications but delivering them in impossible time frames, methodologies are pushed aside. Possibly, certain techniques will be used, but usually the tried-and-true methods will simply be used overtime. Methodologies that offer future advantages but with more time spent in the early stages are simply unattractive. A CASE framework, such as IPSE, is valuable in presenting the concepts to management. Management may have trouble comprehending a new detailed design methodology, but they understand a system that puts all of the development activities in perspective. In fact, although the term IPSE will probably never catch on universally in America, there are many signs that the concept of an integrated planning, design, development, and control environment has already caught on with many firms, particularly those with very large systems development staffs and consequently large budgets. The full environment and its full budget are usually managed at a single point, and most information services managers recognize that all the parts interact and are interdependent. *There is a continuum of CASE methods.*

The key to increased productivity in systems development is the integration of all systems development activities so that advantages in one activity will aid another activity, possibly under a different supervisor. In the last analysis, while many tools may be very helpful, and all the tools offered may be helpful somewhere, future productivity gains are only realized when there is an effective way of managing the people resources. To manage the people resources, there must be effective ways of:

- Training people in new techniques.
- Planning and budgeting the use of people.
- Using project management systems that provide useful information.
- Reviewing accomplishments based on planned activity and actual results.

This means that planning tools, project management tools, and control tools are as important in systems development as the more obvious CASE tools. They all work together and are part of the whole picture. Whether the term IPSE is used or not is immaterial. What is important is that management understands that a whole environment of acceptance of the new techniques is required for the successful implementation of CASE.

1.5   *THE MAJOR ELEMENTS OF SYSTEMS ENGINEERING*

Engineering is a discipline. The acceptance of such an approach requires management commitment, substantial investment, time for training and experimentation, an accepted control structure, and a cooperative effort by a number of groups under different managers. These are not easily obtained; there will be technical, political, and staff capability problems. But the successful results will be highly profitable, and will have considerable, long-term, beneficial effects. What, then, are the areas of systems development that will be favorably affected? They are the areas in which systems engineering is proving to have an impact in the systems development process. The principal areas are:

- The *Software Development Life Cycle* (SDLC) is being markedly modified, as will be discussed in Chapter 3, "How to Manage CASE." The emphasis on the early phases of the SDLC is changing relative amounts of effort in the different phases.

- The *software development* process is being automated in a number of areas, particularly in design and coding. The automation makes the phases more systematic and controllable.

- *Documentation* is obtained automatically, in a consistent and verifiable manner, and is automatically updated whenever modifications or extensions are made.

- *Metrics and instrumentation* are given a more substantive basis, because the data comes from reproducible activities automatically.

- *Planning techniques* are substantially aided and are incorporated into the systems effort. Strategic planning results can flow directly into the automated management process for requirements, analysis, design, and development.

- *Project estimation* is considerably improved because of the numerous automated parts of the system and the consequent reproducibility of the tasks.

- *Structured methodologies* are used that put the complete development process on a defined basis, with standard transfer of information between the phases. These allow greater group participation with recognized interfaces of information.

- *Formal specification methods* allow nonprofessionals to follow and check the applicability of the specifications and provide a means of testing the completeness of the specifications.

- *Verification and validation* of each part of the process produce applications that are much more error-free and that provide the necessary information for quality assurance that should be an integral part of the whole process.

- *Testing* is markedly improved because of the systematization and the automation of the transfer of files between phases, and because the points of testing are clearly noted.

- *Reusability* of code, including small sections, subroutines, and programs, not only provides tested code expeditiously, but also greatly reduces the amount of coding that must be done. Recoding of duplicate programs is eliminated.

- *Technical support* of the system development process is easier and more efficient, since all participants are working with the same systems and the transformations between the systems are clearly understood by the technical support staff.

- *Reverse engineering* (or reengineering) is becoming feasible and effective. This may well be the element of systems engineering that has the greatest long-term benefit. The technical problems are great, but solutions are being developed. The reason reengineering is such an important element is that there exists a vast library of operating COBOL and PL/1 code that is inefficient, full of errors, and requires a disproportionate number of professionals to maintain. Reengineering offers the promise of attacking this voluminous array of programs in a systematic, engineering style.

Automation of many of the steps is an essential part of a structured, clearly defined engineering approach. It is particularly important in the transformations between phases. It provides correctness, reproducibility, and control to the handling of information at all stages. The future of systems engineering is that the great bulk of the staff development effort will be in the definition of requirements and the analysis of the problem. More and more of the subsequent effort will become automated.

Systems Engineering Today

Many systems engineering tools, or CASE tools, are available on the market today in an extremely wide range of automation and interoperability. They have been sufficient, however, to justify the use of CASE approaches and to prove the considerable advantages of the use of CASE. Some of the elements of systems engineering have been noted. Their use is most obvious, and their position in systems development most clear, when the tools that support and define those elements are shown in parallel to the Systems Development Life Cycle. This is done in Figure 6. The SDLC, or software development life cycle, is shown as the basis for the placement and relationship of a number of systems engineering tools and areas simply because it is fundamental in showing what needs to be integrated and where it resides in the process.

The traditional SDLC is shown in the curve labeled "Old Development Methods." Little effort is put into the requirements definition and the analysis. The bulk of the work is expended for system construction, testing, and implementation. The result, almost invariably, is that the work is never finished. Completed projects are recycled for more analysis and development. Maintenance and enhancements are called for indefinitely and become harder to accomplish as time passes, and the original knowledge of the system dissipates. This is because "system knowledge" is held by individuals in an unstructured way, and individuals continually change their jobs. Maintenance never becomes easy.

The new CASE development methods are shown in the companion curve in Figure 6 with a marked skew to the beginning phases, when users and professional staff are meant to come to understanding and agreement. It stands to reason that, if more time is spent on the requirements definition in discussion with the ultimate users, then those users will be more satisfied with the final product. Similarly, if time is spent during analysis and design to express the details of the application in a standardized fashion, those details can be automatically taken by CASE systems and transformed in a series of steps to the final, desired product. By spending more effort and using automated CASE tools in the early phases, the application is finished in the desired form much earlier, and far less effort is required for later maintenance.

FIGURE 6. CASE tools and the software life cycle.

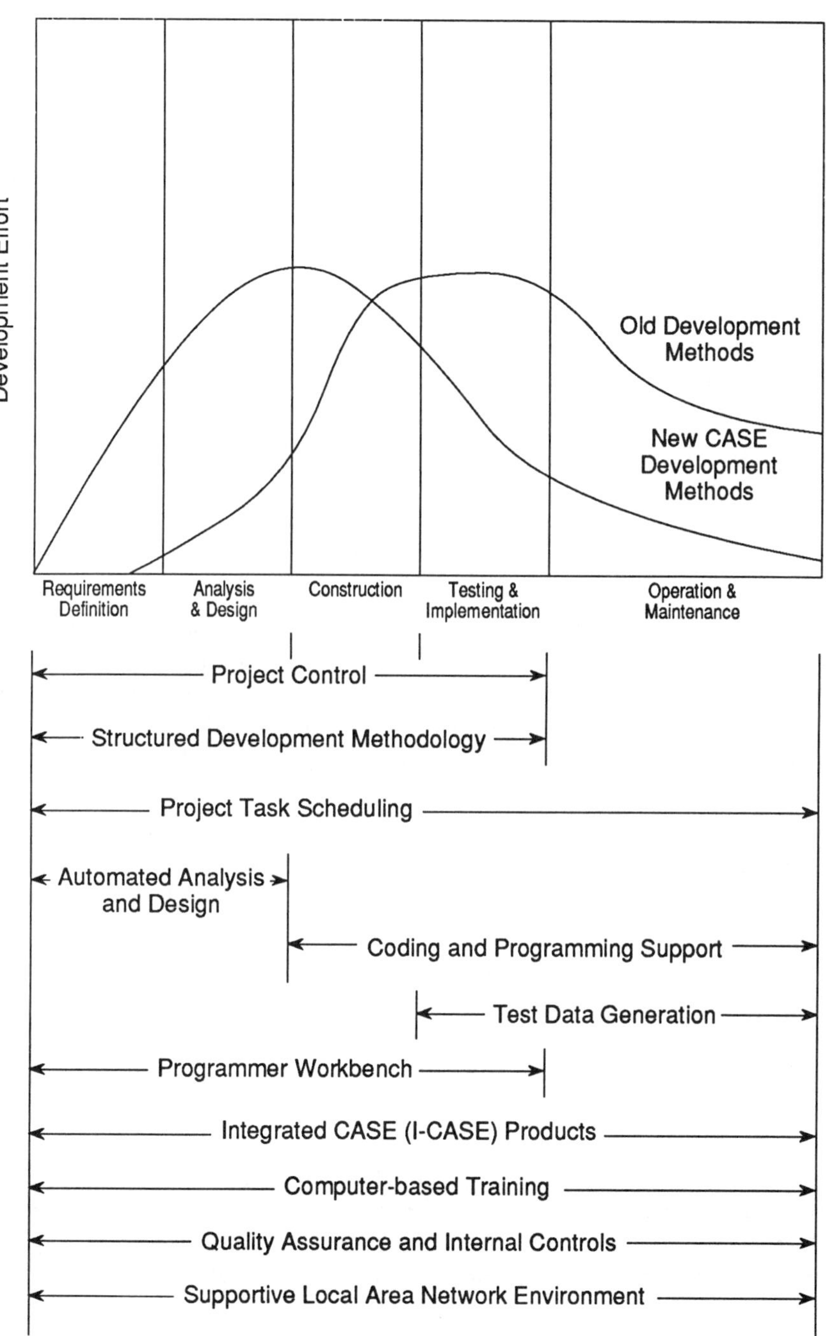

The new CASE method of managing application system development has clearly proven to be profitable. Figure 6 shows how a variety of CASE tools fit different areas of the software life cycle. The examples shown are not all-inclusive but are common CASE tools, and are representative of the full array of CASE tools.

Some Integrated CASE (or I-CASE) products span most of the software life cycle. They usually include a structured methodology, but do not necessarily include project control and scheduling, and such management concerns as QA and internal controls.

Figure 6 is not intended to indicate definitive boundaries between the phases of the system life cycle. In practice, those boundaries are not sharp, and there is recycling across them. A proper approach to CASE, however, will pull together all the illustrated tools and methods, and provide a manageable environment with considerable information available and passed across phase boundaries.

It is important to repeat the basic purpose of shifting the system life-cycle curve to the left in Figure 6. Although the use of CASE requires much more effort to be expended early in the SDLC, this effort pays off in the much-reduced requirements for staff work later in the life cycle. In addition, the improved quality of the product produced will then require less and easier maintenance in the future. The old development method usually had a rush to get started and to produce *any* results early in the cycle, with the effect of requiring continuous repair work in the future. The new CASE development method is based on known engineering principles: Use systematic, comprehensive, early analysis, based on any known and useful products, and finish the project cleanly, as planned.

In the past, there seemed to be an inverse relationship between the ability to respond to change and the work with engineering rigor, and to produce quality. Experience with the old SDLC approach showed that the greater the demands that are imposed, and the more rapidly we have to respond to change, the less can be the rigor of the method used and the less will be the quality of the product. Colloquially, this is sometimes called "quick and dirty," and is believed to be forced on system developers. With CASE methods, the reverse is true. The more CASE systems are automated, the more rigor they have and the more rapidly they operate. The quicker operation produces better product quality. CASE has the advantage for attaining better quality because more of the many, detailed decisions about the application systems are made much earlier in the systems life cycle. There is, consequently, a much higher level of rigor obtained with the CASE approach. In engineering terms, rigor refers to the ability of a method to always produce a correct and predictable solution. If a rigorous approach is taken in the early stages of a development effort, the final result will be:

- Correctness
- Consistency
- Completeness
- Coherency

A rigorous approach to application system development will reveal the details of the levels of structure very early, and will subsequently improve the quality of the architecture—the base structure in which the application must operate. The result is that it reduces defects and improves the quality of the execution of the development effort.

Management Perspective of Systems Engineering

Much about CASE methods is highly technical. Illustrations such as Figure 6 tend to be drawn from the technician's viewpoint. Figure 7 is drawn more from management's viewpoint. The software life cycle numbers clearly show the amounts of effort to be planned for and paid for. The percentages shown will certainly not hold true in all cases, but they are indicative of the situation. The issues facing management are those labeled "infrastructure issues." Management must do something in each of these areas, and they always have the hope that the technical ideas will fit the areas naturally.

The control area is fundamental management. This was noted in Figures 3 and 4, as well as in Figure 7. Here, management is looking for an overall CASE methodology that will carry from the definition to the maintenance, with clear ways of planning the process, and of measuring the results.

FIGURE 7. Key issues in the software life cycle.

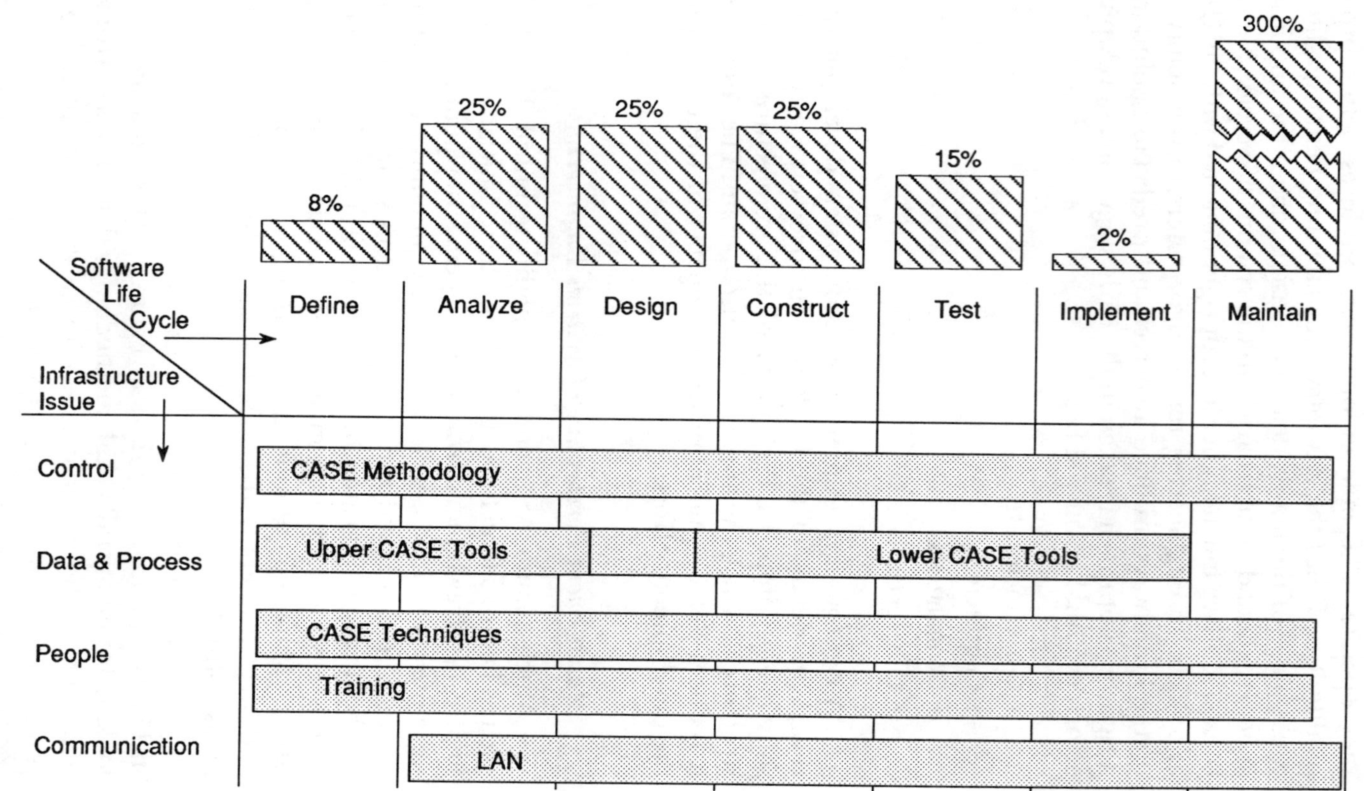

The data and process area is the world of the technician, but it still requires management. Here are the "upper CASE" tools—those for analysis and design—and the "lower CASE" tools—those for coding and testing. Here also are a number of CASE techniques that are partially automated and partially people dependent. What is the overlap between these tools and techniques? How can they be integrated? These are management questions that must be answered, but not necessarily answered immediately. With many professionals, and many groups of people working independently, management may prefer not to make any early decisions among the legion of possibilities, but rather to let a number of methods be tested and then try to evaluate them and select the best.

The people area is pure management, yet it is intertwined with the technicalities of the CASE techniques because they are all people dependent at various levels. The main infrastructure issue here is training. For CASE introduces the problem that not only must its direct practitioners be trained, but anyone related to the systems, including users, managers, and operators, also must be brought up to speed with this new technological approach. There is a real management problem here because even the trainers need training in the new concepts.

The communications area is always a difficult one for management because they usually must rely on a different group for information than the systems developers, yet it is all part of the same package. As Local Area Networks (LAN) become more prevalent, and as systems are developed with Cooperative Processing across such networks, the complexity of the system will become much greater, and new management decisions will be necessary.

Categories of Systems Engineering Tools

Management's basic problem is that their vision must expand in system development work from thinking about tools that are obviously for the traditional analysts and programmers to thinking about CASE tools that span the system life cycle and are used by all support staff in information services—from the systems programmer to the secretary. The vision of what constitutes a CASE tool must be expanded from technical areas such as test data generation, to general areas such as word processing. Word processing is a particularly apt example, incidentally, because a fundamental element of CASE methods is automatic documentation, and such documentation requires sophisticated word processing to be able to produce it automatically and modify it manually at the same levels of control.

The following is a listing of some categories of systems engineering tools. Since it is taken from various sources in the literature, there is no indication of the relative importance of the categories. They are simply subjects that must be investigated in CASE development work.

Requirements Definition, Analysis, and Design Tools

- Analysis
  - Fourth-generation languages
  - Rapid prototyping

- Design
  - Business modeling
  - Entity relationship modeling
  - Process modeling
  - Data modeling
  - Screen design modeling
  - Design documentation
  - Design testing

- Verification and validation
  - Design review
  - Compliance testing
  - Change control
  - Quality assurance
  - Archiving

Construction, Testing and Implementation Tools

- Construction
  - Configuration management
  - Decomposition

- –Editing and checking
- –Automatic code generation
- –Code reusability
- –Reverse engineering
- –Compilation and linking
- –Documentation
- –Performance optimization

- • Validation, testing and implementation
  - –Test data generation
  - –Automatic testing
  - –Debugging
  - –Documentation
  - –Standards control
  - –Symbolic evaluation

- • Tool management
  - –Tool selection
  - –Tool development and customization
  - –Tool integration

Management and Project Support Tools

- • Project Management
  - –Strategic and operational planning
  - –Setting objectives
  - –Budgeting and resource allocation
  - –Project scheduling
  - –Quality assurance
  - –Metrics, monitoring and review

- • Object management
  - –System version control
  - –Configuration management
  - –Requirements tracing
  - –Dependency management
  - –Code and design reuse

- −Access control
- −Defect tracking
- −Security and disaster recovery
- Communications management
  - −Local area network operation
  - −Join application development
  - −Cooperative design and development
- Personnel and office automation
  - −Personnel assignment and training schedules
  - −Job assignment: plan-versus-actual
  - −Word processing
  - −Electronic publishing
  - −Graphics and presentation support
  - −Electronic mail
  - −Personal work management tools

Considering Communications and Office Automation as parts of CASE technology indicates the modern movement to CASE as a complete environment of systems development. For example, those developing systems have long been lax and uninterested in their documentation efforts, even when automatic systems were available. Now, CASE thinking is pointing out that documentation is fundamental, and that a "system" for extracting the elements of an application from its code is insufficient documentation. Other material must be entered in, using word processing automation, and well-presented documentation can easily be prepared with electronic publishing.

As another example, CASE is moving fast from independent efforts to group efforts such as Joint Application Development (JAD). Co-workers are linked on LANs. The only way that they can effectively communicate today is through electronic mail. Thus electronic mail becomes one of the packages in the CASE tool kit.

1.6   TRENDS IN CASE TECHNOLOGIES

The idea of computer-aided software engineering has not sprung up suddenly as a completely new concept with all its facets in place. It has grown over the years from several roots and a number of tested and proven approaches. Recently, a number of the methods have been pulled together because they make sense being used together. Writers who have long clamored for an engineering, or scientific, approach to the development of software have begun to be heard. The commercialization of CASE has sprung up. Astute managers will be able to distinguish between vendor offerings that truly fit into an integrated CASE portfolio of products and those that are merely labeled as CASE for convenience. This book can be of great help in such an analysis.

Two of the major areas where CASE concepts have been formulated over the years have been in the advances in the reusability of program code and in the evolution of operational application systems.

Reusability of Program Code

It has long been recognized that far too much program code is written and rewritten repeatedly and uneconomically. In most business application systems, over three-quarters of the program code modules are common to other programs that have previously been written and the earlier code modules have been tested and proven. This reusability of program code is a fundamental element of CASE. It has been very slow in coming however, because of many technical difficulties. The background of reusability spans forty years.

In the 1950s, libraries of code for mathematical routines were developed, principally in the SHARE group of IBM scientific users and other user groups. These libraries of code were primarily for FORTRAN subroutines which fit easily into other programs. They were developed for Assembly routines and other languages also. The reuse of code became very common in the scientific and engineering communities.

In the 1960s, operating systems and the use of higher-level languages became central to MIS efforts, particularly with the introduction of the IBM 360 series. The complex operating systems, in essence, made considerable amounts of "computer housekeeping" code reusable, and this is some of the most difficult code to write. A new era started in which systems programmers and application programmers were distinguished.

In the 1970s, databases and communications packages became necessary to handle the tremendous complexity of data being moved from program to program. Databases made data reusable by sharing a common set of controlled data with all users. Communications packages extended this reusability to other locations.

In the 1980s, business application modules began to be reused in COBOL and other higher-level languages. The dramatic increase in the use of program generators made code for the production of code reusable. That is, it became practical to reuse code with many modifications with almost the same ease as reusing unchanged code modules.

In the 1990s, there will be the reuse of architecture. Proven elements of architecture and broad segments of the related code will be able to be used as building blocks in newer architectures.

One of the most important movements into the 1990s will be, of course, the increased practicality of reverse engineering, which is, essentially, the substantial reuse of the whole application system. There are practical reengineering approaches today, but there is much work to be done to attack the mountains of existing code readily and convert them to engineered code. Reverse engineering involves beginning the development life cycle with an existing system or programs rather than starting from the beginning with the application system specifications. Reengineering systems recover the design specifications from existing code and reuse them. They then restructure the code and convert the data in the database or change the whole database itself, such as from hierarchical to relational.

Evolution of Operational Application Systems

The time to use CASE methods has now arrived, partly because of the evolution of operational application systems. Such systems started individually for specific departments. They grew to be highly controlled centralized systems. The microcomputer revolution has driven them out throughout the organization and they need to have more built-in generality.

From 1950 to 1965, application systems were laboriously put onto computers with such tight coding that they were exceedingly specific and individualized. Modifications, changes, and expansions to other groups were most difficult.

From 1965 to 1980, again with the popularity of the IBM 360, there was a widespread movement to the mechanization of accounting procedures. Since the programming was in COBOL and PL/1, there was some good documentation and some reusability of elements of the systems, but generally the push was simply to get certain accounting programs mechanized from keypunching the data to the distribution of detailed reports. The demand was for data volume under control. The users of the reports were principally clerks and supervisors. The systems analysis was based on "fields of data."

In the 1980s, there has been a reaction leading to widespread demands for cost reduction and, at the same time, provision of needed information to management. The emphasis has shifted from the mechanization of accounting procedures to the automation of business procedures. This means that more attention is paid to the production of a wider variety of outputs, to special reports, and to the sharing of data between a number of programs. One significant part of this is that systems analysis became more complex. More departments and individuals have had to be consulted to determine the data to be used and the information to be produced. Systems analysts can no longer develop the obvious solutions, but must analyze the data flow and handling in more complex ways. The idea of taking an engineering approach to the analysis has become attractive.

In the 1990s, the emphasis will be on more information for analysis and decision. The search for competitive advantage through the use of information will intensify. The demands for very rapid development of applications will accelerate. This means that:

- There will be even greater demands for the sharing of data and the network transmission of data, calling for uniformity and compliance with standards at all levels of data storage and program modules.

- There will be even greater demands for program modules that can be used by different groups in different types of applications, rapidly yet with confidence in their integrity.

- "Creative" operational people will be doing analysis for systems rather than technical professionals. They will need simplified tools for the technical tasks.

- Small professional teams will handle complex computer architectures, with many other people within those architectural structures expecting program modules and data on demand.

- The increased productivity demanded for both professionals and end users will be realized by systemization and sharing.

- The estimates that about 90 percent of future systems will be from reused code will be realized.

Background of CASE

There were a number of programming tools produced over the past 25 years that could well be called precursors to CASE because their essential structures were oriented to analysis rather than to individual processes. Two of these were:

- Report Program Generator (RPG) from IBM.
- MARK IV and its predecessors from Informatics General Corp.

Programs such as these allowed software developers to create and modify structured specifications easily, first on fixed form sheets, then on-line on structured form sheets on the CRT. They also created their own documentation. They were exceedingly productive but had limitations that are rapidly disappearing in more recent tools. Such tools were the first indications of the possibilities of new approaches to systems analysis.

The first ideas about information engineering were put forward by Clive Finkelstein in Australia around 1980. He crystallized the idea that systems analysis could be engineered. The principles are well described in a book by James Martin and Clive Finkelstein, *Information Engineering*, published by the Savant Institute in 1981. It describes the rationale and techniques of information engineering for use by departmental systems and corporate-wide systems. Martin later consulted with Texas Instruments as they produced the Information Engineering Facility.

At about the same time, a study came out from the Department of Defense on the "software crisis." Its concern was what could be done about:

- The lack of trained people for complex software development.
- The cost and time overruns that always seemed to accompany systems development.

- The problems of software quality and the need for constant maintenance.

It was clear that an order of magnitude improvement was soon needed in the work of developing software, yet there were no new technologies evident that could rapidly provide such improvement. But it was also clear that there were some organizations that had far superior productivity than other organizations in software development. Evidently, they used practices and techniques within the same tools and approaches others used to gain considerable development advantage. These problems and observations intrigued many people and, in 1984, the Software Engineering Institute was formed at Carnegie-Mellon University to investigate this phenomenon. The first director of the institute was Nico Habermann. He was followed by John Manley who did much to popularize the concepts of software engineering. The present director of the institute is Larry Druffel.

The emerging technology was soon described and dissected in detail by many articles in the literature. One of particular interest for the record is John Manley's *Industrial-Strength Software Engineering for Large Organizations* (FJCC, p. 102-4, 1987). It suggests that large automated systems development and lifetime support require industrial-strength management and engineering, and advises the reader to take a close look at what people really do in other large organizations in general and in software-intensive organizations in particular.

There is sometimes discussion about the difference between "information engineering" and "software engineering." Some, in the literature, have said that information engineering deals with how people process and use information, while software engineering deals with how people create large software systems. There are even others who say that the present thrust should be called "systems engineering" to be closer to the truth. The fact is that these terms have now coalesced and there are no clear distinctions between them. For example, Texas Instrument's Information Engineering Facility is made up, principally, of what others would call software engineering modules, linked in a coherent and communicating system. There has been a blurring of boundaries between the terms and they are frequently used interchangeably.

In the early 1980s, there were many "CASE" systems emerging in the areas of systems specification, syntax checking, modularization of design, application generation, word processing for documentation, automatic drafting, and so on. It became obvious that such systems, each in its own area at the time, could substantially decrease the time to develop and check system specifications, check on syntax and other error sources, and develop repetitive code. After Martin, Manley and others pointed out the interconnection between such systems, and the software vendors supplied usable packages that could perform the necessary joining of the data sets in the various systems, the idea that there could be larger sets of CASE systems soon became obvious. So, more and more linkages of systems development applications have been successfully made, and now the CASE approach is obviously viable and highly productive.

The definition of CASE as the disciplined and structured engineering approach to systems development is sufficiently inclusive to cover its recent and forthcoming developments. The practical areas in which the term "CASE" is used are continually broadening, however. Some writers and vendors now include under CASE:

- PC-based front-end analysis and design tools
- Code generation
- Graphic human interface elements
- Agreed elements of rigor and standardization
- Approaches to systems integration
- Analysts' "tool kits" of CASE systems
- Reusable design and program modules
- Data dictionary and repository integrators
- Particular elements of workstations
- Application generators
- Reengineering and maintenance approaches
- Project support environments

When faced with the conflicting claims of individual CASE products and the variety of articles in the literature, it is important for managers to have a perspective that there is currently a convergence of CASE technologies occurring, and that all CASE tools will be forced to be compatible and communicative with other CASE tools in the future. The purpose of CASE is not simply to increase programmer productivity with a number of tools. The purpose of CASE is to achieve an overall increase in productivity among the programmers, analysts, users, and managers together.

The technologies that are now converging are not simply the tools within the various CASE tool kits, but are the related information services technologies that affect the use of CASE approaches. Rapid advances in personal computers are making more complex and sophisticated procedures readily available. A few of the technologies that are converging are listed below:

- *Personal workstation hardware* is becoming more powerful and easy to use, and is therefore being accepted as the standard environment for the delivery of software. The typical CASE workbench is a PC with a complete software development environment that supports the entire life-cycle process. It can be customized for individual users. It has highly interactive, responsive design techniques. It has its own large information repository with ready connections to other databases. In essence, it can support a full life-cycle coverage for an individual with a tightly integrated tool set that is tailored to that individual.

- *Graphics* systems are being integrated with all other parts of CASE and with available graphics devices in addition to those on the PCs. They include the automatic checking for completeness and consistency and they support the increasing acceptance of entity and data modeling. They are a prime tool in many systems for automatic code generation.

- *Relational databases* are fundamental to the most effective use of CASE. As the technology of relational databases moves from the central computer to PCs and, further, to distributed databases, there will be a profound effect on the ease of use of CASE approaches, and the controls that will be available over accuracy, security and consistency of data.

- *Fourth-generation languages* are being used for the automatic code generation in many CASE tools, and there will be much more use as the entire life-cycle process is automated. As they develop so that there is more generation of efficient code that does not impose a run-time performance penalty, there will be a complete coupling from the front-end CASE products to the back-end COBOL generator.

- *Communications* have become an increasingly important factor in the selection of CASE tools as more developers are working together with LAN connections.

- *Expert systems* are being increasingly used in CASE tools to expedite the selection of choices and to bring more uniformity into the decisions made by individuals within groups of developers. The incorporation of knowledge-based rules of inference can greatly facilitate some decision processes.

- *Human factors* are being included in analyses and selection of CASE tools. Many improvements are being made in human interfaces, including the use of simplified, intuitive command interfaces, the elimination of alien syntax, and the extensive use of graphics screens. When such factors are properly considered in the design of CASE tools, the efficiency and effectiveness of the end user increases.

In compatible systems and interconnected groupings, CASE tools are fundamentally altering the way application systems are specified, designed, implemented, and maintained. Many CASE tools are designed to operate on personal workstations, which are rapidly becoming the standard environment for the development of software. This new generation of tools is helping to apply rigorous engineering principles to the analysis and development of software. CASE technology now represents a new approach to the implementation of complex computer systems. The future will bring the automation of all phases of the life-cycle process and will tie application development more closely to the strategic planning of the business.

1.7 AN OVERVIEW OF THIS BOOK

This CASE book is designed to bring together accepted advanced ideas and proven practices and approaches for optimizing the benefits that may be realized by the use of CASE approaches. It is based on information received from successful senior managers in information services, people who have proven the value of CASE in their own work, and consultants who have been useful in introducing CASE to practitioners. It is also based on recent articles in the literature on this subject. It is a "how-to" book, with step-wise methods for reviewing the possibilities of CASE, implementing CASE activities, and improving on present CASE efforts. The sections in this book are:

Chapter 1: "What Is CASE?"
An introduction that defines CASE, fits CASE into the overall area of Application Development and Maintenance, lists the major elements of systems engineering and the main categories of CASE, and describes the trends in CASE methodologies.

Chapter 2: "Why Use CASE?"
A brief review of the software crisis and a number of opportunities for productivity improvement in systems development. A discussion of the need to improve systems quality, and of the greater advantages in this improvement over the reduction of development time, because of the long-term effect of quality improvements. A review of the economics of CASE and its uses and functions.

Chapter 3: "How to Manage CASE"
Gives practical reviews and advice on the introduction, implementation, and management of CASE in an organization. Describes the CASE-oriented System Development Life Cycle. Stresses the importance of planning and project management in the delivery of CASE applications. Notes strategies for the successful adoption of CASE.

Chapter 4: "Components and Functions of CASE Products"
Discusses integrated CASE architectures. Describes the key components of CASE products, including diagramming techniques, design analyzer, code generator, information repository, expert systems, and life-cycle development methodology. Shows how the front-end CASE tools and the back-end COBOL generator support the life cycle. Reviews reverse engineering.

Chapter 5: "Management Considerations in CASE"
Discusses the cooperation of experts and end users in the development and implementation of computer sys-

tems over the life of the application, which is a generic CASE environment called *cooperative applications development*. Describes requirements definition prototyping, which is becoming a standard CASE tool. Reviews related systems development concerns, which do not usually fall under CASE but are an integral part of CASE management, including relational databases, 4GLs, applications generators, expert systems, QA, training, security, and disaster recovery.

Chapter 6: "How to Evaluate and Select CASE Products"
Gives practical proven approaches for establishing the functional requirements of CASE tool acquisitions and for evaluating CASE methodologies. A how-to section with tested checklists on evaluating and selecting CASE products and managing their introduction.

Chapter 7: "Experiences with CASE Tools"
Reviews the capabilities of a number of CASE tools and approaches and summarizes the experiences and opinions of some corporations with their use of the CASE tools. The tools include Excelerator, the Bachman Methodology, AION, and the Information Engineering Facility.

"Appendix"
Compares the product functionality of a number of CASE products. Supplies a glossary of CASE terms.

CHAPTER 2

Why Use CASE?

Overview

*C*ASE has been presented as an answer to the "software crisis," the large backlog of software development, and the increasing complexity of software. The productivity improvement of CASE comes from more nearly meeting the users' requirements, from the automated transformation of specifications through to the code, from the better documentation and modularization of the system, and from the ease of maintenance. CASE provides a rigorous approach to application system development.

The advantages of CASE come from the automation of the activities of software developers. Productivity is increased and quality is increased at the same time. The flow of the work becomes smoother and requires fewer resources than traditional approaches. A principal advantage is that CASE aids considerably in making systems that meet the needs of the users.

The measurement of productivity and quality, though difficult, is important in the management of CASE. Definitions of productivity and its measurement are discussed in detail. The need for measurements is emphasized. A Texas Instruments model for the calculation of the economics of CASE is given. A Net Present Value calculation is described.

CASE technology is in its early stages of development, but it is important to begin using those technologies that are basic, such as relational database, data management, and standards, to start gaining advantages from the use of CASE. A planning checklist is provided that covers the management concerns about CASE technology.

2.1   THE SOFTWARE CRISIS

Much has been written about the software crisis that is confronting all information services groups and getting headlines in the lay press as well as the technical journals. The study in the Department of Defense in the early 1980s has already been mentioned. The stated reasons for the crisis fall into the following groups:

- The *software development backlog* is growing rather than disappearing, as was predicted when microcomputers first became popular. Although the use of PCs takes many requests from the average backlog, the greater understanding of and trust in computers is causing many new and larger projects to be proposed that require a full networked solution rather than a PC solution.

- The *size and complexity of applications* is increasing as more large and small computers are interconnected in networks for organization-wide solutions.

- *More is being spent on software* relative to total computer costs because there is far more maintenance and enhancement work required to keep the systems operating as desired. The software maintenance share of total system costs has increased markedly in the past ten years.

- *Software development times* are being stretched out as the increased complexity of on-line, real-time, PC-networked solutions is faced. Simple, standalone systems are now often relegated to the PCs, while company-wide solutions require the interaction of many devices. In many system development projects there are still cost and time overruns.

- *Higher costs of programmers,* plus the meager availability of experienced programmers, is forcing the search for increased programmer productivity. There is a lack of trained people for complex software development.

- There have been problems with software quality and a need for constant maintenance.

- *Experience with failed systems*, many of them large, is increasing the interest in quality assurance programs that review the progress against expectation from the design to the operation of the systems.

- *Many large systems have failed* to deliver the functions that management needed and have been scrapped or greatly modified. Most large companies have had such experiences but have not publicized them. The trade press has described in great detail the problems encountered by the Bank of America's institutional trust accounts system and by the State of New Jersey's automobile registration system, for example.

- *Automated methods for the development of systems* are being widely publicized, and it has become imperative that they be considered.

A few statistics can be quoted that reinforce one or more of the factors listed above:

- Applied Data Research, of Princeton, New Jersey, has determined in surveys that up to 75 percent of all software projects are canceled.

- T. Capers Jones has pointed out that, on average, six generations of programmers maintain a program during its lifetime! Up to 25 percent of very large projects are canceled before completion. The average large system is a year late and costs twice as much as the original estimate!

- A U.S. Army study of several federal projects found that:

    –47 percent were delivered, but not used

    –29 percent were paid for, but not delivered

    –19 percent were abandoned or reworked

    –3 percent were used after changes were made

    –only 2 percent were used as delivered.

- For a U.S. Air Force command and control system:

    –the initial estimate was $1.5 million

    –the winner's bid was $400,000

    –the actual project cost was $3.7 million.

All of these generalizations and cost statistics about the reality of a software crisis today do not necessarily point to the same diagnosis, however, and do not lead to the same solutions. Some advocate more widespread training, as they say most systems will move to the personal computers. This approach is helpful, but it cannot alone meet the increasing demand for the very large data processing systems with complex networking and huge databases. It is clear that it is fundamentally necessary to search for more efficiency in software development. It is possible that sufficiently increasing systems analyst and programmer productivity will meet the shortage of professionals.

The CASE approach has been suggested as one of the best directions to take to confront the software crisis. The reason for the advantage of CASE is more complex than simple "productivity improvement" of the technical staff. CASE emphasizes the concept of doing the right thing first, rather than trying to do things faster. Actually, early use of CASE systems usually shows very little, if any, advantage in the time it takes to implement a system. What CASE does do to alleviate the software crisis is to introduce systematization and control to the system development process. CASE produces better systems under management control with better documentation. This is where the word "engineering" can be used. The engineering approach has several beneficial effects:

- There is better *validation* that the user's requirements will be met by the system. The definition of the originally defined requirements is maintained throughout the system transformations during development.

- *Quality* is considered in detail throughout the life cycle. There is continuing review that the users' expectations are being met by ongoing quality assurance.

- The *information system architecture* is used to maintain a cohesive system structure. Application systems are not separate entities, but are part of the designed architecture.

- File and code *transformations* are automated when moving from one stage of development to another, such as from design to development. Since they are reproducibly automated, the transformations are handled in a completely consistent fashion.

- A high degree of *standardization* is mandated and maintained through the automation. The standards requirements are built into the automated systems.

- Consistent and accurate *documentation* of the system is made automatically available as the development proceeds. If there is later maintenance through the use of the same automated system, the documentation is updated accordingly.

Figure 8 shows the typical distribution of effort over the life cycle of an application system. Clearly, the problem is that the average system requires too much maintenance effort. The solution is to provide small improvements in the development process prior to the maintenance phase because they can have significant impact on the level of effort required to maintain the system. The intent of CASE is to build systems in such a way that the maintenance costs can be brought under control. If the maintenance work can be appreciably reduced, one of the largest problem areas causing the software crisis is effectively attacked. The experiences with CASE to date have clearly shown an advantage in this area. Because working with the rigor of CASE improves quality, it has the effect of greatly improving system development productivity, especially over the full life cycle of the application system.

Why use CASE? Because system development and maintenance productivity is improved at every step in the life cycle:

- In *requirements analysis*, CASE methods make the process objective and crystallize it for both the users and the analysts. In the old SDLC approaches, it was never quite clear when the requirements analysis was complete and users never really cut off their requests. The 3 percent of the costs noted in Figure 8 is actually deceptive because much more time of highly paid staff was always involved.

- In *specification*, the amount of time spent is relatively small, but CASE methods increase staff productivity tremendously here. Again, it becomes a completely objective process.

- In *design, code, module test, integration,* and *test,* Figure 8 indicates that 27 percent of the total system life cycle cost is expended. This is equivalent to 90 percent of the application system development cost. In these phases, CASE methods clearly show ap-

FIGURE 8. System life cycle cost distribution.

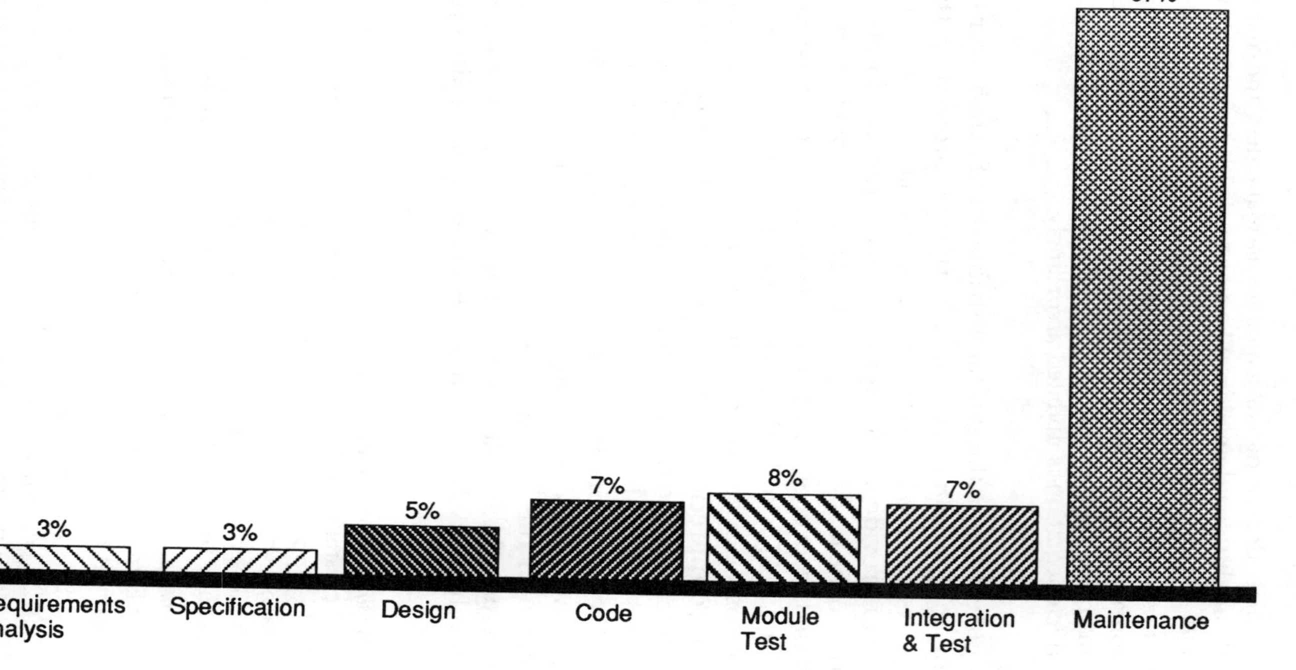

(Source: Institute of Data Processing Management, 1986)

preciable productivity improvement to the extent that development staff can be reduced in these areas.

- Finally, in *maintenance*, CASE provides outstanding productivity improvement from two sources. First, the quality of the product is superior if it has been developed with an integrated CASE methodology. Second, the maintenance itself is more rapid and more accurate because CASE systems maintain information that allows the maintenance to be done back at the specification phase and carried through automatically. The maintenance updates are automatic and accurate; they are not "patches."

In summary, the advantages of using CASE come from productivity improvement in several areas:

- The application systems will more nearly meet the original requirements of the users, so fewer changes are required when the users see the systems operating.

- Automating the transformation of specifications to design, then to code, then to program, results in fewer errors and less need for maintenance in the future.

- The better documentation and modularization of the system components makes maintenance easier and more accurate.

- Maintenance is faster because of the automated code generation and the complete central information repository.

Not only does CASE do things faster, it does them right. Future operating modifications and enhancements are readily handled. The application systems that are built are well structured and easily maintained.

It is clear that quality improvement and professional productivity are inextricably interwoven. When systems development productivity arises from the automation of the process in CASE and greater attention to rigor, the quality of the system is automatically improved. CASE approaches are all objective enough so that quality assurance methods can be applied at every step of the process. This attention to QA within the productive, automated systems will guarantee higher productivity in producing acceptable systems products.

The software crisis is with us, to a great extent, because of the repetitive efforts that have been common in the old software development process. In the past, individuals have often worked essentially isolated from the users, and there has been insufficient coordination for the completion of the desired product. Programmers have written, rewritten, and rewritten the same code segments and routines, unable to take advantage of code written by others or even code written previously by themselves. Coded subroutines were recreated each time they were needed. Coders often inserted "interesting" segments of code that took time to produce, did not improve the overall product, and were difficult to debug or modify. Even worse, the occasional programmer could insert damaging code routines such as viruses, trojan horses, trapdoors, and logic bombs, and they would be exceedingly difficult to detect.

In the past, there has been no easy way for management to know in detail how the programming was progressing. There has been no easy way to check on the efficiency of the programming work or to maintain security control over the coding detail. Nor have managers had direct ways of checking on the quality of the product of skilled programmers. Some CASE methods provide an answer to these management problems. They can best be confronted by the "engineering" approach, which involves detailed standard specifications, group efforts, modular construction, automatic transfer of information at interfaces, reuse of proven sections, and continuous quality assurance.

CASE thus offers a proven solution to the software crisis through systematic management, better problem analysis, use of tested methods, and effective quality assurance. Today, the recognized management decision is not *whether* to use CASE, but rather *when* to use CASE and *which* CASE tools to employ. This decision is, of course, dictated individually in each organization by the present state of management practices and systems development methodologies. A CASE tool set that is unplanned, in the hands of the untrained or unprepared can produce negative results.

2.2 *IMPROVING SYSTEM DEVELOPMENT PRODUCTIVITY*

It was pointed out that the main purpose of CASE is to facilitate a marked improvement in application system development productivity. As the automated tools are used, there is first experienced a definite increase in productivity in the early stages of systems development. Much more effective effort is put into the requirements definition, the systems analysis, and the design of the application. Although the use of CASE requires this extra effort early in the system development life cycle, it pays off in the much reduced requirements for effort later due to the automation of the coding process. In addition, there is improved quality and control of the resultant product, so there is less and easier maintenance required in the future. The old development method usually had a rush to get started and to produce any results early in the cycle. The new development method follows time-proven engineering principles. There is systematic, comprehensive, early analysis, and all the information is kept in the database so that its flow can be analyzed or changed. The project is finished cleanly and as planned, and whenever maintenance is required, the whole process can be reconstructed for change at the appropriate place, moving automatically from a statement of the new requirements. The result is an increase in productivity in all phases of system development and maintenance.

The purpose of CASE is to automate the activities of the software developers. The effect of CASE is complex because software products are not designed, built, and boxed for perpetual use. They are continually changed to adapt to new business demands. Some of the changes are incremental, while others are structural. Because software products are adaptable over time, the tendency is seldom to retire them but to just keep adding to them and modifying them indefinitely. We are therefore not looking for a single set of CASE products that will improve development productivity for a given size of new application systems. We are looking for a whole portfolio of CASE products that will:

- Improve the productivity of requirements definition and design, sometimes called "Upper CASE."

- Improve the productivity of coding, debugging, and testing, sometimes called "Lower CASE."

- Improve the productivity of modifying the application being developed at any stage of its development.

- Improve the productive application of quality assurance techniques throughout the system life cycle.

- Improve the productivity of the integration of application systems through the sharing of data, program modules, and development steps.
- Improve the productivity of maintaining application systems by retaining in the database all the information used in the system development.
- Improve the quality and productivity of the many older operational application systems by reverse-engineering them and building maintainable systems with other CASE tools.

Clearly, this broad spectrum of productivity increases is a lot to ask from any particular set of CASE tools and a lot for a manager to expect. The fact is that such advantages in productivity are only attained through experience and through the use of a number of different types of CASE tools managed coherently. The encouraging fact is that, especially with the increasing complexity of software, productivity improvements are definitely available through the use of CASE, and there is also an associated improvement in system quality. This is illustrated in Figure 9.

This figure shows that in the traditional, hand-crafted system development approaches, system quality has usually been sacrificed to productivity demands. The only way to make high-quality systems was to test and retest, to write code and to rewrite code, and to find out how the system operated and then patch it until it operated more efficiently. Quality was only obtained through more time and more effort. When management demanded more productivity by getting the job done faster using the same resources, quality always deteriorated. There was an accepted, inverse relationship between quality and productivity.

CASE methods have changed this relationship. As Figure 9 shows, there is now a direct relationship between quality and productivity. The improvement in software quality comes largely, in CASE, from the automation of the design and coding process. This automation not only speeds up the process, but also makes it more accurate and reproducible, yielding higher quality.

The productive CASE methods also produce higher quality because of the extra effort spent in the early phases of requirements definition, analysis, and design. There is, consequently, a much higher level of rigor in application system development

FIGURE 9. Relationship between productivity and quality.

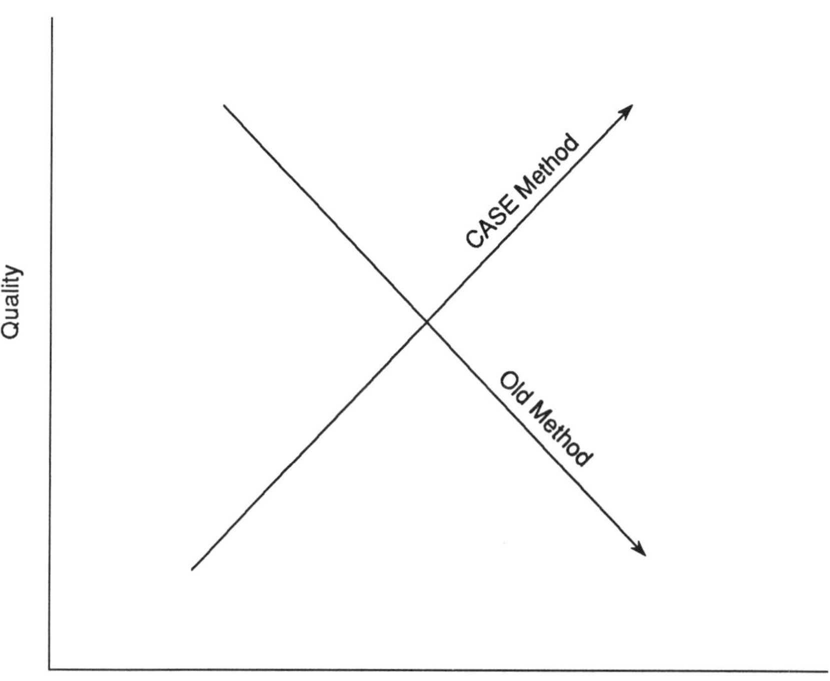

obtained with the CASE approach. In engineering terms, rigor refers to the ability of a method to always produce a correct and predictable solution. If a rigorous approach is taken in the early stages of a development effort, as in CASE, the final result will be better in:

- Correctness
- Consistency
- Completeness
- Coherency

A rigorous approach to application system development will reveal the details of the levels of structure very early and substantially improve the quality of the architecture. The result is that it will reduce defects and improve the quality of the execution of the development effort. Thus CASE helps to improve system development productivity and improves system quality at the same time.

Some articles in the literature have emphasized the quality improvement aspects of CASE and have neglected to see that the better quality comes from the methods used that first increase productivity. This is usually because, although we are less comfortable in the measurement of productivity, as will be discussed in the next chapter, we can readily measure quality. Writers then see the CASE world in terms of quality, which, in reality, is an effect of the productivity increase rather than a cause of it. Quality can be readily measured. Errors can be reported, ABEND listed, and poorly designed reports sent back for correction. Productivity is less obviously measured and managers are less inclined to believe productivity reports. To move CASE forward on a sound basis, with the approval of higher management, there simply must be more attention paid to the measurement and reporting of productivity. For one thing, productivity means better use of resources and approval of more attractive budgets. Quality is less easily translated into dollars.

Productivity in the Building of Systems

The way CASE improves system development productivity is expressed graphically in Figure 10. This figure illustrates the normal progress in an application systems development effort. In the traditional SDLC approach, called here the "old method," there is a first rush from requirements definition to programming. Coding work is started as soon as possible because it will take so long to do. Soon after the first tests are in, however, it is perceived that there are changes needed in the system. Users complain or change their requirements and the effort repeats, going back to analysis and quickly down to coding again and again. Frequently, enough time has passed by so that the users have decided that their original defined requirements are no longer applicable and changes need to be made in them. Again, the cycle is repeated.

The CASE method does not operate this way. First, there is relatively constant communication between the end users and the

FIGURE 10. The building of systems.

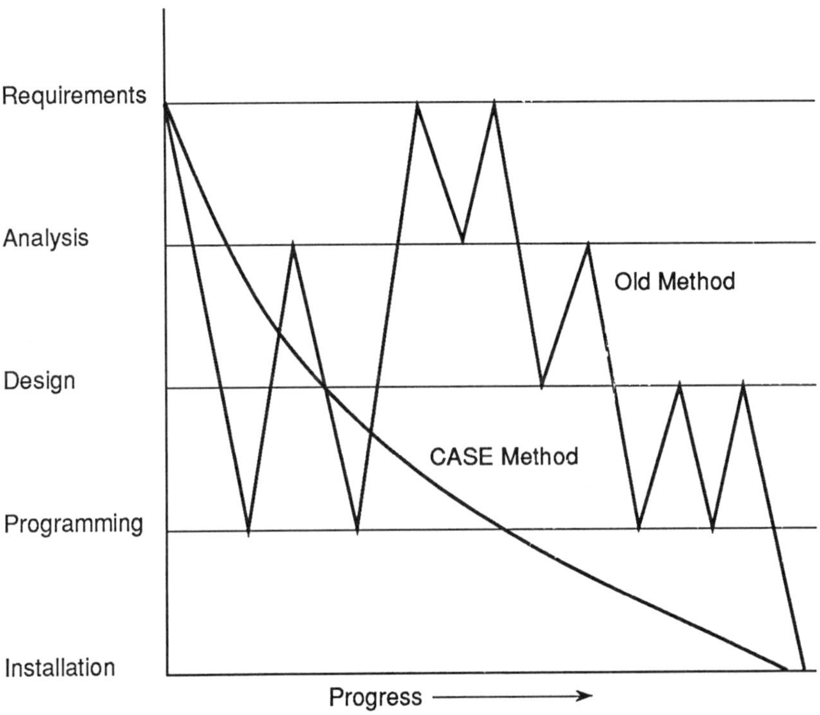

programmers, so that changes can be introduced incrementally. Second, when appreciable program changes are required as the work progresses, the subsequent flow from the new requirements to the new analysis to the new design to the new program is handled relatively automatically. Little personnel time is lost and there is no discontinuity in the flow of the work. In reality, there are also many fewer system changes expected in a CASE project because much more time is spent in the initial discussion and design stages. Possibly, prototypes are developed for review and the users are imbedded into the process.

The building of application systems by the older and the newer methods can also be illustrated by comparing the "waterfall" models of the two approaches. Both approaches are waterfalls. The work flows from one stage to the next and time cannot be backtracked. The subsequent stage receives the exact output of the preceding stage. As the flow proceeds, energy is expended in the form of personnel and machine resources.

In the traditional SDLC, with its handcrafting of software, the theoretical waterfall flow is shown in the upper part of Figure 11. The reality is shown in the lower half of the figure. At every stage, changes are made, errors are found, new requirements are introduced, and much energy is lost as the work is "pumped" back up to the higher stages to flow back again. The system eddies

FIGURE 11. The waterfall model of the traditional SDLC.

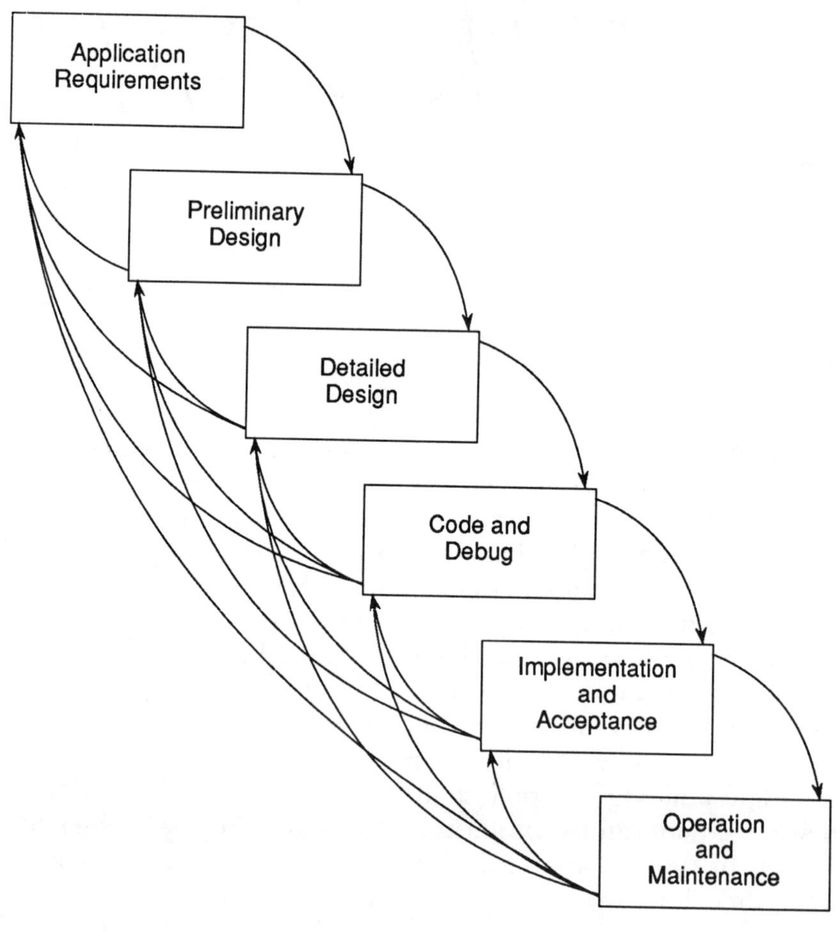

about as the work cycles and recycles. To carry the waterfall analogy further, the turbulence is increased, the confusion is increased, and the status of any particular system element is always uncertain.

The situation is quite different in the CASE waterfall of system development. This is shown in Figure 12. The same general SDLC is followed, but the flow of the work changes markedly and becomes much smoother, with the expenditure of much less energy in terms of resources. In the CASE waterfall, there is no

FIGURE 12. The waterfall model of software engineering.

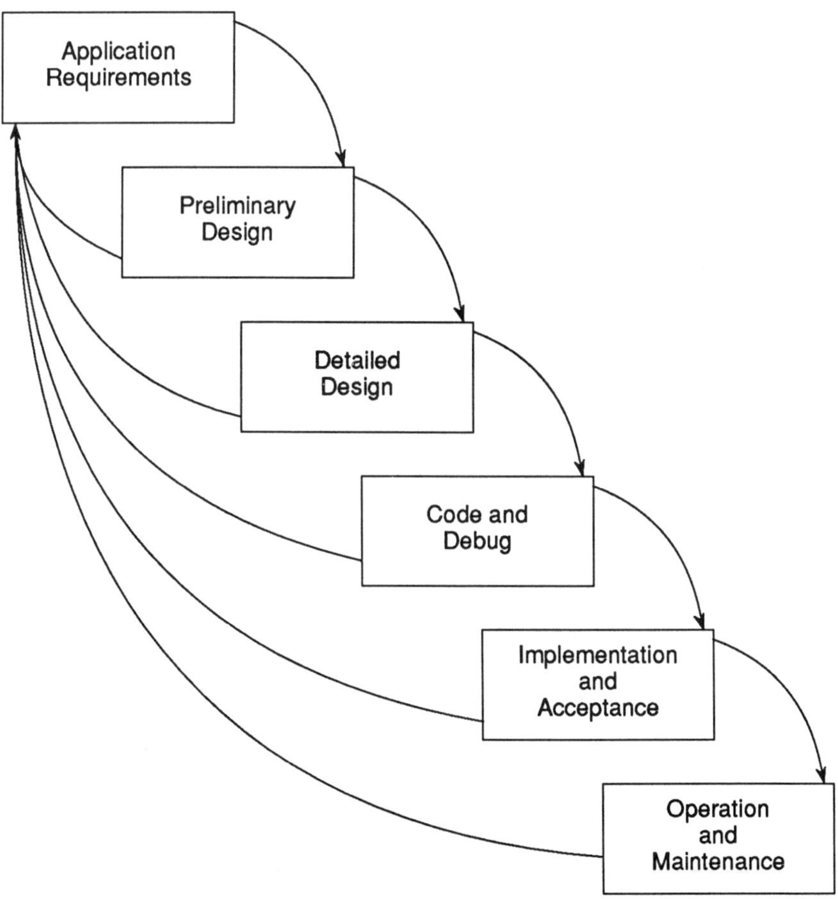

"eddying about" with handcrafted changes and patches and modifications that do not fit the requirements. The process flows smoothly and relatively automatically. Whenever changes are needed, at any stage of the waterfall, the work is pumped back up to the top, to the requirements definition, and allowed to go through the whole process relatively automatically, resulting in a smooth, consistent flow of the work. The automation means that there is greatly reduced use of resources. This simply means that the productivity of the streamlined CASE flow is greater than that of the turbulent, traditional SDLC flow.

Productivity in the Meeting of User Needs

There are thus four principal sources of increased application system development productivity when CASE is used. These are:

- Better definition of system requirements, which leads to fewer changes and modifications later.
- Improved quality of the system, which leads to greater user satisfaction and fewer corrections that must be made.
- Greatly increased automation of the system development process, giving better consistency and smoother flow of the work effort.
- Closer meeting of user needs, resulting in fewer system change requests and more rapid use of the system by the user.

The improved convergence of the system to the needs of the users is illustrated in Figure 13. No computer system is going to meet the needs of the users fully. Some systems exceed expectations and are praised for their capabilities. Many large systems cause a complete restructuring of the way the business is conducted, the organization of the staff, and the needs of specific users. The world progresses, however. Business changes, competitive efforts force rethinking, and new inventions change the environment. The question is, then, how can the application systems be made to meet changed and increased user needs?

In Figure 13, user needs are shown as continuously demanding more system functionality over time. Even as the application systems are originally designed, user needs have already advanced further. As time progresses, with the traditional systems

FIGURE 13. The meeting of user needs.

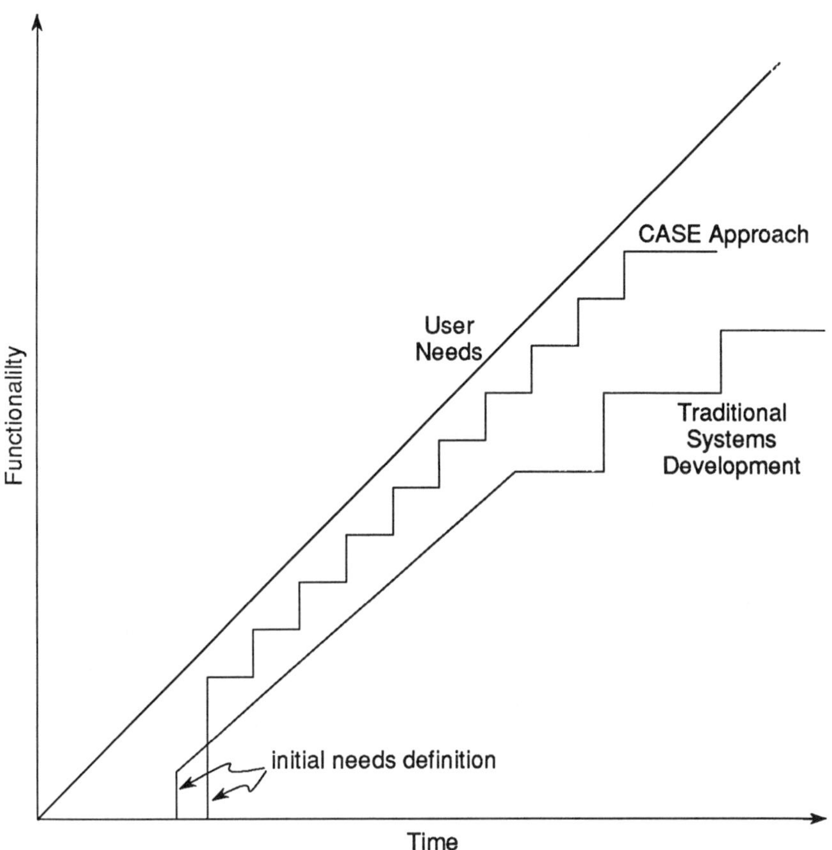

development methods, there is continued divergence of the system functionality and the needs of the users. Occasional major modifications are made to the system to bring it a little closer to new user needs, but the fight is a losing one, and the divergence increases.

With the CASE approach, more time is taken to create the initial definition of user needs, but when they are created they are closer to reality. As time advances, CASE systems can be modified frequently and readily, because of the automation of the handling of the changes. This means that CASE-developed systems can always be kept much more convergent to the needs of the users, with much less effort than was required in the traditional SDLC modifications. There is simply a better meeting of user needs. Any user will describe this advantage as increased productivity.

2.3 THE MEASUREMENT OF PRODUCTIVITY AND QUALITY

Productivity in application system development would appear to be recognizable when it is obtained, but such is not always the case. There is a practical dilemma in the measurement of productivity in application development and maintenance, which arises from the difficulty of obtaining baseline information and of capturing comparative numbers.

> *Productivity is the ratio of quality work products completed per unit of time.* Increases in productivity are caused by more quality work products being produced in a given time, or by less time being required to complete a constant level of quality work products.

How marvelously simple it is to define productivity, yet how exquisitely complicated it seems to be to measure the productivity of the application development functions. There are all sorts of reasons for not measuring the productivity of the applications developers. Notorious rationalizations follow such classic logic as:

Systems development is an art.

There are too many variables to measure.

Good system developers hate to be measured.

Measurement cannot be done objectively.

There is no such thing as an error-free program.

I don't have time to measure. (One of the all-time favorites)

If any improvement in productivity is to be expected, in all cases, a crude measurement is better than none at all. As time progresses, the measurement process can be refined and the ambiguity can be reduced. Ambiguity does not always mean lack of direction, nor does an overall framework imply a fixed set of references. We must successfully evaluate the alternatives.

In the development of computer applications there are many factors that influence productivity, both positively and adversely. Which factors are important? How important are they? Are the same factors important in all environments? How does the productivity of one group of developers compare with the productivity of other groups? Is there a norm that can be applied? These are reasonable questions. To know the answers to these questions, and to others, it is necessary to apply defined measurements regularly and systematically. Analyses must be made and reported over time until there is some rational understanding of the factors involved.

Productivity is currently a popular word in the literature and in CASE product advertising. It is used to describe hardware, software, and combinations of systems and management methods that purport to aid the organization's operations and reduce its costs. It has a valid, technical meaning in industrial engineering as a measure of how effectively the total assigned resources are used to produce desired products. This can be reduced to an equation where productivity equals the value of the output products produced, divided by the assigned cost of producing those output products. This measurement will be enlarged upon later.

It is clear, however, that the concept of productivity does not have a consistent meaning among the many CASE areas where it is used. At one extreme, productivity is measured by efficiency alone or by the number of tasks that are accomplished with given resources. At the other extreme, productivity is measured by effectiveness, which is the perceived impact of conducting work in a given way. Yet over this whole range, from analytical measurement to intuitive perception, there is general agreement that, in the final analysis, nothing can be claimed to increase productivity that does not have a positive influence on attaining the objectives of the overall organization, which usually means an increase in profit, possible by a reduction of costs. For reasons of consistency and communication, basic definitions of productivity, to have any meaning, must be agreed upon and accepted in practice, and therefore some are described here. On the other hand, this does not preclude the use of the term in areas that are most difficult to measure, such as management activity and "competitive advantage." Productivity is too recognizable a concept to limit it to areas where industrial engineers can apply metrics to it.

The Measure of Productivity Improvement

For clerical work, and for many of the end users of application systems, productivity improvement can be measured. Normal work measurement and timing methods can be used, since many of the uses of applications are repetitive and definable. A great deal of such measurement has been done in office automation studies and has been reported in the literature. There is absolutely no doubt that better application systems, produced sooner and with fewer errors, can substantially increase the productivity of clerical workers. Accepted industrial engineering methods can be used to check this assertion.

There is also a substantial body of literature available on the measurement of the productivity of systems analysts and programmers. Much of this applies to the delivery of applications through the use of software productivity tools, application generators, and a variety of programmer aids that are now thought of as part of CASE.

In professional programming, the software metrics used must give yardsticks of system quality as well as project productivity. They are inseparable. There is no programming productivity obtained unless there are comparable advances in the measures of program efficiency, correctness, integrity, maintainability, reliability, testability, and usability. Measures of lines of code and the numbers of defects are meaningless unless the desired results are produced on time, within a budget, and to the satisfaction of the manager involved. Interestingly, these factors have been understood for many years in the measurement of productivity, and they are exactly the same factors that CASE advocates claim for CASE methods.

Productivity can be measured either directly or indirectly. Direct measurement requires that a model of the process be built that includes all of the significant variables and their relationships to each other, or their relative impacts on each other. It also requires that a common unit of measure be defined, such that the work products during problem definition can be compared with programs written or with advice given. Finding something meaningful that can be counted under all circumstances is impossible. Finding a few things that can be counted and then being able to relate them one to another is difficult. The favorite old measurement of "lines of code produced in a unit of time" is seldom valid anymore because of the variety of languages used and the application of code generators. Fourth-generation languages have negated comparisons to COBOL coding. Even COBOL-to-COBOL can still be compared only if the same compilers are used.

Indirect measurement requires that someone develop a model and then run a sufficient number of cases through the model to determine a norm. These, then, become believable answers. The results of such an analytical study will translate into the number of hours required to do a certain task. If the sample is large enough, the results will be reproducible. If the sample is consistent with the types of projects that you handle, then the answers can be compared. Once someone else has performed and published all this work, you can compare the time it takes for you to do the set of tasks with the norm to arrive at an indirect relative measure of productivity.

There is value in using both direct and indirect approaches when testing CASE tools! First, the indirect, or relative, method establishes some useful comparative values for your own shop. Second, the direct method gives you an ongoing check on the accuracy of the relative measure. While there is no single factor that can be counted on for all types of application development work, a small number of variables, other than time, can be readily collected, categorized, reported, and reviewed as different CASE tools are used.

In considering the measurement of productivity, there is another important distinction to be made, which is between the productivity of the workers involved and the effective productivity to the organization as a whole. At the clerical and end-user level, the productivity focus is on cost reduction and efficiency. This important concept is that of economic productivity, which means goods or services produced per unit of labor or expense. At the executive and manager level, the productivity focus is on advantage to the organization. The key concept here is that of common productivity, which simply means finishing a desired and acceptable job as rapidly as possible. Speed is needed to be useful for management decision. There has often been a lack of distinction between these two concepts, particularly since they have areas of intersection. In the following discussion on productivity measures, the emphasis will be on economic productivity, or efficiency, because it is clearly measurable under agreed conditions. The problems of measuring effectiveness, quality, and appropriateness are great, although metrics may be occasionally available. The essence of the measurement of common productivity in the high payoff areas of management will be in the perception of the managers themselves. All measures that may be appropriate should be taken, plans should be written for productivity improvement, and the actual results received should be compared in writing to the plans. The human perspective on the success of CASE implementations will remain paramount. Managers will be satisfied if they and their staffs can get analyses and reports more efficiently, and in better form, than they had previously.

Thus the measure of productivity improvement should always be understood as possibly in one or more of three distinct measurement areas: efficiency, quality, and effectiveness.

Efficiency is the economic measure of the use of resources and the achievement of specific, defined goals. In data processing, it must include computer performance evaluation, professional time utilization, and work product measurement. It may be simply represented by a surrogate, such as the number of jobs processed per month, or it may be represented by a total factor efficiency approach where the value of all the output produced is divided by the total cost of production, or all the input. Such measures are expensive to obtain and track and may not be worth the effort.

Quality is a measure of the general usefulness of a product in the condition in which it is produced. There is no great value in the efficient production of low-quality results. Factors of accuracy, completeness, consistency, error tolerance, security, traceability, auditability, and information commonality are the key criteria in the acceptance of the computer products. No productivity improvement can be claimed for computer results that are not of more than acceptable quality. Quality is indeed measurable, and there is a body of literature available on quality assurance of computer processes.

Effectiveness is the most important component of productivity improvement. It is the perceived increase in managerial productivity that is obtained. It is the satisfaction of the users and their managers that the functions are being performed in a more superior manner. Managers will be satisfied that there has been a productivity increase in the work of their staffs and their own work if the results of projects:

- Are obtained in an acceptable time for their decisions.
- Fit with their understanding of the problem.
- Are testable, consistent, and apparently accurate.
- Can be modified whenever desired, as conditions or assumptions change.
- Can be verified with a variety of calculation approaches.
- Are what they wanted, when they wanted them, at a cost that was understood.

Technical staff must always be concerned with the objective measurement of productivity improvement and should analyze a variety of approaches to the metric involved. They should be satisfied, however, that some of the critical areas of assessing productivity improvement will remain subjective. If management perceives that the profitability of the organization has been enhanced by the use of CASE methods, then there has been productivity improvement.

Productivity Measures

Productivity is usually a perception of management. If more items are produced than normal or if the "bottom line" of an operation comes out well, it then appears that productivity has been increased. Whether the increase was due to better management, harder work, or the new CASE methods may well be open to debate if there has been no attempt to analyze and measure the productivity of existing and planned systems. In some cases, if the new systems appear to be more productive, there may be no interest in finding out why they are so. In other cases, there may be great advantage in finding the sources of the productivity increases in numeric terms so that extensions and further use of them may be planned and approved. In this section, a few productivity measures that have been tried are discussed, and the principal productivity performance factors are described.

It is important in productivity measures and analyses to use the most objective figures that can be reported and that are accepted by all concerned. In the order of preference, the following numbers should be attempted for stating the output and cost figures:

- *Use actual production and cost figures* when they are available. These will normally be the "standard cost" figures to remove detailed operational differences.

- *Use agreed-on assigned costs and estimated production and efficiency figures* if actuals are not available. These are usually accepted as objective.

- *Use user estimates of advantages of the system and approximate costs of the operation from an analysis* if no routinely reported figures are available.

- *Use qualitative improvement benefits* if the user agrees to weigh them against the costs. This may be completely adequate if the system is installed because the user says it is an "operational necessity."

Actual cost and benefit figures can be considered as "hard dollars." Estimated numbers to which the user agrees can be considered as "soft dollars."

Hard Dollar Savings.

Hard dollar savings are reductions in costs that are clearly reflected in actual balance sheets. Normally, they can be readily obtained on agreement with the accounting department. It may be necessary, of course, to establish new accounting line items to gather such numbers systematically and routinely. The numbers will be allocated according to existing budgets and accounting rules. Some of the figures may be directly attributable to savings in the department concerned, such as:

- Reduction in computing costs
- Reduction in communications costs
- Reduction in clerical costs

Other figures may depend on the agreed-on cost assignments within the organization, such as the reduction in the charged use on the central computer. This may be offset by increased technical support costs and must be examined. Other hard dollar savings will depend upon the overall organizational procedures, such as reduction in floor space requirements. This may be difficult to find as a stated savings for a project because of other shifts and changes in floor space usage.

Soft-Dollar Benefits.

There are a number of very real benefits that need management agreement on evaluating the advantages of time savings, more efficient use of staff, and less future increase in staff. If the ground rules are discussed, it may be possible to state substantial benefits that have been gained operationally by the CASE methods. These are usually soft dollars because they do not show directly on the bottom line and depend upon management perception of the advantages that have been achieved. Some of the benefits on which agreed-on figures can be placed are:

- More rapid access to databases that are used with consequently faster analyses or customer response.
- Faster response to management requests for information and analyses.
- Reduced lead time in installing systems.
- More efficient use of the analytical staff when they have priority use of sufficient data and computer power and get improved problem turnaround.

Definitions of Productivity

It is helpful to define mathematically such concepts as productivity, efficiency and effectiveness to show how they are ultimately measured in terms of real costs and real operational advantages. Such terms have been clearly defined in economics and industrial engineering literature. The problem is to focus the definition on the computer systems rather than on the general economy or manufacturing procedures.

Figure 14 lists four statements that may be directly applied to information services activities.

First, productivity is a measure of how effectively the total assigned resources are used to produce desired products. The desired products are, of course, information and the data stored to produce information at a later date. Note that the information must be "desired" and appropriate for some useful function in the organization. The "information resource" frequently discussed includes the whole body of useful information in an organization and the systems available to manipulate and report it. The size of the information resource does not help to measure productivity, however. Productivity is a measure of the effectiveness of the information-generating resources in producing the appropriate information resources desired for management decisions.

FIGURE 14. Definitions of productivity.

A. Productivity is a measure of how effectively the total assigned resources are used to produce desired products.

B. $$\text{Productivity} = \frac{\text{Output}}{\text{Input}} = \frac{\text{Value of the Output Products Produced}}{\text{Assigned Cost of Producing the Output Products}}$$

C. To increase productivity means to increase the yield of results, benefits, or profits, while following processing standards with sufficient quality control, to satisfy the specified requirements at a lower cost.

D. Productivity = (Efficiency) x (Effectiveness)

or

$$\frac{\text{Useful Results Delivered}}{\text{Cost}} = \frac{\text{Production}}{\text{Cost}} \times \frac{\text{Useful Results Delivered}}{\text{Production}}$$

Second, the classical definition of productivity is (output) divided by (input). This definition can be handled in either a macro or micro sense. In information services, the best definition of output is the value of the output products produced, while input is the assigned cost of producing these output products. Obviously, these are not simple numbers to obtain. These are really (benefits) divided by (costs), however, and most information services personnel are familiar with the various approaches to quantify benefits and costs in order to justify new systems. Much has been written and published on the subject. One of the critical problems in assigning costs in data processing work is the decision on data gathering and controlling costs in the user areas. This problem is usually solved by following the procedures in force in the organization for budgeting and cost reporting. This helps give a repeatable base for productivity measures. When part of the effort is in the user areas, the related costs there must be considered.

The third definition of productivity is its attainment. To increase productivity means to increase the yield of results, benefits, or profits while following processing standards, with sufficient quality control to satisfy the specified requirements at a lower cost. Data processing productivity is not a matter of manufacturing a product less expensively as long as it sells at the same cost; the value of data processing products is principally in their accuracy and timeliness. Quality assurance of the product is a critical factor. Standards and procedures must be followed and the specified requirements satisfied, or the output is inadequate.

The fourth definition is:

```
Productivity    = (Efficiency) × (Effectiveness) where:
Productivity    = (Useful Results Delivered) ÷ (Cost)
Efficiency      = (Production) ÷ (Cost)
Effectiveness   = (Useful Products Delivered) ÷ (Production)
```

In this fourth definition, the classical definition of productivity as (output) divided by (input) is extended to show that it is the product of efficiency and effectiveness. Efficiency is essentially the unit cost of accomplishing the results, while effectiveness is the amount of useful results delivered per production unit. There is one extra dimension that is not readily apparent in the equation.

That dimension is the usefulness, quality, and appropriateness of the results. It is assumed that the results are those desired by management.

Thus the definition of productivity is apparently simple. The elements that make up productivity are clear. The questions arise: How are these elements measured? How can it be objectively determined if the installation of a computer system has increased productivity? Can ratios be developed that will indicate the degree of success in increasing productivity? The answers to these questions will be discussed, but the numeric application of the definition will depend upon the individual circumstances and on what factors management wishes to have reported as the measurement. In the final analysis, productivity with microcomputers is always a perception by responsible managers.

Measuring Efficiency

Efficiency represents the cost to prepare output products, or the ratio of production to cost, as defined above. It is the unit cost of production. The improvement of efficiency is the production of defined outputs with a lesser amount of human, software, and hardware resources. Improvement of efficiency is action taken to avoid loss. It is readily measured by industrial engineering and management science techniques. Efficiency answers the question, Is the information organization developing systems and producing information at the lowest possible cost?

Efficiency will be attained by:

- Maintaining the necessary management controls over the information organization's resources.

- Using the proper procedures, techniques, and standards in developing computer-based systems at all levels in the organization.

- Maintaining an optimal balance of personnel, hardware, and software.

- Staffing and equipping functions at the correct level for their needs.

- Systematically reviewing all information services areas to ascertain their costs and operational efficiency.

The steps in the measurement of efficiency are outlined in Figure 15. They will not be further developed here, as the subject is general. Note that a measure of efficiency can only be discussed after a detailed system design has been accomplished so that the data work flow is clearly understood. Indicators that will then be developed to calculate and report efficiency will be entities such

FIGURE 15. Measuring efficiency.

Analyze Information Flow in System

- Identify critical inputs
- Identify system activities
- Identify critical outputs
- Develop indicators that are related to the work flow, and are reportable and repetitive

Establish a Work Product Reporting System

- Use computer system to generate counts
- Apply quality control criteria
- Use regular production reporting to measure production

Allocate Costs to Production Steps

- Identify cost elements
- Develop standard costs for functions
- Agree on cost allocation algorithms
- Collect cost data to measure costs

Apply Quality Standards and Controls

- Measure objective quality (timeliness, accuracy, response, etc.)
- Measure perceived quality (user acceptance and complaints)
- Develop level of acceptable quality

Analyze Efficiency

- Relate cost data to production data, where standards have been met
- Develop unit costs
- Compare against standards and over time

as data counts, calculations accomplished, output report lines, and so forth. The counting of the indicators must be systematic and repetitive so that a work/product reporting system can be designed with results that are automatically generated, after they have been screened for quality. Standard costs can be useful in such a reporting system.

The problem of assigning costs to production steps is normally considered to be difficult in data processing work with large computers, because of the complexity of the operating systems and the concurrent operation of several unrelated applications. The problem is much more straightforward with microcomputer systems, however, and the cost allocation algorithms can be easily developed after a few initial assumptions have been made to assign overhead costs.

The application of quality standards and controls to the results that are produced brings in the third dimension mentioned above. Arbitrary distinctions can be made relative to quality to produce some objective quality measures that can be directly factored against the efficiency numbers. It is not efficient to produce late, inaccurate, or nonresponsive information. There are some less objective measures of quality, however. The reported information may pass a control screen, but the users may perceive it to be less useful, or they may even complain about it. Counts of complaints may be of interest to management, but they are not real numbers to apply in an equation. A level of acceptable quality and appropriate results must be developed by analysis and discussion with the users. It can then be applied against the production figures used to calculate an efficiency factor.

The analysis of efficiency is, therefore, the relating of cost data to production data where appropriate standards have been met in the production. For the ongoing measure of efficiency, criteria are established for these measurements and standards, and, generally, unit costs are developed. The principles of standard costing may be applied if the measure is to be regularly examined, with the unit costs being routinely compared to the standard costs over time.

Measuring Effectiveness

Effectiveness is the use of the output information products to further the goals of the organization. It is a measure of the fulfillment of the purpose and the accomplishment of the desired results, and it is the leveraging of value throughout the organization. It may be measurable as the attainment of a planned increase in value of the organization's information resources, in proportion to the production effort expended to attain the increased value.

Effectiveness answers the question, Are the organization's resources being applied to the most profitable and useful application of computer-based systems?

Effectiveness will be attained by:

- Giving proper priorities to systems implementation based on business needs and objectives.
- Using the installed systems in accordance with the profitability and cost objectives originally established.
- Modifying the systems as required by a changing business and economic environment.
- Determining if significant opportunity has been lost by lack of certain systems in the development plan and program.
- Analyzing the usefulness and quality of the information products that are delivered by the system.

Effectiveness is not as readily measurable as efficiency because it frequently depends upon opinion as to the outcome of the process. In some cases, it can be quite specific, such as the number of useful reports produced for a given amount of effort. The actual usefulness of the reports may be called into question, however, and some measure of their quality may be required from a survey of the perception of the users.

The steps in making a statistical measure of effectiveness are outlined in Figure 16. Again, they will not be further developed here because only the idea of effectiveness is important in the management of microcomputer system productivity. For a given application, and after a user survey, some useful measures of effectiveness may become apparent.

FIGURE 16. Measuring effectiveness.

Define the System Objectives
- Results to be delivered
- Quality level to be attained
- Indicators of useful results delivered

Relate to Efficiency Measures
- Use same work/product reporting system
- Get figures from regular production reporting
- Apply scale to quality standards

Collect Data on User Perception of Effectiveness
- Apply scale to objective quality measures (timeliness, accuracy, response time, consistency, reruns, etc.)
- Conduct routine surveys of user perception of the accomplishment of the desired results
- Apply statistical scale to the data related to efficiency

Analyze the Effectiveness and Efficiency Ratios
- Reject areas of strong dissatisfaction (noneffective)
- Compare the statistical effectiveness data to the measured efficiency data
- Analyze whether results are homogeneous and normal, or if they consist of irregular, outlying data

The first step in discussing effectiveness is obviously to define the system objectives, with the results to be delivered and the quality level to be attained. Then, some indicators of useful results to be delivered may become apparent and may be measurable. Effectiveness measures should be related to the efficiency measures if a reasonable criterion of productivity is to be established. Thus, the data from the same work/product reporting system should be used from the regular production reporting. Scales should be applied to quality standards because a given quality is accepted or not accepted in efficiency calculations, but the range of acceptable quality will have a bearing on effectiveness as it is perceived.

The best method of collecting data on the effectiveness of information system products is to gather results of surveys of the user perception of particular areas of effectiveness. Some data can come from user-accepted scales applied to the objective quality measures, such as timeliness, accuracy, response time, consistency, reruns, and so on. Other data can come from routine surveys of the user perception of the accomplishment of desired results. All such information is essentially opinion research and should be handled statistically. The numbers are not mathematically "real."

In analyzing the effectiveness and efficiency ratios, areas of strong dissatisfaction should be rejected. If the system is noneffective, it cannot be used indefinitely, and there will be no good measure of effectiveness. If the statistical effectiveness data are then compared to the measured efficiency data at set periods over time, the results can probably be accepted and used for discussion if they are homogeneous and close to what is normally expected. If the results show irregular and outlying data, the figures are of little value as they are probably not reproducible.

These approaches to measuring efficiency and effectiveness can become quite complex and difficult if large systems with many users and many system interconnections are being studied. Only agreed, specific data should be gathered after broad assumptions have been made. The approaches are much more straightforward with microcomputer systems, however. If there is a decision to analyze and report efficiency and effectiveness, it is possible to agree on specific measures and ways of reporting them, and to come up with reproducible data that will show significant trends in improvement or other factors.

Measuring Quality or Appropriateness

Quality, usefulness, or appropriateness is an even more elusive number to arrive at. It is essentially a "yes/no" or a "go/no go" screen that can be applied to the efficiency numbers to determine if the results are adequate for further consideration. Quality control, or quality assurance, is greatly needed in data processing work, but the results are, by nature, qualitative even though quality "metrics" may be used in the reporting. A report on quality as a performance factor may be, in essence, simply a remark or footnote if "sufficient" quality has been attained. It is still a factor of considerable interest, however.

Quality, or appropriateness, may be defined in several ways, depending on the purpose of the applications being run. It may be described as the degree of excellence of the operation of the system. It may be described on the basis of whether it is valid or appropriate to the end in view being justified, correctly defined and developed, and legally efficacious. It may be described on the basis of whether there is sufficient control, direction, regulation, and coordination of the business activity in question. Quality or appropriateness answers the question, Is the information produced usable and timely enough to meet the operational decision requirements of management, as well as accurate enough to meet financial and statutory requirements?

Quality and appropriateness will be attained by:

- Reviewing that all operations are appropriate to the end in view.
- Maintaining adequate controls and direction over computer processing and utilization, which are commensurate with good operating principles.
- Setting, maintaining, and reviewing proper quality control standards and procedures.
- Determining that the output of the information organization meets all financial and statutory requirements.
- Determining that the information processed meets operational, decision, and technical needs, according to the specifications and requirements.
- Having written, approved procedures and trained employees.
- Being aware of user opinions and attempting to improve the user perception of the operation.

Measurement of Quality

It has been generally found that productivity can be measured by the systems development group involved, since they should have routine collection mechanisms for most of the effort and time data that is required for such analyses. The measurement of quality, however, is best handled by third parties who were not part of the application development work. Organizations that are interested in substantially improving the effectiveness of their systems development efforts usually find it necessary to have a formal quality assurance program handled by an independent group reporting to the highest level in information services. An effective QA program will play an important role in ensuring the best economics in systems development, as well as the most favorable use of human and other resources. QA fits well with the management structures that are needed with CASE methodologies. Doing things over or working with less than desirable products are not satisfactory alternatives. Establishing and running a formal QA program is an effective way to reduce human errors and nonhuman faults, and it is clearly appropriate to involve it with CASE. The professional handling of QA can provide the objective proof that may be necessary to establish and enlarge a CASE effort.

Quality Assurance is normally a staff function within information services that analyzes, develops, and implements control and review systems in all areas of information analysis and production. Usually a small staff, it does not perform the full quality review work itself, but develops the necessary review methodologies and oversees them. It usually raises the organization's consciousness of quality information products. If involved early in the analysis of CASE efforts, QA could well be instrumental in proving the value of CASE to the corporation.

Quality Assurance should be considered in its relationship to CASE work, whether it is for improving the quality of the resultant CASE products or for proving to management the value of the CASE approach in creating excellent products. For a comprehensive description and analysis of the organization, management, and implementation of QA work, a very useful manual is the three-volume *Quality Assurance*, available from the Chantico Publishing Company.

The creation of computer applications is not simple; nor is maintaining the applications. Good computer applications depend upon finding a sense of order or structure for the things that are done by people. Unfortunately, different people have their own ways of doing jobs. Each one sees a certain piece of the work and is biased toward his own tasks. The developer of applications must try to be systematic and analytical, must find the overall pattern, and must successfully describe that pattern to the affected people.

The mechanism for finding those patterns—for building applications—is neither as neat nor as orderly as the mechanism for building databases. Data remains stable within an organization. The processes for using that data are continually changing. There is no way to define the minimum, nonredundant processes. In other words, there is no one right answer.

Structured development methodologies have helped to order our thinking about processes, but structured methodologies create extra paper. The problem for the application developer is that, with the exception of small, textbook cases, it is essentially impossible to perform all of the correct transformations manually that create the logical models of an application from the physical model. The complexity of the translation is immense, which is the reason why some CASE tools are directed to this area.

No permanent solution to our productivity problem can afford to be that complex. Many of the quantum leaps of knowledge within the physical sciences have come from a change in perspective that simplifies the observations: Newton's laws of physics; the world is round; the planets circle the sun and not the earth. Each of these conclusions simplified the assumptions.

For most real applications, no one can rationally and logically create, let alone explain, the Current Logical Model and the Future Logical Model, and precisely how they were derived. With enough time and patience, you might be able to create the Current Logical Model for a large application, although it will be changing. The results would be in the form of three generic functions: input, transform, output. All control processes will be gone. Either all data will enter a function and be stored somewhere, or they will be removed from where they were stored and sent somewhere. How can the transition to this bland set of diagrams be explained? How do you justify the required controls?

On the other hand, for data, there is a set of correct and provable rules for translating physical data into logical data. The mechanism is called normalization, which can be defined as the process by which a group of data elements is logically ordered to form the smallest set of data (entities) possible. When data are grouped logically (referred to as the Third Normal Form), they will remain stable even when the processes that use the data change. There are specific rules for translating a given set of data elements into a stable data model. These rules move the data elements from the nonnormalized state in the Current Physical Model to the Third Normal Form, which is recommended for stable database implementations. From an academic point of view, the process, and therefore the result, is mathematically provable and correct.

There is no Third Normal Form for processes. Processes are messy functions, particularly since they involve people. How then can this mess be sorted out? How can you improve productivity and quality? More fundamentally, how do you measure productivity? What should be happening in the application development function? Which of the new technologies are most promising? What overall methodologies should you use to integrate these technologies? How can you determine the potential value of any particular approach for your organization?

These and other questions are explored in this book. Practices are described that others have found successful, and checklists are provided to aid in their selection. You must evaluate where you are and how to get to places where others have been. There are a variety of approaches that may enhance your ability to service your customers.

In all aspects of productivity and quality, your people are the key to effectiveness. They must comprehend the intent and possibilities of any approaches that are selected, and learn to use them in an integrated, cooperative fashion.

2.4 THE ECONOMICS OF CASE

As an example of the calculation of the economics of CASE, this section gives an overview of the approach used by Texas Instruments for the use of their *Information Engineering Facility*.

Texas Instruments developed a Lotus 1-2-3 model to compute the Net Present Value (NPV) resulting from a decision to implement their Information Engineering Facility (IEF). The example of the investment in this model is their perception of what a commercial customer would make.

If this model is useful, Texas Instruments (TI) would welcome your comments and suggestions and share them with those who are interested.

The IEF integrated CASE product from TI is a powerful

piece of software. While many software packages promise cost savings through operating efficiencies or productivity gains, these gains and savings are difficult to measure. The IEF promises productivity gains, not in percentages, but in multiples. The multiples may also be difficult to measure, however. The tolerance for error is also much greater. If $2\times$ or $3\times$ multiples are profitable, it matters less that we cannot say for sure whether the gain is really $4\times$ or $5\times$. In either case, the decision to use the IEF is clearly one that is profitable to the user.

Early experience with IEF projects that have gone through to code generation at TI have provided productivity lifts of three and four times, with the promise of five times and, in subsequent maintenance, even more. Since TI is already a heavy user of the IEF and plans to achieve significant penetration of its systems activity, the question has arisen within TI about what to expect in terms of staffing and savings under varying assumptions.

Their Lotus 1-2-3 model, IEFNPV, was prepared for internal evaluation of the IEF at TI. The assumptions may or may not fit another situation. It is intended to demonstrate a method for economic analysis of a software decision. No warranty is expressed or implied for specific results in any particular environment.

Figure 17 summarizes key assumptions contained in the IEF Productivity Model. In Figure 18, TI has 1000 analyst/programmers who will be affected by the IEF. Their annual cost to TI is about $100,000 a year, fully loaded for salary, benefits, and overhead, including supervision, facilities, terminals, supplies, and mainframe access. They expect that IEF users will consume more mainframe time in their development of systems. Experience to date indicates that this usage costs TI about $1000 per month per IEF programmer/analyst. While this may be a temporary situation, offset by the fact that less senior analysts become effective more quickly with the IEF, they have assumed in the model that people with IEF cost $12,000 a year more than non-IEF people.

TI has a large installed base of information systems operating on DL/1 databases. The target environment for new systems development is DB2. While TI will be aggressive in transferring technology to those now developing systems, it will take six or seven years to reach significant penetration goals. The first natural target is new systems development, followed by major modifica-

FIGURE 17. Information Systems and Services IEF™ productivity model.

Key Assumptions

Fixed
- TI population impacted by IEF is 1000 analyst/programmers
- Annual cost (fully loaded) is $100K per analyst/programmer
- IEF analyst/programmers will use more resources

Variable
- Penetration of IEF (% of population):

	'88	'89	'90	'91	'92	'93	'94

Aggressive Penetration

	'88	'89	'90	'91	'92	'93	'94
1. Modest	2	6	11	17	23	27	30
2. Moderate	5	12	21	33	45	54	60
3. Rapid	7	18	32	50	68	81	90

Very Aggressive Penetration

	'88	'89	'90	'91	'92	'93	'94
1. Modest	5	10	15	20	25	30	30
2. Moderate	10	20	30	40	50	60	60
3. Rapid	14	30	45	60	76	90	90

- Increasing complexity of systems requirements (compound annual growth)
  0%;   6%;   10%;   25%   (BW)
- Productivity impact of IEF (times current level)
  1;   2;   3;   4;   5

tions to existing systems. Existing systems will be converted only when there is a valid business reason to do so, and some systems will never be converted. Maintenance on those systems will be required as long as they are used. They have analyzed two rates of penetration and, within each, three penetration goals.

System complexity is growing at some rate between zero for a stagnant operation and 25 percent, as projected in *Business Week* in the May 9, 1988 issue. TI estimates, from function point analysis, that their systems complexity has been growing at 6 percent per year. Their DL/1 databases grew at 17 percent per year from 1984 to 1987. Since they are applying this complexity factor to the number of people required, one might also look at the historic rate of growth of employees in systems analysis and programming.

FIGURE 18. Information Systems and Services IEF™ productivity model.

Example

Assumptions: Complexity factor growth rate – 6%
IEF penetration — YR 1 = 5%, YR 2 = 12%, YR 3 = 21%
IEF productivity impact = 3 Times
Cost per analyst/prog = $100K/YR (Non-IEF)
$112K/YR (IEF)

		YR 1	YR 2	YR 3
A.	Base MIS staff	1000	1000	1000
B.	Complexity factor	1.00	1.06	1.124
C.	Required MIS w/o IEF (A x B)	1000	1060	1124
D.	IEF penetration	5%	12%	21%
E.	Staff using conventional tech. (C - H AVG x G)	976	973	942
F.	Applications using IEF (C x D)	48	126	237
G.	IEF productivity factor	3x	3x	3x
H.	Staff using IEF (F/G)	16	42	79
I.	Required MIS staff (E + H)	992	1015	1021
J.	People impact of IEF (C - I)	8	45	103
K.	Net savings (J x $100K) - (H x $12K) $M	-0.3	3.2	8.4

Given the assumption shown in Figure 18 that IEF programmers cost 12 percent more, it is clearly unprofitable to go to IEF with anything less than a 50 percent productivity lift. Their experience with a library management system (3:1) and a source inspection system (4:1) confirmed their expectation that 5:1 is achievable. The model also assumes that new IEF users are only 50 percent effective the first year (or use the IEF on average for only six months at full effectiveness). There is a learning curve for new users and an organizational curve as the encyclopedia of reuseable diagrams is built. Productivity will improve with time, but is fixed in this early model.

The investment assumptions in Figure 19 are typical for buying software, training, consulting, and maintenance at published prices. One-year Volume Purchase Agreement (VPA) discounts are used, although two-year VPAs would be more advantageous in some cases. TI will use four mainframe packages, and they believe that these four mainframe encyclopedias will support up to 1000 IEF programmers. To get the productivity lift, most users

FIGURE 19. Information Systems and Services IEF℠ productivity model.

Investment Assumptions

Software
- One workstation tool set per A/P at $13,900 each, less VPA
- Four mainframes over three years, at $265,000 each, less VPA
- One year VPAs based on actual quantities

Training
- 15 days per workstation at $350/day the first year
- Training per workstation halves each year of experience

Consulting
- 40 days per first year project at $1500/day
- One project for every four analysts with IEF
- Consulting needs halve each year

Maintenance
- 15% of installed base

will want to buy one mainframe package the first year, and it may be all they ever need.

Training is tied to the number of workbenches, as each new user must receive some training. They have assumed 15 days training the first year, decreasing by 50 percent each year as those previously trained coach the new analysts on projects. TI's experience with other software indicates that this phenomenon holds true. Similarly, the amount of consulting is assumed to halve each year, from a fixed amount the first year, based on the aggressiveness of the penetration goal and rate. They assume 40 days of consulting per first-year project with one project for every four IEF programmer analysts. Project leaders and assistants can increase the number on a project to five or six people. A project is expected to last six months—the same effective time assumed for first-year IEF analysts.

Because the investment is made over time, with savings being realized concurrently, return on investment analysis and internal rate of return calculations do not prove useful over this range of assumptions. Net present value is used in Figure 20 as an index of merit to compare relative penetration goals and rates. As expected, the present value of the decision increases with productivity factor, complexity growth rate, aggressiveness of penetration, and penetration goals. This is one good thing you cannot do too much of.

One can look at NPV at a bank rate of 10 percent, at an opportunity rate of 25 percent, or at an average cost of capital of 17 percent. They have elected to use the 17 percent rate in Figure 20, but the others are also computed in the model.

The results are shown in Figure 21. The model also computes NPV for each year to show the breakeven period and the NPV if the IEF development were to be discontinued after each successive year. The user is free to chose a period other than seven years.

The model does not take into account quality improvements and other opportunities for return on investment that result from using the IEF. These may include developing the right system for competitive advantage, developing a more timely system because of the reduced development cycle time, catching errors earlier in the development cycle when they are easier and less costly to fix, and maintaining documentation and code integrity at the level of

Net Present Value at 17% Cost of Capital ($M)

Product Factor	Complexity GR Rate	Aggressive Penetration			Very Aggressive Penetration		
		30% $M	60% $M	90% $M	30% $M	60% $M	90% $M
2X	0%	12	26	40	16	34	51
	25%	27	55	84	34	69	104
3X	0%	23	46	70	29	59	89
	25%	52	106	160	63	128	192
4X	0%	28	57	86	35	72	108
	25%	65	132	198	78	157	236
5X	0%	31	63	95	39	80	120
	25%	73	147	220	87	175	263

FIGURE 21. Texas Instruments Information Engineering Facility™ (IEF) net present value model.*

Base MIS Staff	1000	Number of programmer/analysts.
Annual Cost/Staff Now	100	Annual cost of non-IEF user ($000).
Annual Cost/IEF Staff	112	Annual cost of IEF user ($000).
Complexity Growth	10%	Annual growth in systems complexity.
Productivity Multiple	3	Impact of IEF (times current level).
Penetration Rate	2	1 = Aggressive, 2 = Very Aggressive.
Penetration Goal	3	Target % IEF (1=30%, 2=60%, 3=90%).
Net Present Value @ 17%	136.2	Figure of merit for using IEF ($M).

* This model has been developed by Texas Instruments for internal use and is intended to demonstrate a method for economic analysis of a software decision. While TI is eager to work with users of the IEF to achieve successful results, no warranty is expressed or implied for specific results in any particular environment.

FIGURE 21. (Cont.)

Information Systems and Services IEF Productivity Fanout Model

	1987	1988	1989	1990	1991	1992	1993	Year
Productivity Factor	3.0		Productivity of IEF users.					
MIS People	1000		Starting head count.					
IEF Penetration	14%	36%	57%	72%	81%	90%	90%	From table.
Complexity	1.00	1.10	1.21	1.33	1.46	1.61	1.77	Of systems.
People w/o IEF	1000	1100	1210	1331	1464	1611	1772	Head count.
People w/ IEF								
Conventional	928	830	669	509	393	294	251	Non-IEF.
IEF Applic	48	132	229	319	395	483	531	IEF Staff.
Total	976	962	898	828	788	777	782	Head Count.
Delta People	24	138	313	503	676	834	990	Unit Savings.
Annual Savings $M	1.8	12.2	28.5	46.5	62.9	77.6	92.6	$M Savings.

FIGURE 21. (Cont.)

Investment: Units of software and days of training and consulting.

New Workstations	48	84	97	90	76	88	48	Purchases.
CUM Workstations	48	132	229	319	395	483	531	Instald base
New Mainframes	2	1	1					purchases
CUM Mainframes	2	3	4	4	4	4	4	Instald base
VPA Discount	30%	35%	35%	35%	35%	35%	30%	One-yr VPA.
Training Days	720	630	364	169	71	41	11	15 days / WS.
Consulting Days	480	240	120	60	30	15	8	40 days / proj
No. of Projects	12	33	57	80	99	121	133	CUM WS / 4

Investment: $M

Software	0.84	0.93	1.05	0.81	0.69	0.80	0.47	Purchases.
Train. & Consult	0.97	0.58	0.31	0.15	0.07	0.04	0.02	Purchases.
Maintenance		0.18	0.39	0.64	0.82	0.98	1.17	15% of base
Annual $M	1.81	1.69	1.75	1.60	1.58	1.81	1.65	Invest. / year

Net Savings ($M)	0.0	10.5	26.8	44.9	61.3	75.8	91.0	Cash flow
NPV @ 10% $M	0.0	8.7	28.8	59.9	97.5	140.3	187.0	Present
NPV @ 17% $M	0.0	7.7	24.4	48.3	76.3	105.8	136.2	Value
NPV @ 25% $M	0.0	6.7	20.4	38.8	58.9	78.8	97.9	(to date)

Aggressive Penetration

Modest	2%	6%	11%	17%	23%	27%	30%
Moderate	5%	12%	21%	33%	45%	54%	60%
Rapid	7%	18%	32%	50%	68%	81%	90%

Very Aggressive Penetration

Modest	5%	12%	19%	24%	27%	30%	30%
Moderate	10%	24%	38%	48%	54%	60%	60%
Rapid	14%	36%	57%	72%	81%	90%	90%

FIGURE 21. (Cont.)

VPA Discounts	Workstations		Mainframes		One-Year Volume Purchase
	Qty	Disc	Qty	Disc	
	0	0%	0	0%	
	10	15%	2	15%	
	15	20%	3	20%	
	25	25%	4	25%	
	40	30%	5	30%	
	65	35%	6	35%	
	100	39%	9999	35%	
	150	42%			
	200	45%			
	9999	45%			

new systems. The fact is that the systems being developed are generally being selected on an ROI basis, and bringing them into production more quickly with the IEF can only increase the return on those systems. There are many benefits provided by IEF that are not included in this simple model that can multiply the net present value of the decision to use the Information Engineering Facility.

If this model is useful, TI would welcome your comments and suggestions, and would share it with those who are interested.

2.5   MANAGEMENT CONCERNS ABOUT CASE TECHNOLOGY

CASE technology is only in its second generation of sophistication. In the first generation, a few companies produced a number of CASE tools that handled specific parts of the software development life cycle, and many were quite effective for the areas they covered. In the second generation of CASE tools, in the later 1980s, some integration of the software development tools has taken place. A few tools span several phases of the development life cycle. A number have been linked under standard operating systems so that information can be readily passed between them.

The third generation of CASE technology is already emerging. In this third generation, not only will the software development tools through the SDLC be linked, but also part of the system will be:

- Structured methodology for management of the project.
- Project task scheduling throughout the project.
- Computer-based training (CBT).
- Supportive local area network (LAN) environment.

But there is a management concern about how deeply to move into CASE today. In the literature, they read a variety of comments, such as:

- "CASE can not yet produce the productivity increase that is needed."
- "CASE is excellent for new projects, but poor for maintenance."

- "The existing program logic is too unstructured, and database navigation access is too complex."
- "There is no way that logic constructs can be transformed into graphical objects, reorganized, checked for integrity, and then resubmitted to the central repository."
- "Systems analysts will not accept the discipline of integrated CASE."

Much of the CASE activity is on disconnected tools on PCs, while some is independently on the mainframes. At the same time, the bulk of the CASE environments center on an IBM mainframe with 3270-based on-line transaction processing, where the organization is essentially committed to move with IBM to its final Systems Application Architecture (SAA). Since all the promised facilities are not yet available, there is no easy integration of all the CASE activities in an organization into an overall idea-to-production system with all the possible CASE third-generation attributes.

Management, therefore, has a dilemma as to what direction to follow for immediate benefits and how to bring the efforts together at a later date for maximum benefits. Since most organizations have a principal concern about the plan-vs-actual with an annual budget system, immediate benefits normally prevail at the expense of greater benefits that are promised over a longer time.

There are a number of things that management can do immediately, however, that will reap short-term benefits and guarantee greater benefits in the long term. Some of these are:

1. Begin to move towards a shared relational database despite the time and the organizational and procedural changes that this will entail. Consider IBM's DB2 or other SQL-based systems, and train all the staff in relational rules and data definition and the accessing of data at abstract, set-oriented, value-driven levels.

2. Introduce useful standards for CASE, but not inhibiting standards. Remember that the systems will change and there will be even further integration of CASE and related methods. Standardize sufficiently to have all the staff moving in the same direction, with plenty of room left for experimentation and innovation.

3. Have standards for data representation and control and for approaches to represent process. If the database is properly designed, data can remain firm for some time. Process is much less stable than data, however, and much work is currently being done on how best to represent it. Leave plenty of room to experiment with and move to new ideas in handling process.

5. Encourage training and information exchange in all areas of CASE and its related technologies. There are some decisions that do not have to be made yet, but the systems engineering approach is the future of all information services work, and your staff must be prepared to move into this new era to gain the greatest value from its use. There is big money to be saved.

The main management concern is how to get started with CASE and how much to use it this year. Management should have their staff investigating and experimenting with a variety of CASE approaches, and should determine where CASE can best be used this year, even if only tentatively, so that the staff will be ready to move into CASE methods wherever they are appropriate another year. Figure 22 is a checklist to help managers make a logical review of the possibilities with CASE and determine at what level to move.

This checklist can be useful directly for planning the introduction or expansion of a CASE effort, and it can be used in strategic planning for determining where the best next moves might be. It can be used by managers to understand what ideas they may have to grasp, and where suggestions that have come up may fit in the overall scheme of CASE introduction. This checklist is not intended to be either exhaustive or explanatory. It simply lists the principal ideas that must be considered in CASE management. The explanations for all of these ideas are found in this manual. If you are already roughly familiar with most of these ideas, you can quickly estimate where you stand and what your priorities should be. In short, this is a planning checklist. It is not a set of action steps in any particular order.

FIGURE 22. Management concerns about CASE technology.

No.	Concern	Responses		
		Yes	No	N/A	Comments

Could CASE Technology be of Value to Us?

1. Are effective application systems critical to our company's future?

2. Are our present systems methods out of date, indicated by:

   a. No structured methodology for systems development management?

   b. Individual systems development projects, not controlled by management?

   c. Use of on-line 3270-type terminals in a batch environment?

   d. Little adherence to Systems Development Life Cycle controls?

   e. Few automated systems development support tools?

   f. Little effort or agreement on movement to relational databases?

   g. Very large backlog of systems requests?

   h. Little accurate management reporting of the status of systems development?

   i. Frequent time and cost overruns in systems development?

FIGURE 22. (Cont.)

No.	Concern	Responses			
		Yes	No	N/A	Comments
3.	Is there a growing need to support business-critical applications being demanded by high-level strategic planning?				
4.	Are strategic planning concepts applying pressure for more responsive systems development management?				
5.	Are there regular problems occurring in systems development?				
6.	Are user groups developing systems on PCs that should be on a central computer network?				

Are We Ready To Adopt CASE Technology?

No.	Concern	Yes	No	N/A	Comments
7.	Does our systems organization have effective, uniform central management?				
8.	Are our lead and senior systems analysts open to new ideas?				
9.	Have they been experimenting with some CASE tools?				
10.	Are the majority of supervisors advocating a move to CASE methodologies?				
11.	Would a systems development methodology tool be generally accepted?				

No.	Concern	Yes	No	N/A	Comments
12.	Is there an interest in increasing professional productivity with an acceptance of measurement of professional effort?				
13.	Do the various information services groups work well together, with a minimum of politics?				
14.	Can we implement a formal methodology in the major areas of systems development and make it stick?				
15.	Is there senior management pressure to bring systems development under better control?				
16.	Do we have some smaller, new systems projects that could be used as test cases?				
17.	Are we prepared to define and enforce standards?				
18.	Are we ready for detailed configuration management?				
19.	Are we organized for control of uniform documentation standards?				
20.	Can our training group handle a general move to the new CASE technologies?				

FIGURE 22. (Cont.)

No.	Concern	Responses			
		Yes	No	N/A	Comments
	Are CASE Tools Available for our Situation?				
21.	Have we analyzed where CASE tools might be appropriate to use?				
22.	Do we have projects for development in these areas?				
23.	Are there CASE tools specific to these areas?				
24.	Are we prepared to work in a rapidly changing CASE environment?				
25.	Do the professional staff agree that there are problems that could be solved with CASE methods?				
26.	Can we fund the level of support that will be needed for the useful CASE tools?				
27.	Can we solve the organization's political problems with the introduction of CASE tools?				
28.	Are we prepared to provide or obtain the training and support that the useful CASE tools will require?				
29.	Are we prepared to solve the problems of control and documentation that will arise?				

No.	Concern	Responses			
		Yes	No	N/A	Comments

Systems Analysis Productivity Tools

30. Can our group be ready for:

    a. Improving the discipline of analysts, programmers, and project leaders?

    b. Accepting the overhead of detailed project management?

    c. Operating in a structured design and programming environment?

31. Should we start with the available tools supported on:

    a. Mainframe computer system?

    b. Personal computers?

    c. Powerful workstations?

    d. Network (LAN) operation?

32. Do we have an operational relational database?

33. Are our analysts and programmers familiar with relational methods?

FIGURE 22. (Cont.)

No.	Concern	Responses			
		Yes	No	N/A	Comments
34.	Should the early areas of use be:				
	a. Developing a full relational database system?				
	b. Installing the encyclopedia concept?				
	c. Creating a design database?				
	d. Accepting strategic data planning techniques?				
	e. Using computable specification languages?				
	f. Using formal data modeling tools?				
	g. Experimenting with, and assembling, an analyst tool kit?				
35.	Would it be preferable to move straight to a full information engineering concept?				
36.	Should the analyst and programming tools be integrated from the start?				
37.	Do we have standalone, centralized information systems, with few conversion problems, that would be good candidates for CASE experiment?				

No.	Concern	Responses			
		Yes	No	N/A	Comments

Programmer Productivity Tools

38. Are our programmers familiar with nonprocedural languages?

39. Should the first areas of use be:

    a. Computer-aided graphics and narrative documentation?

    b. Automatic code generators?

    c. Application generators?

    d. Design database with specifications and cross-references stored?

    e. Rigorous verification techniques?

    f. PC workstations with mouse-driven graphics?

    g. Languages for rapid prototyping?

    h. Fourth-generation languages?

    i. Expert systems?

40. Would it be preferable to start with integrated design and programming tools?

FIGURE 22. (Cont.)

No.	Concern	Yes	No	N/A	Comments
				Responses	
41.	Have the human factors been considered in educational and technology transition support?				
	Development Support Productivity Tools				
42.	Is there agreement on a system development methodology that should be followed?				
43.	Will the department accept and use a structured development support methodology?				
44.	Is there readiness to install a development support process with a shared database and a shared interface with the design and programming tools?				
45.	Would a complete, structured development methodology be feasible at this stage?				
46.	Would there be acceptance of, and cooperation with, project task scheduling?				
47.	Can a full Computer-Based Training (CBT) system be implemented?				
48.	Can an effective standards and procedures group be given sufficient technical support?				

No.	Concern	Responses			
		Yes	No	N/A	Comments
49.	Can the Local Area Network (LAN) be implemented with all who may be involved?				
50.	Is the LAN environment supportive to the developers?				
51.	Is there sufficient management support and commitment to the needed management and support structures as well as the CASE tools?				

CHAPTER 3

How to Manage CASE

Overview

*C*ASE is clearly in evolution. In looking at the management and planning of CASE implementation, it is helpful to construct a reference framework to show systems relationships and to enable objective choices to be compared. The most satisfactory framework for analyzing most CASE tools is the logical systems architecture that is centered around data management tools.

Another framework that can be considered, particularly for discussions with management, is the systems development life cycle. CASE approaches can be shown as systematizing and automating the traditional SDLC phases. The new information engineering life cycle, with automated transformations between the phases, is described. The constant functions in all systems development methodologies are noted.

CASE has strategic implications for an organization. Strategic planning for CASE projects is emphasized because of the CASE fit with a "top-down" approach to system planning and development. Key points in the project management and control of CASE efforts are emphasized because of their necessity for practical management.

The use of CASE in Application Development Centers (ADCs)

is discussed because of the natural fit of the two concepts. ADCs give the type of structure needed for successful CASE work.

Strategies for the successful adoption of CASE are briefly outlined.

3.1 THE TRANSITION TO CASE

The introduction and effective use of CASE will cause a major change in any organization. From management's viewpoint, there will be a greater emphasis on the application projects that may have strategic implications to the organization, and there will be greater responsiveness from information services. They will see faster delivery of high-quality applications that are readily maintained. From the technical staff's viewpoint, there may be disruption and reorganization, with much more emphasis on business systems analysis, possibly by nonprofessionals, and much less emphasis on programming and maintenance. The full use of CASE in an organization usually leads to new job titles and new job descriptions.

Some organizations have been moving towards CASE steadily over the years through the use of structured system development technologies and the early forms of program generators. Many others have been experimenting with a number of CASE tools and techniques. Most companies, however, have been working principally with traditional systems development methods and life cycles. Probably, all organizations still have a substantial part of their systems staff working on a variety of systems maintenance and enhancement problems. Thus nearly everyone faces the problem of making substantial changes in their systems development efforts in the near future, and of transferring technology from their experimental groups and from the vendors to the bulk of their staffs. The question is, then, *How do we successfully introduce CASE technology and manage the transition from our present methods?*

There is no question that considerable effort must be expended before any dramatic results are achieved. Remember, as was pointed out earlier, the use of CASE is, first and foremost, a productivity issue, but no rapid increase in productivity is to be expected in the first year of the introduction of CASE. It will take time to learn and implement the new techniques. As systems are developed, however, there should be a quality improvement apparent to the users and to management. It is this quality improvement that will provide even more productivity improvement as systems enter the maintenance stage. Under CASE, when systems are properly engineered, they will meet user specifications, be well constructed, and be relatively easy to maintain rapidly.

The successful introduction of CASE technology is based on several standard management practices:

- Recognize that the decision to move to CASE has *strategic* implications and that it must be correlated with the strategic thrust of the corporation.
- Prepare for *transition management* by having a change plan that accounts for the expected resistance to organizational change and supplies the needed technical and management support.
- Define a complete set of *functional requirements* that consider the technical aspects, the organizational aspects, and the personnel skill mix that will be needed.
- Carefully *evaluate* the available CASE technologies, tools, and other products to determine their fit with the requirements.
- *Select* the best CASE products and approaches for the specific requirements of your business.
- *Plan and manage* the introduction of the CASE technologies and tool sets.

Such management practices will go a long way towards the effective introduction of CASE to any organization. They are all discussed in this book. There will also be other questions that arise during the transition to CASE. Some of the questions that keep recurring are:

- How do we change the *skill mix* in our organization during the transition to CASE? Whom do we hire, whom do we train, and what consultants do we employ?
- How far do we move from our *existing technologies*, such as structured analysis and programming techniques?
- Can *end-user development*, with its 4GLs and prototypes, be factored in?

- Do we move to a full *information engineering* approach or develop a number of CASE tool sets?

- What do we do about all the *old systems* that we must keep operational, despite their heavy maintenance load?

- How do we interest *top management* in our plans to spend a considerable amount of money and time to move to our planned goal?

- How do we manage the *recurring replacement* of expensive systems technologies that we will be faced with?

- Can we expect *business support* from the operational groups within the organization?

The use of CASE methodologies will have a profound effect on the systems development organization at all levels. Many CASE products include major improvements in human factors, the use of intelligent workstations, design automation techniques, prototyping, and expert systems. Although many CASE tools are for only part of the system development process, they are being integrated and combined to provide support for the entire life-cycle process. The basic question then becomes, How integrated should our CASE tool sets and methodologies be? Should we simply continue developing a variety of structured techniques that have been used since the early 1970s, adding more features and functions with various CASE tools, or should we commit to a full information engineering approach with a single, integrated set of tools? In either approach, there will be a trend towards developing a knowledge base of enterprise models, data models, and process models to create and maintain the applications, as long as there is an emphasis on data integration and management.

When the approach to CASE is *not* coordinated and standardized, there can be many efforts that are neither efficient nor effective. Many CASE tools may exist and actually be installed but the purported benefits are not realized. The symptoms are:

- Fragmented use of the CASE tools.
- Little transfer of knowledge between the different groups working on CASE.

- No integration between the various CASE tools.
- Considerable difficulty in changing the CASE approaches used to realize conformity and efficiency.

There is a clear need in planning the introduction of CASE to set a goal of the integrated use of tools, techniques, standards, and methodologies to realize a predictable development environment and maximum benefits. This may be through an information engineering product, or it may be through coordinating a variety of CASE tools. In either case, it is the whole environment that must be planned, not just an Information Engineering subset. It must include the management, planning, life-cycle management, control, and quality assurance aspects of development. The whole integrated development environment must be driven by business requirements, key roles taken by planning, and by the management of technology change and control. There must also be a formalization of organizational support to include:

- Central selection and coordination of CASE tools.
- Integration of the design and programming workbench environment.
- Applied standards and procedures.
- Full coverage of education and training.
- Routine productivity measurement.
- A quality assurance program.

The transition to CASE requires the automation of system development. In the past, system developers have automated other processes. With the adoption of CASE, they must begin automating their own processes. This requires a complete change in their traditional thinking, indicating that there must be considerable management planning performed and a large effort put into education and training. Automation always requires strategy preceding it. There must be a transition strategy developed by the responsible managers, advertised among the participants, and followed under control. A new transition strategy has three components:

1. A managed *transition plan* should be put into effect. This starts with a study that determines where you are—a baseline—and proceeds to where you are heading, with checkpoints planned along the way.

2. A *change management plan* should be prepared for handling problems along the way. Points of resistance should be considered and prepared for. A management steering committee may be helpful. It would agree to the transition plan, be prepared to help carry out the plan, and discuss the best solution to problems that arise.

3. A *transition support plan* should be part of the transition plan as it develops, to systematically handle the concerns of technology evaluation and selection, technology transfer, and methods transfer.

The management of CASE implementation is the management of an evolving process. First, it requires some centralization of planning and control to give direction and to follow the work in progression. Second, it is a continuous increase in the automation of systems efforts and will meet with various opposition along the way. Third, there must be a continually changing balance between the development engineering and the program mechanics. The theory is excellent, but there will be continually recurring technical problems. Fourth, the management of CASE is basically people management. The tools are available and the methodologies have been tested, but there are always very real problems installing the approach in any particular organization.

Figure 23 is a useful checklist to review these points and to help determine whether your organization is ready for a smooth transition to CASE. If there are too many "Nos" checked off, it probably means that the best approach is to do more testing of CASE approaches while more management support is gathered. Management backing for CASE is the fundamental key to success, but it only comes if the sponsors of CASE are knowledgeable in all the aspects of its introduction and use.

3.2 A FRAMEWORK FOR EVOLUTION

CASE includes various tools and numerous methods and most organizations work into its use carefully, with planned steps

FIGURE 23. Critical success factors for the transition to CASE.

(Use standard Checklist format)

1. Has high-level sponsorship, or a **"champion,"** for the CASE initiative been obtained?

2. Is there planning alignment between the corporate **business strategy** and the information services plans?

3. Are senior management prepared to be committed to the CASE initiative and budget for the transition?

4. Is information services committed to establish and support a **single architecture** in all its efforts?

5. Is information services planning all its resources (information resource management approach) together with its specific CASE plans?

6. Is the **management of organizational change** foremost in the CASE planning, including:

   a. A managed transition plan?

   b. A change management plan?

   c. A transition support plan?

7. Is there a strong group of analysts and users on the internal support/transition support/implementation team?

8. Are key **end users** willing to be involved throughout the CASE development life cycle?

9. Are there active lines of communication and good relationships with the staff involved so there can be good **people** management?

10. Has an **education/training** plan been outlined, and have preparations for it been discussed with appropriate individuals?

and with long-term objectives in mind. It is important that those in charge of planning for information services see the larger picture, and design and describe a framework for the evolution from present to future methods.

CASE can be many things to many people. There is no generally accepted definition of CASE in the offerings in the marketplace. Among the vendors of CASE tools, some describe CASE in terms of single tools; others talk of tool sets of design tools or code generators; others have linked several steps into engineering systems. This overlapping of terms and variation in definitions is not unexpected, as CASE is in its infancy, from an engineering viewpoint, and there will be many new ideas, new groupings of CASE tools, and new areas of inclusion in the CASE field. It is preferable not to try to contain CASE within a single set of current ideas, but to look at CASE as a developing area of engineering with expanding boundaries. A general frame of reference needs to be built for any organization to sort out and classify the ideas that are put forward and to consider their relationship with existing systems.

A useful reference framework will show relationships and areas of use, and will enable objective choices to be compared and analyzed. Following today's literature, there are many frameworks that can be constructed. Two will be outlined here. The first will be a general operational framework centered around data management. The second will be a comparison of system development life cycles. The differences between software engineering, systems engineering, and information engineering will be elucidated, together with their impacts on the organization.

Data Management Framework for Evolution

A framework centered around data management tools can be comprehensive enough to evaluate the impact of IBM's System Application Architecture (SAA), simple enough to describe your current environment, and flexible enough to be expanded to fit into your own organizational needs as they grow (Figure 24).

The full-functioned relational database management system (RDBMS) operates with an active data dictionary to store all of the definitions and the relationships among the items defined. In CASE work there is a need to store much more than simple data and their relationships, so the dictionary is often expanded to an encyclopedia, or a central information repository. This will be described in Chapter 4 as the real heart of any CASE tool kit. It is more than an ordinary data dictionary because it stores the logical meaning of the entire design rather than merely data definitions. What is sometimes not remembered in the literature is that some of the fundamentals of an RDBMS include a three-schema architecture, integrity, and security at both the database

FIGURE 24. Logical systems architecture: a framework for evolution.

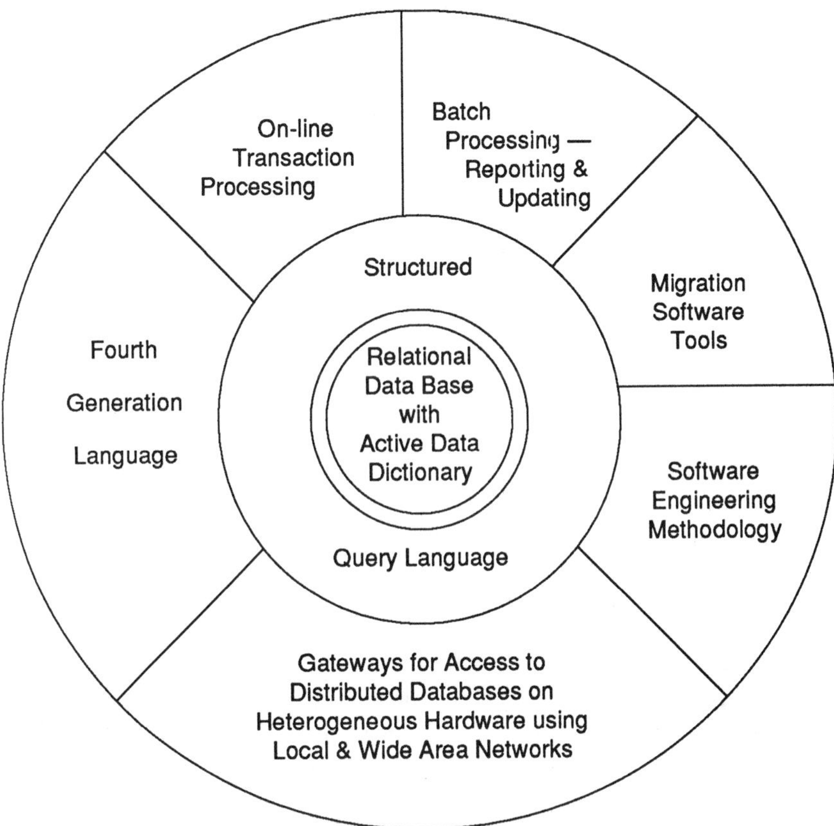

Data Security is the second ring around the RDBMS

and the field value levels. It can be measured against the standards established by E.F. Codd.

Structured Query Language (SQL) has evolved into the standard interface mechanism. The American National Standards Institute (ANSI) has issued standards for the language. Many vendors have adopted the language as part of their current offerings. Many more will follow. It is SAA compliant and therefore part of IBM's strategic direction. SQL will manage the interfaces to the relational database for a wide variety of products.

Surrounding this shell of RDBMS and SQL are a set of state-of-the-art tools. These tools can be thought of in groups as the basis of the areas for which application development productivity can be measured and improved. Of course, different systems will overlap these groups or include several of them.

One of the key areas is that of the gateways. The gateways provide the ability to access and to transfer data among distributed databases that exist on heterogeneous hardware, and that may be linked by a variety of local and wide area networks. They offer the future capability of not having to program where to look for data into each program, while still being able to get that data from anywhere that it is stored within the computer network.

Other key areas in this framework for evolution are:

Batch processing, both reporting and updating functions
Fourth-generation languages
On-line transaction processing
Traditional software life cycle methodologies
Automated software life cycle methodologies
Migration tools
Standards, policies, and procedures.

Even with a well-delineated conceptual framework, there is a need to examine the process of building applications within that framework. Within each organization, there are both the formally-documented procedures and the commonly-used (but undocumented) practices. Knowing the processes that exist will enable an organization to change them and to automate them. There is no easy way to automate functions that are not clearly defined.

There is currently some controversy over what steps are required to develop applications on a computer. There are many vendors of systems who naturally become proponents of methodologies specific to their products, and who claim that the other ways are either wrong or less desirable. The difficulty is that there is no recognized yardstick for us to compare objectively among the methodologies. This makes the issue of selecting the right tools for an organization difficult to address. Chapter 6, "How to Evaluate and Select CASE Products," provides some tools to overcome this dilemma. The relative comparison of the value of particular software tools is complex.

The objective of all software development efforts should be to solve a business problem. If we build a general model of the problem-solving process, we can possibly envision a way to answer the following questions:

- What are the high payback areas in the organization?
- How can this be shown objectively?
- Are there automated tools to support those areas?
- Are there manual methods that will be of sufficient help?
- What is the currently used system development methodology?
- Can this current methodology be supplemented?
- Must the current methodology be scrapped?
- What tools are available that fit your selected approach?
- Which is the best of these tools?
- How does the tool enhance your ability to:
    - Control and measure what is going on?
    - Understand the business processes or functions?
    - Understand what data are required?

Approaches to finding the answers to these questions will be supplied in the following chapters of this book. The development model that you select needs to be applicable to the existing structured methodologies, the available prototyping approaches, and the new CASE approaches, many of which will be described. The structured methodologies define a straight-line, once-through series of discrete steps as the approach to problem solving. The prototyping approach defines an iterative set of discrete steps that converge to an answer. Both are intertwined with CASE approaches.

Any generalized model for solving problems must include the following seven activities:

DEFINE the problem and its REQUIREMENTS.
ANALYZE the process and the alternate solutions.
DESIGN the best alternate system.
CONSTRUCT the application system.
TEST the operation of the system and the results.
IMPLEMENT the solution.
MAINTAIN the operating application system.

Different approaches are suggested in this book, and each does not necessarily fall into a specific category. Therefore, rather than viewing the problem-solving process as a series of discrete steps, or individual CASE tools, with precise beginnings and endings, it may be more productive to compare system development to fluid flowing through a pipeline. There are no precise beginnings or endings of the stages, but when you are in the middle of a process, you know where you are (Figure 25). When a radioactive isotope is placed in the bloodstream it can be traced. It is difficult to say that the isotope is exactly from this point to that point. Now imagine injecting a second, and then a third and fourth isotope at the same point that the first one was injected. The transition points between each isotope and another become fuzzy. Similarly, the interface points from "step" to "step" within any application development life cycle are fuzzy. There are always several activities going on together.

System Development Life Cycle Framework for Evolution

Application Systems Development and Maintenance (ADAM) has a general structure centered around the System Development Life Cycle (SDLC) that is widely understood in principle, but that has many variations in detailed descriptions. Some are illustrated in Figure 26. Such a comparison offers another useful reference framework to show the relationships of CASE tools and their specific areas of use in system development. Some CASE tools are designed to handle individual blocks in this diagram. Others are designed to combine and integrate a number of the blocks. The columns of activities are separated in Figure 26, but in actual use they may be brought together in various combinations. For example, a CASE methodology may allow for prototyping of requirements definition and for the purchase of certain modules, but still use automated design tools and code generators. The activities shown are not always carried out in the same sequential order, and there may be recycling through some of the activities at the time of testing and modifying. The purpose of Figure 26 is to assist in understanding where the different vendor offerings fit to enable objective choices to be compared and analyzed.

FIGURE 25. The problem-solving pipeline.

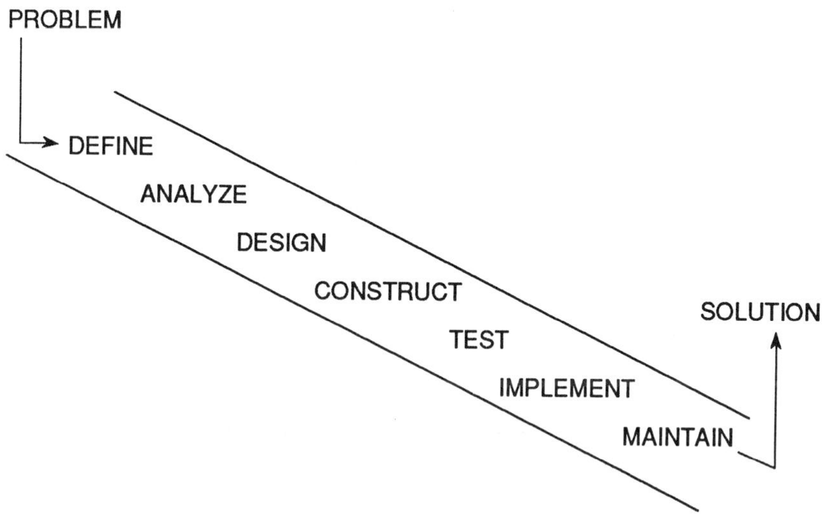

Blocked out in the center of Figure 26 is the classical system development life cycle. The SDLC has been written about at great length in the technical literature because it is fundamental to the understanding of where improvements can be made in application development productivity and where CASE tools fit in the process. There are many times that the advertising for a particular software system package is not clear as to where it is most useful and to what other packages it is directly competitive. It is basic to keep the SDLC in mind at all times. It represents the minimum set of activities that must be accomplished, either manually or automatically.

Activities in the System Development Life Cycle

Structure of operation and formality of control have proven to be the most effective approach to system development. Systematic management has a recognized payoff in system development. The System Development Life Cycle may be followed with either structured or unstructured methodologies. The structured approach may apply anywhere in the SDLC. It is essentially a process in which the inputs to every step are defined specifically and there

FIGURE 26. Variations in the system development life cycle.

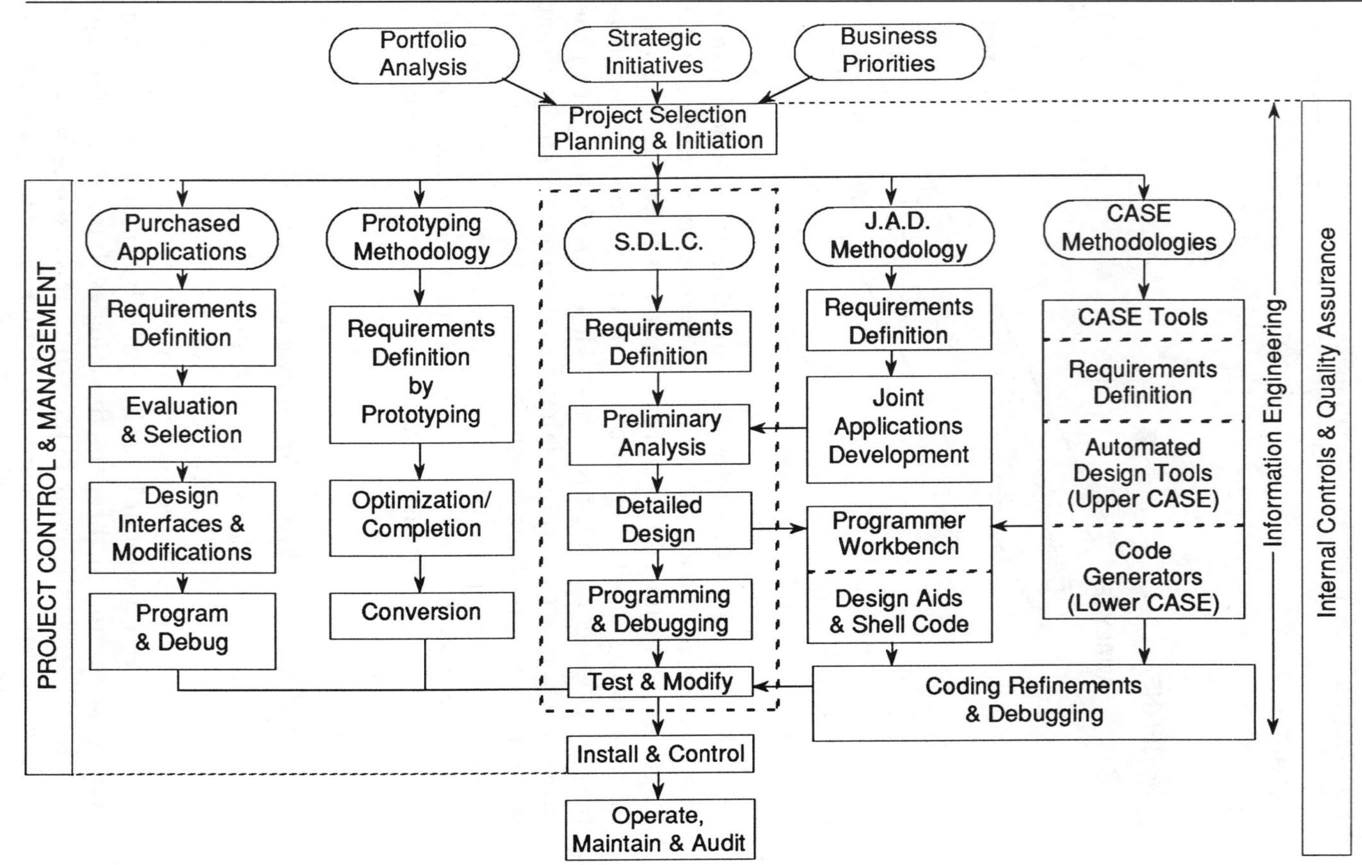

is formal checking of consistency, control, and quality at the end of each step. Automation creates structure. Thus, wherever a CASE tool is used, that step becomes structured.

Requirements Definition.

The steps in the SDLC are familiar, but are worth repeating. Experience has proven that they are equally valid for large corporate systems and smaller departmental systems, for complex systems on both mainframes and personal computers, and for both business and governmental systems. After the initiation of the project, the next step is the functional requirements definition. This step is the critical one in developing, modifying, or purchasing a satisfactory application system. It is omitted at great peril, even when analysts feel that everyone "knows" what the requirements are, or when vendors offer an apparently attractive application package. The analysts involved should be given a free hand to develop conceptually the overall desired system with enough detail so that the various possibilities to solve it can be analyzed and management decisions can be made to progress or not. The requirements definition is usually determined before anything else is started, but in the newer methods of prototyping systems, as will be later explained, the requirements may be developed as the prototyping proceeds. Some requirements must always be stated initially, however.

The requirements phase is usually top-down. The system requirements analysis begins with the original project selection information, after discussions with the senior management who are requesting the system. The analysis then moves down to those who will actually be using the system. The scope of the system and the considerable outline of its structure are defined, and the results are taken back to senior management for approval. Enough information should be gathered to develop a stated need, a general design, and a cost justification for the recommended system. In the prototyping approach, such information is gathered as the prototyping proceeds.

As soon as the early work on the functional requirements definition and the cost analysis and justification of the proposed application appear to be acceptable, the project should be formally brought under the project management and control system that is being used. This will set the timing for the remaining phases. The internal controls group will have been involved early in following the budget considerations. They can also point out the necessary areas of control to be implemented. If there is a quality assurance staff, they should be made aware of the details of the proposed system at the earliest possible time, so that they can begin developing a time table for the application system and planning its quality control points.

Preliminary Analysis.

A preliminary, or conceptual, analysis is then developed in some detail if management has agreed to proceed with the project. At this point, a great deal of information is asked of the users regarding the data that will be used in the application, the calculations that will be made, and the types of reports that will be produced. This will be much less than the information needed for the detailed design, however. At this point, it is important to clarify all the concepts involved and to get agreement from all levels of management as to the specific intent of each step of the program. This is an area for which there are a number of CASE tools available and for which prototyping is frequently indicated. The modern approach to preliminary analysis is screen-centered. The requirements are viewed as typical screens, and the calculations and transformations to be made are tested at the terminal or PC.

The preliminary analysis and design should be completely flowcharted or similarly documented. This is normally done automatically with CASE tools, but the first steps may be manual. It is necessary to communicate and document the following:

- The *data flow* in the application
- The *data requirements*
- The *system structure*
- The use of the *database*
- The overall *program specifications*
- The *reports* that will be produced

The preliminary analysis and design are the break points between systems analysis and programming. If there are both types of staff, they will cooperate as they get into more detail in design. If the system is automated with CASE tools, there may be no "programmers" as such, but the application may be automatically generated and checked by the analysts. By the time the preliminary analysis is completed, however it is done, the classical management controls that should be applied should be clearly defined and applied. These include:

- Define the subsequent SDLC steps, with checkpoints and approvals.
- Define the user and system requirements, with management approvals.
- Define the overall system design, with approvals.
- Prepare the test data and define the production requirements.
- Establish the work within the project management and control system.
- State the quality assurance requirements and control points.
- Obtain approval of the budget and time schedule.

Detailed Design.

When approval has been gained and management controls have been established, the development work will normally proceed at the technical level within information services. The types of questions that are then asked by the analysts handling the work will principally be those that can be answered at the lower levels of operating management and the people who will be running and using the application system. The work should proceed systematically, reporting in at the project management check points. If it is handled by an integrated CASE method, the technical information will be passed from one step of the process to the next, but reports will be available at each step. Classically, the detailed design work includes:

- Perform the detailed systems analysis based on the preliminary design and the functional requirements definition.

- Confirm that the general system design satisfies all the defined requirements and ties into the operating system, other application systems, and possible future enhancements.
- Develop a detailed system design, including file structures, program modules, data input and output, controls, and coding instructions.
- Prepare details of the test methods and the data that will be used for the tests.
- Determine the hardware and communications requirements.
- Determine the development and operating costs in detail.

Programming and Debugging.

The programming classically commences only after the detailed design has been completed and approved. With some CASE tools, the programming will be an automatic result of the analysis and will be handled by the analyst running the tool. In the prototyping approach, much of the programming will be accomplished as the design is being refined. If programmers take over at this step, or if there is a discontinuity between the CASE tools being used, there will usually be no leeway in the interpretation of the system according to the requirements. The detailed system design must be followed, and the test data that have been provided must be used successfully. If the debugging of the system points up some logical or structural errors in the design, then it must be taken back to the analysts rather than solved by the surface indicators. This has traditionally been the most difficult and complex area, but there are now many code generators and other CASE tools that can be applied to make the step essentially automatic.

Test and Modify.

In any structured methodology, all tests will have been predefined, and the system must produce output exactly the way it was planned to do. Any modifications that may prove necessary at this point must cycle back through the earlier design and analysis steps to ensure that they will not adversely affect the defined requirements and any related systems.

This has been a very brief review of the system development life cycle, both in the classical sense and in using a modern, structured methodology. This SDLC should be kept in mind as the basic framework for evolution that shows where new methods and vendor offerings fit.

One of the problems with the standard SDLC approach has always been that it is very time-consuming, which, in practice, has often resulted in shortcuts being taken to meet organizational pressures. This frequently proved disastrous to the schedule because, for example, programming may be started before all the details of the system are described and approved. The common result has been that part of the programming then has to be repeated because of changes in the specifications. Because this has always been an onerous task, the newly defined requirements and additions may be patched into the original code in a less than optimal manner. Not only would the schedule then slip for the completion of the system, but the projected throughput and capabilities of the system would then deteriorate. One of the big advantages of integrated, automated CASE tools is that code is generated automatically, which means that such changes are readily handled in an optimal fashion.

If the classical approach to the SDLC is handled carefully with the controls mentioned, and, particularly, if it is handled in a structured manner, there is no reason why a good application system that meets all the functional requirements should not be developed. This cannot be rushed will all-manual methods, however. For any large system, it always seems to take so much time that the functional specification desired will actually change as the work is underway. This is one of the reasons why the newer, faster methodologies and tools have been developed. They have been produced in response to these queries:

- How can development be speeded up, yet kept under control?
- How can the shortage of highly specialized professional analysts and programmers be handled?
- How can the demands of time-fragile strategic business initiatives be met?
- How can the cost-effectiveness of application system development be improved?

Responses to these questions are found in CASE technologies as described in this book. There are also responses to questions that come to management about the development process itself, such as:

- How can we divide the problem and attack the most costly and time-consuming areas specifically?
- How can we understand where the highly acclaimed development tools fit into the scheme of our development process?
- How can we select new methodologies and tools systematically?
- How can we be aware of the possibilities that are open to us?

Figure 26 begins to show where such questions may be answered, and illustrates where to look for methodologies and tools for specific problem areas.

Purchased Applications.

There is a markedly different SDLC for purchased applications, but it is only satisfactory if the system requirements are first defined carefully. The chances of acquiring the optimum software package for a specific installation are greatly enhanced if time and care are taken to step through the management portions of the SDLC in a systematic manner. Rushing through the initial specification and selection phases to bring up a purchased application quickly can be a complete waste of time and money if the resulting system does not meet the basic operational needs of the users. If a reasonable analysis is first performed, the solution and the decision to select a particular software package will become fairly obvious.

Prototyping Methodology.

Application prototyping is the development of application systems of new design by first creating functional models of parts of the application to test and verify the specifications and assumptions. It first uses small models of the desired system to communicate between the participants in the project and to review the functional requirements with demonstrations on the CRT screen. Parts of the SDLC are still retained. The original requirements definition should not be omitted simply because someone gets a bright idea and can implement it rapidly with prototyping. The great strength of prototyping is in refining the requirements definition by getting the end user involved in the analysis. Prototyping fits naturally with CASE methodologies. By the time a prototyping effort is complete, the requirements are defined sufficiently to move directly into CASE automated design tools and then code generators.

Joint Application Development (JAD).

The IBM concept of Joint Application Development is not so much a methodology for system development as it is a technique. It arose from the understanding that the operational department staff would rather stay in the application system development cycle throughout than simply enter their requirements and wait for a solution. The great many systems being developed on PCs or departmental minicomputers outside of the information services department's system development procedures has forced a need for more cooperative development of all applications. They may proceed through the SDLC in the classical manner, or with automated approaches, but the control of the application development is essentially passed to a matrix management approach. JAD as a technique increases the interaction between the users and the systems professionals throughout the development process.

CASE Methodologies.

CASE methodologies consist of groups of automated development tools that fit one, or span more than one, of the SDLC steps. There are numerous, different CASE tools, each designed for its own niche on the SDLC stages. Some are simple, and some are complex and integrated. They vary from automated design tools, which have occasionally been called "Upper CASE," to such tools as the code generators, called "Lower CASE." They can be grouped by development phase, by function, or by specific application area. A number of these are categorized and defined in this book. A large group fits into what is sometimes called the "Programmer's Workbench." These include design aids, shell codes, and code generators, together with many utility programs. The possibilities are almost unlimited for increasing efficiency, productivity, and quality of product using these CASE tools in their optimum areas of application.

3.3 THE NEW INFORMATION ENGINEERING LIFE CYCLE

There has been such an evolution in development methodology in the new CASE-oriented system development life cycle that it must be thought of in a new way. It is clear in Figure 26 that the CASE methodologies and prototyping do not exactly fit the old SDLC. That is, they do not "map" directly on it. There are two main differences between the two approaches. These are:

- The *transformations are automatic* between the phases and can easily be automatically repeated with modifications.
- The *application information repository* maintains the information model and all the data that are needed to retrace the steps and modify them, or to document the process.

The traditional SDLC was designed for manual methods of system development. It is oriented to the tactics in each phase and not to the overall plan. It is standardized only in its major phases and not in its detail and transformations. Hence, it is often difficult to retrace and repeat the steps taken after the passage of time. The biggest problem of the traditional SDLC approach is that it cannot respond adequately to the users' frequent requests for maintenance and modifications. The hand-built systems were not made for easy maintenance, so it now costs much more to keep them usefully updated than it cost to build them originally.

In recent years, both approaches have been used to try to respond to management's demands for strategic information systems, built in time to be operationally useful to the organization. The traditional SDLC manual approach has failed. It has simply taken too long to construct new or modified systems. The information engineering approach, on the other hand, has succeeded. It has demonstrated that systems can be built in a manner, and with a speed, that is responsive to management, and so that more control can be exercised over maintenance work.

Figure 27 illustrates the comparison between the two approaches. Both approaches should start with a system portfolio analysis, with an understanding of the strategic priorities of the organization, and with an establishment of the business priorities from management's view. There is no reason why they should not both first look at where the business is going in strategic enterprise planning with full management participation. From that point they differ, however. They then handle this information with different outlooks. The traditional SDLC goes through a number of familiar, consecutive phases with manual methods of transformation between the phases. The sequence shown in this figure is a restatement of the phases shown in Figure 26. The information engineering SDLC has a number of significant differences because of the automatic transformations between the phases. The phases cover broader areas, and the detailed analysis, programming, debugging, and testing phases are handled very rapidly, principally by the CASE systems. It is relatively easy to recycle through the phases at any time, so the final result can more closely represent the current thinking about the application's requirements.

The differences between the two approaches can therefore be enlarged upon, beyond the two major differences stated above. The relatively unique features of the information engineering SDLC are that:

- It depends on the use of an Information System Architecture. There must be a systematic framework in which it works.

- It is centered on the use of automated development systems. These create the transformations between the phases and leave a clear record of those transformations in the information repository. This is why they can be repeated automatically whenever changes are needed.

- It is based on a set of structured techniques and diagrams that are handled consistently and recorded in detail. A clear trail is left.

- It forces a high degree of standardization to allow the automation of the transformations.

FIGURE 27. Comparison of SDLCs.

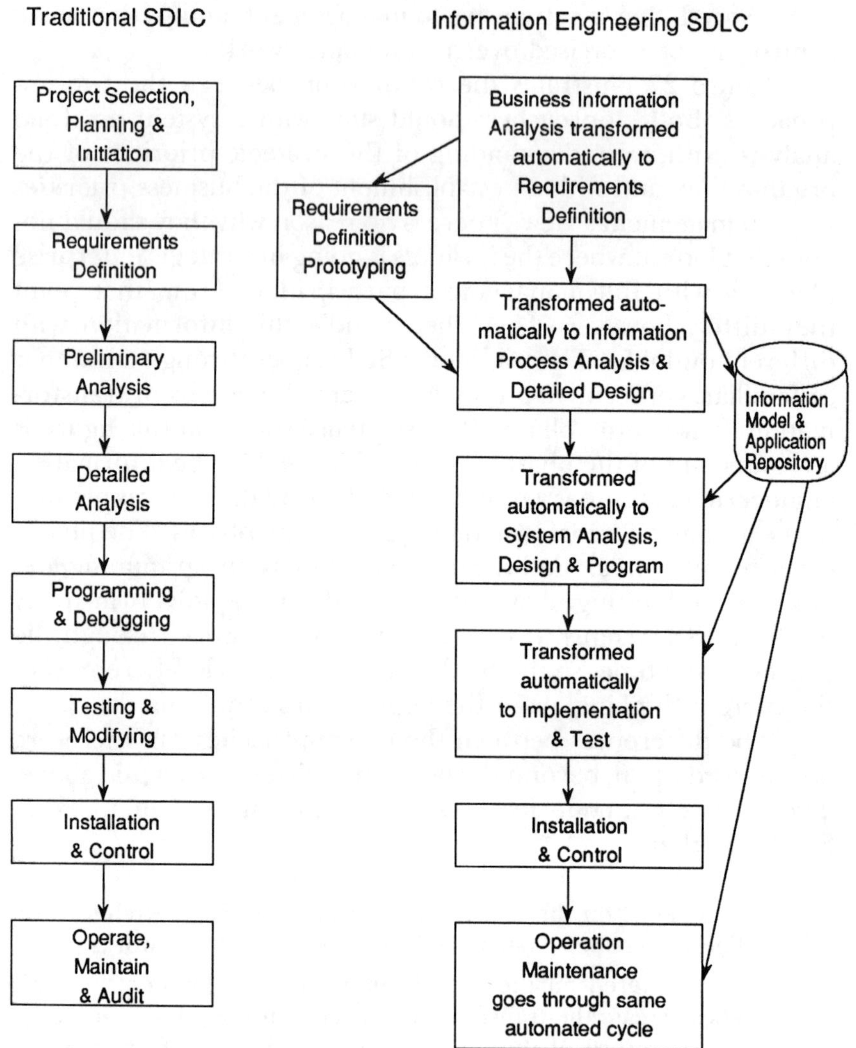

- The information model is maintained from the start, and this application repository holds a full set of correlated information regarding the application.

- Requirements definition prototyping naturally follows such an SDLC, although it is difficult to fit it into the traditional SDLC. The prototyping brings together the old requirements phase and the preliminary analysis and design phases.

- It is a completely *integrated* system, because of the information repository and the automated transformations. This greatly facilitates testing and maintenance.

An interesting thought is that information engineering approaches essentially treat application system development as an application. The application development has its own data, entities, data flow, and entity relationships. It has its own data administration and its own process. The development can be designed and managed as an application, which is managed with the expectation that the users will request many changes. The systems are designed to accommodate such changes. At any time, the key segments can be redefined and regenerated.

Not only is the information engineering life cycle not a direct mapping of the traditional SDLC, but the differences are significant. There is considerably more coordination with business plans and a coupling with business professional efforts. Application systems are not structured principally for reasons of technical efficiency on the computer, but are developed as business models that can be fine-tuned by business analysts to give the greatest efficiency to the business operation. The strategic phases move deeper into the life cycle than they did in the traditional approach. The tactical phases, formerly handled principally by information systems professionals, are all handled by automated transformations. This means that business changes, or simply new desires of management, can be introduced into the information model, and the changes will be automatically rolled through the development system and reflected in the result.

Because the information engineering life cycle is qualitatively different from the traditional SDLC, a number of new terms have been used to describe the phases. These will vary depending upon the vendors of the CASE systems and the methodologies employed. Some examples are:

- *Definition* is called *strategic enterprise planning* and *information strategy planning.*
- *Analysis* is called *business area information analysis* and *process analysis.*
- *General design* is called *business system design* and *logical analysis and design.*
- *Detailed design* is called *physical design* or *technical systems design.*
- *Implementation* is called *construction* and *transition.*

The key to the information engineering SDLC's success is that there is a focused approach that always keeps the business problem in the fore, from planning to implementation, and there is automation of the transformations from one stage to the next in every case.

Information engineering starts, as does all good systems development, with strategic enterprise planning. It then excels because it maintains the alignment of the system development with the business. It does this by keeping business analysts in the development cycle, and whenever business changes are needed in the system, the modification is automatically fed through the series of transformations in the CASE system.

Because of the systematization, interchangeability, and documentation that information engineering offers, there are greater opportunities to exploit the organization's information assets. Analysis models, design models, sections of code, and system documentation can all be looked upon as "information assets" because the engineering approach makes them readily reusable. Such assets can be engineered and reused as useful segments of other systems. They can be customized for any number of other applications. These existing assets can be assembled, modified, used, and put into operation whenever they may be useful.

Information engineering methodologies can be distinguished from separate CASE tools in that they not only have mechanisms for automating the technical system development steps, but they also integrate a number of necessary management functions into the development process, such as:

- Relating system development to strategic planning.
- Making direct connections to Information Resource Management and planning.

- Making the estimation of development efforts systematic.
- Allowing better monitoring because of better consistency of process.
- Simplifying scheduling with the automatic transformations.

It was pointed out that information engineering concepts appear to have been first developed by Clive Finkelstein in Australia in the late 1970s. The idea has been since popularized in America by James Martin and the publications of James Martin Associates. Since then, a number of companies have started to implement the philosophy of information engineering system development. A few have produced comprehensive systems for sale, such as Texas Instrument's Information Engineering Facility™, which is a very large CASE tool set. Arthur Young has developed another interpretation of information engineering. The IPSE approach in Europe is approaching a full implementation of the present status of information engineering. It is not likely that America will adopt the term IPSE, but there will certainly be a convergence of the international methodologies in the future. Each of the various systems that are being developed seems to have many attractive advantages.

Richard Frankel of Amoco Corporation has produced what is probably one of the best definitions of information engineering as it is currently understood. He defines Information Engineering as:

A rigorous, data-driven methodology consisting of a set of interrelated formal techniques used to build and maintain information systems for a computerized enterprise.

It is important that it is a data-driven methodology. It is an integrated set of formal techniques that begin with the creation of the model of the enterprise. In practice, you build multiple models of portions of the enterprise at desired levels. Information strategy planning dictates the particular portions of the enterprise to be modeled. A business area analysis is made of that portion. Particular parts of the business area are then selected and a business systems design is developed. The business systems design is transformed into a technical systems design of the business area.

This is followed in an automatic transformation cycle through construction, transition, and production.

3.4 CONSTANT FUNCTIONS IN ALL SDLC METHODOLOGIES

Figure 26 also shows a number of constant management and planning functions that are fundamental to all application system development methodologies, including CASE. Some of these functions are seldom considered by the technical staff, but they are basic to the successful management of application system development. In the selection of CASE approaches, these functions should always be kept in mind. They are listed in Figure 28. As CASE evolves and becomes more integrated and IPSE-like, these functions will become imbedded in the better systems that are offered, although they will not all become part of integrated CASE systems. On the surface, they may appear to be obvious. This is why they are sometimes neglected in planning. They are frequently handled inadequately, and should be given attention in any planning process for the installation of CASE development

FIGURE 28. Constant functions in all development methodologies.

- Systems planning
- Resource management
- Project selection and initiation
- Project management and control
- Database administration
- Application installation, modification, and control
- Systems operation training
- Systems and program maintenance
- Internal controls
- Security and disaster recovery management
- Standards and procedures administration
- Quality assurance
- Audit review

methodologies. They are generally staff functions, but the main responsibility for them must remain with the system development group. They will be discussed in the appropriate areas in this book where they are significant. Some comments about them follow.

Systems Planning

For any large or complex application systems development, it is imperative to formally plan the activity at several levels and to regularly review the accomplishments versus the plan. In practice, it is less obvious that detailed planning should be done for smaller application systems and for purchased software packages, but experience has proven that all systems should be planned. As long as corporate resources are used in developing an application, there should be planning and resource management. Even at the level of personal computers, the development of unplanned application systems is more costly, and the lack of any management control over application development can be detrimental to the business. Planning has repeatedly been shown to be a necessity to:

- Ensure that the application systems fit the organization's objectives.
- Keep the costs of application system acquisition under control.
- Prevent development of systems that are already available.
- Report to management on the goals to be met.
- Obtain adequate approved funding in the budget.
- Facilitate the sharing of application systems in the organization.
- Allow for the planning of sufficient hardware and communications resources.

These are clearly sufficient reasons to demand the routine and careful planning of all application systems development or acquisition. These are the reasons why *Project Selection, Planning, and Initiation* is the starting point for all the methodologies shown in Figure 26. Notice also, in Figure 26, that the key inputs to the planning for application systems are *Strategic Initiatives, Business Priorities, and Portfolio Analysis*. There are, of course, many other inputs to the planning process, but these three have special significance to application development.

Planning is the process of determining in advance the optimum direction of the application system development efforts by establishing goals, budgeting for achievement, and analyzing the actions that are taken. Planning is never the sole responsibility of the "planning group" in information services, but is a management responsibility at all levels in the organization. Those who are developing the application systems should be expected to participate in the planning processes and analyses, to help establish the stated goals, and to refer to the plans when reviewing their accomplishments through the planning period.

Various phases of application systems planning are handled by the technical and operational groups involved:

- Systems development usually handles project and system planning through a methodology that includes a system development life cycle.

- Database administration usually handles the database planning.

- Computer operations usually handles capacity measurement.

- Technical services usually handles hardware and software capacity analysis and forecasting.

The IS Planning Group should be made aware of the progress in all these planning activities that are taking place, and should coordinate their consolidated reporting in the department's operational plans, budget plans, and annual report. In organizations with mature IS management, there is usually active support for a full range of IS planning activities, including:

- *Strategic planning* in direct and timely response to corporate business initiatives, in order to produce applications that will support such initiatives.

- *Long-range operational planning* to establish an effective and efficient framework to meet future IS responsibilities with appropriate systems.

- *Short-range operational planning* to establish IS priorities and application systems plans for accomplishment in the following year.

- *Annual financial and personnel plans,* or budgets, to set priorities, limits, and responsibilities on IS projects and operations in the following year.

- *Annual report*, and other plan-vs-actual periodic reports, to show accomplishment in application development against the plans, and to help fine-tune IS directions.

All IS application systems planning is interrelated, since it all depends on the same base of information and the same environmental forecasts. Planning is the distillation of forecasts of environmental effects, current status conditions, and future business needs to produce a vision of the future with goals and priorities for application system implementation.

Resource Management

Resource management covers the concerns of managing specific resources, such as hardware operation and capacity. It is particularly critical for any application system development that includes networking of equipment and of systems that span the central computers and the PCs. The government concept of overall Information Resource Management is far more inclusive than the management of resources for specific applications, but the principles are the same. Resource management decisions include whether to use in-house personnel or contractors, and whether to develop or purchase software packages. Such decisions become increasingly complex with larger applications.

Project Selection and Initiation

Project selection and initiation is principally a management function, but it must be supported by considerable staff effort in preparing the application candidates for management selection. When business priorities call for strategic initiatives in the development of applications, the selection process is finalized at higher levels of management.

Project Management and Control

This function is shown in Figure 26 as spanning all the areas of development methodologies and tools. The reason seems clear. The most effective methodology or tool can be used inappropriately or inefficiently if it is not introduced and used in a planned manner under some measure of management control. It is of little use to the organization as a whole if one department has great success with a new methodology or tool but does not communicate the details of that success to other departments. In addition, the apparently successful use of new approaches may be greatly exaggerated if expectations and results are not documented. There is always enthusiasm in an interesting project. Only if the reasons for the enthusiasm can be objectively stated and compared can greater value be gained.

Database Administration

Database administration includes all aspects of establishing and operating the database, the data dictionary, data control, and data ownership. All these must be managed more carefully as more participants are involved in developing applications that use each other's data. The data dictionary work becomes much more complex with CASE approaches as the central repositories hold much more than simply data elements.

Application Installation, Modification, and Control

Though the functions of application installation, modification, and control are common to all applications, there is little commonality in their application. However applications are developed with CASE methodologies, the controls and reviews at testing and installation should be standard practice for all approaches. Substantial modifications should all go through the same cycle as the original application.

Systems Operation Training

The development of applications more rapidly or more automatically does not make training more difficult. The developers may have less knowledge of the inner workings of the systems, but the users have no more difficulty because the development operation is transparent to them. Actually, many CASE methods have more user interaction in the specification and development process, and consequently the users are more readily trained at the time of installation.

Systems and Program Maintenance

Any CASE systems with automatic code generation are far more readily maintained than manually developed systems. There is more consistency in the handling of functions, usually better documentation, and the facility to maintain the system at a higher level.

Internal Controls

Internal control is handled by a staff functionary whose responsibility spans any methodologies that may be used. Management has a responsibility to see that valid and useful controls are imposed at all points of the system design and the operating program. The problem with CASE approaches is that newly trained technical people may not have sufficient background in the necessity of controls and their application. Some systems allow the automatic imposition of controls. Most require the design and installation of the necessary controls one at a time, however. No matter how many arrangements are made for the handling of controls for data input, operations, and output reports, the involved staff are seldom completely aware of the overall organizational concerns of data control, completeness, integrity, and accuracy. This is particularly true of the nonprofessional user staff who taste the capabilities of the new methodologies and tools and do not understand the rigid controls that are needed on the basic information that is involved.

Security and Disaster Recovery Management

The problems of security and disaster recovery are generally obvious to the professional data processor, but are far from obvious to the many users who become involved in the system development process with the use of CASE tools. This is not just a concern of the internal audit group. It is a concern of information services management, which should be addressed with well-publicized standards and procedures to be followed.

Standards and Procedures Administration

The development and administration of standards and procedures are usually handled by a staff group within information services. It often has relatively low priority in the concerns of management, but it is a fundamental effort that must be supported. The problem that CASE methodologies introduce is that a number of completely new standards and procedures must be developed, disseminated, and enforced, yet often little is done about it because of the pressure of introducing the new CASE technologies. Standards and procedures are generally not popular, but, like controls, they are basically necessary to any successful operation.

Quality Assurance

QA is another staff function that should span the complete system development life cycle. QA analyzes, develops, and implements control and review systems in all areas of information analysis and production. It is a staff that does not usually perform the full quality review work itself, but develops review methodologies and oversees them. QA attempts to implement a system that is targeted at ensuring that system products meet the level of quality described in the specifications and also meet a prescribed level of service. CASE methodologies are admirably suited to impose QA on the effort, but frequently the necessary guidelines and policies are not put into place rapidly enough to give the QA staff the opportunity to set the needed standards. When new techniques are introduced into system development, the QA staff must develop new techniques to help manage the accuracy and quality of the results.

Audit Review

Every application system in an organization may be subject to an audit review. In the immediate past, auditors have principally worked with the larger financial systems that were very likely developed under a traditional SDLC, with a clear statement of all the controls that were in place. Auditors now realize that substantive and sensitive work is now being accomplished with the newer languages and the CASE tools, however, and are reaching in to review such applications in many forward organizations.

Strategic Initiatives and Business Priorities

Despite the normal systematization of the planning process for application systems, there are frequently organizational situations that arise calling for immediate and rapid action by the systems development group. These are the strategic initiatives that call for planning and action in direct response to corporate business thrust. It may be that a specific, new systems technology is required, or it may be that a system development project must be given the highest priority. The project planning and initiation is then forced by the business priorities. (See Figure 38)

Strategic initiatives are those that link business and computer systems strategies and require a plan to afford the maximum support to adopted policies. The requirement is to develop systems that facilitate and enhance the efforts of the business that are considered most critical. Near-term systems decisions are demanded that coincide with the longer-term direction of the organization.

When there is a new business priority that has strategic implications, it may call for specific, new systems technology to be developed that is completely different from the development efforts that have been undertaken previously. If the priority is great enough, the project will usually bypass the normal budget process and introduce a major budget modification. An often-used example of strategic initiative driving the system planning process is the introduction of automated teller machines in the banking industry. When that happened, and the need to include them in the bank's strategy became obvious to senior management, all levels of information services and systems development planning had to be modified rapidly to accommodate the new technological requirement and the new data processing systems to be installed.

Response to business priorities should always be central in

the systems development planning process. Response to strategic initiatives frequently enters as a special planning situation that has different time demands and may have a wide range of management interest and urgency. The development process must adapt to the requirements of the unique business situations, and must be timed according to the business necessity that is dictated by higher management. Interestingly, it is frequently the situations demanding prompt and rapid action that start the introduction and use of the many effective and efficient development tools that are becoming available.

Strategic initiatives and new business priorities can only be effectively met and handled if the routine, basic work of gathering systems data, comparing possible methodologies, tools and techniques, and routinely reporting findings and status has been done. Such standard, calendarized work is absolutely necessary in systems planning as a base from which a strategic business response can be developed when a priority situation arises. Long-range technological forecasting is insufficient alone. It must be accompanied by data gathering, testing, and experimentation in new approaches to systems development.

Strategic application systems are inherently time fragile. If there is a business opportunity to be seized, it must be while the conditions are right. If the business operations involved are large and complex, then the systems development time will be considerable. In recent years, however, many strategic application systems have been assembled rapidly with the new, efficient CASE tools and techniques that are available.

Portfolio Analysis

A comprehensive analysis of the existing portfolio of application systems in the organization (Figure 26) is neither strategic nor exciting, but it is one of the key aspects of data gathering that should be accomplished in the system development area, whether or not CASE is used. Computer application systems are assets to the organization and should be treated as such. They are costly and time-consuming to develop, and every system should be completely documented both from an operational viewpoint and for an assessment of its present and possible value. Vendors supply lists of the application systems they can supply and charge for. There are many good reasons why an information services organization should gather documentation on all the application systems that may be available internally, distribute this information throughout the organization on request, and analyze it to determine whether there are applications that can meet current requirements by direct use or with modification.

The full library of application systems in a corporation is often extensive, and there is little use in simply listing all systems without classifying them, arranging them by language and type, and producing summaries of the assembled information for perusal by interested departments. It is assumed that each system will have satisfactory documentation on file somewhere. That documentation can be studied when there is possible interest in a particular system. Even when a completely new system design is contemplated, with a complete rewrite of the programs, the basic documentation of the system frequently supplies information about the underlying operation that is valuable to the concerned analysts.

The documents that may be of use to an organization in a portfolio analysis are the following:

Figure 29: Significant Applications by Business Function
Figure 30: Assessment of Current Application Systems
Figure 31: Description of Ongoing Projects
Figure 32: Description of Planned Projects

The use of these form sheets is self-explanatory. They are presented more for the type of information that should be gathered and made available to system analysts than for the detail in them. There is not a particularly great effort in gathering such information, at least annually, from all departments. The assembled information can then be analyzed for possible value whenever an application development is initiated. Systems need not be reinvented to be useful, and internally available systems are frequently as valuable as the commercially available packaged systems.

The available application systems in an organization are usually called the systems portfolio simply because they are of value. A portfolio is classically the listing of the securities held by an

FIGURE 29. Significant applications by business function.

Reporting Unit:		Date:
Business Function		Application

FIGURE 30. Assessment of current application systems.

A. Application System Description
1.   Name of the system:
2.   User department:
3.   Frequency of runs:
4.   Type of system (interactive, batch, etc.):
5.   Planning, control, or operational function:
6.   Year originally started: _____ Year put into production: _______.
7.   Current annual operating cost (if availaible):
     a.   Information services cost
     b.   User cost
8.   Volumes of transactions going through the system:

B. Assessment of the Application System
1.   Original intent of the system:
2.   What it actually does, and its impact on user areas:
3.   Benefits derived from the system:
4.   Outstanding problem areas:
     a.   User perspective
     b.   Information services perspective
5.   Adequacy of documentation:
     a.   Are user procedures developed such that only limited
          training is required for new personnel?
     b.   Is user documentation current?
     c.   Is the system and program documentation current?
     d.   Is extensive training required for analysts and programmers
          before they can be effective in the system?

C. Currently Indentified Plans
1.   Life expectancy of the system:
2.   Brief description of major changes or enhancements to the system:
3.   Need for a rewrite or design:
4.   Cost of identified plans:
5.   Level of ongoing effort:
     a.   modification, enhancements
     b.   maintenance
6.   Cost of:
     a.   modification
     b.   maintenance

D. Summation of Assessment
1.   User perspective
2.   Information services perspective

FIGURE 31. Description of ongoing projects.

Reporting Unit: Date:

1. Project no.________________ Title: _________________________________
   Sponsored by (function/client, etc.):_______________________________
   ____

2. Purpose of project: ____
   ____

3. General description (including input and output data and run frequency):

4. Mandated or not mandated:_____________________________________

5. Development effort:
   a. Systems/programming —expended to ______   \$___ M/M____
                                                             (date)
      19___ \$___ M/M____
      19___ \$___ M/M____
      19___ \$___ M/M____
      19___ \$___ M/M____

   b. Testing —   expended to ______   \$___ HRS.____
                                                           (date)
      19___ \$___ HRS.____
      19___ \$___ HRS.____
      19___ \$___ HRS.____
      19___ \$___ HRS.____

   c. Other Costs —   expended to ______
                                                    (date)
      (Feasibility, design, etc.)   19___ \$___   ____
      19___ \$___   ____
      19___ \$___   ____

FIGURE 31. (Cont.)

Reporting Unit:	Date:

6. Operational Requirements:

    a. Forecast annual computer use

       Upon completion   19 ___ $ ___

       (indicate computer model and location)   19 ___ $ ___

                                          19 ___ $ ___

                                        19 ___ $ ___

    b. Estimated annual maintenance costs   19 ___ $ ___ M/M ___

                                          19 ___ $ ___ M/M ___

                                        19 ___ $ ___ M/M ___

                                        19 ___ $ ___ M/M ___

    c. Other costs (itemized)   19 ___ $ ___

                                        19 ___ $ ___

                                        19 ___ $ ___

                                        19 ___ $ ___

7. Annual benefits: Savings
                           ____

		Headcount $	Other $	Total $
a. Tangible	19 ___	_________	_____	_____
	19 ___	_________	_____	_____
	19 ___	_________	_____	_____

    b. Intangible (specify)

FIGURE 32. Description of planned projects.

Reporting Unit: Date:

1. Project no: _______________ Title: _________________________________
   Sponsored by (function/client, etc.):___________________________________
   ____

2. Purpose of project____
   ____

3. General description (including input and output data and run frequency):

4. Mandated or not mandated: ____

5. Total development cost $_______________

6. Operational requirements:
   a. Current annual computer use $ _______
   b. Annual maintenance costs $ _______   M/M_______
   c. Other costs (itemized) $ _______

7. Annual benefits:
   a. Tangible   Savings
                        Headcount _______
                        Personnel $_______
                        Other $_______
   b. Intangible (specify)

8. General comments:
   a. Strengths and weaknesses:

   b. Major redesign plans:

FIGURE 32. (Cont.)

Reporting Unit:		Date:
9. Project phases and target dates:		
Phase	**Start date**	**End date**
Study, definition, feasibility		
Function spec., design,		
Systems, programming		
Testing, etc.		

investor. The systems portfolio is a listing of a class of valuable assets held by an organization.

3.5 STRATEGIC PLANNING FOR CASE PROJECTS

Structured planning at all levels is fundamental to the success of CASE projects, and all the planning processes must begin with the corporate strategic planning thrust. Traditionally, information services has had a "bottom-up" approach to application system planning, as shown on the left of Figure 33. Most of the ideas, support, and cooperation came from the control level in the organization. These are the staff managers and information services management. Most of the information for the design of the application came from the operations level in the organization. Thus, the application was designed to satisfy the needs of the clerical and supervisory operations personnel, with the general structure dictated by information services. By the time the information in the systems reached the strategic level in the organization, it was too mundane to be of great use in management.

The systems that have been developed using the bottom-up approach have been implemented following the traditional system development life cycle. This means that information needed at the lower levels became imbedded as the core information of the system. This approach has frequently worked reasonably well for operational and financial computer applications, where the output is used in routine line operations. All too often, however, the time involved during system design and construction has been considerable. Since there traditionally has been little management contact during these development phases, the resulting system has frequently diverged from the original intent and ideas of the managers involved.

CASE and its subset, information engineering, use a "top-down" approach, which is also shown in Figure 33. It starts at the top level of the organization with strategic enterprise planning, and moves down through business area analysis, logical analysis and design, physical design, implementation, and management. Note that the use of individual CASE tools alone can readily lead to a regression to the traditional SDLC, with little management attention and support. Individual CASE tools, used separately, simply automate specific areas of the SDLC. Computer-aided software engineering, however, and the better implementations of information engineering, start with the basic premise that the foundation of application systems is the strategic thrusts that are being planned by upper management.

FIGURE 33. Planning approaches.

Top-down planning is strategic planning, because it is focused on the interests of top management and the strategic initiatives of the organization. When the planning focus progresses down to the analysis of the business area, the systems considered will be those that help to implement the desired strategic initiatives. Of course, CASE is not the only approach that centers on strategic initiatives, but CASE is well structured to move in that direction. To get the management cooperation and the end-user participation that are necessary for the successful implementation of applications, CASE offers an excellent environment to center on strategic systems and to implement strategic initiatives. Those are the projects of management interest that need the efficient and accurate implementation that CASE promises.

Potential strategic information systems are usually identified by a conscious, coordinated effort of opportunity analysis. It is necessary to develop a good line of communication between the developers of information systems and the senior managers who are looking for ways to improve the business. Opportunity analysis, or the identification of strategic systems, must itself be handled systematically.

There are two main phases to a strategic systems planning effort. The first is the opportunity analysis, or the identification of potential strategic information systems. The second is the strategic systems planning itself. Much of the literature on strategic systems is concerned primarily with the opportunity analysis, because the information services group has been positioned in the organization in such a way that they have little access to the decision makers who can most readily identify strategic system possibilities. In the past, information systems have been used principally in business automation areas to reduce clerical costs, reduce inventory levels, provide operational information, computerize the company's books, and so on. Many of these systems have been most effective in saving money and in making information more readily available. Some of these systems have actually had strategic impact on the firm. There has not always been a good line of communication, however, between the developers of information systems and the senior management who are looking for business successes. Information services has generally asked what to do with automation by talking to those with immediate operational problems that can benefit from the use of the computer. They usually have not asked how they should position their systems resources to provide the greatest support to the business thrust.

The investment in automation, therefore, has been mainly to improve business operations. Most of the systems have shown a measurable economic return. There have also been many intangible benefits obtained from the system, mostly in the areas of providing information and control to management in a way that allows them to move strategically with the business. The problem has been that the information services planners have not understood management thinking because they have not been part of management discussions and because possible strategic thrusts have not been recognized during the development of the systems.

The purpose of strategic analysis is to find automation opportunities that will improve the competitive position of the business, to find ways to direct the information services staff to gain meaningful advantage for the firm, and to move into new and profitable areas. Information services capabilities can then be planned with a strategic view of the potential business impact of the computer systems. Many computer applications are on the verge of being strategically important, if they are only recognized as containing capabilities and information that can be directly applied to business thrusts. Information is obviously a key vehicle for effecting business change. The problem in realizing the potential is usually in the mutual lack of understanding between the key business managers and the information system developers. The identification of opportunities for business advances using information systems lies in having a mutual, concerted approach by both the responsible managers and the system developers. Methodologies are available. The technology is available. Only the applied communication is normally lacking. If senior business management desires to look into the possibilities of gaining strategic advantage by use of information systems, the first task is to organize the effort so that there is meaningful communication and systematic review of the possibilities.

Thus, the opportunity analysis, or the identification of strategic systems, must itself be handled systematically. There are two common approaches to such opportunity analysis. One of the most attractive, to many, has always been the use of experienced consultants. These may be the authors of papers on strategic systems and their staffs or professional consultants who have had some successes in uncovering strategic opportunities. The advantages of using such consultants are that:

- They have recent experience to draw on and many ideas already formed.
- Access can be gained to the higher levels of management who are interested in the use of the systems that might result.
- They have worked through their methodologies several times and know the strong areas and the pitfalls.
- If they do not discover a strategic breakthrough, no internal staff are blamed.

The other approach to opportunity analysis and strategic planning is to train capable internal staff people and to encourage them to make presentations to higher levels of management. Use the existing systems development staff, who certainly understand the present and possible capabilities of information technology, and give them a chance to work on planning critical, strategic systems. The advantages of the use of internal staff are that:

- They will likely remain with the organization and retain the experience there.
- They can train other staff members over time.
- They can apply the knowledge gained from one success directly to other systems in the organization.
- An understanding of and a desire for strategic information systems will be diffused throughout the organization.

Whichever approach is used—external consultants or internal staff—the first, and probably the most interesting, part is the opportunity analysis, and the second part is the detailed planning of the strategic system and the execution of the plan.

A number of approaches to identifying strategic information systems possibilities have been described in the literature. If a consultant is used, clearly the methodology preferred by that consultant will be central. It is not necessary to have a single methodology, however, as a syncretic mixture of the ideas that appear to best fit the organization's culture may prove to be the best because of the likelihood of its acceptability. There are several important criteria in the selection of a strategic system identification approach:

- Move in the key operational areas of the business, where strategic successes can be highly profitable.

- Adopt a *proactive*, rather than a passive style. Strategic systems are seldom found by waiting for system requests to come through the mail. It is helpful to give classes and seminars, talk up the possibilities, and seek interested managers.

- Use proven techniques for systems development. Do not confuse the problem of identifying strategic opportunities with the problem of realizing their benefits. Identification requires management interaction. Realization requires proven systems development methods.

- Leave contingency room in the information services plans. Do not fill the allocated budget with mundane automation projects. Budget for opportunity search and be ready to ask for other funds. Their use will be multiplied by the existing information services capabilities.

- Experiment with different methods for identifying strategic systems. These may be Critical Success Factors, Pressure Points Analysis, Key External Factors, or even IBM's Business Systems Planning. Any good systematic analysis can lay an excellent base for the education of management and the search for strategic opportunities.

Structured approaches offer the best solution for internal staff efforts to find possible strategic information systems. First, they can be preidentified as the approach that will be followed and funded. Second, they carry with them a degree of authenticity, having been proven elsewhere. Third, they provide understood checkpoints for supplying plan-vs-actual information to management. Fourth, the documentation is useful for training purposes. A few of the structured approaches that are available are:

- IBM's Business Systems Planning and Business System Information Planning.

- McAuto's Information Systems Transition Planning.
- Price Waterhouse's Strategic Information Systems Planning.

These have all had many successful users and are well documented. Unfortunately, they have less psychological appeal than consultant approaches. For example, Charles Wiseman's idea to have small groups brainstorming for strategic system opportunities, to discuss and evaluate the ideas, and to pick out the "blockbusters," combines training and communication with some enthusiasm for the outcome. Such enthusiasm can be equaled by any approach, of course, if a responsible operations manager comes away from the planning with a perception of gaining strategic advantage in a particular area. Obviously, the best approach to take to uncover strategic opportunities will vary according to the company culture. It will take experience to learn how to identify potential strategic system opportunities, to alert the corporation to the possibilities in such systems, and to sustain the effort required to implement them.

Pilot projects can be one way of introducing the strategic concepts. Frequently, such projects are already partially implemented on personal computers at the staff level. What is then needed is cooperation with the analysts who have implemented the approach, interest in its further development, and a reasonable amount of management interest. Unfortunately, pilot projects seldom offer great strategic advantage in themselves, but merely point to the possibilities. They are great training tools and an excellent way of developing technical skills among the management staff. Since many people are using personal computers, there are many more opportunities to identify strategic systems, experimentation is encouraged, and there can be calculated risk taking at a reasonable level. The proliferation of analytical systems of many types is teaching senior management about the real applications of technology. There is great awareness and consciousness raising, and widespread assimilation of information systems concepts. All this leads to better opportunities for identifying and pursuing strategic information systems.

The key element in thinking strategically is the development of a new way of approaching information systems planning. The operational way of thinking about a system is to pursue what labor and equipment costs can be cut, how more accurate information can be made available, and how operations can be made to run more smoothly. Exactly the same system can be looked at from a strategic point of view and the results will be different. Now the thinking is on the impact of the change. Will it increase productivity? Will it open more markets? Will it increase the business? Not only does the thinking change, but the system itself will be designed from a different perspective. Operationally, people look for the most data processing for the dollar. Strategically, people look at the competitive and informational opportunities, then ask how much they will cost.

Those participating in the search for strategic opportunities must start thinking in terms of business changes. Information technology is becoming a primary vehicle for effecting business changes.

- *Productivity changes* must be in terms of reducing the overall product costs significantly. The elimination of labor and the processing of clerical volume may be involved, as it was in the older operational systems. The thinking, however, is directed toward reducing the overall market costs.

- *Product and service changes* can come from information technology in providing product-related services. The services may even function as new products.

- *Communications changes* are becoming more realizable. Separate entities can be linked geographically and organizationally. A new view of organization-wide coordination is possible.

- *Managerial changes* also come with coordinated efforts. Decisions are implemented, performance is analyzed, and the future is forecast from a whole-company viewpoint, rather than by department. When a strategic system appears to be a winner, the staff relationships may change markedly.

This sort of change can be found and planned when the overall, strategic view is taken. It is the facilitation of corporate effectiveness rather than efficiency. The thinking is directed toward improving the competitive position to gain meaningful advantage, and improving the business operations to effect economic return and intangible competitive benefits. Information technology is used as a primary vehicle to effect business change. The momentum of the information services activities must be shifted from producing automation to following the thrust of the business.

3.6 *PROJECT MANAGEMENT AND CONTROL OF CASE*

The purpose of a project management system is to help management define the tasks necessary to complete a project, control the progress of the activities, and account for the resources expended through the project. There is no reason why a CASE application development project should not be managed as carefully as traditional projects in the information services department. Of course, there will be problems with the accuracy of the initial estimates, but experience will improve the estimates. No project should be started without some measure of management control. If it is a short-term project, it may be sufficient to simply state its objectives, its justification, its general design, and the time and resources that will be expended in accomplishing it. If it is a larger project, the project director should apply a full project control system. No attempt should be made to develop such a system. There are plenty of them on the market that have been time-tested and shaken out. Most information services departments have project management systems that are well documented and ready to be used for CASE projects.

There are over 200 project management systems available on the market. The cost of these ranges from about $50 for a simple microcomputer program to $100,000 for a complex system on a mainframe computer. The simpler, less expensive programs usually give only time estimates of tasks, with responsibility for the task completion. There may be costs listed, and times and costs may be totalled and compared with the plan as the project proceeds. The more sophisticated programs supply complete planning and scheduling tools, usually based on standard methodologies such as PERT (Project Evaluation and Review Technique) or CPM (Critical Path Method). Some packages provide the capability for budgeting, resource leveling, and loading, as well as performance and cost monitoring and reporting.

Any project management system should provide management reports that include the start, completion, and deadline dates for each task and the costs per task. As the project proceeds, the reports should include percentage of completion, days remaining, and actual start and finish dates. The planned and actual costs should be listed, with the cost variance.

With CASE application development, the responsibility for the control of the effort lies with both the operating manager and the systems staff. Together, they will have the responsibility for:

- Initiating and defining the scope of the project.
- Considering the project's impact on other information systems.
- Preparing the business justification and project plans.
- Budgeting and controlling the required resources.
- Monitoring the progress against the plan.
- Obtaining all required authorizations and approvals.
- Certifying that all deliverable items meet the specifications.
- Ensuring that there are adequate security, control, and disaster recovery provisions.

The operating manager starts such a project and may terminate it at any time. All application development should fall within the managing and budgeting authority of the area manager.

The information services department should be available with technical support, as requested, to aid the planning, development, installation, and operation of CASE systems. The responsibility of information services management includes:

- Assisting in definition of the project scope.
- Approving the functional requirements definition.
- Assisting in the systems design process.
- Assisting in the analysis and selection of vendor proposals.
- Informing the CASE team of existing standards and procedures and authorizing exceptions from them, if appropriate.

The complexity of the management of a CASE development project will depend on the needs of the particular system and its relationship to other data processing operations. It will also be related to the expected business growth of the area and, hence, the possible growth of the system in size and sophistication. The level of project management to be applied will, of course, depend on the number of employees involved, whether there are concurrent projects, the number of tasks, and the level of resource usage. There are project management systems available that can handle any level of complexity appropriately. Pick a project management system that will give the ability to:

- Plan project schedules.
- Compare project plans with actual job performance.
- Highlight the percentage of project completion.
- Forecast future time, manpower, and cost requirements.
- Be useful to simulate possible modification decisions.

It should also provide management reports at the level desired that will give the:

- Costs per task
- Start, completion, and deadline dates for each task
- Actual start and finish dates
- Percentage of completion and days remaining
- Cost variance relative to plan

The use of the more sophisticated project management systems that integrate with other systems, produce accounting reports, and have integrated text processors will depend on the established requirements of the organization.

Many organizations will have their own project management systems running on the mainframe and handled by a dedicated staff. CASE users may use such systems for their project management, or they may prefer to set up their own systems on their microcomputers. Some of the available systems for the latter approach are:

BSO/Planner, Boston Systems Office, Inc., 469 Moody St., Waltham, MA, 02154, for use on VAX, PDP-11, and Micro-11 computers.

Harvard Total Project Manager, Harvard Software, Inc., 521 Great Road, Littleton, MA, 01460, for use on IBM PC and compatibles.

MicroGantt, Earth Data Corp., Richmond, VA, for use with PCDOS- and MSDOS-based systems.

Microsoft Project, Microsoft Corp., 10700 Northrup Way, Bellevue, WA, 98004, for use with IBM PC and compatibles.

Primavera Project Planner, Primavera Systems, Bala Cynwyd, PA, for use with the DEC Rainbow and Data General DG Model 10.

Project Management System (PMS-II), North America MICA Inc., San Diego, CA, for use with CP/M-, MP/M-, and CP/M 86-based systems.

Project Scheduler 5000, Scitor Corp., 256 Gibraltar Drive, Sunnyvale, CA, 94089, for use with IBM PC and compatibles.

In the management of project schedules for CASE application development, it is important to understand that the types of effort involved are quite different from the traditional management of project schedules for large applications on large computer systems. In the past, planning for systems was only about 10 percent of the total effort. The bulk of the effort was in systems design and programming. Today, most central systems development is still handled the way it has been for some years, but CASE application development is highly automated, using many modern tools that have at least quadrupled programming productivity in terms of delivered functions. In some CASE application development now, planning and system design account for about 80 percent of the time expended, and programming and testing amounts to only about 6 percent of the total effort. This means that project management must now start earlier in the planning portion of the project cycle, and the old rules of thumb for the amount of effort expended are invalid.

This change in the proportion of effort in the different system life cycle phases comes from several sources. First, much of the application-dependent effort is in screen designs, and the screen sketches are produced during planning. It is relatively straightforward to enter them into a system that produces code. Second, many designs are data driven and automated, and record layouts emerge from data negotiations with the owner of the data, or with the data administration group. Once agreement has been reached, the data has been defined. Third, the standards for data usage and reusable program modules will expedite, rather than hinder, programming. Models that have been proven are used again and the wheel is not reinvented.

The overall result is that CASE application development, which tends to be data-driven, has new problems of project management. It is simpler in concept, but the steps may be quite difficult to estimate. The bulk of the effort is in the planning and system design stages, areas that are traditionally difficult to estimate. On the other hand, good project management remains an imperative if high-quality work is to be done on time, within budget, and with the expected results.

3.7   USE OF CASE IN APPLICATION DEVELOPMENT CENTERS

The Application Development Center (ADC) is a concept of bringing together some of the better system developers and programmers, giving them CASE, modern application development tools, workstations and computer power, and trying for high productivity and rapid application system development. It is not a competitive breakaway from the system development group; rather, it is a group with enough budget to:

- Use advanced programmer's workbench techniques including all aspects of CASE.
- Speed the system development process.
- Try new system development approaches and introduce CASE to others.
- Test fourth-generation languages and new programming methods.
- Test the automation of system development with newer CASE approaches.
- Experiment with application prototyping methods.
- Document the methods and techniques tested.
- Provide training in the successful processes that result.

There is a great need to accelerate the development of large applications and to tie them into relational databases, to optimize them, and to ensure their quality when they are completed. The use of computers has become absolutely imperative to meet competitive marketing and operating conditions. Most organizations have their accounting and general operating programs firmly in place in central computers, using the COBOL language and inefficient databases. The success of this automation, together with the difficulty of getting specific items of information rapidly from the massive files that have been generated, has created an immense backlog in the demands for usable, timely information and computer control of new areas. The only feasible way of removing this backlog appears to be the development of large relational databases, together with optimized, specialized application programs that can deliver controlled information to critical operational areas. This is no small task. It is effective to develop a special task force to handle it.

A large array of CASE system development tools and programming aids is currently on the market. It is certainly not clear by reading the sales literature which vendor offerings are superior for any specific application and for the group that is working on it. There are many factors that come into play, including efficiency of computer use, the learning curve, the ability to optimize, the availability of many required functions, and ease in tying in to existing systems. The fact is, however, that CASE tools are available to achieve a manifold increase in the efficiency of system development and installation. But there are many of them and the problem is simply finding out which are the preferred tools for a particular organization and its applications. This effort requires trained, experienced personnel.

One solution to the backlog problem frequently put forward is the purchase of packaged application systems. This is an excellent solution when proprietary packages are available that meet all the required specifications of the desired system. Very frequently, for standalone programs, excellent packaged systems can be purchased and installed. They sometimes require a slight bending of the functional requirements specifications, and they sometimes need a few modifications to be acceptable. In general, however, the purchase of packaged, vendor-developed systems can be a useful way of meeting a number of demands. It is most effective when there is a systematic, experienced review of the desired specifications.

Another solution to the backlog problem is the hiring of contract systems development staff, or working with an outside firm to develop systems that exactly meet internal specifications. This is a solution that is adopted very frequently by government agencies and by corporations that have difficult deadlines to meet and rigid staff limitations. It is a relatively easy solution to manage, and usually the systems developers made available are experienced professionals. The problems with this solution are that the cost is high, control of staff is more limited, and adherence to internal standards is seldom assured. If they do not use CASE approaches, the resulting system quality is seldom satisfactory. Such contract staffs must be given considerable freedom if they are to produce results efficiently. In addition, the helpful experience they gain in the development and in working with operational managers is all lost to the organization at the end of the contract.

Purchased application systems may even interrelate with each other, but they are generally limited in handling all the requirements of any organization. Hiring outside staff is helpful when it is needed at a point of urgency, but it is generally not helpful in the long run because the organization loses all the experience that they gain in system development. The Application Development Center (ADC), however, is an approach that combines some of the best features of these other approaches and offers unique advantages. It is a good organizational structure to test and develop CASE. It is an excellent focal point to oversee the purchase of application packages. It gives quality experience to the better technical analysts and programmers who are likely to stay with the organization. It is not a replacement for these other approaches, however, but a specific, companion approach that has its own important niche in the organization.

In summary, the ADC is an organizational approach of concentrating staff and resources to manage the CASE approach and to build quality systems products in less time and at less cost. It requires management commitment and interest, and a substantial investment in people and equipment. Its focus is on productivity and quality improvement in system development, and its main objectives are to:

- Get applications into production quickly.
- Meet the demands by users for systems.
- Profit from changes and advances in CASE methodologies.

The ADC is a combination of:

- Experienced support staff of analysts and programmers.
- High-productivity application development software and other CASE tools.
- Dedicated, powerful workstations and central computer availability.

The support staff must be well-trained professionals who are interested in experimentation and new methods. Their mission is to implement application development software methods, experiment in optimizing software development, and support both end users and other system development professionals.

The application development software should be in an integrated CASE methodology. It must be high-level languages designed for interactive use. It must be interfaced with data administration and, preferably, relational database systems. There must be strong emphasis on project management, documentation, and training, and these should all be automated as much as possible.

The hardware resources required are terminal availability, CPU accessibility with good response time, and substantial on-line libraries of support systems.

The Application Development Center concept is a strategic solution to the management issues of:

- End-user demand for more and better systems, delivered rapidly.
- Introduction of CASE to improve system development productivity and morale.
- The overload of backlog and maintenance requests.

It requires an assessment of the:

- Attitudes of the users towards the system development work.
- Existing backlog of user requests for systems.
- Possible level of user requests if systems were delivered promptly and accurately.
- Capabilities of the staff for running an ADC and learning CASE.
- Availability of hardware resources.
- Available support from vendors.

It also requires a study and an action plan, with management involvement at every step.

Position in the Information Services Organization

The ADC fits well into an effective, centralized information services function. Figure 34 shows the generally accepted organizational structure of information services, greatly simplified. Its purpose is to show where the responsibilities of the ADC fit into an overall structure. There is no attempt to show a specific, relative position. The ADC may well be part of the system development group, or fit elsewhere. The purpose of Figure 34 is simply to show how the responsibilities both interface and interconnect, and the types of methods and approaches that are central to each of the types of groups. It is obvious that there will be overlap between the methods and responsibilities that are shown. Each individual organization must define the interfaces for its own situation.

It is important to note that the ADC is structured principally to be in the forefront of trying out new application development methods, not simply to develop complex applications rapidly and well. It is provided with the best equipment and systems to perform the systems development function efficiently and effectively, so that the methods, when proven, may be used by the rest of the system development group. It is not a substitute or a replacement for the system development and programming group. Rather, it is a task force for priority, urgent applications, and a test center for new approaches.

FIGURE 34. Information services organization and responsibilities.

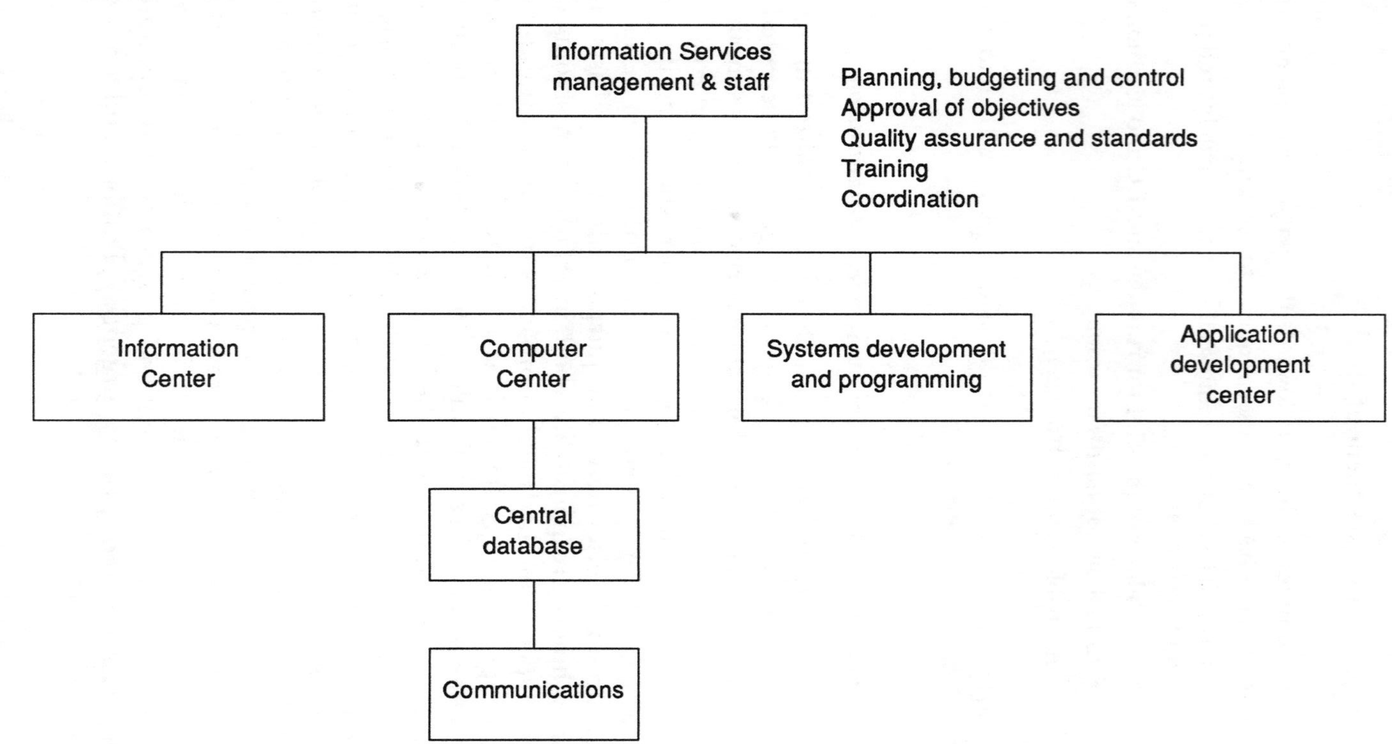

EQUIVALENT METHODS AND RESPONSIBILITIES

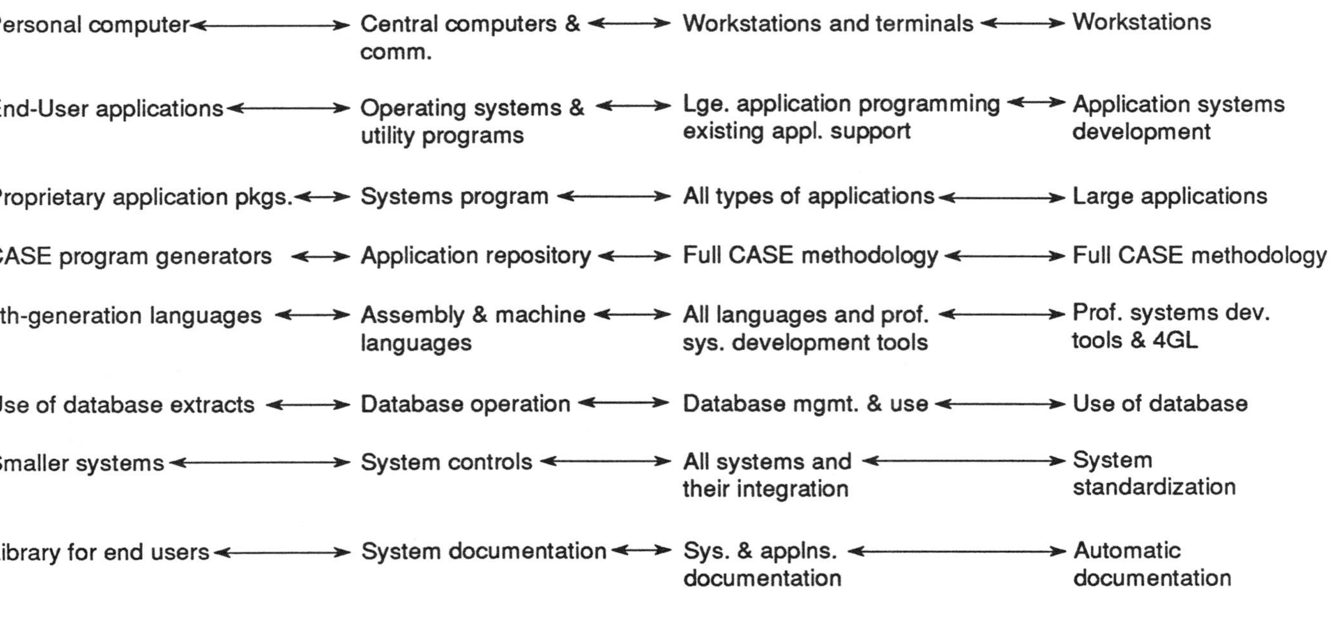

Figure 34 shows information services divided into one management and four operational areas. Some of the responsibilities listed under information services management and staff may well be under the control of other areas. For example, quality assurance may be a system development activity. Also, quality assurance will be a key factor in the ADC. The equivalent methods and responsibilities of the operational areas are summarized comparatively. Once again, there may be considerable overlap, but the comparative emphases are indicated.

Hardware.

In the use of computer hardware, the ADC will normally require workstations. These are simply powerful PCs or terminals that have extra memory and considerably more function than most programmers or end users require. They will generally include disk memory and printers. The type of application development that is done in CASE will need rapid turnaround and considerable local power. Other system development and programming personnel may well have similar workstations, but most programmers who are working on modifications and enhancements to programs can work well on terminals, and receive their printouts centrally.

Application Development.

ADCs normally work with the development of large, different, or test systems, concentrating on CASE approaches. They are less likely to be involved in maintenance activities, unless new methods are being tested. Smaller systems are seldom worth the power that is concentrated in the ADC. System development continues to work on the traditional large application systems. Over 60 percent of their effort, however, is usually involved in maintenance and enhancement work. Some estimates are that, without CASE, this will increase to 80 or 90 percent of their effort. Other than the operational programs that it runs, the computer center is only concerned with operating systems and utility programs. This can be a substantial amount of work, of course, requiring highly experienced systems programmers to handle it. These systems are usually provided by the computer vendor or software vendors, however, and are seldom developed in-house. The effort is in installing and debugging them. The information center is ordinarily involved only with standalone end-user applications and the setup of extract databases. They usually defer to the other groups for work on any systems on the central computer.

Types of Programs.

ADCs are concerned with large application programs. For more rapid development, this may include the use of prototyping methods which can give a spinoff to other programs. The system development group will work as professionals with all types of programs, large and small. They may also find CASE and prototyping advantageous, but usually only after it has been tested by a special group, such as the ADC. The information center will be mainly involved with proprietary application programs because they are easier to use. Some users may develop programs and some may even try prototyping which is mainly of use with large systems.

Languages Used.

Fourth-generation languages (4GLs), imbedded in CASE methodologies, are one of the keys to the success of ADCs in the rapid development of applications. 4GLs come in a great variety of complexities, however, and the types of languages used by the ADC will generally be larger and have far more functionality than the 4GLs used in the information center. The experienced programmers in the ADC will be sufficiently competent to handle any degree of language complexity. They will be looking for all the power they can get, and the ability to work with multiple files and programs at the same time. End users generally look for simplicity in learning and operation in selecting a language. Of course, the system development group will also be ready to use the more complex 4GLs, but, too often, most of their work is bogged down in modifying existing COBOL programs.

Database.

The capabilities and flexibility of relational database systems so far exceed other types of databases that it is likely the ADC will concentrate on them. Relational is needed to support CASE. It offers the greater speed of application development that is the central purpose of the ADC. On the other hand, the central system development group will have a far more complex task. It will be up to them to keep all the existing databases in operation, and there will probably be a database management group with that main function. Once again, they will also have the responsibility of maintaining any existing database applications. Most end users, working with the information center, will be content with extracts from databases.

System Concerns.

The ADC will have a central interest in system standardization within a CASE approach. Only through establishing and holding to standards will their maximum efficiency in system development be ensured. The ease of use of existing code and subroutines, and the standardization of as many programs as possible, will be critical to their work. The system development group would be pleased to have similar conditions, but, again, they are forced to maintain and enhance all the existing application programs, some of which may be far from standard. They will also make an ongoing effort at system integration, but, in many cases, this will only come through the writing of much interconnection code. The computer center accepts most application systems as they are delivered, and must spend the most time on establishing system controls and in seeing that all applications use those controls. The information center end users work generally with smaller systems, and the standards and procedures for them are less complex.

Documentation.

The ADC system development with CASE must be optimized in all areas, and one of the more important areas is documentation. This is normally a slow, bothersome, and bug-ridden function, so it should always be handled by an automatic documentation system. This system should also be used by the system development group, of course, but they are tied up by many older systems that have been manually documented. The computer center is principally concerned with system documentation from an operational viewpoint, although they may always insist that complete documentation exists for any application that is accepted for routine operation. The information center has less control over the actions of the end users in creating documentation for their programs, and can only hope that, through training and advice, they can get the point across regarding the necessity for documentation. Their main thrust in this area will usually be in maintaining a complete library for end users of all the programs that will likely be used, and to show the advantage of documentation through example.

Training.

The ADC will have little involvement in the training of other people. Rather, they will have a great interest in the training of their own people, and any cooperating systems analysts and programmers, in the use of advanced system development methods. The field is always moving fast, and newer approaches are regularly being made available. The ADC will always be interested in new ideas and in training for better development systems. The system development group is concerned with all aspects of training for large systems, for analysts, programmers, management, and the system users. That group has so much training to accomplish that it may be put in charge of the training function. The computer center is only interested in the training of its own operators, unless, of course, there is an on-line system with inadequately trained terminal users. The information center emphasis is on the training of its own staff and the end users. This training is generally at a much less complex level than that for larger systems, but the people being trained know less about computers, so the effort is just as great.

Note that this view of the ADC is that it is one of three similar types of centers: the information center, the computer center (which is sometimes called the production center), and the application development center. One factor that these three types of centers have in common is that they are assemblies of specialties to service all other departments in the organization that need their services. They are specialty service organizations. The system development and programming group, on the other hand, is not specialized, and may be involved with other departments in a great variety of ways. Their staff works in variable groupings, depending upon the work to be done, and teams are frequently under the control of user management, or are intermixed with users. They do not necessarily stay in a "center," but may be scattered throughout the organization.

The Mission of the Application Development Center

The creation of an ADC is a strategic move by information services. Most IS groups are faced with a critical business problem, which is the delivery of required information to the operating departments of the organization. Computer-developed information is now accepted as a necessity. The demand for that information far exceeds the capabilities of IS response by traditional system development methods. End-user computing and information centers only supply part of the need for systems, and it is usually at the simpler, less complex end of the spectrum. Business strategies are being based on the availability of information or customer computer services. IS must link that business strategy to their computer strategy and come up with new ideas. New business initiatives require more computer information. The IS strategic response must be to supply it as required. This simply means the use of new tools and new methods. The older system development methods are just not responsive enough. CASE methods, hailed by professionals, are needed.

The ADC must be established with a clear understanding of meeting this strategic need. It is no longer realistic to throw more people into the programming pool—the availability of competent people and the company's budget preclude that approach. It is now a matter of working smarter, concentrating the effort on priority projects, and putting business needs first. The ADC must be planned strategically to match the IS resources to the meeting of strategic business opportunities where the computer systems will have an impact on the business products and operations. Despite these strategic ends for ADCs, however, they must be planned carefully to be effective, with data gathering, comparison of equipment and systems, the application of technical expertise, and routine project reporting.

ADCs must, therefore, be established on a business basis, and their role must be understood clearly by all involved. One of the first management steps is to agree upon and to state the *mission* of the ADC. The mission statement is not just a nicely worded phrase that is filed away. It is the basis for the work, and it establishes the business boundaries of the team. Mission setting specifies the sectors in IS in which the unit will conduct its business, broadly describes how the unit will operate, and states any constraints. Early in the planning process, the tentative mission statement should be reviewed with responsible management. At a minimum, this is the senior IS executive. The ADC is being created as a matter of policy, and the person who decides the policy should be completely aware of the implications.

A good place to start thinking about the possible mission of the proposed ADC is the mission statement that IBM, Toronto, established for its development center. Essentially, it was: "The Development Center is to find the means to improve the productivity of information system developers and to enhance the application development process." The statement could also be: *"The ADC is to test improved productivity tools for system development, and to demonstrate improved application production methods."* This leads directly to CASE.

It is no less important that groups other than system development and any concerned senior management and user management are also made aware of the mission of the ADC. It should be written in memos, well distributed, and discussed. It represents a planned effort by information services to do something constructive about the backlog of requests and the quality of systems, and if it is made to appear attractive enough, the users and managers involved will all want to cooperate and follow the effort. Therefore, state the mission of the ADC, advertise and discuss it, and move on to establishing specific objectives.

Objectives of the Application Development Center

The objectives will include specific statements of ends, or business goals, to be gained and management targets to be attained. Some of the possible objectives have already been mentioned. There are usually main objectives and lesser objectives. They all need to be stated, since some effort may be put into an uninteresting area, like improving documentation, while the bulk of the effort is put into new system development processes. There are four main objectives of an ADC:

- Improve the application development process.
- Evaluate development tools and integrate them into the develpment process.
- Provide support for the new, improved development methods.
- Standardize and measure the development process.

In improving the application development process, the objective is to find ways to make the computer systems do more, and lift the burden from the developers. CASE is indicated. It is essentially the automation of the process. The ADC staff are to find systems and methods, test them in practice, standardize on them for particular areas, document them, and provide the necessary training. Improvement of the process is generally obtained by experimentation and testing of approaches. The attainment of this objective can be measured in several ways. One is the shortening of the development cycle and the reduction of the program development effort. Another is improving the management of the process, so that projects can be estimated and delivered according to the estimation. A third is improving the user participation and communication. If improving the application development process is to be stated as an objective, it needs to be further modified to say what will be improved, and how the improvement will be noticed. All these ways are found in CASE approaches.

In evaluating and integrating development tools, the objective can be stated simply, but in practice the effort may be great. There are a large number of vendors, each of whom claims to have the best solution to the problems, although those may be different from your problems. The most useful tools, with the greatest functionality, are not simple to install and test on any objective basis. The functions of the many vendor offerings all seem to vary in specific areas. The only realistic way for an ADC staff to approach this objective is to be systematic and objective in their analyses of the tools. First, written functional requirements for the projects being considered must be established. Second, the vendors must be approached with a statement of the prioritized functional requirements and asked to respond. Third, the evaluations must be on an equal basis, pertaining to the same requirements. This does not mean, of course, that new package systems with great advances in certain areas that were not originally contemplated should not be considered on their own merits. It simply means that the comparison between packages should be made on a systematic basis, and that desired functions be given greater weight than other, perhaps interesting, functions. The tools should be selected according to the applications to be installed and the resources that are available. The ADC may be better off with "lean and mean" tools that fit their particular jobs than they would be with very complex tools that can do anything but use up many personnel and computer resources.

In providing support for new and improved development methods, the ADC staff must be prepared for giving consultation and direct aid with the new CASE development tools and processes. Once an ADC is created and staffed with competent analysts, they should also be considered as the focal point of the use of 4GLs and productivity aids for complex problems. The staff should select, learn, and maintain the systems selected, and be prepared to train and help others with those methods. The productivity tools may not be particularly expensive, but they are complex to maintain and support.

The ADC should be in the loop whenever a CASE productivity software package is being considered, and the systems available through the ADC should always be given preference by managers.

In standardizing and measuring the development process, the ADC group must try to take measurements of baseline development systems, and compare newer approaches analytically. Some sort of measurement base should be established that indicates where the organization is in its development productivity.

Advances should then be compared to that baseline. This is an analytical approach that directly fits management's thinking as they watch the plan-vs-actual figures in dollars and headcount. The objective of the ADC is not just to develop applications faster, it is also to develop them cheaper and better. Standardization helps everyone to use one of the better approaches to system development, and puts all the development activities on the same footing. Timings and cost measurements begin to have real meaning. Some control can be exercised over the use of resources. Measurement proves the standards and the selections, and shows whether there have been any advances in productivity. The development of standards will normally be part of the function of the ADC staff. The measurement of productivity, machine usage, timings, and so forth, may be in the ADC, or may be handled by the capacity planning group in information services.

The main objective of the ADC should be a concern about the CASE process, or the development methodology. In trying out new systems, the staff can handle high priority application jobs and satisfy the user customers, but it will always be a minor part of the total systems development group. They must keep focusing on how to help the large staff of analysts and programmers in their department, and think about how to increase their productivity. They are the ones who are producing the bulk of the applications for the users, and most of the users are looking for faster, better development methods so that real business deadlines will be met.

3.8 STRATEGIES FOR THE SUCCESSFUL ADOPTION OF CASE

CASE should be managed the same way systems development has traditionally been successfully managed, by:

- Relating it to the strategic planning of the organization.
- Doing traditional analyses with operational budget planning.
- Applying project management over the effort.
- Applying the necessary controls at all levels.
- Making both good technical and feasibility analyses of system acquisitions.

- Considering training, security, and disaster recovery planning.
- Applying quality assurance control over the whole project.

These points have all been discussed in this chapter. There are also strategies involved in the timing of the implementation of CASE, and the relationships that should be developed to attain success. Some of the key steps in a successful strategy for the adoption of CASE are listed in Figure 35.

1. Define the Functional Requirements

You have to know what you want to do before you start doing it. It is imperative to define the functional requirements of a CASE project before it is started if it is to be successful. Certainly, the final, accurate statement of the definition of functional requirements will come out of the enterprise and systems modeling that is done with CASE tools. Also, the detailed functional requirements will come out of the data and process modeling, again with CASE tools. There is a clear need to define the general functional requirements before starting, however, for several strong reasons:

- To get senior management support for the project.
- To make preliminary budget estimates so the project can start.

FIGURE 35. Strategies for the successful adoption of CASE.

1. Define the general functional requirements before starting.

2. Start with pilot projects to gain understanding and experience.

3. Analytically determine the methodology and the CASE tools to use.

4. For the first projects, pick ones in which CASE has obvious strengths.

5. Select CASE products that are indicated for the types of projects you have.

6. Implement the selected CASE products in a planned and systematic way.

7. Introduce CASE to other professionals only when the first group is experienced and comfortable with it.

8. Introduce the results of the early CASE efforts against the planned expectations.

- To understand clearly what direction the effort should take before it is truly started.

General functional requirements should be stated in order to know if the effort is truly going to support a certain business strategic initiative. Also, there is no way to select, plan, and initiate a project professionally without having a clear understanding of the functional requirements that management anticipates. Even if the early systems attacked are small test systems, they must be defined and handled systematically if there is to be any assurance to management that the CASE group knows what it is doing.

2. *Start with Pilot Projects*

The process of implementing CASE and producing substantive results is long and tedious. Major results cannot be expected in only a few months. Also, if management is expecting CASE to "increase productivity," they will be very discouraged with the CASE effort if they expect to see noticeable productivity results in one year.

Remember that the increase in productivity that is to be expected from CASE will not occur in the early phases of the SDLC. On the contrary, the early work will take longer than in the traditional SDLC. In addition, many new tools are involved, and the learning curve will be lengthy. If management expects productivity results in the first budget year, they will probably be disappointed and may cancel further CASE efforts. It must be impressed upon management that productivity results can be expected probably in the second year, when a number of professionals will have become familiar with the tools. In subsequent years, there will be dramatic improvement noted in the quality of the CASE products and in their ease of maintenance. Then there will be proven productivity.

Since most management is impatient for results, the best strategy for CASE, therefore, is to start with fairly small pilot projects that can supply the understanding and experience to the professionals involved, and show some measured, even though small, productivity advantages in a time frame that holds the interest of management.

3. Analytically Select the CASE Tools to Acquire

Do not pick the CASE methodologies or tools to use in your environment from a few articles in periodicals or visits by vendor salesmen. Your own situation may well be unique. Use a systematic, analytical method to review and select the CASE environment tools that will serve you best. Chapter 6 of this book, "How to Evaluate and Select CASE Products," offers the proven methodology for the selection process.

There are many factors involved in the selection and acquisition of CASE tools. Some of the questions that arise are:

- Does the CASE product fit our environment?
- Does the CASE product fit the batch or on-line or shared type of system being considered?
- Do the individual CASE products fit the overall CASE methodology that is being selected?
- Does the vendor support appear to match your own requirements?

4. Does CASE Have Obvious Strengths for the Selected Project?

Some CASE tools are specifically designed for the analysis and design phases of application development, so they will fit such an application where they can best be used. Others are built for the automation of programming. Still others concentrate on expert systems as an integral tool. Then there are CASE environments that span a large part of the system development life cycle. Any of these may be useful for very large projects. For initial, smaller projects, however, some CASE tools will clearly be more valuable than others. It is clearly an advantage to select the particular CASE products that will be most useful for the selected pilot projects, even 'though they may be less useful for larger projects that will be considered later. Pick CASE tools with obvious strengths to be able to prove the advantages of the approach.

5. Pick Projects Where CASE Has Obvious Strengths

Some applications lend themselves to the CASE approach and are more useful to prove the value of CASE. These are applications that have fairly complex models, with some difficulty in relating the data and the process throughout the application. They may also be applications with a good deal of model and code that could be reusable throughout the system. CASE is particularly useful when there is complexity in the data relationships. Select a project in which CASE can show its advantages quickly. Even though the first project may be small, do not pick one with simplistic design and easily structured data files with simple use of the data elements.

6. Implement in a Planned and Systematic Way

Management will get no proof of the value of CASE if what is expected is not stated up front, and then the actual results are compared to the promises. Giving management plan-vs-actual tools is the simplest way to install confidence in the CASE effort. Vague promises are useless. This CASE book gives many points to follow in the proper and fruitful management of CASE projects. Follow the theory, because it has been proven to be the way management prefers. Select, install, and implement the chosen CASE products with plans that are familiar to management, and in a systematic way that is familiar to the participants.

7. Spread CASE Slowly

The professionals who work with CASE early on may become very enthusiastic and forget the length of their own learning curve. They may well feel that they can spread the word about CASE much faster than they received it themselves. In the early stages of CASE introduction, set up a CASE personnel environment, just as a CASE technical systems environment is set up with a support staff. Remember the importance of systematic training at all levels.

Establish CASE firmly as a proven and practical approach. Set up a formal training program. Do not have the technical staff trying to influence others to use CASE until they themselves are experienced with CASE, sure that it is useful, and comfortable with all aspects of it.

8. *Evaluate CASE Efforts Against Expectations*

Follow the principles of successful data processing planning. Analyze and set goals carefully. Present them to management and convince them to fund the work. When the work is completed, or a specific phase is completed, analyze the situation and prepare a plan-vs-actual report. Give management realistic expectations and then evaluate the CASE efforts against those expectations and report accordingly. Do not try to evaluate against unexpected profitable (or unprofitable) results. Use those findings for the next set of CASE plans. Always evaluate against your best estimate at the start of the project.

There are, of course, exceptions to such evaluation. There are many situations that can arise that will markedly change the expectations as the work progresses. These may include staff changes, organizational changes, management changes, unexpected technological difficulties, lack of continued funding for unrelated reasons, and so on. If such is the situation, the "expectations" are adjusted, and the adjustment is described to management in the plan-vs-actual report. Success must be objective to impress management—This is what was expected. This is what actually happened.

CHAPTER 4

Components and Functions of CASE Products

Overview

*C*ASE products come in many packages at many levels. They may be classified by function or life-cycle usage. By function, the three areas of categorization are assistance, analysis, and automation. The classification by life-cycle usage usually breaks into the "Upper CASE", or design and analysis tools, and the "Lower CASE", or coding and screen painting tools.

An integrated information architecture is a necessity to gain the optimum advantages from the use of CASE. A planned architecture is a necessity in CASE work. Several ways of looking at information architectures are briefly noted.

A diagram is given of the possible integration of the typical components of CASE products, and the various components are defined. The place of prototyping and of expert system components is noted. The central information repository is described as the key to productivity.

It is clear that CASE products vary widely in their capacity to support the application development life cycle process. A number of examples, and their place in the life cycle, are given.

CASE methods are an extension of the use of structured techniques and diagrams. The relationship of different diagrams and the generated code is shown. Some of the more useful and necessary types of diagramming needed to represent the requirements and the application system are briefly discussed and illustrated.

The importance of COBOL Reverse Engineering technology is discussed, and the Bachman Methodology is reviewed.

A number of desirable features of CASE products are outlined.

4.1 THE CLASSIFICATION OF CASE PRODUCTS

CASE products come in many packages at many levels. Some are single CASE programs, while others are packages of integrated components. They can be classified by function or by life-cycle usage, although such classifications will not include all available CASE offerings.

Classification by Function

A useful way of categorizing CASE products is by the functional area in which they are employed. Three areas are: assistance in managing and accomplishing the CASE process; analysis in areas that are difficult to handle manually; and automation of previously manual tasks. These functions are not mutually exclusive, and CASE products may operate in more than one area, but they help to categorize the wide array of available CASE products.

The assistance function includes any CASE tools that accumulate and track information, or make information available in an organized way that is readily handled by other systems or manually. These tools thus assist the managers of CASE efforts in accumulating and tracking information that will be of value in directing the CASE effort towards increases in efficiency and effectiveness, while reducing the staff effort and the error rate. They are tools that control the system development process or aid in the handling of data that is used.

Some of the CASE assistance tools are:

- *Supervisory tools,* such as planning, project control, project management, and quality assurance.
- *Dictionary reporting tools,* such as

—Storage and retrieval of information from the information repository

—Editors for information capture, including diagram, form, matrix, and text

—Screen reporting systems

—Hardcopy reports for validation, verification, and the production of deliverables

—Production of tables of information and cross-references.

- *Layout design tools* for screens and reports, which are linked to the information repository and produce high-quality, reusable layouts.

- *Drawing tools* for creating, modifying, and producing design diagrams, and for producing visual reports that will provide entry into the database.

The analysis function includes the CASE tools that aid in work that is otherwise too complex to handle manually. Such analytical tools augment the capabilities of the CASE application developer. They allow things to be done that might otherwise be too complex, too difficult to do accurately, or too time-consuming with manual methods. In general, the analysis tools ensure a higher level of system quality and the ability to use the best analytical systems available.

Some of the CASE analysis tools are:

- The ability to provide *design verifications*, such as consistency checks and the level-to-level balancing of a data flow diagram set.

- The provision of *cross references* through the application system.

- The production of *complex reports* accurately.

- The application of *known design rules* to a design.

- The offering of *suggestions* to a system developer.

- The analysis of possible *inconsistencies and redundancies* in the data design, including overlaps in the structure and content of data sets.

- The enforcement of *configuration management* rules.

- The *tracking* of all *components* during the development of a large system, including the code, the specifications, and the design modules.

- The sharing of *design modules*, with suggestions concerning overlaps.
- The *what-if analysis* of design alternatives.

The automation function includes the CASE tools that bridge the life-cycle phases. The tools provide matrices of information that have been prepared in one phase for use in another. The CASE system automatically bridges between development phases, eliminating some manual activities and making others more accurate.

Some of the CASE automation techniques are:

- The *generation of programs*, up to a complete operational system, from design information, producing output code, screen forms, application reports, and so on.
- The *generation of standard information* from a COBOL or CICS environment.
- The *production of program code* with greatly reduced error rate, and increased consistency.
- The ability to produce many lines of code from nonprocedural descriptions.
- The *creation of bridges* between the life-cycle phases, and between the various CASE techniques and tools.
- The making of *transformations* between the modeling components and the various levels of abstraction.
- *Database normalization*, producing first, second, or third normal form relations, prompting the user for missing information and making deductions from the general rules of normalization.

The ideal CASE system will move the information from the end users' requirements to an executable system automatically. All information in the process will be maintained in the information repository, and accurate documentation will be automatically produced. CASE is having a significant impact on the way systems are being produced. Productivity gains of 5 to 10 are not uncommon across a broad domain of system development problems. There are three areas where CASE has proven to be particularly effective. These are:

- *Iteration in the design phase.* CASE is offering the promise of moving automatically from the design phase to coded and tested system product. This indicates that system developers will be spending far more time in the design phase, iterating the designs and testing at the design level. The use of prototyping will become much more common. The transition from the formally stated system specifications, through the models to the operational specifications will include validation and verification of completeness and consistency. Since the detailed design and coding will later be done automatically, the developer can spend much more time optimizing the design checking it against the specifications.

- *Management of large system complexity.* The complexity of a large system development project has long confounded the ability to manage it in detail by manual methods. CASE systems can handle the complexity down to individual system components. It provides top-down decomposition and simplification of abstractions that enable the handling of complexity.

- *Provision of expert assistance.* Expert systems are a natural adjunct to CASE development systems. They allow the analysis of many parts of the development to assist the developer with expert guidance. This can range from simple, local guidance to global guidance. Simple guidance can provide intelligent analyses, statements about transforms, and useful error messages. Global guidance can make suggestions to the system developer as the development work proceeds. It will take time to develop sufficient proven and accepted expert rules to do a comprehensive job of system development guidance, but there are many known rules that can be applied today, particularly in areas such as database design. It is a profitable area for an analysis by knowledge engineers.

Classification by Life-Cycle Usage

Another useful and common way of categorizing CASE products is by the life-cycle phase, or phases, in which they are employed. Figure 36 is essentially an extract from Figure 26. It simply shows the phases in systems development into which the various CASE tools may be slotted. Any particular CASE tool may be in one or more of these life-cycle phases, or in part of a phase. When the tools are categorized in this way, their use can be readily explained to management.

FIGURE 36. CASE tools through the development life cycle.

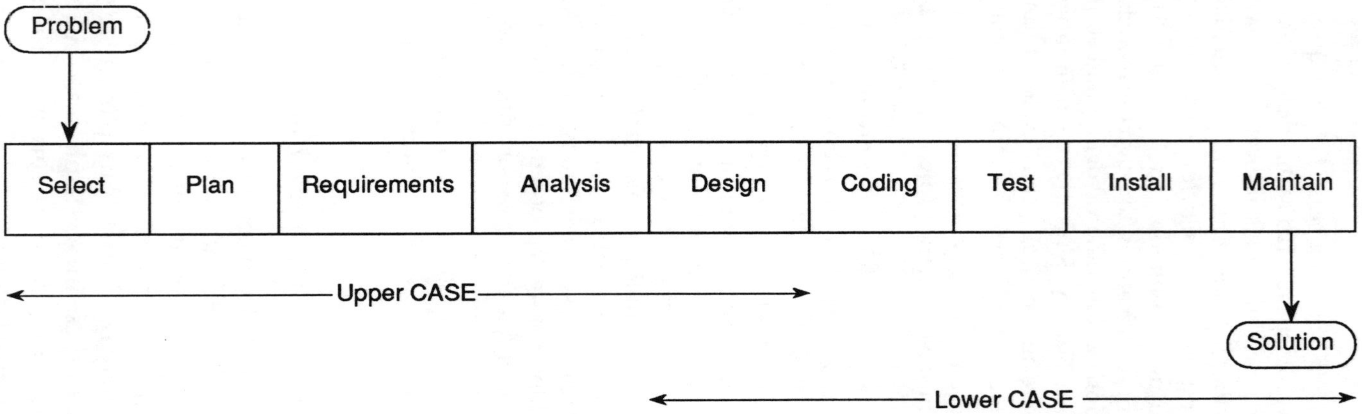

The *Upper CASE* tools are the most common on the market today. They are the tools and methods used in the initial activities of software development. This means that they interface with both the end users and the analysts, and are critical in getting the system development started correctly. The key to the greatest useability of Upper CASE tools is their capability of transporting, or transforming, data between the various tools, such as from the information repository to the tool, or from the tool to application generators. Many CASE tools are generic, and are useful with a variety of other CASE tools. Other tools are specific to certain methodologies, such as the Information Engineering Facility. It is fundamental that any Upper CASE tool selected should have free communication with the central information repository, or the project design database. Many CASE systems on the market today are in the process of being updated so that they can readily communicate with a set of other CASE tools that are necessary for a full methodology. Descriptions of tools a year or two old may not have the most updated information about interoperability, since the field is progressing rapidly.

Most Upper CASE systems have a project design database. The key to compatibility is whether such a database maps on your information repository. Many CASE systems can be readily customized to be useful in a given situation.

Some of the Upper CASE tools are:

- System *selection and planning*, including enterprise modeling, relationship modeling, system planning, profitability calculations, gap analysis, and presentation graphics.

- System *requirements definition*, including graphical specification, screen utilities, data flow diagrams, and integrated word processing.

- System *analysis*, including structured analysis, entity-relationship modeling, data model diagrams, integrated dictionary, integrated analysis facility, and report design.

- System *design*, including structured design, object-oriented design, structure charts, structure diagrams, data model diagrams, process description, module description, record layout, element description, and entity-relationship diagrams.

Index Technology's *Excelerator* is a good example of a composite Upper CASE methodology. It contains an integrated set of tools using a common design repository with a number of different "workbenches" of tools. It is critical to remember that the tools must be so designed that one or a number of people may use them with the same information repository.

Some of the Lower CASE tools are:

- System *design* tools used in workbench groupings that produce code.

- System *coding* tools, including source code generation, copy libraries, screen maps, and use of reusable code.

- System *test* tools, including data flow diagrams, structure charts, structure diagrams, screen design, and report design.

- System *implementation* tools, including automatic documentation, integrated word processing, and presentation graphics.

- System *maintenance* tools, including operational reporting, error analysis, and any of the above.

4.2 INTEGRATED CASE ARCHITECTURES

An *integrated information architecture* is a necessity to gain the optimum advantages from the use of CASE. An architecture can be defined as a structure, or coordination, of information technology components designed to best accomplish specific business purposes. The objective of an information architecture is to match the objectives of the business in order to produce the required information effectively, efficiently, and under control.

The idea of an information architecture can be used at any level of an information processing effort. For example, computer manufacturers talk about the architecture of their computers and communications systems. In CASE work, we are talking about a combination of hardware, software, and communications systems. Others may talk of an architecture for a specific application. An architecture gives structure; it does not supply detail. But a planned architecture is a necessity to assemble and coordinate a number of tools, such as in CASE, in an efficient way. Developing an architecture does not mean searching for the newest technologies. It simply means setting a clear overall objective when acquiring individual CASE tools, and sticking to that objective in all acquisition decisions.

An architecture has a number of different facets, which is why the term at some times appears confusing, as it is used differently by different groups. An excellent perspective of an information architecture was published by John Zachman, of IBM. This is shown in Figure 37. He was one of the first authors to relate the situation in building a system to that of an architect designing a building. When an architect talks to a customer about building a house, he sketches initial drawings of the plans. The drawings are the architect's interpretation of what the customer desires in the building. An architecture for information provides the same overview.

Note in Figure 37 that data, function, and network are three relatively independent areas in systems design. Data should be completely independent and free standing. It should preferably be maintained in a relational database, and any data used by any systems or programs should be identical at the entity level. Function is the organizational or business process. It can also be analyzed as a free-standing area. Functional programs can be developed that call on data and release information to the network. Network is the third area, which simply deals with the distribution of data and function throughout the organization and related organizations. Data, function, and network can be developed independently with CASE tools, although they obviously have to be completely coordinated at some point.

A number of "descriptions" are also noted in Figure 37, such as scope description and business description. Each of these is an area that must be addressed by a CASE tool. All of the descriptions, diagrams, charts, and programs noted are required parts in the development of application systems. Zachman's figure, *Information Architecture* (Figure 37), is an excellent point of reference in analyzing CASE systems. It helps to sort out, and show the relationships of, the results of many of the structured techniques and diagrams that are a normal part of the CASE products.

It is important to study the concept of information architecture seriously when determining how to use computer technology for competitive advantage. The business thrust should predominate when analyzing when and how to integrate the CASE tech-

FIGURE 37. Information architecture.

	DATA	FUNCTION	NETWORK
SCOPE DESCRIPTION	LIST OF THINGS IMPORTANT TO THE BUSINESS  ENTITY = CLASS OF BUSINESS THING	LIST OF FUNCTIONS THE BUSINESS PERFORMS  FUNCTION = CLASS OF BUSINESS PROCESS	LIST OF LOCATIONS IN WHICH THE BUSINESS OPERATES  NODE = BUSINESS LOCATION
BUSINESS DESCRIPTION	"ENTITY-RELATIONSHIP DIAGRAM" 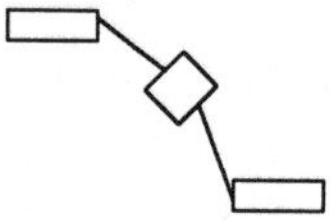 ENT. = BUS. ENTITY RELN. = BUSINESS RULE	"FUNCTION FLOW DIAGRAM" 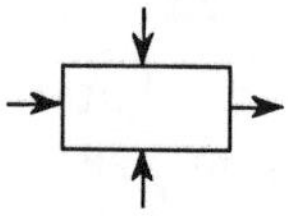 PROC = BUS. PROCESS I/O = BUS. RESOURCES (INCLUDING INFO.)	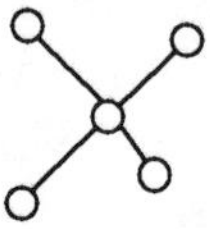 MODE = BUS. UNIT LINK = BUS. RELATIONSHIP (ORG., PRODUCT, INFO.)
INFORMATION SYSTEM DESCRIPTION	"DATA MODEL" 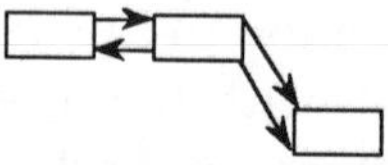 ENT. = DATA ENTITY RELN. = DATA RELN.	"DATA FLOW DIAGRAM" 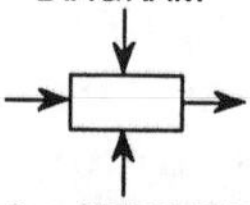 PROC. = APPLICATION FUNCTION I/O = SCREEN/DEVICE FORMATS	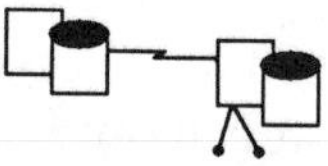 NODE = I/S FUNCTION (PROCESSOR, STORAGE ACCESS, ETC.) LINK = LINE CHARACTERISTICS
TECHNOLOGY CONSTRAINED DESCRIPTION	"DATA DESIGN" 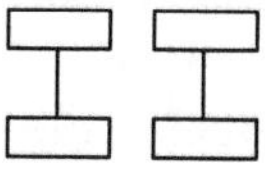 ENT. = SEGMENT/ROW RELN. = POINTER/KEY	"STRUCTURE CHART" 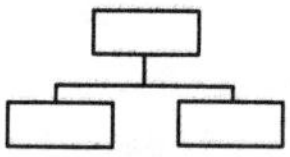 PROC. = COMPUTER FUNCTION I/O = SCREEN/DEVICE FORMATS	"SYSTEM ARCHITECTURE" 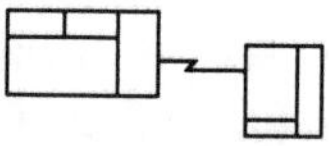 NODE = HARDWARE/SYS SOFTWARE LINK = LINE SPECIFICATIONS
DETAIL DESCRIPTION	"DATA BASE DESCRIPTION"  ENT = FIELDS RELN. = ADDRESSES	"PROGRAM"  PROC. = LANGUAGE STMTS I/O = CONTROL BLOCKS	 NODE = ADDRESSES LINK = PROTOCOLS
ACTUAL DESCRIPTION	DATA	FUNCTION	COMMUNICATIONS

nologies selected, how to link computing with the mainstream of the business, how to manage computing with fragmented organizational responsibility, and how to define a clear and shared vision for the organization.

There are four basic objectives for any CASE information systems study. These are:

- Develop a one-year and a five-year CASE systems plan within the framework of the one-year and five-year information services plan.

- Develop a comprehensive CASE information architecture that gives everyone in the organization a shared vision of its future computing environment. Link this architecture directly to the strategy of the business, and tie it in closely with the information plans.

- Develop and acquire appropriate and integrated CASE tools that will guide and direct the building of application systems. Tie these into the databases, communications network, and technology that are focused on supporting the business strategy.

- Obtain management's approval on effective guidelines and policies for the management of organizational data as a valuable resource.

After the overall information architecture has been agreed upon, it must be put on paper with details that fit the particular organizational circumstances. A good example of such a picture of the architecture is shown in Figure 38. This figure was developed by AT&T in their large and successful effort in determining their CASE strategic decisions, establishing their requirements, evaluating and selecting CASE tools, and developing information products with CASE. Figure 38 shows how they pictured their CASE architecture from a physical viewpoint. This proved to be of great help in their selection of CASE tools.

Another organization may not want to accept the specific hardware and software selections made by AT&T. They should use similar methods in approaching and describing the architecture, however. Such information is most helpful to systems analysts who are working with the system, and is readily understood by analysts and management as they discuss detailed selections and decisions in acquiring CASE tools.

FIGURE 38. Integrated CASE architecture.

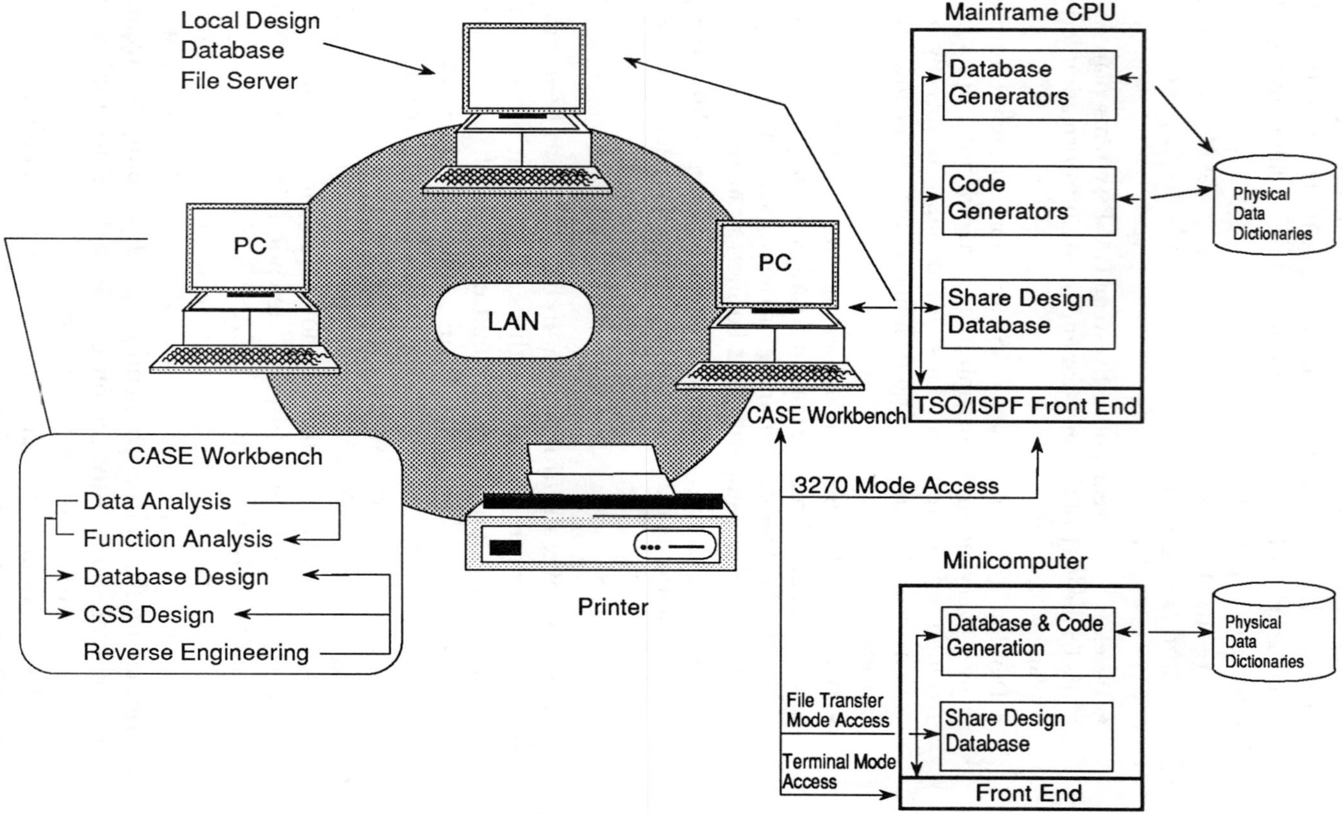

A third way of looking at an information architecture is shown in Figure 39. This diagram is used by Texas Instruments in explaining their Information Engineering Facility™. It obviously covers a wide area in the CASE field and simply shows general relationships. Although it has little detail, it helps to show the fit of the various components to management, and visually explains the necessity of cooperative action among a number of different organizational groups. It is a diagram more of organizational structure in the CASE effort, rather than information structure, but it clearly shows the general flow of information from the bottom to the top.

There are obviously a variety of CASE architectures. One categorization of them is as one-tier, two-tier, or three-tier architectures. This is illustrated in Figure 40. The simplest is the one-tier architecture, probably best represented by Excelerator. Excelerator runs entirely on a PC, although it is not limited, and does run on other levels of computers. The repository is local to that PC. If you want to collect the work of several users, then you manually transfer the ASCII files from one PC to another. This is, of course, a simple architecture that is easy to install. It is personal, it is responsive to the local users, and individuals can make quick progress. It is necessary to get procedures in place to manage group efforts, however, if such a one-tier environment is to be productive. Many CASE installations today are successfully running in this mode, particularly those with a variety of CASE tools that are not completely integrated.

A more sophisticated approach, shown in Figure 40, is the distributed, two-tier architecture. The real information repository resides on the mainframe. There are also some check in/check out capabilities, and usually LAN support. The entire CASE product cannot be described as being either mainframe or PC. The graphics editors are probably PC-based, but the control of the system is mainframe-based. For example, the code generation piece may be on the mainframe. Texas Instruments Information Engineering Facility™ is of this architecture. It is essentially a cooperative processing environment, using the PC for what it is best suited, and using the mainframe for what it is best suited.

There are also three-tier, distributed architectures, as shown in Figure 40. A LAN network runs against an intelligent server.

FIGURE 39. Information engineering framework.

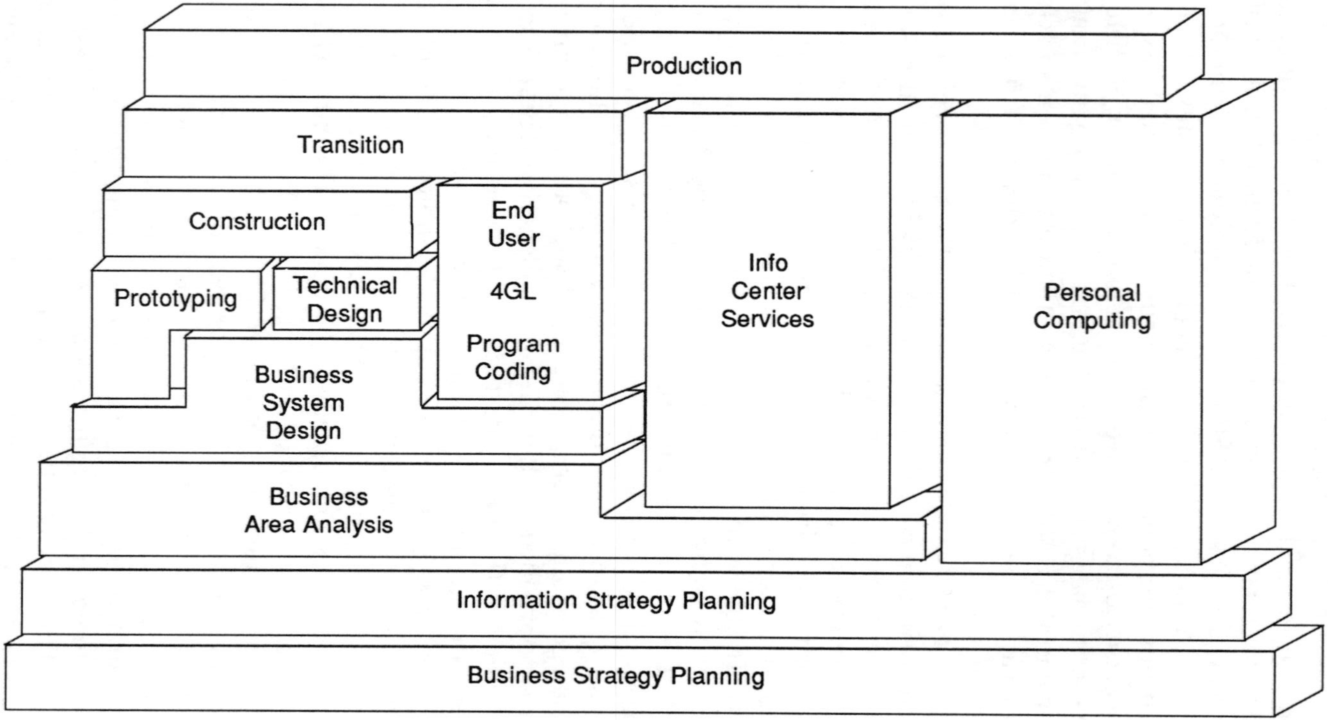

Production

Personal Computing

Info Center Services

Transition

End User

4GL

Program Coding

Construction

Technical Design

Prototyping

Business System Design

Business Area Analysis

Information Strategy Planning

Business Strategy Planning

FIGURE 40. CASE architectures.

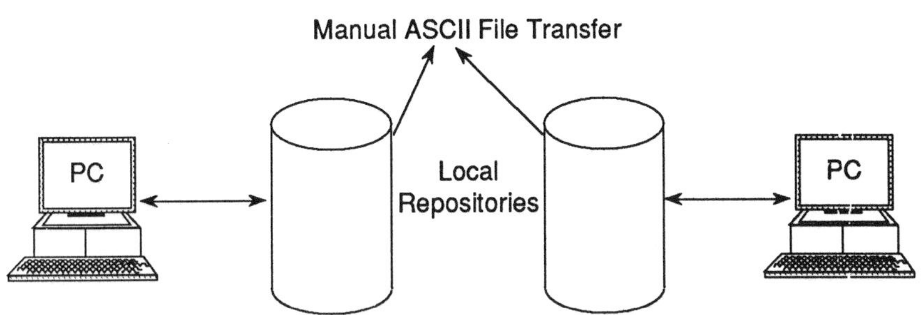

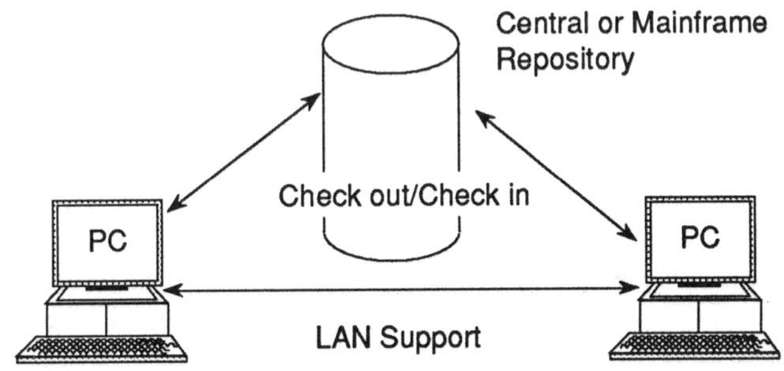

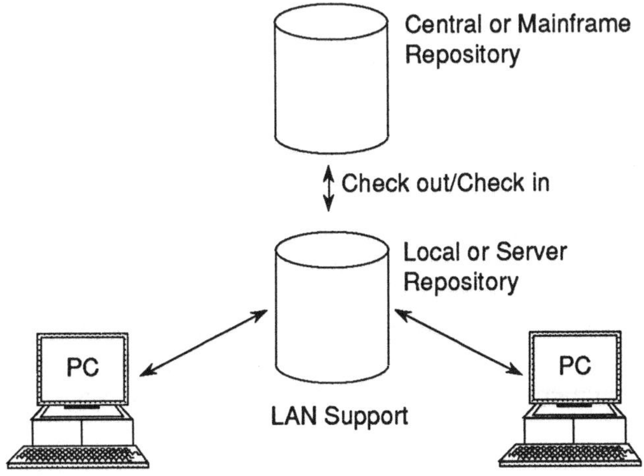

This is a popular architecture in Europe, where the server is often a Motorola minicomputer. It is less popular in the United States at this time.

4.3 COMPONENTS OF CASE PRODUCTS

The information architecture for CASE gives an overview of the framework in which the CASE tools will be operated. In practice, however, CASE tools will often be selected, and CASE training will be applied, at the component level of the CASE products. Very few CASE products are integrated with all the components. The complexity of the component level is shown in Figure 41. This figure essentially shows the operating relationship between the various functions noted in Figure 37. Figure 41 shows the overall design of a typical CASE environment for information system software development, broken into its principal components. CASE products will vary widely as to which of these components are contained in them. The functions that are illustrated in this figure and handled by CASE components and exchanged with other components are as follows:

- The *systems administration* component has a number of functions, not all of which are shown in Figure 41. Systems administration essentially consists of the project management functions of integrated CASE tools. This will include planning, budgeting, life-cycle management, and monitoring.

  The systems administration component may also manage both the central information repository and the application diagrams, and handle such functions as version control. It may have security and control elements, including access control, which gives permission to make changes in the requirements or the models. It may also manage the document formats database. If there is a planning function in the systems administration component, it will have elements that feed the business system design.

- The *business system design* component combines elements of planning, organizational structure, and business analysis. It is business modeling rather than system modeling. It is difficult to structure it completely, as different business problems will require different amounts of enterprise modeling, organizational analysis, management science analysis, and business impact analysis.

FIGURE 41. Typical components of CASE products.

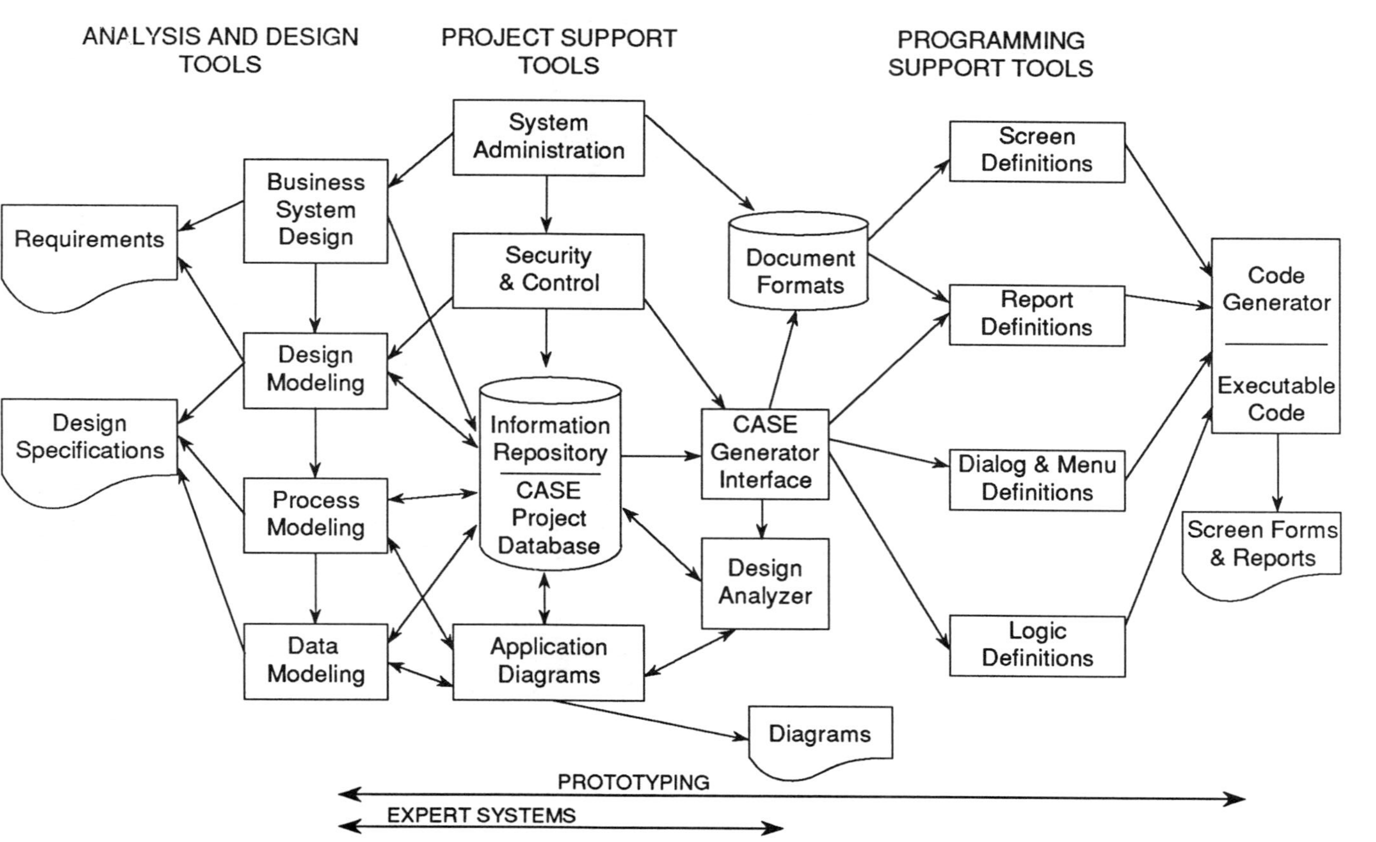

- The *design modeling* component moves from the business model to the system model. *Design automation techniques* are appearing in more products. These use front-end graphical design techniques that provide automatic analysis. Systems are specified in graphical form, and the diagrams are analyzed automatically for design errors and inconsistencies. In some systems, the specifications are converted automatically into code. Relative to Figure 41, this means that automatic design CASE products may incorporate all the tools needed to go from the design specification to the code generator, supplying information to the information repository en route.

- The *process modeling* techniques include data flow diagramming, structure charts, dialog flow, and state transition, which are at the heart of CASE methods. CASE programs evaluate the diagrams and the semantics, and can check for syntax, consistency, and the cohesive structure of the program. This component creates, and transmits to the central information repository, the requirements definition, functional decomposition, program structure, and program logic. It transmits data flow diagrams and program structure charts to the application diagrams database.

- The *data modeling* component creates and transmits to the information repository information on the data entities, data relationships, and data elements. It transmits entity-relationship diagrams to the application diagrams database. Entity modeling is clearly meaningful to end users, and an excellent mode of communication. They understand their own data and rules, and the diagrams become a common language. The highest level of entity modeling is an excellent presentation layer. As the process progresses through lower levels (there may be up to five), however, it becomes more technically esoteric, and gets into integrity constraints.

- The *security and control* component provides the necessary access and change controls that may be needed, and keeps records of accesses and changes. This component is a critical element in CASE that is frequently given little attention. In manual methods of application system development, it was possible for individuals to introduce erroneous code, self-serving code, viruses, Trojan Horses, and so on. The automatic code generation features of CASE now make it possible to control such deception. However, it will only work if attention is paid to it and if it is managed.

The security and control component is at the heart of *object management*, and may include:

−Version control

−Configuration management

−Defect tracking

−Requirements tracing

−Dependency management

−Code and design reuse

−Access control

- The *central information repository* component handles all the information resources and the data dictionary. This will include: functional models, database description, program logic, screen and report definitions, program structures, and change information. It will also include all the administrative and security information. This will be developed further in the next section.

- The *application diagrams* component handles data flow diagrams, data structure diagrams, and program structure charts. This will be developed further in Section 4.6, "Structured Techniques and Diagrams."

- The *document formats* component contains information about all screen definitions and report definitions. It is a critical element, as it eliminates all further work on document definitions, it maintains document standards, and it is a factor in the security of the program output.

- The *CASE generator interface* component is a system element within any set of integrated CASE tools, and will therefore be individual to any CASE tool developer. It handles data from the CASE project database and makes it available in the correct formats for the code generator and the reporting programs.

- The *design analyzer* component detects internal inconsistencies, ambiguities, and incompleteness in the design specifications. It is based on the underlying formal information model so that it can provide rigorous consistency and completeness checks. Newer design analyzers in CASE tools are being built with smart editors and intelligent assistants to use the power of expert systems.

- The *screen definitions* component receives screen and report definitions from the central repository, and transmits screen forms and reports to the output files. There may be screen painters, which support the definition of the formatted screens, menus, and data-entry procedures.

- The *report definitions* component manages diagrams on the report layout that are used to create and format reports, including the specification of data items, page headings and footings, column headings, sort breaks, control breaks, totaling and subtotaling, page numbering, and so on.

- The *dialog and menu definitions* component stores and makes available the programming for screen dialogs and menus.

- The *logic definitions* component stores and makes available the programming for logic definitions and logic handling in the reporting phase of the program.

- The *code generator* component receives information on the functional model and the database description from the central repository. It receives information from the application diagrams database and receives the sequence and layout of graphics and text from the document formats file and the definitions files.

  The problem of code generation is that there is not one-to-one mapping of what the CASE front-end products produce and pass to the information repository, and what is needed to generate code. Thus, the CASE generator interface, the screen definitions, the report definitions, the dialog and menu definitions, the logic definitions, and the document formats are all needed to provide the detail to generate code. They couple the front-end CASE and the code generation. In only a few products is this coupling tight. Many products in CASE modeling and analysis are free standing, and similarly, many of the CASE reporting tools are independent of the other tools that may be available. These functions in programming support are handled differently, and grouped differently, in different CASE tools. They are at the heart of the problem of integration of CASE tools. No integration is any stronger than the weakest link in the connections from the analysis and design tools to the programming support tools.

- *Prototyping* components may be integral with any CASE tools and products. Prototyping will be discussed further in Section 5.2, "Requirements Definition Prototyping." Although centered on the requirements definition phase, prototyping may be valuable in other phases, such as document formats. There are two general approaches to prototyping, which have different spans of use in system development:

—The *rapid throwaway* prototyping approach is used essentially in the CASE front end. It entails prototyping the software system to learn more about the problem and its solution. It may be simply producing screens for the user to look at. The idea may be to partially implement the system to provide early functionality. The results are usually discarded after the desired knowledge is gained.

—The *evolutionary* prototyping approach starts by learning about the problem and its solution, then proceeds through the full development cycle by being built on, or expanded, repeatedly until it becomes the final system.

• *Expert system* components may be imbedded as "black box" systems within any of the CASE analysis and design tools or in the design of the database. Such systems will be further described in Section 5.6, "The Use of Expert Systems in Case."

4.4 CENTRAL INFORMATION REPOSITORY

The central information repository, or encyclopedia, is the critical and essential element of any integrated set of CASE tools, CASE toolkits, or CASE workbenches. It is the *CASE* project database, but it is called a repository rather than a database, because it is much more than a collection of related data elements. It is the basis by which CASE tools can be integrated, standardized, and documented. It is the source of information for code generation. It is the mechanism for code reusability. It is the knowledge base to store information about the enterprise, including its structure, functions, procedures, data models, data entities, entity relationships, process models, design models, and so on. It maintains sufficient detail about the design of a system and its procedures so that program code can be generated automatically.

The central information repository is the database for storing and organizing all the components of an application system, including architectural design, data structures, process logic, screen definitions, report definitions, logic definitions, system diagrams, source code, test data cases, project management information, system documentation, etc., etc. It is the key to productivity because:

- It provides all developers with consistent information that is controlled.
- It provides information when it is needed and in a form that is directly useful.

The repository will normally contain a database of consistent and proven specifications, stored in abstract form, that can be viewed in a variety of related graphical formats, including data flow diagrams, structure charts, entity relationship diagrams, action diagrams, navigation charts, etc. It provides the facility for translating from one view to another while maintaining consistency between all the views. There is a difference between a data dictionary of a DBMS and an information repository of a CASE development system, although some CASE workbenches offer only a data dictionary. A data dictionary merely records information in a usable, organized form. An information repository, or encyclopedia, offers a higher level of information management by supplying the ability to coordinate and analyze the information as well.

An information repository stores the logical meaning of the entire system design. It includes the principles of an expert system knowledge base, because it contains facts and rules for checking the completeness and consistency of the data stored within it, as well as having a full database management system. In essence, this makes the repository an intelligent tool that not only provides multiple views of the information when they are needed, but also can choose which information is to be used. It performs an active control role in maintaining data integrity and consistency.

The repository is central to CASE application development because it not only provides the management control that is necessary over the data, and documents the data in diagrams; it also greatly facilitates the use of the data and the understanding of the data structures in rapid application development. It collects and disseminates all the information that is needed in the application development process, and provides automatic methods of converting the information into the necessary usable forms.

In all integrated CASE development systems, the information repository is the single required source of all information relative to the data and the procedures being used. It can display information, and it can generate control blocks and data structures to insert information into any phase of the output functions. The information repository:

- Manages the data resources.
- Provides an information system about the data.
- Provides many different views and models of the data.
- Is the principal program development aid.
- Systematically gathers all requirements and changes.
- Maintains the responsibilities for, and the physical uses of, the data.
- Provides information in formats required for program access.

The information repository is well named as the CASE project database. It maintains many administrative rules and procedures. It is also the centralized repository for a library of functions, processes, procedures, data models, process models, and design models, all stored in abstract form. It may contain design analyzer information, and will definitely contain expert system rules.

4.5 SUPPORT OF THE LIFE-CYCLE PROCESS

It is clear that CASE products vary widely in their capacity to support the application development life-cycle process. The variations come from the number of the components shown in Figure 41, which are either included or integrated in them. CASE tools are not necessarily needed for the simpler problems of applications development. Their great strength lies in being able to handle the increasingly complex systems that are required to support the strategic use of computers. In essence, this simply means that the important systems required to be developed today are not just the self-contained operational systems, however large and complex those may be. They are, rather, the complex applications in which data are gathered from a number of sources; the users have varied requirements, and the demands for information may change markedly at any time. The traditional techniques, such as the manual coding of applications in COBOL, have proven inadequate to handle these new demands. In fact, the problems of modifications and revisions have essentially overwhelmed most groups of COBOL programmers. It has proven impossible for human analysts to keep track of all the data elements, data links, and process interconnections in large and complex systems. Most manually developed COBOL systems have grown to be full of inconsistencies and design errors as they have been patched and changed.

It was hoped that COBOL generators would be the solution to the problem. Indeed, they proved to be the solution to the problem of size and consistency, but not of complexity. A number of COBOL generators have been used successfully, and have proven to be two to three times more productive than manual COBOL coding. Some of these COBOL generators are:

- APS, from Sage Systems, Inc.
- Gamma, from Knowledgeware, Inc.
- Pacbase, from CGI Systems, Inc.
- Telon, from Pansophic Systems, Inc.
- Transform, from Transform Logic Corp.

The difficulty with these useful systems is that they did not provide support for the analysis and design of the programs—the front-end design tools that are appearing in CASE. They also did not produce all the COBOL code automatically, and those portions of the application that still had to be coded by hand were still as prone to error and to difficulty in modification.

Fourth-generation language (4GL) tools were developed with essentially simplified design statements of the problem and a wide variety of integrated functions, including database management systems, a high-level procedural language, and nonprocedural functions, such as decision support, screen and report generation, database queries, and graphics. Some of these integrated, 4GLs are:

- ADS/OnLine, from Cullinet Software
- Application Factory, from Cortex Corp.

- Ideal, from Applied Data Research, Inc.
- Mantis, from Cincom Systems, Inc.
- Model 204, from Computer Corporation of America
- Natural, from Software AG

The 4GLs proved to be exceedingly efficient when they were applicable, and achieved tenfold increase in programming productivity over the use of COBOL. They never became accepted by systems professionals for the development of complex systems, however, for a variety of reasons, including:

- 4GLs could not perform in on-line transaction processing environments at the level of manually generated COBOL programs. Their automatic generation of code did not allow for the fine-tuning that can be accomplished in COBOL, and caused severe performance penalties.
- 4GLs did not have the functional capabilities and the programming flexibility of COBOL.
- 4GLs were excellent in the programming and code generation phases, but gave no support to the analysis and design phases.

There has been a natural transition from the 4GLs to some of the CASE tools. This has been led by some of the above tool developers. The first CASE tools, however, were front-end tools that supported the analysis and design phases, but did not link to the code generators. They were excellent for entering specifications in graphical form, and for checking the logical consistency and completeness of the specifications. There are manual steps involved in the transition to the coding process, however.

Index Technology, with Excelerator and other vendors, developed very useful analysis and design tools. They then began to provide flexible linkages between their tools and a variety of application generators and code generators. This approach has been advanced in the industry by pushing for a standard electronic data interchange format (CASE/EDIF) governing the transition of text and graphic data. CASE products are now being interfaced to a wide variety of code generators and 4GL application generators.

Some CASE tools are coupled with COBOL generators, such

as APS, Gamma, Pacbase, Telon, or Transform. These break out of some of the limits of 4GL language products. In this way, front-end CASE tools can enter and check specifications, and then link to back-end generators which convert those specifications into COBOL code. Many products use import/export file facilities to link the CASE tools information repository to the data dictionary facilities of the code generator system. This combination of a front-end CASE tool and a back-end COBOL generator essentially supports the full life-cycle process, and some have been designed to generate highly efficient code. They have captured many of the elements of CASE, and interface with the investment that may have been made in mainframe code generation facilities.

CASE tools are now being interfaced to the traditional 4GL language products, such as ADS/OnLine, Application Factory, Ideal, Mantis, Model 204, and Natural. Application Factory, from Cortex Corp., was the first traditional 4GL application generator to be interfaced to a CASE front end. The front end product is called CorVision, and the combination runs in a DEC VAX/VMS environment.

A major trend today is to provide an integrated architecture over the whole CASE application development life-cycle process from business system design to code generation. These products do not simply link the functions, but also supply the management information and control that is necessary for successful system development and maintenance. They maintain full information repositories that are useful in the maintenance phase. They generate code automatically from logically consistent and complete graphical specifications. One of the more successful of these integrated products is *The Information Engineering Facility (IEF)* from Texas Instruments, Inc. Examples of its diagrams will be given in Section 4.7, "Structured Techniques and Diagrams." Other vendors that are linking the full application development cycle include Knowledgeware, Inc., Cortex Corp., and CGI Systems, Inc.

There are other advanced systems that are using an open CASE architecture based on the use of the widely accepted DB2 database management system from IBM as the standard system repository. This is illustrated in Figure 42. The relational DB2 database is interfaced to a variety of front-end CASE analysis and design tools and to back-end programming support tools and code

FIGURE 42. Use of DB2 as the central information repository.

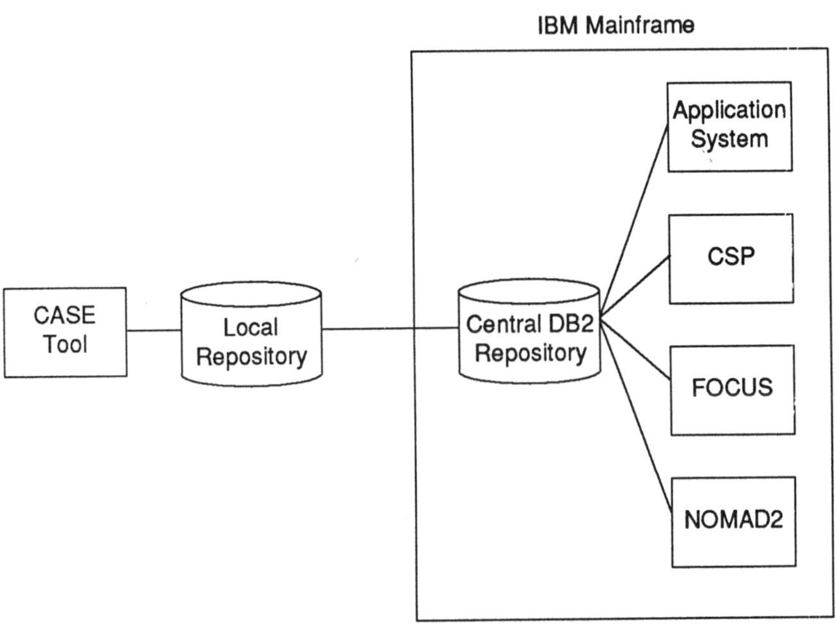

generators. Some of the application generators that provide read/write interfaces to DB2 include Application System and CSP from IBM, Focus from Information Builders, Inc., Nomad2 from Must Software International, Oracle from Oracle Corporation, and Ingres from Relational Technology, Inc. This approach is gaining rapidly, since DB2 is becoming generally accepted and can be the source of system-wide data and process definitions. It is particularly appealing to large IBM users, since it provides the flexibility of selecting from a wide variety of front-end CASE products and back-end application generator options.

4.6 STRUCTURED TECHNIQUES AND DIAGRAMS

Application systems development methods have always incorporated some sort of diagramming to document the processes and relationships that describe the environment of the application. In early work, organizational charts showed hierarchy with little relation to the application process. System flow charts described the flow of the information in the 1950s and 1960s, and they showed some details of complex logic. They contained insufficient information to translate the logic directly into code, however. When structured techniques became accepted as ways of accurately defining systems, in the 1970s, the diagramming became more structured and formal, and carried with it much more information. Structured diagramming techniques, such as data flow diagrams and structure charts, were introduced and widely accepted. The diagrams used in CASE are a further development of the structured techniques diagrams. In many CASE systems, the diagrams have become the main method of information input into the system, and therefore must be highly controlled and accurately drawn. The process of using diagrams has grown naturally as PCs and larger workstations have become the prime tool of systems analysts. It is now possible to edit the diagrams rapidly, and to transmit them on-line to other workstations.

Diagrams have become the language of software modeling because they offer a clear, concise, and unambiguous method of describing processes, elements, and their attributes. Diagrams are an aid to the conceptualization and visualization of application flow, and they serve as an effective communications tool. They have become fundamental to software analysis and design. Different structured methodologies have different diagramming techniques, but the use of diagrams is so well understood that professionals can move readily from one to another.

Most CASE tools use computer-aided design and programming techniques to create diagrams of the system design. Analyst/programmers can use them to create, verify, and modify the diagrams interactively on the screen. Different CASE tools support diagramming techniques associated with a variety of application development methodologies. Some use modern techniques based on formal information models. Others follow the older, proven, manually oriented structured engineering techniques such as those of Yourdon-DeMarco, Gane and Sarson, Jackson, and Warnier-Orr.

There are many different structured diagramming techniques in use. The essential requirement is that the set of diagramming types be sufficient for representing a software system. One grouping of different diagrams that show their relationship to the generated code is shown in Figure 43. Here the different diagrams include: entity relationship, process hierarchy, process dependency, process action, dialog flow, screen design, procedure action, and data structure. This figure shows their usage in Texas Instrument's Information Engineering Facility (IEF).

In the entity-relationship diagram, you model the data. In the process hierarchy diagram, you decompose the functions and processes within the organization. The dependency diagram shows the dependencies between those processes. Each of the diagrams in this figure may or may not be used in generating code.

The entity relationship diagram goes into the data structure diagram, and is used to generate DB2 tables. The IEF is generating code from COBOL, so the data structure in Figure 43 is a COBOL program. The structure does not have to be COBOL, as long as the data model created is involved in the segment layers and the data access statements. In the same way, the screen designer paints the screens and is used for generating code. The process dependency diagram and the process action diagram are not used for generating code, but are used for documentation.

The natural modularization of the diagrams makes them readily used in the future for adding some types of knowledge-based decisions, or expert systems. The procedure action diagram describes the logic of the processing procedure. An action diagram in the business area analysis describes what the process does. The next level of business system design describes how to do that process.

The result of putting this logic into these action diagrams is a new programming language. This must be understood, as there has to be enough specified detail to generate code. This has its problems. On the one hand, good systems like the IEF provide syntax guides for things in the action diagrams. They check that you do not put something in there that should not be there. They provide useful guidance. On the other hand, in using the IEF for action diagramming, for example, the view matching is tedious. All the information needed in an action diagram must be in that action diagram, and the work is time consuming. The information needed for an action diagram must be described, and view matching must be performed on it. The information that is passed between action diagrams and the information on the screens must

FIGURE 43. Different diagrams and the generated code.

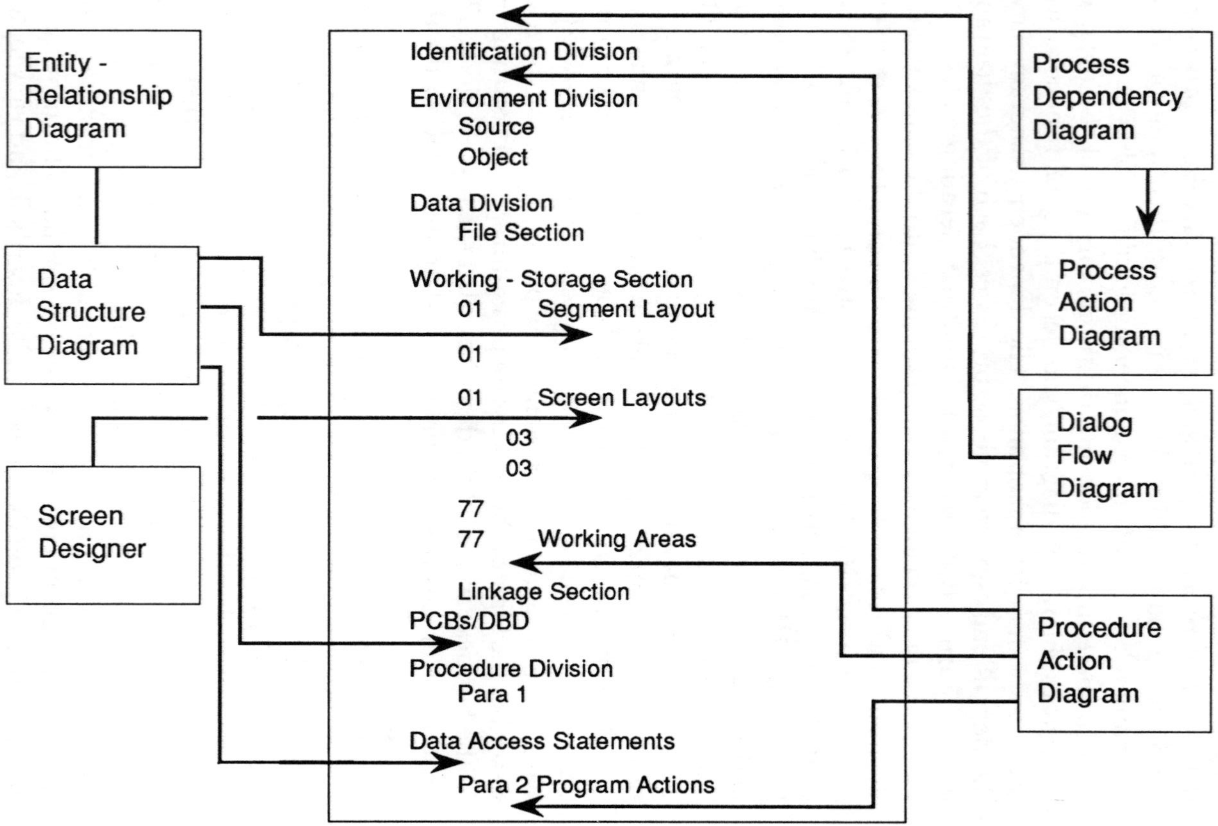

be matched. Stereotypical transactions and processing should provide some relief in that area.

Because of the required view matching, it is also difficult to simply copy and edit routines from previous programs. In traditional COBOL programming, old programs were copied, edited, and then globally changed to create new programs. This cannot be done using systems like the IEF. The process here is slower, with an additional level of rigor. Additionally, these programming systems are new, and therefore the richness of the language is limited. For example, IEF has no string manipulation, although it will probably be available in the future.

One of the important things to remember about the new structured techniques and diagrams is that good programming practices, learned over the years, should not be forgotten. They are simply providing a new, more automatic way of programming, but the results are programs, and the lessons of the past are still valid.

Graphics capability is an important factor in increasing productivity. In CASE systems, the graphics capability should always go beyond simply automatic drawing functions. The underlying logical meaning associated with the graphics is stored and used. Because of this:

- When the logical meaning is derived from the graphics, the correctness and completeness of the diagrams can be checked.

- When the meaning associated with the symbols is stored, the necessary information is available for automatically generating code from the diagram.

- When the meaning associated with the symnbols is stored, that information can be represented in different, but equivalent, forms. For example, the activities represented in a data flow diagram can be viewed in the corresponding decomposition diagram. Similarly, the lowest-level leaf nodes in a tree structure diagram can be automatically converted to an action diagram. The same information is thus represented in different forms. Different approaches can be taken to the diagramming with the same end result.

The logical meaning of the diagram is stored when a diagram is drawn on a screen and captured. Most CASE tools store the diagram and its logical meaning in the information repository. The diagrams can thus be changed quickly and redrawn, and automatic changes can be made to all of the associated diagrams affected by the first change. Such equivalent changes have always been most difficult and tedious in manual development efforts.

The use of diagramming standards and improved diagramming techniques is absolutely necessary for the successful use of CASE tool sets. When automated diagramming facilities are used, they can provide the following major benefits:

- Automatic code generation.
- Automatic conversion from one type of diagram to another.
- Rapid and easy design modification.
- Effective synchronization of all diagrams.
- Faster development time and improved quality of work.
- Capability of integrated project management.
- Automatic generation of consistent system documentation.
- Ready enforcement of organizational development standards.
- Improved capability for error tracking and debugging.

There are many different structured techniques and diagrams in use. Some of the more useful and necessary types of diagramming needed to represent the requirements and the application system are:

- *Entity-relationship diagram*—give the ability to define entities that are of interest and the relationships between them. These are in most CASE tools. An example is shown in Figure 44.
- *Process decomposition diagram*—a hierarchical, or tree structure, diagram used during structured analysis and design to represent program structure. It shows program functions and their hierarchical relationship. An example is shown in Figure 45.
- *Process dependency diagram*—used to show process activities and their dependency on each other. It may show the data that were created by one activity and used by another. An example is shown in Figure 46.
- *Data flow diagram*—the traditional diagram used in systems analysis to show flows of data between processes or procedures. It

FIGURE 44. Entity-relationship diagram.

Entity-Relationship Diagram of Texas Instruments' Information Engineering Facility ™

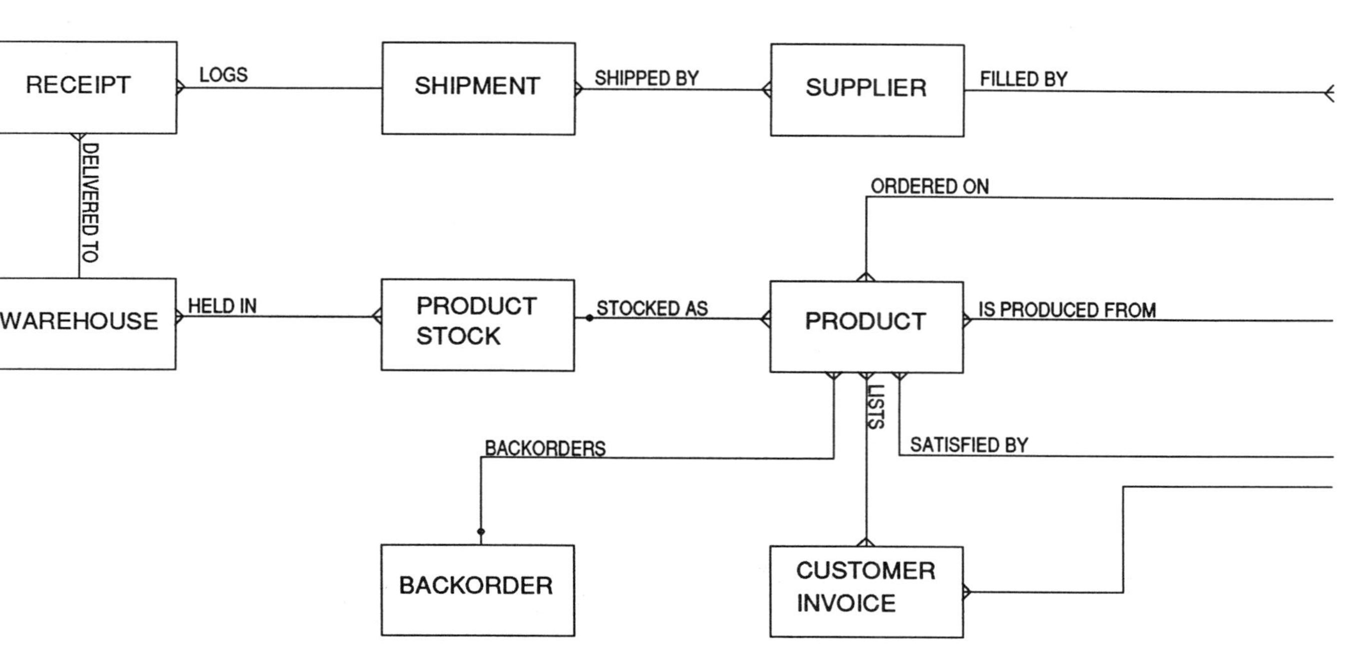

FIGURE 45. Process decomposition diagram.

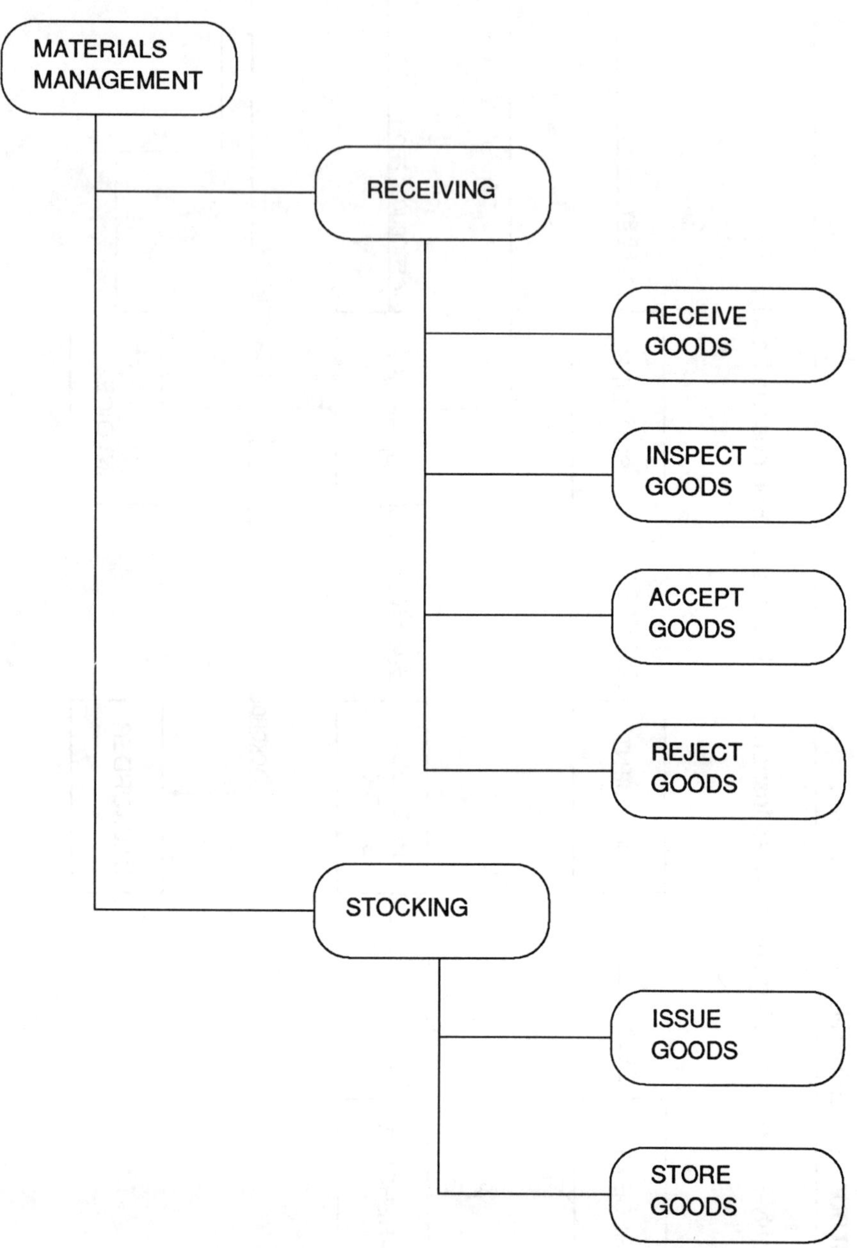

FIGURE 46. Process dependency diagram.

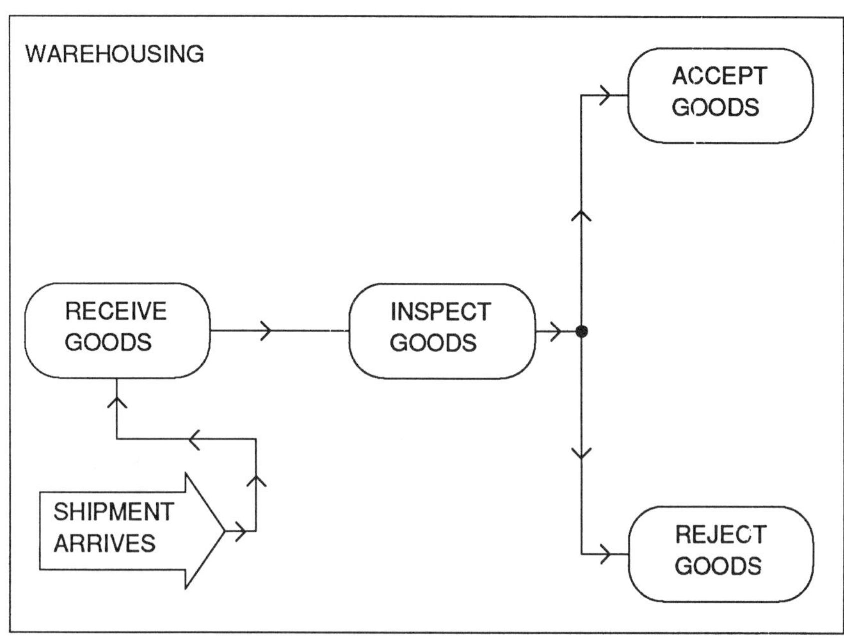

shows data sources, data sinks, and data stores. An example is shown in Figure 47.

- *Data structure diagram*—used during data modeling to show system data entities and the logical relationships among entity types. Entity-relationship diagrams are the basis of higher-level data models. An example is shown in Figure 48.

- *Process action diagrams*—used to specify the detailed program control structures, or the detailed logic of a process. Will contain procedural constructs, such as: DO WHILE, DO UNTIL, and so on. May be used for high-level decomposition, program structure overviews, and detailed control structures. An example is shown in Figure 49.

- *Business function/entity type usage matrix*—relates entity type business functions, employing weighted patterns of usage. The results of the cluster analysis are used to assist in the identification of natural business systems. An example is shown in Figure 50.

FIGURE 47. Data flow diagram.

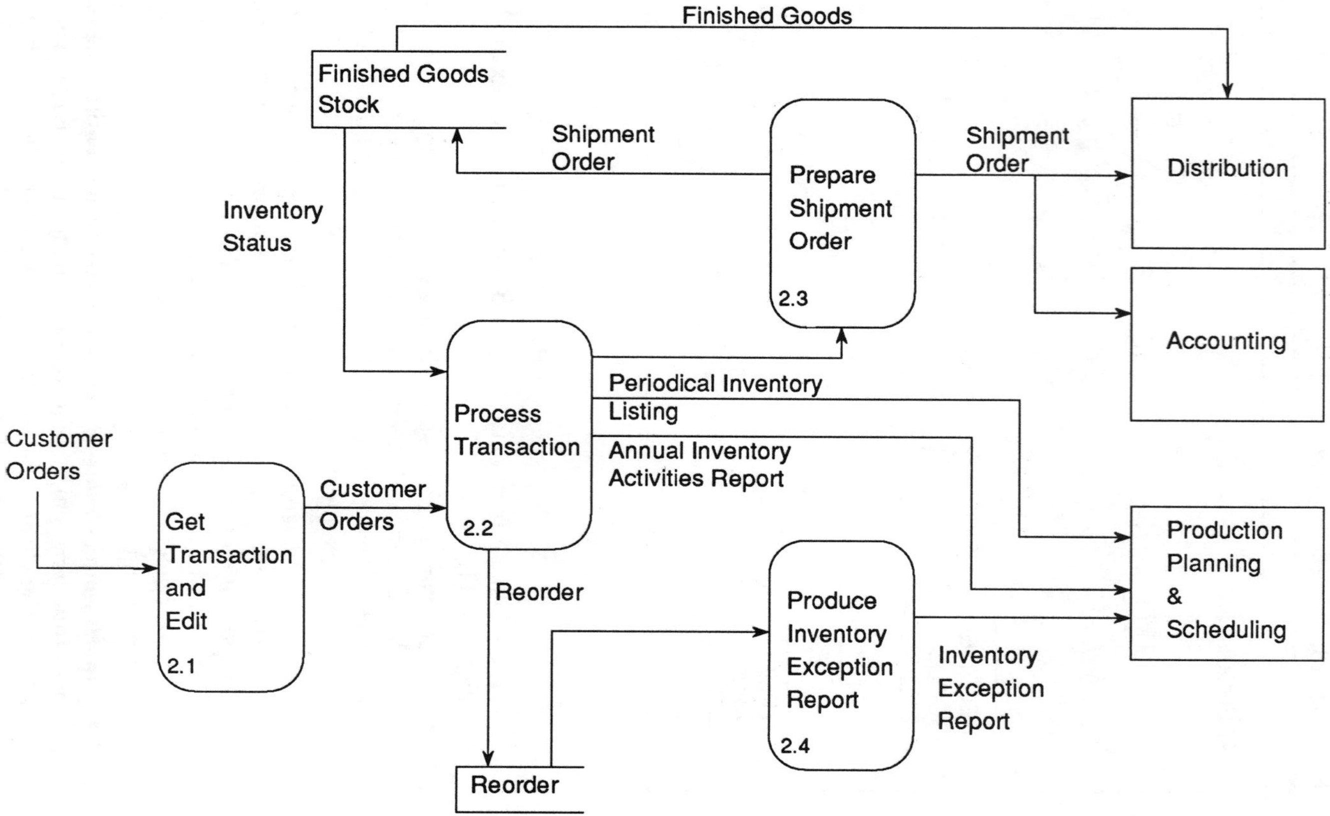

FIGURE 48. Data structure diagram.

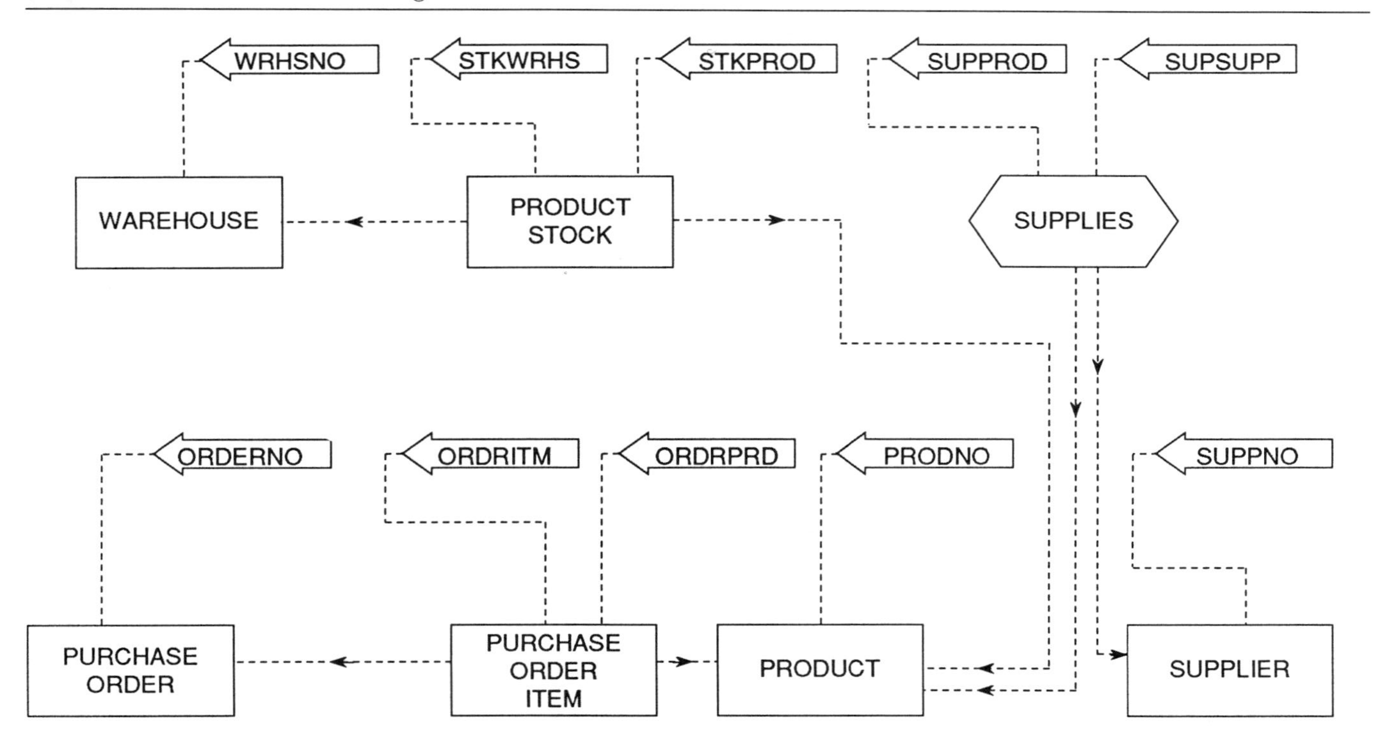

FIGURE 49. Process action diagram.

```
┌ RECEIVE GOODS
│     IMPORTS: Entity View receiving warehouse
│                  Entity View received product
│     EXPORTS: Entity View updated product_inventory
│     ENTITY ACTIONS: Entity View required warehouse
│                        Entity View required product
│                        Entity View required product_inventory
│
│   ┌ READ required product
│   │      WITH number EQUAL TO received product number
│   └
│
│   ┌ READ required warehouse
│   │      WITH location EQUAL TO receiving warehouse location
│   └
│
│   ┌ READ required product_inventory
│   │      WHICH is_held_in required warehouse
│   │          AND is_stock_for required product
│   └
│
│   ┌ UPDATE required product_inventory
│   │      SET quantity USING update_inventory_calcs
│   └
│
└
```

There are a number of other diagrams used in different CASE systems. These include:

- Structure charts.
- State transition diagrams for real-time systems.
- Dialog diagram for screen control and sequences.
- Data Navigation diagrams.
- Compound data access diagrams.
- Decision trees and table diagrams.
- Screen painting and report diagrams.

The problem with any diagram is that it can get quite large, much too big for a typical workstation screen. Some products are

FIGURE 50. Business function/entity type usage matrix.

Key: (Enter highest classification only)

C = CREATE
D = DELETE
U = UPDATE
R = READ ONLY

ENTITY TYPES	GOVERNMENT_CONTRACTS	PURCHASING	RECEIVING	WAREHOUSING	LEGAL_SERVICES	GENERAL_ACCOUNTING	COST_ACCOUNTING	ORDER_PROCESSING	SHIPPING	PACKING	MATERIAL_REQUIREMENTS	RELEASE_PLANNING	FINITE_CAPACITY_SCHEDU	FACTORY_MONITORING	METHODS_ENGINEERING	FACILITIES_MAINTENANC	BASIC_RESEARCH	PRODUCT_DESIGN	SCRAP_DISPOSAL	EMPLOYEE_RECORDS_MAIN	PAYROLL_AND_BENEFITS	EMPLOYEE_TRAINING	SECURITY	TRANSPORTATION_PLANNI	FLEET_MANAGEMENT	FLEET_ACQUISITION	FLEET_MAINTENANCE	VEHICLE_DISPOSAL
SALES_ORDER						R	R	C	U	U	R	R	R				R						R	R				
CUSTOMER								U	R	R							R							R				
CONTRACT	C																R											
SHIPMENT			C																					R				
SUPPLIER	R	R	U		R	R											R							R				
PURCHASE_ORDER					R	R					R	R	R				R						R					
PRODUCT		R	R			R		R	R	R	R	R	R				R	C	R				R					
RAW_MATERIAL		U	U								U						R											
CHEMICAL		U	U								U						R											
SHOP_SUPPLY		C										R	R															
WORK_ORDER											R	C	U	R														
WAREHOUSE			R	C												U												
BIN			U	C						R						U												
SUPPLIER_INVOICE	U	C			R	U																						
LEDGER_ENTRY						C	C																					
PRODUCT_INVENTORY		R	U	R				U		U		R	R										U					

Information Engineering Facility is a trademark of Texas Instruments Incorporated.
Copyright © 1986 Texas Instruments.

creative in the way they supply a usable environment on the terminal—for example, giving windows over larger diagrams. These may be called zoom facilities. You can work with a magnified piece of a diagram, then move in with multiple levels of zoom. Some products allow editing at any level of zoom. Different products have different ways of navigating around diagrams.

Products also differ in the rigor of handling the diagrams. The Information Engineering Facility concept views existing systems as irrelevant. It does not try to automate existing problems, but tries to produce a better solution. The flow of information is strictly controlled throughout the development cycle. Knowledgeware's Information Engineering Workbench has much less rigor, and can be entered at different places.

4.7 COBOL REVERSE ENGINEERING TECHNOLOGY

CASE offers great advantages in the development of new application programs and systems, and in the future, it will offer even greater advantages in the maintenance of systems that were developed under CASE technology. The problem for most organizations, however, is that the major part (usually over 80 percent) of their current systems work load is the maintenance and modification of older systems, most of which were written in COBOL. This means that the biggest job facing most information services managers is the restructuring and rewriting of these old COBOL systems so that they can be brought under the CASE maintenance umbrella. This is a problem of COBOL reverse engineering, and several companies are active in the field today with considerable success.

The concept of reverse engineering is to begin the development life cycle with existing systems, or with parts of existing systems, at the abstract specification level of the original system rather than at the strategic planning, requirements specification, and analysis levels. The idea is to recover the original design specification, as it has been modified over the years, from the current physical implementation, the databases, and the program code in those existing systems or system parts. One of the problems in this process is to determine whether the existing systems really are an accurate reflection of the original design specifications that management requested, and whether it is worth enhancing rather than rewriting. If six generations of programmers have maintained the average system, as has been estimated, and if several different managers have requested modifications or enhancements, is it a good system that is worth saving?

Many consultants have expressed concern about COBOL reverse engineering because it may simply perpetuate the problems of the past. If the system was built the wrong way, for the wrong reasons, it is hardly worth saving. The gospel of information engineering is that old systems are too riddled with error to save, and are too inefficient in their mode of operation. So do away with them and start from scratch. This is certainly a worthy idea from a technical person's viewpoint. The reality, however, is that many large, operating COBOL systems are quite satisfactory in design and general structure, but are exceedingly difficult and expensive to maintain. It is well worth reengineering them if the overall effort is markedly less than starting from scratch again.

One idea that appears to be of great value is that of database conversion, as will be described. There appears to be considerable value and opportunities in going from existing IMS applications to DB2 applications to get the benefits of the relational capabilities of DB2 while retaining a solid base on which to build. The rigid consultant's concept that says you have to leave your past behind and start over again is theoretically pure from an engineering viewpoint, but not necessarily practical in many cases. Unfortunately, when you are sitting on top of 14 million lines of code with several hundred users, and you are supporting a $2 billion enterprise whose very existence depends upon those 14 million lines of code, you simply do not have the luxury of telling your developers to start over.

Charles Bachman, of Bachman Information Systems, Inc., Cambridge, Mass., has pointed out that the primary information services development activities have, in the past, been new applications development and the maintenance, enhancement, and migration of existing applications. The long-term trend, however, is that IS resources will be increasingly redeployed into maintenance work rather than new development. This includes many substantial enhancements of the old systems.

Most organizations have already installed financial, customer, marketing, manufacturing, and personnel systems that are adequate. What is needed in CASE, therefore, is the ability to revise the existing applications readily as new requirements arise. Therefore, the tool kit of CASE products must be expanded to include the maintenance, enhancement, and migration of existing application systems. For example, there are an estimated 77 billion lines of COBOL code residing in IBM production systems alone!

Bachman points out that reverse engineering allows the extraction of business rules from old applications, and their use for restructuring and maintaining those applications. The original source code, which is the base of running the applications, is not enough for them to be automatically reverse engineered. There are missing pieces to identify and fill in. There must be a systematic analysis made of the applications, consulting with those who have business understanding of it. This is an extensive and difficult task, but it has been found that expert systems can be used to determine the pieces that are missing.

COBOL reverse engineering efforts do not follow a simple top-down approach, as is advocated by CASE consultants, because there has been too much interaction between various levels of the organization as the system has grown and been changed. Decisions from many different corporate levels may have to be reviewed at the same time. Bachman notes that there must be give and take by which changes can be propagated up and down at any point in the design process, as shown in Figure 51. In such an area of CASE activity, both forward and reverse engineering are happening at the same time. The data analyst and the database administrator focus on the data problems. The systems analysts deal with the process problems. Design objects at the various levels—requirements, specifications, implementation, and operation—are interrelated from the conceptual considerations at the top to the machine code at the bottom.

Reverse engineering begins at the bottom with the definition of existing applications; it then moves to successively higher levels of abstraction. On the other hand, forward engineering begins at the top with the business analyst and at the bottom right with the new or revised application. In reality, this is a mature CASE life cycle because it shows the continuity of the applications and their

FIGURE 51. The reengineering cycle.

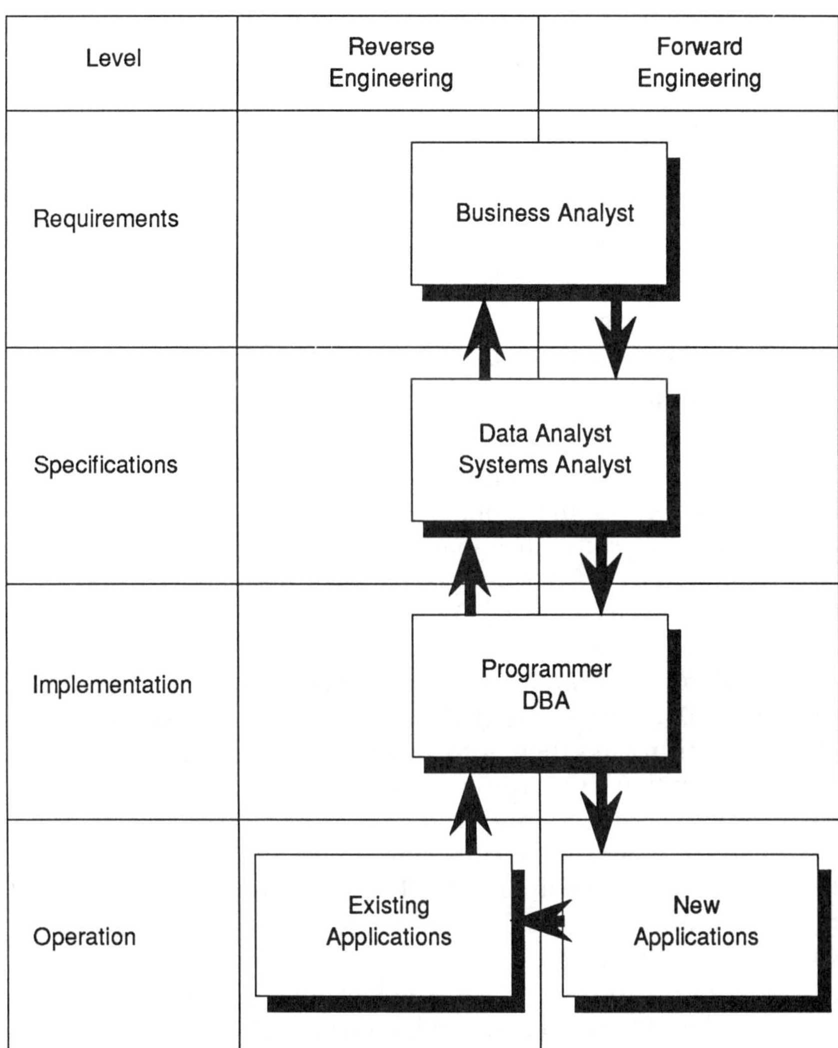

From Bachman Information Systems, Cambridge, MA.

modification and maintenance over time. Thus reengineering clearly fits into the CASE approach.

Reengineering Development Steps

There are six basic development steps in reengineering:

- Capture and generate the source code
- Reverse engineering
- Enhancement and validation of the system
- Forward engineering
- Design and optimization
- Generation of source code

These steps are listed in Figure 52. They may blend together and be repeated in any cooperative design process, but they are identifiable. In reality, they may be used in any combination.

The capture source code step is a fully defined translator that translates the original COBOL source code, the database descriptions, and the implementation-level design objects without the loss of information. It accepts source code for file and database designs (DDL), programs (COBOL), and job control language (JCL), and translates them into a semantic equivalent without human intervention. The result is stored in the design repository for reference. Syntactic and other errors are noted.

The generate source code step is also a fully defined translator. It takes implementation-level design objects from the design repository and translates them into source code—again the DDL, COBOL, and JCL.

The other four steps are problems of incomplete information, and therefore entail human interaction. It will be a profitable area in the future for the use of expert systems to check the details, handle routine tasks, and advise on decisions. The reverse engineering step cannot automatically handle a file, a database definition, or a program automatically, because some of the information needed is not present in the existing code. Future products built with expert systems will be valuable for interactive work with a professional. The system will be able to identify missing infor-

FIGURE 52. Steps used in various CASE activities.

	Maint.	Enhance	New. Dev.	Migrate
Capture Source Code	yes	yes	no	yes
Reverse Engineer	yes	yes	no	yes
Enhance / Validate	no	yes	yes	no
Forward Engineer	no	yes	yes	yes
Design / Optimize	yes	yes	yes	yes
Generate Source Code	yes	yes	yes	yes

From Bachman Information Systems, Cambridge, MA

mation, determine its nature, propose alternatives, and follow the user's instructions. This is a complex task, however.

The enhancement and validation step is where the analyst enhances or creates the specifications-level definitions of applications. These definitions may be available, may be in libraries, or may be created by the analyst. They include the definition of information structures, information flow, and the business procedures. Again, expert systems will prove valuable here.

The forward engineering step is where the specifications that define the applications system are implemented. The entities defined in the information structure, and their attributes and relationships, are translated into the records, tables, or segments known to the target DBMS. The transaction monitor, the program language, and the operating system are also designated.

The design and optimization step accepts the file and database design and program specifications and upgrades them into an optimized design ready for compilation and use. It must be able to accept and use additional descriptive information about the operating environment in which the data is to be stored and communicated, and in which the programs are to be executed. This may include designing indices to assist in the retrieval of the most frequently accessed information. Expert systems will be helpful in this step, also.

These six steps provide the capability for CASE to maintain, enhance, and migrate existing applications, if necessary, because of technological change or business conditions. CASE products that are part of this reverse engineering life cycle will be most valuable to handle the great number of existing systems. They will help to install CASE firmly in the systems development arena. There is clearly a tenfold advantage in using such products compared to starting manually with redesign of older systems.

4.8 DESIRABLE FEATURES OF CASE PRODUCTS

The selection of CASE products will be discussed in detail in Chapter 6, "How to Evaluate and Select CASE Products," and checklists will be supplied to review product functionality. The most desirable features to look for in CASE products will, of course, depend upon the environment in which the products will be used. There are certain features, however, that are generally considered to be most important in CASE products. These are:

- *Support for the entire application development life cycle,* which will include the automatic generation of most of the executable code from graphical specifications. Some products support only low-level code generation functions, such as the generation of the COBOL data division. For most efficient development and best performance, the front end of the CASE tool should be tightly integrated with an automatic COBOL generator.

- *Use of an information repository* to store both the forms of the diagrams and the meaning of the diagrams in abstract form. The specifications should be convertible automatically from one consistent graphical view to another. The repository should provide an information system about the data, control the physical use of the data, and systematically gather all requirements and changes.

- *Support for at least a basic set of diagramming techniques* that represent the software system in software engineering. The minimum should be entity-relationship diagrams, process decomposition diagrams, process dependency diagrams, data flow diagrams, and process action diagrams. It must include rigorous completeness and consistency checking, and should be based on a formal information model. The product should allow flexible conversion from one graphical format to another.

- *Availability of most of the product components* shown in Figure 41. If it is simply a front-end CASE product, of course, only the applicable components should be sought.

- *Availability of the product on the workstation to be used,* whether this is the IBM PS/2 or a DEC MicroVAX.

- *Networking capability permitting the interconnection of multiple workstations,* and facilitating access to corporate mainframe databases.

- *Central mainframe information repository* shared by all in the network, with version control, project management facilities, global consistency and completeness checking, security and disaster recovery controls, and so on.

- *Open software architecture,* including MS-DOS compatibility, to make available the many MS-DOS compatible support programs that are available in the workstation environment.

- *Compatibility with any widely used software facilities* that are available in the particular environment, including the database management systems (frequently DB2), utilities, application generators, and COBOL generators.

- *Support for a rigorous, structured methodology* that integrates planning, specification, design, and coding.

- *Possible support for recent methodologies* that may be adopted.

- *Support for prototyping tools* that integrate well with the other systems using a well-structured, high-level procedural language.

- *Use of a well-defined life cycle process* so that all follow the same process, and improvments in development can be measured.

- *Useful human factoring,* including the elimination of complex command mnemonics, intuitive system operation, on-line diagnostic and HELP facilities, and sub-second response to on-line interaction.

CHAPTER 5

Management Considerations in CASE

Overview

*C*ooperative applications development is becoming more understood in CASE. It includes the cooperation of experts and end users in the development and implementation of computer systems over the life of the application. Its evolution and process steps are described. It is one generic CASE environment.

Requirements definition prototyping is becoming a standard CASE tool, so it is described in some detail. It is a subset of CASE centered on modeling, evolutionary development, and successive refinement. Benefits of prototyping are noted, and good and bad applications for prototyping are reviewed.

The accepted use of relational databases for the CASE environment is outlined, with some of the benefits of the relational system.

Fourth-generation languages (4GLs) have become an accepted part of the CASE environment. They are described, and their advantages are outlined. Application generators are a special class of 4GLs that are in all CASE back-end tools. Program code generators, report program generators, query languages, and screen design programs and generators are discussed.

Expert systems are frequently used in CASE for the automation of technical decisions. They are used in the development process in many CASE packages, and are imbedded in the resulting applications. They have found particular use in methodology integrity enforcement, life-cycle process support, and code generation.

There is a necessity for quality assurance in CASE, since one of the key reasons for using CASE is to meet the demand for quality application systems. Relationships and distinctions between quality assurance, quality control, audit, and security are given.

Types of training for the use of CASE, and its evaluation and implementation, are noted.

Security and disaster recovery planning considerations are reviewed.

5.1 COOPERATIVE APPLICATIONS DEVELOPMENT

CASE is not limited to any particular set of tools available from vendors today, nor is it limited to use by a particular group of professionals in the systems department. CASE has collapsed the traditional boundaries, so that the most effective approaches can be taken in systems development to yield stategic advantage to the organization. This section will summarize the continuum of CASE methods that are available, the ideas of joint application development, and the resulting direction towards cooperative application development.

CASE tools do not stand alone as a unique set of system development tools that are available to a select group, such as professional systems analysts on the central computer. CASE is definitely not limited to the tools that are mentioned in this book at this time, or to any particular vendor's integrated set of CASE tools. There is a continuum of methods in the CASE arena, that stretches from productivity aids for users developing systems on personal computers, to the familiar CASE tool sets on mixed configurations of central computers and workstations, to the advanced networked systems of the future developed with cooperative application development, and operating under cooperative processing. The CASE approach will be developed rapidly in the future, with such features as:

- Full coverage of the whole system life cycle.
- Coordination of multiple CASE systems from various vendors.

- Reverse engineering of code imbedded in development systems.
- The capture of physical usage information even in complex networks.
- Technology selection during the modeling phase.
- The simulation of advanced production systems.
- User specification leading directly to system design and development.

The key feature of CASE work in the future will be the concatenation of tools and systems, as a result of the design phase, to link together the optimum group of CASE tools for a particular application design. Also, the problem space will extend far beyond the types of applications that are now being handled to complex configurations and to mixtures of new development and reverse engineering.

CASE is not a certain set of tools. *CASE* is a concept that application systems can be "engineered." CASE includes any approach where science and mathematics are applied in tested and recognizable ways to use the properties of computers and computer languages to develop computer systems that can be validated and reproduced in a consistent way. This means that:

- In any organization, there exists a *common set of data* with properties that can be described.
- There exists a wide and growing *range of CASE tools* that are essentially standard analytical and design methods, and that can be cataloged, used when needed, and strung together in different combinations.
- Different trained professionals who understand the data sets and the use of the tools can be *interchangeably and cooperatively* involved in the development process.
- Those who are not systems professionals, but who will be using the final, engineered products, have a key role to play throughout the development cycle—in the analysis, design, development, and testing phases. They will gain systems expertise as they participate.
- As an engineered system is developed, it is thoroughly documented in a coordinated manner at every step of the way.
- The final CASE software product is never an absolute, with fixed and rigid design, but can be further and continually developed

in an *evolutionary way*. Every further development or maintenance effort will be able to draw on all that has been learned in the previous efforts with that system.

This also means that systems development under the CASE approach can employ varying tools and methods, so long as these tools and methods can integrate with the data files and the documentation system. They do not all have to be labeled as CASE tools, but can be a variety of systems and methodologies that fit together and can be managed. They will soon span the full system development cycle. A good example is described later in this book as the leading-edge experiences of The Hartford Insurance Company efforts in the CASE arena. They have been in the forefront, and have swept to new capabilities by linking their own selection of a group of packages and developed systems to provide a new, effective, controlled environment for applications development.

Do not put CASE tools in a labeled box to distinguish them from all other tools. For example, there is no reason that the many high-productivity applications development systems on microcomputers, such as screen generators, cross tabulation systems, fourth-generation languages, and so on, cannot be included in the range of CASE tools as long as they are integrated with the existing CASE tools, and are controlled in their use in an engineering sense.

Thus, cooperative applications development on a number of PCs in a LAN, usually connected to a central computer for data sharing, is rapidly becoming a new and profitable frontier for CASE work. Essentially, users doing their own develpment are joining with professional developers to produce a coordinated result with an engineering approach.

Expand your horizons when thinking of CASE, far beyond the current vendor literature, because the bounds of CASE are moving outward rapidly. For example, prototyping for application system requirements has been developing as a standalone approach with considerable profitable return in breaking down the user–developer barriers. Prototyping is rapidly finding its niche, and becoming a key component of the requirements analysis phase of CASE efforts.

A further example of this opening of horizons is IBM's Joint

Application Development (JAD) for rapid analysis. JAD was conceived some years ago as an effective way of bringing users and systems people together in the design phases. Companies have found that JAD can be a useful part of the CASE effort, and it exists as a fully described approach that can be taught to people and used immediately. Information services was looking to become more efficient in developing the systems of the future. The divisions were coming to IS for help in technical consulting. When a division does a study, they have found that the group method of doing the study had many benefits. As a result, together they started experimenting with some of the graphics requirements definition activities, such as IBM's JAD, for rapid analysis.

A 3M company group, for example, was then faced with trying to take CASE architecture to the next level for implementation. They wanted the divisions to take entity-relationship diagrams and function flow diagrams to the next level. They therefore developed the joint requirements definition (JRD) process, as shown in Figure 53. To do this, they took what they felt were the best parts out of JAD, and out of other rapid analysis methodologies that were data-oriented processes, and put them together in a process to meet the needs of the 3M Company. Their workshop-oriented method uses the data and the process approach to define documents and to verify user requirements. Figure 53 is simply a brief overview of what JRD is about. The initial scoping workshop defines the number of detail requirements workshops needed. The detail requirements workshops follow the manner of the SIP process in that there is emphasis on functions and processes, and decomposition of these into more detailed levels. Emphasis is also on the entity side, doing data-entity relationship modeling, where data modeling breaks them down and attaches the data to the functions.

Defining Cooperative Applications Development

First, cooperative applications development will be defined, and compared to cooperative applications processing. The two concepts are quite different. Cooperative applications development includes the cooperation of experts and end users in the development and implementation of computer solutions over the life of the application. It is evolutionary definition and develop-

FIGURE 53. Joint requirements definition process.

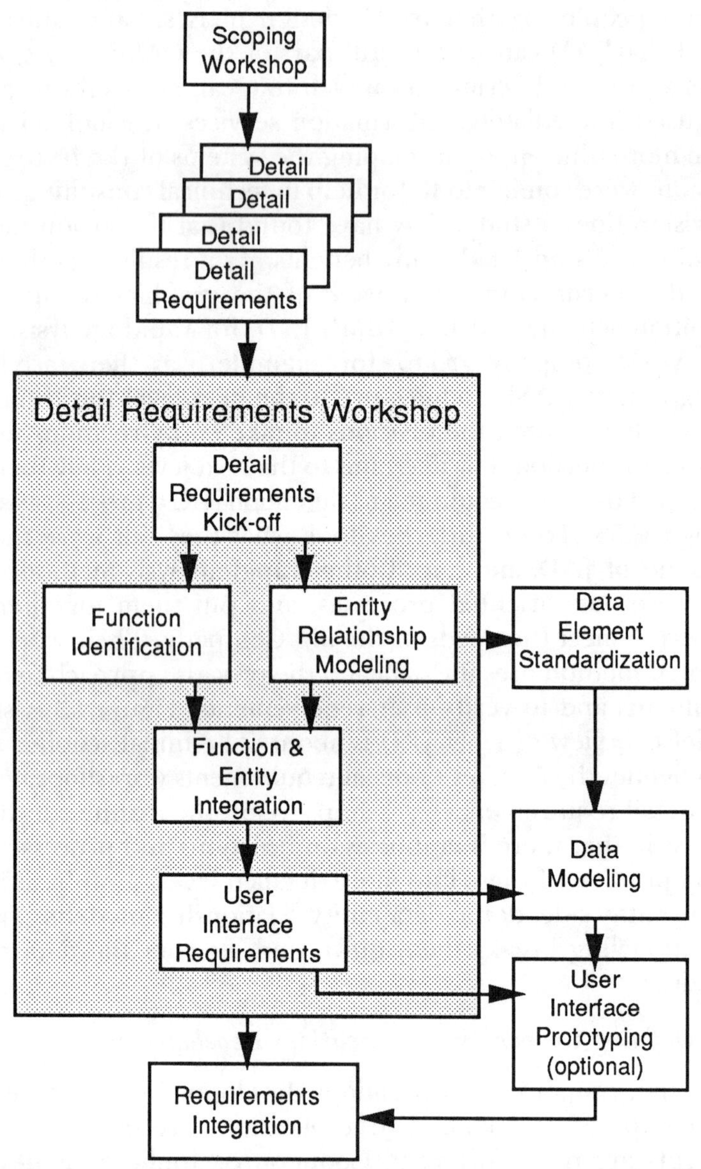

ment based on an agreed set of assumptions. It is the controlled management of work on both the mainframe and the PCs to develop and maintain application systems. It is preferable for interactive systems that are data intensive, rather than algorithm intensive. It is basically a prototyping approach with the heavy use of recognized CASE tools. It helps provide early user satisfaction and meets ongoing and changing business needs.

Cooperative applications processing, on the other hand, is the modern development of the old ideas of distributed data processing. It is a computer operations concept. It is IBM's goal in SAA for software portability and consistency across heterogeneous computer environments, which are the now largely isolated computing architectures such as S/370, S/3X, and PS/2. Cooperative processing is not strictly portability across a number of system lines, such as DEC has already accomplished, however. Portability is an essential part of the picture, but the whole includes all the aspects of distributed data processing that have long been sought. It should be possible to run systems, essentially unchanged, in networks of different configurations, on the mainframe, or on PCs.

IBM's concept of cooperative applications processing will have the applications and data residing on the central S/370, in any combination. It will then have, through the 372X, a variety and mixture of applications and data being processed on networks of PCs, PS/2s, S/36s, S/38s, and their successors. Cooperative processing is characterized by:

- Either hierarchical or peer-to-peer relationships
- Intelligent workstations
- Distributed applications
- Distributed data

Cooperative processing is the culmination of the development of distributed data processing by the execution of an application across networks of personal computers, mid-range computers, and mainframes.

The two concepts of cooperative applications development and cooperative processing will not long remain separate, however, after SAA is more fully developed. This is because SAA's programming and data access interfaces will allow users to develop a variety of applications directly. The problems of database tuning and applications optimization will be handled more automatically. Therefore, keep the two concepts separate, but realize that they will closely interact in the future.

Summary of Cooperative Applications Development

NOTE: This section on cooperative applications development is a summary of a paper presented by Arun K. Gupta, DataEase International, Inc., Trumbull, CT. The DataEase line of products started with a high-productivity applications generator, linking microcomputers to a central database. As their vision grew, and their products grew richer in features, they incorporated a number of tools that are in the CASE arena, and used CASE approaches, to build up a systems development line of products that fill connected CASE niches from query processing with custom menus, to graphics systems, to automatic system development and documentation, and to the shared environment of a local area network (LAN). While many CASE approaches have started with a concentration of systems development on the mainframe, using PCs as work stations, DataEase and others have started with user development on the PCs, then have integrated systems into a full networked environment. Both approaches are rapidly meeting on a common ground, where the most useful mainframe approaches and the most useful PC approaches are being integrated.

There has been an evolution in the application development process, as follows:

Traditional—The process was centered on experts. It required rigorous initial definition; then the application was developed in one continuous pass, with recycling only for maintenance changes.

Accelerated design—New ways of getting user cooperation in design were tried, using a variety of staff meetings and user involvement in the effort.

Prototyping—The project goals are defined initially, but the definition of the project requirements is handled cooperatively, with considerable iteration to develop the product.

Cooperative/evolutionary—All phases of development are handled cooperatively, and prototyping is extended. The system is codeveloped by users and professionals. The system evolves over the life of the application.

There is a need to bring the computer expert and the end user together, in close working relationship, over the life of the application. The end user understands the business needs, will be involved with the system over time, and has enthusiasm for the project. The computer expert has the technical skills, and can analyze the business needs, implement the solution, and enforce the systems standards. All of these skills are needed together over the project life.

There is also a need to bring together both third- and fourth-generation languages. The third-generation languages are powerful, are used in many computer-aided development systems, and provide the best performance on the computer in operation. The fourth-generation languages, on the other hand, are suitable for end users, increase the speed of system development, are easy to change and modify, are self-documenting, and portable. All of these attributes are needed together over the project life.

There is a big difference, however, between the way application systems are defined in traditional approaches and evolutionary approaches. Traditional approaches start with a rigorous definition:

- You do not proceed with an incomplete definition.
- Change of the definition becomes more expensive as the work proceeds.

In evolutionary approaches, including a variety of cooperative application development, prototyping, and CASE approaches:

- You do *not* proceed with *incorrect assumptions.*
- Change is inevitable, because the users can never fully visualize or communicate their needs. Also, a rigorous definition is expensive, the fulfillment of the project extends the user's needs, and the business needs always change.

There is also a difference between the traditional systems development on the mainframe and cooperative development, which uses a combination of mainframe and PCs, with most of the input being from highly versatile workstations. The mainframe offers full access to all data available, and provides a high degree of security and integrity. It also has excellent performance if there is not too much impact of the ongoing operations. The PCs, on the other hand, offer immediate accessibility, which leads to greater speed of system development. The cost of their operation is also considerably lower. Again, the combination of the two in a cooperative development linkage can offer the best of both worlds.

Figure 54 clearly shows the process steps and some of the strong areas of cooperative application development. It also indicates many of the steps which can use what have become standard CASE tools. The capability of giving cooperative application development the rigor of an engineering approach is obvious. The details of the process steps noted in this figure will not be spelled out, because many are obvious, and those that are CASE-oriented are described elsewhere in this book. For example, the tools required for the requirements and design phases of cooperative process development are strictly out of a CASE handbook. They include:

- Automated requirements and decision making
- Data design from source documents
- Auto-normalization
- Entity-relationship models
- Data flow models

The tools for implementation can again be the better CASE tools, which are easy to use, menu-driven, visual, and non-procedural. They must provide for comprehensive transaction processing, be quick to learn and use, and be liked by both experts and end users.

In the product phase of cooperative application development, the typical tools are again the CASE tools:

- Automated system documentation
- Automated user documentation
- Automated test set generation
- Performance fine-tuning and measurements
- Installation and upgrade

FIGURE 54. Cooperative application development process.

---

1. **Requirements**
   - Application goals
   - Complexity
   - Capacity and performance
   - Time
2. **Suitability for co-op development**
   - Interactive
   - Data intensive — not algorithm intensive
   - User and expert cooperation
   - 4GL tools available
3. **Design**
   - Blackboard — or napkin
   - Database administration
   - Entities and relationships
   - Data flow
4. **Prototype**
   - Minimum usable application
   - Basic forms, reports and menus
   - Demonstrate, discuss and enhance
5. **Trail run**
   - Meets user needs
   - Estimate benefits
   - Find basic design problems
   - Complete requirements
   - Ongoing implementation
6. **Completion**
   - Correct design problems
   - Complete implementation
   - Redo the menus
7. **Turn it into a product**
   - Rigorous testing
   - User documentation
   - System documentation
   - Areas of improvement
   - Installation
8. **Evolution**
   - Problem logs
   - Enhancement requests
   - Field enhancements
   - Major revisions

The tools for evolution of cooperatively developed systems are automated to the extent that automated CASE tools were used in the development. Here, more of the management tools are required to track and keep retrievable records of the performance of the system, the changes that are made over its life, and the system versions that are used.

The benefits of cooperative application development are, of course, the same as the benefits that have been described for CASE, because cooperative application development is a variation of CASE environments. It is a CASE environment framework that has been thought out from the viewpoint of traditional systems developers who have started system development work on powerful PCs. Some of the clear benefits are:

- Early user satisfaction, through participation, through knowing that their requirements are being satisfied, and through receiving prototype models of the final system.

- The system will meet the ongoing business needs, because of the prototyping effort and because of the continuous review and modification of the system.

- There is less cost in the development in this way, because the user is constantly involved and no wrong steps are imbedded.

- There is much less cost in the evolution and maintenance of the system because of the automated CASE programs that are used throughout the development process.

- The users gain expertise in the system itself, in the maintenance of the system, and in the process of application development on the PCs.

Cooperative application development is simply one generic CASE environment. There are other types of CASE environments, but they tend to all use similar tools, and all count on cooperation from the user throughout the development and maintenance cycles. Similarly, prototyping is becoming a standard CASE tool in many different CASE environments.

5.2   *REQUIREMENTS DEFINITION PROTOTYPING*

Requirements definition prototyping, or application prototyping, is the development of application systems of new design by first creating functional models of parts of the application to test and verify the specifications and the assumptions that lead to the requirements. It uses small models of the proposed system to communicate between the participants in the project, and to review the requirements by means of demonstrations. The full application system is then developed in an iterative manner, being enlarged systematically as particular features are agreed upon.

Requirements definition prototyping is an integral part of cooperative applications development and of many CASE environments. It is not universally used in CASE, but the method is so similar to a number of CASE tool approaches that it is certainly part of the larger CASE portfolio.

Requirements definition prototyping is a strategy for obtaining, observing, and refining the requirements of an application by producing a series of increasingly complex models that converge to the final, required design. It is a process that assumes:

- Users generally do *not* know all their requirements.
- Users do *not* know how to communicate their requirements to systems analysts.
- User's needs are continually changing.

Requirements definition prototyping is similar to the modeling and prototyping that has long been part of the design process for complex engineering projects. It is clearly an "engineering" method. In that design process, engineering theory and physics are first applied to build scale models, which are then tested under stress and in wind tunnels. A full-scale model, or prototype, is then created and subjected to a number of realistic tests. The final design is then modified and agreed upon and put into production. In application prototyping, the scale models are usually screens and reports. The users look at them and can readily determine whether the content and presentation are what they desire. The full-scale prototype is then usually the core programs in the application, without all the exceptions and refinements, and without all the system interconnections that will be made later. A usable, intermediate product is produced that can be tested to see if it fulfills all the functional specifications that have been established, and the desires of the users that may not yet have been established.

Requirements definition prototyping is sometimes called rapid prototyping because interesting and observable models are produced in days, rather than months. It is also called modeling, evolutionary development, or successive refinement because these terms describe the process of prototyping. It is sometimes called simulation, but that term has a somewhat different meaning. Simulation means developing mathematical equations that are like the process, so that factors affecting it may be investigated. On the other hand, prototyping is the mathematical production of the process itself, in a stepwise fashion, which is exactly the CASE approach.

Another term that is misused for prototyping is heuristic development. Heuristic development has a similar, but particular use in developing artificial intelligence programs, where heuristics are the rules of thumb, or empirical rules, that are tested to see if they lead to likely, good solutions. Heuristic development is the use of exploratory problem-solving techniques that use self-evaluation, or feedback, to improve the system performance. Certainly, that is very similar to prototyping, and may even be said to be a kind of prototyping. However, it is generally centered on the algorithm involved, while prototyping is geneally centered on the structure of the application and the form of the screens and reports produced. CASE tends to be more data oriented than algorithm oriented.

The essence of application prototyping is that it is rapid and in context. Large-scale systems, which may have hundreds of screens and dozens of record types in the database, get bogged down in development in the tying down of all the details before any attempt is made to show the user the probable product. In the many months that it takes to coordinate the details of such large systems, the details of the products the user wants will change markedly, and the actual users of the system themselves may change. The slowness of development means that it is unlikely that the final product will be in the form desired by the user at that time. With application prototyping, however, there is very rapid production of the forms of the final products, and the calculations for getting those numbers. The user sees the final result while the discussions about the application are still remembered and appropriate. Similarly, the initial screens the user is asked to look at are in the form that they will be expected to have at the completion of the project. Questions of specifications and conceptual feelings about the form of the screens are completely in context with the whole application system.

Note that just as there is no single term agreed upon for application prototyping, there is no single version of how it should be done. In practice, application prototyping will vary from producing business models with spreadsheet generators and then tying them together, to developing fully integrated systems in a stepwise fashion.

Requirements definition prototyping is a relatively new approach to system development. Elements of it have been tried for a number of years, but few articles were written about it until 1982. The reason is obvious: It is difficult to do rapid prototyping in COBOL. Too many elements have to be predefined, and too much coding is involved in most third-generation languages. The new fourth-generation languages are most useful for prototyping, however, particularly when much of the data required already resides in a database. Application prototyping has become generally useful since the rapid software tools have become available, and since users have felt comfortable sitting in front of CRT screens.

At this point, not only has prototyping been proven as an excellent approach to generate specifications and to bring systems on-line rapidly, but it has also become recognized as a design process that can be handled systematically and under control for even the most sensitive applications.

Caveats. There are two important caveats to keep in mind in making decisions about the use of prototype models in production systems:

1. *Functionality:* Frequently, users will be so pleased with the early prototype models that they will want to use them immediately for production work. This is particularly true when, in the past, they have waited for months or years for systems, then, suddenly, they see what looks like an operable system on their desks in a few days or weeks. They must be warned in advance against this superficiality. There is no way that one can stop an analyst from using a prototype model if it is easy to put the data in and the results are attractive. However, if there is considerable data manipulation that is needed in practice, if more functionality

will be required for regular use of the system, and if there must be checks and controls imposed on a critical system, permission to use a model in production should not be given. The *throwaway prototype* approach must be especially watched for this problem, because users do not like waiting for the final system when they have seen what appears to be a perfectly good sytem on their screens. The *evolutionary prototype* approach does not present this problem.

2. *Operational efficiency:* With the use of any fourth-generation languages, the appearance to the users is that of system production speed and attractiveness of the output. The hidden problems of system efficiency, data search and retrieval, and computer resource utilization are generally hidden in the prototyping process. Some 4GLs can produce efficient code when used by professional programmers, but the prototyping process is not directed to that end result. Rapidly developed prototypes, having all the functions in place that the users require, may be exceedingly inefficient in routine operation. No one worries about machine efficiency during system development. After all, the main point is to trade machine cycles for rapid development. If the system developed through prototyping is to be used in regular and frequent operation, however, the system must be modified to produce efficient production operation. The evolutionary prototype approach must be particularly examined for this problem, as less attention has been paid to the efficiency of the final system design.

Delivery of Business Application Models

Prototyping may be profitably used in any type of application system development where the problems of system specification and agreement upon output design are central to producing an acceptable product. In general, these are business application models. Engineering and technical analysts have long used approaches similar to prototyping, in that they have built up systems equation by equation, report by report, until they have developed a satisfactory application. Business application models present a different problem. They usually must draw on very large, controlled files of information and produce reports that are themselves under the same level of control. Acceptance of a business application model depends on two, quite different factors. First, there must be assurance that the data files were searched correctly and that the data produced truly applies to the particular analysis that is being presented and is maintained under control. Second, it is critical that the information is presented in the form that is wanted, including the amount of data, the types of data, and the display of the data.

For many years, business application models were slow to produce because there was considerable time taken in deciding on all details of the prespecification, and then the COBOL coding of the extraction from the files was laborious. It simply takes great effort to be assured that the COBOL sorts and searches are being handled correctly. This time has been slashed by the use of high-level fourth-generation languages; yet the problem still remains as to whether the output is truly usable as the recipient envisioned it to be.

Prototyping solves the problem of determining the best way of presenting the data in a desired form. Where the non-EDP business people were never very comfortable with trying to pre-specify requirements in unfamiliar terms, they soon become comfortable with stepping through the specifications that are simply screen displays. Within hours, initial models are developed and shown to the user in a way that facilitates communication. There is no pressure to finalize the specifications; there is simply an interactive process started that will lead more quickly to that finalization than any other way of communicating. Most users quickly become familiar with the terminals. After all, that has been expected of their clerks for many years, and CRTs look exactly like television screens. They then become quickly familiar with what is displayed on the terminals because they can say what column and row headings they want, and see them prepared in moments.

Users soon learn that "what you see is what you get," and start interacting with it. They then become enthusiastic when they realize that their changing business requirements can be matched by equally rapid display changes.

A great many business application requirements need a large traditional system development effort. Many financial reporting applications, for example, are already rigidly predefined, and the reports to be received from them are specifically known. A large part of the development effort must be directed to establishing the complex control system that is absolutely necessary and does not lend itself to prototyping.

Many of the outputs from traditional business applications, however, and nearly all the analytical and operational management systems, are admirably suited to prototyping. With these applications, the essence to be captured is the usability of the screens and reports, rather than the legality of them. First, managers want the information fast. That can now be handled with 4GLs. Second, managers want the information on their own terms. They can express those terms by simply pointing at the screen in the use of prototype development.

Possible Benefits and Management Concerns

Some of the benefits of prototyping are:

- Provides clear communication.
- Fits user work patterns.
- Increases system development productivity.
- Reduces the risk of uncertainty.
- Allows early stoppage of unsuccessful projects.
- Provides a dramatic training tool.

It has been repeatedly pointed out that prototyping is fundamentally a method of providing clear communication between the end users and the system developers. The traditional problem of system specification has been that users do not understand the data processing words, methods, and abbreviations, and are not at ease in detailed specification in an abstract sense. The two parties involved both think they are communicating, but they are using different terms that do not map accurately on each other. The analyst does not know if the user understands the stated computer requirement; the user does not know if the analyst has translated it correctly into the computer abbreviations. There is an impasse that is frequently not solved until the "finished" system is being tested. There is an ambiguous communication that cannot be readily resolved. In the prototyping method of system specification, however, the communication centers on a model that is clear, and understood by both sides; they point at the same data items, and agree to the same terms.

Prototyping fits user work patterns. End users typically examine sets of figures and determine their applicability to a particular assumption or problem. They have been trained in a natural way to make calculations, and are not used to dissecting data handling procedures. Their work pattern is one of examination, analysis, and determination. This is exactly what prototyping offers them, screen by screen, report by report. The system analyst's work pattern of reducing everything to its lowest common denominator, assembling uniform tables of mixed data, then writing the procedures to find the highest common factors may be a scientific work pattern, but it is unfamiliar to the business manager. Prototyping brings the two approaches together. The analyst can use data processing methods on data files that are already spread out, and assemble output that is natural and understandable to the user. There can then be cooperative development by following the user's normal approach to analysis.

Prototyping increases system development productivity. This has already been discussed at length in the previous section. Prototyping takes the traditional system development life cycle, with the slight rearrangement of putting more user training at the beginning. It then completely restructures the requirements definition phase, with the result that all the subsequent phases are reduced in effort, and the final modification and acceptance are greatly simplified.

Prototyping reduces the risk of uncertainty. The traditional method of system development does not provide adequate verification of the requirements definition until the system test phase—after most of the work has been done. There is absolutely no guarantee along the way that the large amount of effort is being put into solving the right problem. A considerable amount of uncertainty is inherent in the process.

This problem is compounded by the fact that large system projects will take one or more years to complete, and the uncertainty increases rapidly with time. People change and conditions change; assumptions that were made and statements that were accepted at the beginning of the project may be unfamiliar to the involved people at the end of the project. There is always the risk that a system that would probably work, based on the original theoretical assumptions, will simply be unacceptable when the procedures finally meet operational reality. Prototyping introduces small pieces of reality early in the process, and cuts the risk item by item.

Prototyping allows the early stoppage of unsuccessful projects. The users may have a good idea, and the systems people may believe that they can translate that idea into an operating application; but if it cannot be done within the time and resource limitations allowed by the business, the project should never be completed. Extraordinarily large losses have been taken by organizations who thought they knew what they wanted, but lacked the communication necessary to realize that the system was useless in the designed form until it had been completed. Prototyping gives a simple way to stop a project, with a minimum expenditure of resources, if it does not look like what is wanted. Engineers have long used prototypes of airplanes and automobiles to find out if they should be put into full production. The back lots of many manufacturing firms are full of mechanisms that were tested at minimum expense and then discarded. The front offices of many businesses contain white elephant application systems that should never have been completed, but were too expensive to simply discard. Prototyping offers cheap discarding of poor systems.

Finally, prototyping provides a dramatic training tool. Its use is completely dependent upon the fact that most business people today have some familiarity with microcomputers, and are comfortable working in front of a CRT screen. No longer is very much training necessary in keystroking and in the principles of the computer. Users are looking for training in getting the answers that they need. Traditionally, this would mean building a full system for them; then giving them pedestrian training in walking through the output reports. With prototype models, they are faced with alternatives, and with decisions to be made. They are immediately trained in the computer handling of the details of their problem. They are shown clear documentation of what is being built. They are shown the alternatives that the computer can offer, visually and rapidly. They are opened up to new uses of the computer, new ways of handling their terminals or micros, and new possibilities for computer analysis.

Good and Bad Applications for Prototyping

Prototyping is a technically correct process for developing application systems, and it can offer great productivity increases. It is not a universal panacea, however, and should be strictly limited to use in applicable areas. There are good applications and bad applications for the prototyping process. They are generally the same as for other CASE approaches.

In general, the applications that are most suitable for prototyping are those that have considerable user interaction in operation. One might say that the more user screens and reports that are programmed into the application, the more likely prototyping will offer considerable advantage. These are the dynamic, on-line systems that are transaction oriented and operated from terminals or microcomputers. Whenever the routine key to the operation of the system is action by users and clerks, the specifics of the procedures are best determined through prototyping. When there is extensive use of user dialogues, the users should be able to test and change the structures of the dialogues until they feel comfortable with them—long before the system is finally programmed.

The applications that are least suitable for prototyping are those that involve little or no user interaction. Applications that are batch oriented and produce large reports routinely are also better predefined, as are engineering, technical, and scientific applications that are basically numerical analysis, statistical analysis, or data reduction systems. In these, the algorithm is the most important part of the program, and can be readily predefined. Also, communications systems that involve such things as operational protocols, priority scheduling, and network management are best coded from prespecifications. This does not preclude the development of the output portion with prototype methods for any of these types of applications. In fact, extremely large systems are best not prototyped, but many programs within those systems can be developed using prototype methods.

Prototyping is not limited by size, but it is less useful if the requirements can be defined with little discussion with the users. For example, the output reports from large engineering applications tend to be matrix oriented, so that further analysis can readily be done on the numbers. There is little use prototyping the algorithms and the production of the output matrix; they are readily predefined. It may be useful to prototype the subroutines where graphical displays are built on the terminals, however, because here the users are closely involved and various solutions may give different benefits.

There are many application areas where the traditional system life cycle or structured analysis methods are desirable and preferable. General ledger, accounts receivable, accounts payable, and payroll are typical examples. Generally accepted accounting practices have been clearly established to define the inputs, the process, and the outputs. Discussion with the users is centered more on data volumes, account codes, and periodicity of reporting. There are always hybrid possibilities, however, even with such applications. Once the files have been established and controlled, financial analysts will want to use the information. Since their requirements are relatively unstructured, prototyping may offer the best approach to communicate their needs.

Prototyping is a specific, resource-limited capability. It should only be applied where it offers obvious advantages. Good systems to illustrate prototyping to its greatest advantage are systems that are:

- *Deterministic:* These are systems that perform the same functions in the same way over and over again. Typical systems are order entry and inventory control. These systems have the same screens coming up frequently, so it is important to design them for the optimum use of the end user. Specific answers are expected on the screens each time they are used, and it is clear that they should be designed for optimum, easy, and frequent use. Most users do not know what to ask for until they see a screen on the CRT, but they do know if they are comfortable with a screen that is shown to them.

- Deterministic systems are process driven rather than context driven. *Process driven* means that they appear in a specific form because the application process has reached a predetermined point where that form is expected. *Context driven* means that something seen on one screen prompts what is wanted on the next. An example of a context-driven system is a sales manager who sees columns of figures on a screen and wonders why sales are down in the third quarter. The next screen to be called will be data that will illuminate the reason, not another screen that had assumed there would be no further questions on the first. Some context-driven screens can be prototyped if the manager knows what sort of questions will frequently be asked. All process-driven screens are best prototyped because they will be used frequently in exactly that format, and it is worth the effort to refine the format by the use of prototyping.

- *Screen manipulative:* Frequently in this discussion, the topic is the screens in the system; they are the heart of communication about prototyping. Prototyping is certainly possible with listed output, and has frequently been used that way. The heart of modern prototyping, however, is the manipulation of screens using fourth-generation languages. The combination of the powerful modification language and the easy discussion of what is seen by all parties on the screen is the reason prototyping is useful. Most prototype system development is done in front of CRT tubes, by manipulating the screens that are displayed. When there are algorithms to develop, technical people can go off by themselves and do the work. When there are screens to be manipulated, the user should be able to get eyes and hands on the prototype, and find out immediately if the screens are useful.

- *Record manipulative:* Systems always have far more records than are needed to be exhibited at any one time. Most of the records are substantive, but only some are of interest for a particular review. The problem is that many records are interrelated, and a user may want to see them handled in various ways. If a variety of record manipulations are desired at the screens, and these same manipulations are to be reproduced many times in actual use, prototyping gives a clear exhibit of what will happen and what will be shown on the screen as different records are selected and operated upon.

- *User interactive:* Prototyping is best with systems that have considerable user interaction, because it is at the points of interaction that the prototype discussions are most helpful in determining the optimum design. If a system has little user interaction, it can be more readily prespecified, and there will be little argument about the format of the output or the input. Whenever there is user interaction, however, the user will want to refine the screens or the output in ways that are difficult for them to prespecify. It is always simple to handle the refinements by prototype discussions.

- *Nontrivial:* There is no point in spending time on prototyping systems that are not complicated. Prototyping can be learned on small systems, but there is no payoff with them. Many fourth-generation languages are quite adequate to quickly design small-scale systems, try them out, and redesign them. That is not prototyping, because the final system is no larger than the one that is manipulated. A prototype is a usable model, but is not a full-function design.

  The payoff for prototyping comes with the large-scale systems where there will be a number of users involved, making it difficult to get everyone to agree on the design details without the hands-on experience. Any problem with more than fifty record types, more than one hundred screens, and a large number of users can benefit from prototyping. Whenever there is substantial scale to the proposed system, and complex issues of user handling to resolve, there is enough scope so that prototyping extends the use of the fourth-generation tools to provide iterative, progressive steps that will result in a better design of the application. Prototyping works best for systems that have multiple databases of file interfaces, many user terminals with planned dialogues, and a variety of periodic batch reporting. If users want structured requests, ad hoc requests, and batch reports, they will have a difficult time giving adequate definitions of all the varieties without being shown some working models.

- *High risk:* If there is little risk in the development of a system, it can likely be sufficiently specified and smoothly developed without bringing in a trained prototyping staff. In a large-scale system, however, the time for system development is often so lengthy that there is considerable, built-in risk that many of the users and the specifications will be different by the time the project is complete. If there is the added financial risk that there will be considerable dependence on the system once it is installed and used, prototyping may be of great help. The whole system development life cycle methodology was introduced over the years to reduce the risk of not getting a system on time with the right specifications. It often failed because it was cumbersome and rigid. Prototyping introduces considerable flexibility into the initial phases of the system life cycle, helps to ensure that the specifications will finish up as desired, and greatly reduces the risk.

- *Used by people who understand system development:* It is absolutely essential for successful prototyping to work with people who generally understand the system development activity and realize what part they are playing in it. If they realize the specification and time difficulties, and are committed to getting a useful system, they will be willing to spend the time, maintain the interest, and keep up the participation that are absolutely essential for good prototyping.

  Prototyping includes testing the model on the actual users, and the users must be willing to try to understand the process and to cooperate. No one who simply wants to write his or her system functional requirements specifications in twenty-five words or less, and then leave the work to the systems analysts, will be helpful in prototyping. They must be committed to a somewhat lengthy process that is unfamiliar. This commitment can usually only be obtained if the user management is satisfied that this is the correct process to follow and is willing to fund it and insist on participation.

  The commitment to a prototyping project must be obtained before the prototyping is started, not halfway through the sessions. If prototyping is beginning to draw out the requirements, and the participants suddenly lose interest and do not show up for the sessions, you are left with incomplete specifications and no formal structure to follow. The users must understand the system development process, and be committed to work with the prototyping until the system is specified fully.

Thus, prototype project selection is partially based on the type of project, and partially based on the type of participants. Prototyping is not a substitute for good analysis and design; it is merely an effective tool and a helpful aid in developing systems in cooperation with the users. It is handled in step-by-step fashion with considerable interaction with the users. It is not necessarily useful in very large systems that require structured design methodology and complex programming techniques. However, even in such very large systems, pieces can be broken out into manageable sizes that are suitable for prototyping. There are a number of decomposition techniques that make sense in breaking an extremely large system into smaller pieces, as long as a rigorous life cycle is followed and standards are adhered to.

Prototype project selection must also consider the attitude of the users. If, in the first pass at developing the specifications, only about 60 percent of the job is done, there must be agreement that the users will also cooperate when the analysts come back for further refinement. There must be an understanding that the process will be iterative, and may go on considerably longer than ordinary system specification analysis. The users must be prepared to allow the recycling of the project work. The users must also agree not to run off with a reasonable prototype and ask that it be put into production immediately. The project must be such that they will want the whole system, and not one piece of it that has been mocked up. Part of the education of the users has to be that the pieces of the project are not free standing, but have to be integrated into an operating system before they are all usable. Many of the requirements of an operating production system are missing in a prototype, and the first prototype system cannot be adequately implemented; it is simply an illusion of the finished system. The users cannot have the attitude that they can use each piece of the system as it is developed, without the structure as a whole.

If there appears to be a communication problem for any substantial project, the use of prototyping may well be helpful. With the use of prototype generation, the users can get an immediate view of the probable results during the early discussions, when interest is high. The users can see and work with the system and the screens before agreeing to a final statement of the specifications. Differing interpretations can be worked out. If such an approach appears to be indicated, the project may be a good one to select for prototyping.

Prototyping Staff

As part of the CASE development effort, there should be a group of specialists who can handle particular classes of prototyping problems knowledgeably and effectively. These problems are principally in the functional definition and design of user-oriented data processing applications, but may be in any of the areas of CASE development in the future. The most profitable areas of prototyping have been in concentrating on the interface between the users and the systems analysts. It revolves around the rapid building of program structures in fourth-generation languages, particularly for the screens and outputs that the users require.

Professional prototypers need a powerful workstation, preferably with multiple windows, and they need good response time. When they want to display a relatively trivial item on the screen, they will expect instantaneous results in order to maintain good interaction with the users.

They also need access to a library that gives information about the data models in the organization. Everything available in the way of business and system documentation should be accessible to them. In addition, in the prototype review process, there are frequent consensus meetings, and there needs to be a reasonably good environment for information display and meetings.

An idea that has considerable popularity in prototyping has been the parts department. This is no more than the reusable code emphasis in advanced CASE work. It is imperative to build and to make use of reusable components that will be developed as prototyping progresses in the organization. The inventory of reusable system parts will continue to grow, and will be available for use in subsequent prototypes. In established prototyping environments, as much as 60 percent of the applications can be "parts" from other applications. The more effectively these parts are organized, stored, and managed, the more efficient will be the prototyping work. This, of course, may be integrated with any other facilities for reusable code that are developed for CASE.

In engineering, and in prototyping, the use of reusable code has been called component engineering. This treats software modules as parts of an assembly line process, because similar products are always being produced. Assembly lines are more efficient than individual, hand manufacturing. When software modules are treated as parts in building application systems, as much as 60 to 70 percent of the system can be taken as parts from other systems. They are kept in the existing inventory, or parts dictionary.

A main element of prototyping has always been the integrated, data-driven software architecture. Once again, this has a natural fit with CASE systems. Successful prototyping has many similarities to the CASE approach, and can be readily integrated with it. Prototyping is similar to CASE "manufacturing" in that the documentation must mirror the engineering "bill of materials" that gives the details of what "goes into" what. Each part is made up of subcomponents that go into it. This is not a simple analysis, but it has long been solved by automated engineering systems, and it is being solved by integrated CASE systems. It is necessary to be able to analyze the model and its components on-line, and get the "goes into" details through screen reports while building the model. A good prototyping system can extract 80 to 85 percent of the user manual and documentation in this way, also.

5.3 THE USE OF RELATIONAL DATABASES FOR CASE DEVELOPMENT

The principal problem in data processing system development is an economic one: the number of people and the length of time required to develop and maintain applications. There is an application backlog problem, and the key solutions involve the use of relational DBMS, integrated dictionaries, application generator and development tools, and end-user tools. In short, the answer is in the use of CASE.

A relational DBMS is a major component in CASE, and its choice should be carefully made. Relational database systems are delivering what they promise: faster and cheaper application development with lower skill requirements, and considerably reduced maintenance effort. Relational DBMS helps to lower system modification costs. Relational models should be simple, precise, predictable, robust, and extensible.

The use of relational DBMS, with integrated data dictionaries and application generator tools, is an investment that gives an increased system cost. This investment is more than offset, however, by the fact that there is more work done by the system in application development, and less work per person per application, resulting in markedly decreased people cost.

A good relational database management system will include:

- Central I/O with reusable code
- Concurrent access by multiple users
- Data security and recovery
- Data integrity and consistency

- Logging of all transactions
- Shared, controlled data

A good integrated dictionary, in the central repository, will offer:

- Administrative tool for process control
- Application development tool over the life cycle
- Maintenance and enhancement tool
- Single, controlled defnition of data for all

Good application generator tools, tied to the DBMS, will offer:

- Faster application development
- Simpler application maintenance
- Less skill required in data management
- Easy interface for both professionals and users
- Automated application development

In short, when a relational DBMS is used, integrated with the data dictionary and the reporting facilities, more work is done by the system per application, and less work is done by the person per application. In a CASE environment, there is effective synergy going on between the relational DBMS, the dictionary, the application development tools, and the end-user tools.

The choice of the DBMS may fall automatically into the choice of the CASE system. Most integrated CASE systems have integrated relational DBMS, often DB2. When CASE tools are used that are not integrated, however, there must be a selection made. It is clear that the *DBMS* is not an isolated product in any CASE system. It works with the hardware, the microcode, the CASE tools, other software products, and the applications themselves. The technical capabilities of one DBMS over another are not as important as the whole CASE environment that the product will work in. A DBMS is not a short-term component, and must be usable over more than one generation of CASE tools. The DBMS is a major component in any CASE system, and should:

- Provide required state-of-the-art DBMS functions.
- Have an integrated set of tools.
- Exploit the hardware and software environment to advantage.
- Protect the investment in the applications.

There are many good reasons why most DBMS selected for CASE environments are relational DBMS. Some of these are:

- Of all the DBMS technologies, relational is the simplest. It has been proven to work well.
- Relational is a *precise* DBMS because it is based on proven theory.
- The results from relational DBMS are *predictable*. There are no surprises. This is particularly important as data networks become larger and more complex.
- The relational model is very *robust*. It contains all the function that is needed and can do the job.
- Relational is *extensible* because it is built on three-valued, first-order predicate logic. It is mathematically powerful, and can be extended to do any real work that is required. This is why relational is the selection for expert systems as well as for CASE work.

Relational languages are high-level, set processing languages. They do not deal with a record at a time. They can readily handle any of the Boolean operators. For example, they can collect EVERY or ALL with simple commands. Relational languages are comprehensive. They retrieve data, insert new elements, delete old elements, and modify existing elements in the database with simple commands. With their simple structure, they can be used standalone, for query language, or as the accessing language in any database within the application program. The very simple, generalized structure, with simple operators, is highly effective.

Relational systems are simply collections of values in tabular form. People can be rapidly trained in their use, and can soon devise tables themselves. In relational systems, you deal with data values and data names only. There is nothing in the data manipulation language itself, or the request to the database, that has anything in it other than what you want the system to do. The system does not have to be instructed in what index to use, for example. The request is simply for the value that is being sought.

Finally, relational DBMS are easy for communicating. The relational languages are simple and the constructs are simple, so they are readily understood by the end users and the managers as well as by the application developers.

5.4 THE USE OF FOURTH-GENERATION LANGUAGES IN CASE

Fourth-generation languages (4GLs) are fundamental in CASE. They offer great value in rapid application development. They come in a variety of functions and complexities. Some are really suitable only for end-user application development. Others are very powerful, and can be used for larger systems, particularly as the efficiency of their produced code is improving.

4GLs offer the great advantage of speed of application development. It must always be remembered, however, that they are interpretive systems, and the aid that they give is often at the cost of operating efficiency and user response time. This must be taken into account as they are selected for use. It is usually balanced against the fact that they excel in application development ease and speed.

Fourth-generation languages are suitable for rapid development of applications because they have a limited set of powerful operators that are easily learned, rapid in application, and readily modified. The defining features of 4GLs are:

- They are appropriate for use by both end users and professional programmers.
- They are used with a simplified application development cycle.
- Their operators are easily learned and applied.
- They are debugged at a high language level.
- The applications are readily changed and thus easily maintained.
- They are more concerned with user friendliness than with operational efficiency.

There are a number of features that may be found in fourth-generation languages that help to define them. Note that not all fourth-generation languages will have all these features, and that this list is not considered to be exhaustive. The following features are typical of many 4GLs, however, and may be said to be distinguishing features of a fourth-generation language:

- *Nonprocedural language:* A 4GL specifies what is to be done, but not how to do it. It defines the elements and the operations in general, without saying, step by step, what is to be accomplished.

- *Simple language subsets:* The operations and relationships that will likely be needed for analysis are provided with no attempt to provide all the types of operations that could be used. The effect is that the number of terms to be memorized are kept to a minimum, and the language is readily learned and easily remembered.

- *Capability for application expansion:* Little or no recording of detail is required to handle growth in capability. There is no need to know the actual shape of the records or the size of the files. The 4GL handles all the housekeeping details for the programmer. This does not mean that they are necessarily handled efficiently from an operations point of view, but they are handled expeditiously. This makes 4GLs the ideal medium for *prototyping* applications. Simple subsets can be built up to large systems with no effort on the part of the programmer of sizing the files or remembering the file details.

- *Independent of the hardware environment:* The programmer need not be concerned with the details of the hardware environment or the limitations of the memory systems. Use is dependent only on the operating system, and the connections to it are limited and readily learned.

- *Powerful software facilities:* A great many aids are offered to the programmer. Simple interfaces to the operating system and database are provided. The language terms cover a great variety of operations. Output aids, such as screens and tabulations, are supplied for automatic report generation. Single 4GL commands will call for complex programs for structuring and applying the query or the output request.

- *Multiple database and file interface:* The programmer has little concern with data handling, or with even knowing what particular files are on-line at any given time. The system will have one or more databases and files set up for access on request.

- *Programmer workbench capability:* Complex tools are offered to the end users that may not even be appreciated, although professional programmers will recognize them as the "programmer workbench" capabilities that are tuned to the increased productivity of application development. Such tools as command language facilities and text editing are provided in the minimum subset that is required for program development.

- *Logical user views:* The user accesses data in a relational manner in that logical user views are expected rather than the names of lists and the position of the data within the lists. The user simply states the use of the data logically, rather than descriptively.

- *Integrated data dictionary and directory:* The ability to use a 4GL is based on the existence of a suitable database with an integrated data dictionary and directory. In some cases, the user may develop the data dictionary. In most cases, however, the data dictionary has been developed by professionals and is offered to the end users in a simple format. All they have to do is know how to read and apply it, and all problems of data handling are immediately solved. Note that the incredible productivity advantages of 4GLs are possible because of the foundation of the available database with its integrated data dictionary and directory.

Fourth-generation languages come in many varieties and are designed for specific areas where they are most useful. Different organizations will find that different fourth-generation languages are optimum for their own environments. Selection of a 4GL must start first with a decision as to who the prime users will be and what the principal applications will be. The investigating group should then go to the particular area where the greatest use is expected and determine what functions and features will be emphasized. After this key information has been determined, the decision should then follow the acquisition decision procedure of any software package. It should be systematic and cover all aspects of vendor and package review and the problems of package installation. Fourth-generation language packages can sound most attractive during a sales pitch, and the available sales literature can be voluminous. A reasonable selection is only possible if a systematic approach is used.

Consider the features that may be offered by a 4GL, list them, and rank them in order of need or priority. This list of features will then be the basic screen against which all possible packages must be tested before consideration. Some of the attributes that may be considered include the following:

- *Fit with available database:* The 4GL must fit with the database that will be used for the information being extracted. If the 4GL has its own, unique database, then the conversion of the desired data files to this database format must be able to be done realistically and economically.

- *Efficiency of operation:* The 4GL must be able to operate at the level of efficiency that is expected. If the end users are principally professional analysts, the 4GL efficiency is much less important than the ease of learning and use. If the 4GL is to be used by professional programmers, the features that make for efficient operation are far more important, no matter how complex their use. If the 4GL is to be used for an on-line system, there must be a careful review of the response time that will be achieved.

- *Avoidance of procedural programming:* Once again, if the 4GL users are to be nonprofessionals, the simpler the command structure the better, with little use made of procedural programming. The maximum use should be made of automatic code generators.

- *Speed of compilation:* Users do not like to sit in front of their terminals waiting for compilations. They are not trained to wait in line like professional programmers. The speed of compilation should be estimated for the typical problem with the typical number of terminals on-line. Many fine 4GL systems behave poorly when a large number of users are on-line, but are excellent for a few users.

- *Ability to modify:* Techniques should be available to enable modifications and enhancements to the programs to be readily made. All such changes should be made in the higher-level language.

- *Verification of correctness:* All internal semantics and syntax errors should be caught automatically. Assistance that is provided to easily catch external semantics errors should be reviewed.

- *Communication with the user:* Users should be able to check every stage of system development. The input screens should be clear and easily learned. The error messages should be voluminous and partially in plain English.

- *Simple database linkage:* The part of the database being used, or the extract database, should have clear commands and simple linkage for the user.

- *Fast database extraction:* The key to response time is the speed with which the system can extract information from the database. For very large databases and complex inquiry, this may be impossible to do simply and fast. The limitations of the database extraction commands must be reviewed, and limits possibly placed on the size of the database that is made available.

- *Modularity:* Whenever feasible, the system should allow the division into easily comprehensible and usable modules. This requires effective ways of linking modules. Changes should be possible locally, within a module, with methods of determining the effect of the changes outside the module.

- *Effective library control:* There should be a facility for setting up and constantly enlarging a library of program modules that can be made available to all programmers.

- *Automated change control:* Whenever changes are made, the effects should be shown automatically, enabling further consequential corrections to be made in the library.

- *Higher complexity available:* The system should have an interrelated set of more powerful mechanisms, so it is readily used by an end user but offers more power and complexity for experienced programmers.

- *Integrated set of tools:* Tools that achieve the particular objectives that have been determined, or that have the particular features that have been requested, should all be integrated to work together to avoid manual bridges that introduce errors. They should all use common syntax and graphics where feasible.

- *Good human factoring:* To encourage the use by nonprofessionals, there should be well-designed, interactive display techniques that keep the user focused on the problem definition and that ease the development.

- *User-friendly operation:* The system should be easily understandable at the level of the expected users. It should have numerous on-line prompts, menus, and error messages.

- *Limited memorization:* The system should have a minimum vocabulary, without the need to remember too many specific command sequences, formats, or mnemonics.

- *Useful default assumptions:* There should be intelligent use of default assumptions in the generation of reports, displays, or graphics.

- *Simple debugging:* The debugging of applications should be readily understood by the users.

- *HELP facility:* There should be a comprehensive HELP facility that is readily invoked.
- *Rapid learning:* The average analyst should be able to learn a usable set of the language in a two-day training course.

IBM 4GLs.

IBM strives for connectivity and straightforward migrations from one computer line to another, but it does not, in any sense, have a monolithic approach to systems across all computers, and this is true for its fourth-generation language offerings. Thus, there is no single IBM fourth-generation environment. However, since the IBM PCs are the most popular personal computers, and since the IBM PC/AT and its successors are exceedingly powerful computers that frequently take over the tasks of larger computers, IBM is in the center of the fourth-generation language revolution. The majority of 4GL vendors has prepared products for the various parts of the IBM computer line, and IBM itself has several useful programs.

IBM thus creates de facto standards by definition. IBM strives to maintain the connectivity of its systems and hold its market position by a series of hardware, software, and format standards that have emerged as the changes have taken place. IBM continually encourages the spread of the IBM standards to aid in its growth in both the PC and mainframe environments, and 4GL standards are no exception to this practice. Many software houses make their product development decisions based on these standards.

IBM supports a wide variety of hardware and software environments, including the System/370, System/38, System/36, 5520, 8100, and the PC. While the IBM standards tend to apply across this range of technology, the 4GL application systems that IBM makes available do not, but are designed for each specific, and large, area of computer type. For example, newer high-productivity tools, such as Application System and CSP, are designed for the IBM 370 mainframe environment. But they are being introduced in parallel with significant improvements to COBOL and other third-generation languages. Thus, IBM is not trying for a dramatic change in direction, as some software houses like to advertise, but is trying for the prompt introduction of high-productivity tools that will fit existing standards and that will converge, in time, with the massive base of installed programs that its customers have bought and paid for on their big IBM computers.

A good example of IBM's position in fourth-generation systems is in its database technology. IBM customers have installed large IMS systems, and have invested an exceedingly great amount of money in IMS. There is no intent, on either the major customers' part or on IBM's part, to consider moving away from this considerable investment. IMS may be a more traditional, hierarchically organized DBMS, but it has a great many useful functions and is very widely used for the operational batch applications of most businesses. IBM, therefore, makes a second, independent DBMS available: DB2. DB2 is the IBM database most suitable for CASE work. DB2 is a full database system with many functions, including transaction processing, data inquiry, report generation, and decision support. It is an efficient DBMS, which is satisfactory for most corporate uses. There is sufficient room in the IBM world for the two database systems to exist side by side and perform in their most useful areas.

This does not mean, of course, that the operation of both database types in parallel is the most efficient approach. Naturally, it would be better to have a single DBMS with all other systems integrated with it, which is an approach being offered by several software houses. The preferred direction is an operational and financial decision for every separate organization. IBM offers a fourth-generation environment. It is relatively easy to install and use in an IBM computer operation with the current systems programming staff. The various offerings are mostly individually good, and their installation offers little risk. If computer efficiency for the fourth-generation language work is important, however, and if a fully integrated operating system is economic and indicated, there may be other routes that are preferable. As always, the final selection will be based on the particular features that are considered to be necessary, and the economics and time estimates that are involved. There are many choices that can be made, but IBM support is considered by many to be one of the necessary features to select. This must be balanced, together with the other

IBM features, against some remarkable integrated systems that are becoming available on the open market and gaining in operational efficiency.

5.5 THE USE OF APPLICATION GENERATORS IN CASE

Application generators, application program generators, or application development systems are a special class of fourth-generation languages characterized by their capability of generating complete object programs, or sets of programs, from specifications or parameters, usually without the use of any procedural code. They are an integral part of a CASE environment. They include the capability of interfacing with a variety of data files and other programs to create a complete application system. Thus they are products that can be used to create programs or applications with the simplicity of a high-level language, which would otherwise require extensive programming.

All application generators are fourth-generation languages, but there are many 4GLs that are not called "application generators" because they do not produce full application programs with a single set of powerful commands. These include high-level nonprocedural languages, decision support system tools, graphics generators, and user interface menus.

Application program generators are an assembly of tools and aids that provide control over all phases of application design, testing, implementation, documentation, and maintenance. They may be designed for both programmers and nonprogrammer end users. Typical application program generators offer screen design facilities, program code generators, interactive debugging and testing, documentation, and report generation capabilities.

Application generators are usually interactive programming systems using the available editors, access to compilers, file management facilities, and library structures in the system environment. They are frequently menu driven, using available editors and documentation facilities.

Application generators are sold with a variety of software productivity aids that are helpful in various stages of the system development cycle. This variety complicates the feature comparison of different vendor offerings, as there is no standard structure for an application generator. Some will contain other productivity aids, while others will simply interface with them.

In addition, the basic functions of systems that are called application program generators vary widely. Different programs can be claimed to be application program generators, but their usability for specific requirements does not depend on the way they are named in advertising. Rather, it depends on how the particular functions that are offered match the specific program requirements that have been determined as necessary or desirable in particular situations. Therefore, the more general application program generators will be discussed first, followed by brief discussions of other types of applications that are called application generators in their own right. These include:

- Program code generators
- Report program generators
- Query languages
- Screen design programs and generators

The use of any application generator in the area for which it was designed can speed and simplify the application development process. Whether a generator is used by a professional programmer or an end user, it has the advantage of rapidly showing what the application will look like. This is an excellent way of visually demonstrating the functional requirements that have been discussed. It also allows modifications in the program requirements in the initial development stages, when little effort will have been lost if there are changes to be made. This has the useful effect of shortening the overall development time.

Application program generators are fourth-generation languages in that they have very little conventional procedural logic in their programming, although some, such as subroutines, is allowed. They usually provide a set of precoded function modules that are common to most applications. These modules may be for inquiry, edit, update, report, security, and so on, which are typical of on-line transaction systems. Parameters are selected, possibly from screens, which direct the execution of the modules and tailor the program to the defined requirements. This "selection of modules" takes the place of conventional coding in procedural languages. However, additional code can be written for any particular functions that are desired, but are not available in the system.

Application program generators are systems that produce code from apparently simple command statements and tie it together in a usable program. If the code is used immediately, they are essentially interpreter languages, with the interpretation extending to the data flow and program interactions. They may produce single application programs, or they may be used to generate a number of programs and subroutines that can be assembled for use in a complete application system.

Particular application program generators may thus be oriented toward the delivery of a full application system or more toward the delivery of individual programs or pieces of code that can be used in a system. All application generators produce outputs that are similar to those of third-generation coding systems, be they screens, reports, or listings. The 4GL inputs are much simpler, however, and the commands are much richer from a functional point of view. They are easier to use. This may be at the expense of machine time during development, but the final products are not necessarily less efficient, particularly in the production of the output reports. Their view of the database may be just as good as the others, and complex procedural sections may be coded in 3GL terms.

A product should not be called an application program generator unless it handles a substantial amount of the coding automatically. If too many subroutines have to be written, and if the screen development portion takes the same effort as older systems, then it may not offer as much efficiency as hoped for. Unfortunately, the capabilities of application generators vary greatly among the numerous vendor offerings. Each one must be examined individually to determine what it offers in terms of ease of programming and efficiency in system development. The same adjectives and terms are frequently used by vendors to describe very different capabilities.

Advantages of Application Program Generators.

The general advantages of application program generators may be stated, though perhaps hopefully considering the variety of offerings on the market, as the following:

- Make the application development process more efficient.
- Provide consistent standards across the applications.
- Allow for fast implementation.
- Ease the use of prototyping.
- Promote user participation and user–developer interaction.
- Simplify frequent development iterations.
- Reduce the maintenance effort.
- Provide adequate documentation in a simple way.

Application generators are essentially function and parameter driven and, therefore, force consistent structure across applications. A given input will produce a standard output for the common on-line application functions. Thus for sign-on, function selection, record selection, display, and updating, the same view will be presented each time. There will be consistent procedures for the terminal operators. There is no room for programmer inspiration or experimentation in developing the structures.

They allow for fast implementation if the users are given sufficient training in the available capabilities. The functions that they offer are powerful and complex, and can be used to create results that are out of control. They can also be used to develop large program sections rapidly if they are used properly. There must be a good understanding of the giant programming steps that are taken.

Application program generators are most useful for prototyping applications, as will be discussed further. They are designed so that a prototype can first be generated, and then the set of instructions can be simply expanded to introduce more functions.

Generators promote user participation. In an iterative process, the user defines the program requirements, the developer produces a prototype and designs some screens, the user reviews the screens, and then the developer makes the necessary modifications. The process may start relatively simply, becoming more and more complex as the application is filled out to become a fully usable application system. The user confirms the validity of the results on the screens, and the logic is represented step by step as the system is developed.

The development iterations are greatly simplified, as compared to the classical program development cycle. The normal process is as follows:

> *First:* The screens are designed, as noted above, and the user works with the designer until both are satisfied that the requirements are fulfilled.
>
> *Second:* Simple test data are used against the screens. If there are any problems between the programs and the data, they will become obvious while they are still simple to correct. The problems may be the form of the data exhibited, data overflows in the assigned fields, and so on. When the user first sees real data on the screens, there may be other modifications requested, also.
>
> *Third:* Raw data is introduced at the beginning of the application program process to see how it will flow to the screens. The data may be retrieved from the file or database that will be used, or it may be entered and validated from a terminal. All the application function modules are linked together and to the screen module to test the system. This will be done stepwise, of course, to allow easy customization of various parts of the system. Blocks of reusable code may be introduced at this point.
>
> *Fourth:* Unique or custom program logic may then be added to the application and tested. The functions up to this point may have been provided completely from the generator's common modules that were supplied. Since they have been previously tested, the initial tests were confined to their linkage and the data flow. Now, more complexity may be added and tested step by step. This approach greatly simplifies the overall testing process.

Note that this process is essentially a top-down approach from the user's viewpoint. The user sees the results first and verifies them. The general system structure is then applied and tested. Finally, the details of the actual data available, and the manipulations that must be made to process it to a usable form, are introduced and tested.

One of the results of this approach is that a good system is installed rapidly with many of its facets tested. Another result is that the subsequent maintenance effort is greatly reduced because the user has been able to examine the results and comment on them throughout the process. Misunderstandings are greatly reduced.

The normal maintenance problems of coding errors are also greatly reduced. This is because tested program modules are used throughout, and are simply called for by high-level commands. These commands are rules or parameters that are readily interpreted and changed as is necessary. The code supplied with the generator remains intact and is used so often in a number of applications that it is thoroughly tested.

Finally, but importantly, adequate documentation is readily provided by most generators. The screens themselves are excellent pieces of the documentation. The high-level coding is quickly documented. The development interaction with the user has shaken out any problems with the statements of the program requirements.

Problems with Application Program Generators.

Despite their many advantages, there are, of course, some problems with the use of application program generators. They are simply not optimal for all situations. Some of these problem areas are:

- State of the art in development
- Capabilities of the users involved
- Capabilities of the program developers

The concept of application program generators is excellent, and the available systems will improve rapidly in the near future. One serious problem, however, is that there is tremendous variation in the capabilities of the systems that are currently available on the market. The use of these systems must be studied carefully, and the requirements matched against the reality of the packages that are proposed. Thus the section of this report on the selection of application generators is critical.

The state of the art is in flux. This does not mean that you should wait until it settles down. There are great opportunities to be gained by starting now with even imperfect systems. The concept is excellent and proven. The fit to particular applications and people may not be the best. The area of application generators is very similar to the area of artificial intelligence in that they are both progressing rapidly, and neither offers absolute answers to many classes of problems. However, they both offer many useful solutions right now, and should be analyzed to find out where the profitable applications are. Interestingly, people in both these fields are talking about their future conjunction; that is, it will some day be possible to generate programs using AI approaches. The systems will adapt automatically as the user enters information, problems will be anticipated, and the command structure will simplify.

The capabilities of the system designer are the key to success. All programmers will not fit well with the new thought processes that are involved. Some will want to even get into the system and make modifications where they should not. Others will feel superior to the simplicity of the analysis and programming. Participants must be selected who are adaptable, and are enthusiastic with the new technology.

Developers must come with their technical skills and computer knowledge and be prepared to learn about building systems with end users that will be effective for them. Relatively short classes, one or two days, can expose experienced people to the use of the tools and techniques. Further instruction is needed to orient them to user thinking and the new pace of development. Those who will adapt and grasp the concept will be able to realize the potential of application program generators as powerful development tools.

System generators are now coming on the market with the claim that they can generate entire application systems, with all the required linkages between the applications and support programs within the system. Some system generators may accept existing applications as inputs and build them into the final, generated system. Most system generators provide the linkages to particular database management systems and data dictionaries. This type of application development system is clearly beyond the realm of most end user application development, and should be reserved for professional programmers.

Program Code Generators

Program code generators are programs, rather than development systems, that are designed for writing other programs automatically. These program products increase the efficiency of professional programmers and reduce program development time by providing automatic source code generation for reports, file maintenance, and inquiry functions. Clearly, there is no sharp distinction between application program generators, program code generators, and report program generators. The differentiation is made in this report purposely, however, to reinforce the concept that such program products on the market cover a wide range of capabilities, and the distinctions must be understood to select the right product for a particular job. There are major differences between some products; other differences are marginal between the different classifications. It is important to understand that the steps in functions offered are great, even if individual program offerings tend to blur the differences.

In the IBM mainframe area, the majority of program code generators offered are designed to facilitate the coding of COBOL programs, with, possibly, file handling and screens added. Some use formally coded design documentation to generate COBOL procedure division code directly. Others use nonprocedural statements to generate COBOL programs for an on-line environment. The direction is to produce structured COBOL source code that the user can combine with other code, compile, and execute. This may include file structure support, the copying of source statements from the COBOL library, arithmetic operations, and COBOL subroutines. Some recent generators produce COBOL programs by means of screen painting. They may handle touch screens, color CRTs, and multiple printers.

In the microcomputer area, there is a great variety of program code generators for such languages as BASIC, DIBOL, and dBase, under various operating systems such as CP/M varieties, UNIX, XENIX, DOS, etc. Many microcomputer vendors have constructed their own program code generators to facilitate rapid system design with minimum memory requirements.

Program code generators can thus be characterized as application generators that are designed to either:

- Facilitate COBOL program development by automating important segments of the process, rather than the whole program.
- Develop programs for microcomputers more effectively and efficiently.

If a system is called a program code generator, it is unlikely that it will produce a fully operational application system, even on a small scale. It may, however, greatly improve programming efficiency.

Report Program Generators

Report program generators (RPG), or report generators, were among the earliest productivity aids that were developed to make programming more efficient. They are basically batch-oriented programs, and are quite similar to query languages, which are a more recent development for on-line applications. When this class of packages was first produced in the 1960s, the increase in programming productivity was dramatic, so they have continued to be widely accepted ever since. They were among the earlier program packages that used form sheets and tables rather than procedural statements.

The purpose of RPG packages is to eliminate much of the programming required to produce formatted, printed reports. They are quite formalized in their own structures, but they allow simple expressions of the data content and position to put together complex reports. They usually include some arithmetic capability, some subroutine functions, plus subtotaling and totaling of rows and columns. Some allow subroutines to be written and included. They may be used by both programmers and end users. They can usually be learned in a one-day class.

Thus, report program generators (RPG) are true application generators, but are limited in their scope to the design, coding, and production of output reports from data files or a database. Many databases have, in fact, incorporated the equivalent of RPGs in their system. Most RPGs are compilers. The program is simply written on the specific form sheets, entered, and run. Although they are very rapid to write, they may be quite inefficient in operation. Thus, they are frequently used for one-shot jobs. They are sometimes useful for production jobs, however, when the requirements are changed occasionally and randomly, and special reports are often required. In such cases, programmers can produce a system for a user department and train personnel in the coding. Those users can then make modifications at any time and run special reports that have been requested. There are some control dangers in this type of use, as it is difficult to relate the coding instructions to the results at a later date. If users wish to operate in this way, they must institute their own controls. This only applies to the output reports, of course, since most such programs work from controlled data files.

Some of the more popular RPGs, such as Cullinet Software's Culprit, IBM's ADRS-II (A Departmental Reporting System), and Informatic General's Mark IV, have proceeded far from their early roots, but started basically as batch RPGs. There are many other RPG systems on the market. Some are for specific application areas, or specific microcomputers, while others are general-purpose report producers.

Report program generators do not put together a program that can be used with little or no modification as an executable module of code within a system. For this reason, they are sometimes not considered as application generators because they do not produce a complete software system. From the viewpoint of end users, however, the application developed from an RPG or a query language is executable as a freestanding system, and performs all the desired functions.

Query Languages

Query languages are systems that allow the simple formatting of inquiries against data files or complex databases in an on-line environment. As application generators, they are also directed solely towards the production of output reports. They produce such application programs rapidly, however, and are generally easy to learn. They can be thought of as nothing more than on-line RPG languages. They are nonprocedural languages that provide the required data access to the database and permit the formatting of the data into either printed reports or screen displays through the use of specification parameters. They may be sold as part of a DBMS package.

Query language packages frequently provide some arithmetic capabilities and support some graphics outputs. They are highly productive in programming because the results can be called onto the screen rapidly, and the programs can be changed as frequently as desired in a single session.

Query languages provide the user with a simple report generator that can be readily operated from a terminal with little contact with the computing group. A common example is IBM's Answer/DB-Personal Reporter and Answer/DB-Inquiry. These systems enable the users to enter natural-language report statements and access DL/1 databases and other files without knowing the structure of the data. Report requests are prepared interactively with diagnostics to assist the requester, accessing both on-line and batch databases and files.

There is no functional distinction between query languages and report program generators (RPG). The distinction is made here that the query language is for on-line applications and the RPG is for batch applications, but all vendors may not agree with this.

Screen Design Programs and Generators

Screen design programs and generators, or screen formatting tools, are packages that aid in the design of CRT screen layouts and the definition of data entry fields on the CRT. Elements such as field position, field names, field size, and editing functions can be controlled with these packages.

Screen design programs and generators are usually included as integral parts of application report generators. There are a number of separate programs also available on the market, however. These programs should always be used by end-user system developers. There are sufficient functions offered to make it quite impractical to do any hand coding of screens unless it is an operational system with very specific requirements.

A number of other screen editors are interactive programming aids that provide all the tools necessary to create computer terminal screen formats to be used with new or existing application programs. The systems control the interaction between the application program and the terminal. Features may include error checking, fixed- or variable-length fields, mandatory or optional entry, default values, partial screen scrolling, and hidden fields for data storage. There may also be bold, underlined, and blinking characters, 132-column lines, jump and smooth scrolling, and split and reverse screens. Apple's MacIntosh computer has particularly versatile functions.

IBM offers COBOL-3270 Full Screen Support, Extended Editor and Full Screen Manager, and SDF (Screen Definition Facility). These are typical programs that build screens by defining the screen layout on-line. They define new maps and map sets, and maintain them in the library. The test function formats the screen as displayed, and an editing function is included. SDF offers a demo session that defines and displays sequence for review.

5.6 THE USE OF EXPERT SYSTEMS IN CASE

CASE is a loosely defined subject, and some even claim that CASE itself is an expert system. This may be true philosophically, but, in practice, there is a type of knowledge representation and search that is called an "expert system," and it is helpful to stick to the definitions of expert systems that have evolved. Expert systems are not simplistic subroutines to be inserted into a CASE system. They are fairly complex systems, but they are frequently used in CASE because they are extremely valuable in the automation of technical decisions. They are particularly useful in such areas as reverse engineering, where there are many decisions to be made based on insufficient knowledge. Formerly, such decisions could only be made by professionals, but now professional "knowledge" can be inserted into an automatic system.

An expert system has, involves, or displays specific skill or knowledge that is derived from experience or training. It allows the use of the stored information to enable anyone to make the appropriate decisions based on an existing set of facts. In every area of any business, there is a routine need for problem solving based on voluminous but incomplete, uncertain, and even contradictory information. This type of information can be captured in the computer as data, and can be called "knowledge," which is simply a group of facts or conditions about something. The problem is how to use this data-knowledge to make appropriate decisions. Up until now, conventional data processing has simply printed out large amounts based on the assumption that the questions being asked will always be the same. These computer printouts are of great use for routine, fixed applications such as payroll, but are of little use when decisions are demanded based on a current set of unexpected conditions. The design and use of expert systems can help to solve such problems. They present a powerful, new way to give assistance in decision making from the production line to the boardroom, and are ideally suited as part of CASE.

Expert systems can be described as programs that help the computer make decisions in a similar way to that of an expert in a specific domain, or particular subject area, of interest. They are an attempt to "clone" someone who has developed an expertise in a defined field. It has been shown that there is a wide range of practical applications that can be computerized, from medical diagnosis to diesel engine repair, to space shuttle operational decisions, to rejecting objects on a production line. The critical subsets of decisions that must be made by the experts are analyzed, defined, programmed, and put into a logical sequence for application. These AI systems do not make wide-ranging, random searches through a large body of facts. Instead, they are given a series of specific selection points based on IF-THEN-ELSE logic (meaning IF this condition exists, THEN accept this fact, ELSE step to another decision point). All searches are up defined "trees" of decisions, and the sequence to be followed is prescribed by the decisions that are made following the "branches" of the trees.

Expert systems can be used to help make routine operating decisions that normally require handling by an experienced individual. Each expert system is used only in its own, specific area of decision making or domain, and can handle only those decisions for which it has had sufficient information, including facts and decision rules, stored in its knowledge base or database. When current data is entered into it, an expert system can frequently supply a decision on the condition that it is a close equivalent to the decision that would be supplied by a human expert looking at the same data. An expert system is likely to be used as an intelligent assistant to a human who needs to make a decision, but does not have the experience of an "expert." An expert system simply gives a "best guess" to the human, who can then:

- Use the answer from the system, with reasonable confidence.
- Add more current data, and request another answer.
- Reject the answer from the expert system, and make another decision.

In CASE, the expert system approach has the advantage of speed.

An expert system is thus an aid to thinking and decision making that has the other advantages of:

- Being able to accurately retrieve a great many facts and rules.
- Providing a less-experienced individual with the decision rules of a person who is experienced and expert in the particular field.
- Being portable, and installable at any number of locations.

Professor Edward Feigenbaum, of Stanford University, defined an expert system as follows:

An expert system is an intelligent computer program that uses knowledge and inference procedures to solve problems that are difficult enough to require significant human expertise for their solution. The knowledge necessary to perform at such a level, plus the inference procedures used, can be thought of as a model of the expertise of the best practitioners of the field.

The knowledge of an expert system consists of facts and heuristics. The "facts" constitute a body of information that is widely shared, publicly available, and generally agreed upon by experts in the field. The "heuristics" are mostly private, little-discussed rules of good judgment (rules of plausible reasoning, rules of good guessing) that characterize expert-level decision making in the field. The performance level of an expert system is primarily a function of the size and quality of the knowledge base that it possesses.

An expert system has, involves, or displays special skill or knowledge of a particular subject that derives from training or experience. It may be described as a computer program that stores a large number of facts, assumptions, and miscellaneous pieces of information, and that expedites a search to be made and decisions to be reached that will correspond with decisions that would likely be made by a human expert in that subject. The storage of knowledge (which is a group of facts or conditions about something) in the expert system will usually be systematically accumulated over time by many specialists of diverse experience. In this way, the expert system will continually become more useful, and it may attain a level of ability to solve problems that exceeds the abilities of any one of the experts who contributed to it.

An expert system consists of:

a. A knowledge base of facts, solution methods, and solution rules that are attested by the human experts in the particular field.

b. A program control structure, or inference procedure, that will search the knowledge base for the solution to the problem in a systematic manner related to that of the human expert.

c. A working memory, called a global database, which keeps track of the problem status, the input data for the particular problem, and a trail of the relevant work that has thus far been done.

An expert system can be thought of as an attempt to "clone" a human expert. This means that some part of a routine human activity is systematically broken down into its component parts, and the information involved is put into computer memory. It is then supplied with a search and reasoning process that resembles the way the human makes decisions about the subject. The result is a computer program that can:

- Make an in-depth use of the stored knowledge about a subject area.
- Reason logically to reach decisions or formulate plans.
- Be "trained" with a set of rules or sample cases.
- Generalize from incomplete knowledge.
- Give an explanation of the decisions reached.
- Respond to questions about its knowledge base.

What is the value of an expert system to CASE? It is more stable and consistent than humans, because humans are frequently slow and inconsistent, they get emotional or tired, and they may retire at any time. It is more flexible than the familiar data processing methods because the expert knowledge is completely separated from the program procedures, and is maintainable, transportable, consistent, and in readily retrievable form.

Traditional data processing programs essentially operate in a single mode. That is, they are given specified input data, and produce predefined results in an expected report format. Expert system programs may operate in any of three distinct modes:

1. They may produce answers to problems as other EDP programs do, except that the form of the answers may be unexpected.
2. They may have their store of knowledge and their rule base increased or modified by the human experts without touching the computer program itself.
3. Their knowledge base may be searched independently by a human using a wide variety of assumptions and approaches.

A number of definitions follow, but it must be realized that these are not all strictly defined and accepted. The field is new, the competition for sales and attention is great, and no one has a copyright on the terms. Hence, many of the words used are defined to mean whatever the user wishes them to mean. A good example is calling an on-line spelling checker in a typewriter an example of artificial intelligence. The checker essentially compares the spelling of a word that has just been typed in with the spelling of words in a dictionary that are similar. It indicates those words that differ from the approved list. This useful tool is an exceedingly elementary "artificial intelligence" application, but has every right to use the name because it aids in an unstructured decision. There are similar uses of the term "expert system" in some CASE products. The following definitions are, therefore, useful guides rather than approved statements.

> *Artificial intelligence* is the use of computers to carry out tasks that would require intelligence if the tasks were performed by humans.
> *Domain* is a specific knowledge base for a given subject. It is the set of elements to which a logical variable is limited.

An expert is a person who has special skill or knowledge in a particular subject that has been derived from training or experience.

An expert system is an AI computer program that uses expert knowledge to solve problems more efficiently by relating the facts, assumptions, and inference procedures in the knowledge base through heuristic methods suggested by the human experts.

Heuristic is providing direction in the solution of a problem along the paths most likely to lead to the desired goal. It is the expert's "rule of thumb." It covers exploratory problem-solving techniques that use self-evaluation, or feedback, to improve performance.

Intelligent assistant is an AI expert system that aids a person in the performance of a task. It is thus a computer program that aids the thinking process of an individual.

Knowledge is simply a collection of facts or conditions about something.

Knowledge base is a database containing facts, inferences, and procedures corresponding to the types of information needed for the solutions of particular problems.

Knowledge engineering is the systems analysis of a knowledge base, and of the problems that are to be solved, to determine the best list structures and organization of the knowledge base, and the best modes of search.

Knowledge representation is the formal way of representing facts and rules about a subject, or a special area of interest, in a knowledge base.

Knowledge systems are computer systems that embody knowledge that may consist of facts that are inexact, heuristic, or subjective, in addition to exact, or controlled, facts.

A human expert in the particular "domain" of interest usually collaborates with professional knowledge engineers to help develop the knowledge base and then the expert system. The knowledge engineer is a specialized systems analyst who interrogates the expert about the facts that are needed for any particular decision, the points of decision, and the rules of thumb that have proven to be necessary for obtaining the answer to a particular problem.

The Structure of an Expert System

An expert system is a complex computer program that attempts to replicate the search and inference procedures used by human experts. It solves AI problems more efficiently by relating the facts, assumptions, and inference procedures in the knowledge base through heuristic search methods that have been suggested by the humans who are familiar with the domain. It may also be called a "knowledge-based expert system" or a "knowledge system." Figure 55 shows the general elements of such a system.

The largest part of it, and the most difficult and time consuming to develop, is the knowledge base. This element contains the facts, assumptions, heuristics, and rules that have been derived through consultation with the domain expert. It will also include the suggested heuristics that are associated with the particular problem. If it is a rule-based system, it will contain the knowledge rules and the inference rules. It is the repository of all the knowledge (facts, data, conditions) that will be used in the solution of problems for that particular domain.

Another part of the expert system is the control structure. This is sometimes called the inference engine becauses it handles the inference procedures in the use of the knowledge base for the solution of the problem. It is also called the rule interpreter when the domain knowledge is stored as production rules.

The third large segment of the expert system is the global database, or working memory. This is the classical "data processing" part of the system. It is a combination of the working memory and the knowledge acquisition subsystem. It contains detailed information about the search as it proceeds, and desired information can be drawn from it. The status of the system can be reviewed at any time. It also handles the input data, or knowledge acquisition, putting it in the database in correct form and under control.

The user interface to the expert system is usually a module joined to the control structure that provides a natural language interface for the user. Few research systems have a complex interface, but most commercial systems try to offer a user-friendly, natural-language interface to facilitate the use of the system. This may be in all three modes of use of the system: development, problem solving, and instruction. Each mode has unique problems. Connected to this, an explanation subsystem, or module, is supplied in the better systems. This subsystem allows the user to challenge and examine the reasoning process that has provided the system's answers.

Note that in an expert system, there is a sharp separation of

FIGURE 55. A knowledge-based expert system.

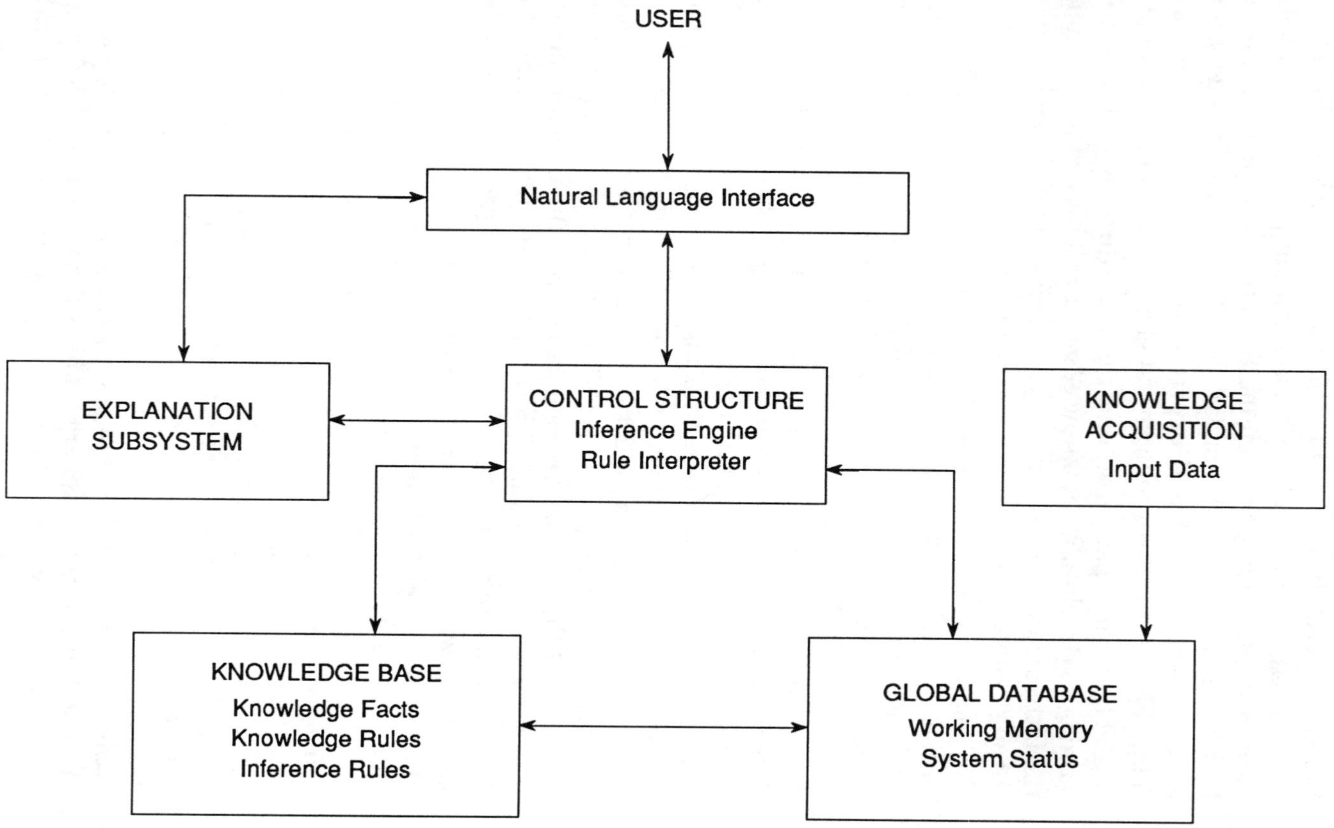

the general knowledge about the problem (the facts and rules in the knowledge base), the information about the current problem (the input data in the global memory), and the program for applying the knowledge base to the current problem (the control structure). This is one of the principal distinctions of expert systems from classical data processing programs. Other characterizations are listed in Figure 56.

FIGURE 56. Expert system distinctions.

- **Separation of knowledge base, control structure, and working memory.**

  Knowledge and methods are not intermixed, as in conventional computer programs. The system can be changed by simply adding or subtracting rules in the knowledge base.

- **Symbolic knowledge representation.**

  Data is not numerically addressed in the database, but is searched for by relationships that are expressed symbolically.

- **Symbolic inference.**

  Processing is not numeric, but is based on inferences and relationships.

- **Heuristic search of complex knowledge.**

  Searches are not algorithmic, but follow rules of thumb (heuristics) that simplify the search tree branching.

- **Extensive use of domain constraints.**

  The stored knowledge is selectively searched according to constraints that have been suggested by the expert.

- **Self-knowledge of reasoning processes.**

  The working memory stores information about the reasoning process, and at any time, an explanation of the decisions made to that point may be retrieved. The processing is highly interactive, and may be modified as it proceeds.

The Knowledge Base

The knowledge base contains the facts and rules that embody the knowledge of the expert in that particular domain, which may be a CASE system. It is usually put together by a knowledge engineer who first becomes familiar with the problem domain and then talks with an expert who describes how decisions are usually made from the available knowledge. The knowledge engineer may use any of five different ways to encode the facts and relationships that make up knowledge. These approaches to the representation of knowledge in the knowledge base include:

- Rules
- Semantic networks
- Object-attribute-value triplets
- Frames and scripts
- Logical expressions

Knowledge representation is a formal way of presenting facts and rules about a subject or a special area of interest. If the knowledge representation is well designed by the knowledge engineer, the expert system will be efficient, and may be useful. If there is not sufficient effort or experience put into the knowledge representation, the system will probably be inefficient and difficult to use.

The purpose of knowledge representation is, thus, to organize the required facts and rules into a system that can be readily accessed by the proposed AI program for whatever purposes are required. In an expert system, it will be organized for making inferences. It will be straightforward to pass from one statement that is considered true to another whose truth is believed to follow from the first.

Knowledge is simply a group of facts or conditions about something, such as CASE information. In ordinary data processing, there is always an attempt to have controlled, or accurate, data. In expert systems, it is acceptable and frequently helpful to have approximate data, or even questionable data, that may throw light on the problem's solution. An example would be clues about a crime in a police investigation system. It is all knowledge.

A knowledge base is, then, a database that is a collection of facts, inferences, and procedures that correspond to the types of information needed for the solution to the problem under consideration. A knowledge base is designed for very specific types of inquiry. This must be determined by the knowledge engineer.

Problem solutions that are reasonably useful to aid human activities have so many possible combinations of data to be searched that the expectation of getting an answer in a useful time is almost nil when the data is not structured specifically to aid the search. It became apparent very early that considerable attention must be paid to the way knowledge is represented in a database if reasonable results are to be obtained from searches. This realization led to the field of knowledge engineering, as a necessity for specialists to study knowledge representation and to design efficient searches. Humans do not have this problem of overcoming slow search times, because they have the facility of very rapidly, though frequently inaccurately, moving directly to the required data. Computers, however, must be instructed to track through to specific data. They cannot yet make leaps of thought to a related idea.

Knowledge engineering has come to mean the systems analysis of a knowledge base and of the problems that are to be solved. Its purpose is to determine the best list structures and organization of the knowledge base. Knowledge engineers design the knowledge representation system.

Knowledge engineers work similarly to systems analysts in that they operate in a consulting role and derive most of their information from interviews. They must talk with the "experts" who understand the particular knowledge area and draw out the items of knowledge that are important to the solution of the particular problem. These items of knowledge will broadly consist of an understanding of the problem in four areas:

- The "road map" of how one goes about solving a particular problem, including the data to be collected and the analytical steps to be taken.
- The particular "knowledge" that is needed for the solution of the problem, such as the instrument readings to be observed, and the environmental factors to be taken into consideration.

- The "rules of thumb," or heuristics, by which the expert normally makes decisions.
- The detailed knowledge of specific, critical areas that will be important to examine after logical reasoning has led to the particular area.

Rules.

The most popular approach to representing the domain knowledge required for CASE expert systems is by production rules, which may also be called IF-THEN rules, or situation-action rules. Many knowledge bases are made up principally of heuristics, or rules of good judgment or actions to take in specific situations. The rules are invoked by pattern matching with features of the problem environment in the global database. The power of the expert system to solve problems will then lie in the number of useful rules that have been assembled in the interviews with the expert.

Production rules are most useful in AI programs that are designed for an individual to follow the steps that an expert would take in solving a problem, such as finding the cause of a machine failure. Procedural representations are small programs that specifically describe what actions to take in a defined situation. Some take a broad view of a problem and are grouped in subroutines. The most common procedural representations, however, identify individual observations and steps to take, which are the production rules. The purpose of the statements is to match the observed situation to the preconditions needed for the procedure to be called for.

Production rules are in a format of the types:

- Pattern-action
- If-then
- Antecedent-consequence
- Situation-procedure

Such production rules represent knowledge in a modular way, and are readily extended or modified. They fit perfectly the type of thought process in CASE that is used by systems analysts.

An analyst can draw them out from an expert in a particular field by stepping through problems in the natural sequence.

Expert Systems and CASE

Some CASE vendors are using expert systems technology as a way of making the CASE tool work. Some of the embedded "black box" systems are described below:

Methodology integrity enforcement—TI's Information Engineering Facility has an expert system. TI's error has been that they forged ahead in expert systems. That experience and that technology are an important piece of what makes the IEF actually work. An expert system understands the rules of the methodology. If you try something that does not conform to the rules, it will not let you do it. It will tell you that this procedure is invalid. KnowledgeWare's Information Engineering Workbench is similarly built around an expert system technology. It is used for methodology and integrity enforcement, and in the human interface. It is giving better HELP subsystems and a more intelligent human interface. With the VS Designer from Visual Software, you tell that product what kind of interface you are accustomed to dealing with. Do you use the WordStar paradigm? The Lotus paradigm? The Mac paradigm? You tell it which one, and the human interface takes on that appearance. That is an intelligent interface.

Life-cycle process support—There is an interesting product from Cortex, called *Vision*, which contains an expert system technology that knows about the life cycle. It also knows what liberties you can take with a life cycle. So it says, "Those of you who have done this, should do this." You say, "I don't want to do that; I want to do this." When you come to the next sync point at the end of an activity, the menu says, "You haven't done this yet, you should do this next. You don't have to, but don't forget that it has to be done." If you choose not to do that, it will remember and the next time it may say, "You cannot go any further, you have to do this now." It is making the methodology a bit more palatable by giving you the support for the methodology.

Code generation—Expert systems are used in code generation. Transform uses an expert system approach to take design specifications and generate code. It understands the rules of good structured code. It understands the rules of reusable architecture and it uses those technologies inside itself that are invisible to you as a way of generating the code. It is also used in *code analysis*. Bachman uses expert systems technology to look at database designs and to figure out what the underlying model was that you were trying to represent in the physical implementation.

Expert systems "shells" are a different way of building systems. AION is an expert system whose positioning is: Why write a traditional data processing system with or without CASE? An expert systems shell is a more productive way of dealing with the same kind of problem. It does not have to be a diagnostic application. A report generator problem can be productively handled with an expert system shell rather than with hand coding or CASE coding. The developers of AION have positioned AION more as a CASE product than an expert systems product.

There are many if-then-else constructs in applications, but they keep changing. You do not have to change the application; it is the rules that change. There will be more expert system technology to handle that automatically.

5.7 *THE NECESSITY FOR QUALITY ASSURANCE*

One of the key reasons for using CASE methods is to meet the demand for quality application systems. Too many systems have simply been enhanced and modified over the past years and fulfill a given function, but cannot claim to be efficient. There are still too many batch systems in operation, and too many systems that have inadequate operational and audit controls in place. Quality assurance is a relatively new function, and has not been applied to many systems that are in operation today. There is a growing demand for computer application systems, but the requirements are for a better quality system than in the past. There are a number of reasons for this new emphasis:

- The cost of hardware has decreased steadily, but the cost of programming has increased steadily. This means that the equipment is available for more and more systems to be installed and readily justified. On the other hand, there are relatively fewer experienced system developers. The gap cannot be filled by simply hiring anybody. The gap can only be filled by working smarter, rather than harder.

- Users now generally understand data processing systems and their possibilities. They are no longer content to have systems analysts do all the design work, and then have to tell them what they really want. They are anxious to be more involved in system development, particularly in the area of design decisions. They want to be offered options, and not to be told that the discussion of options will greatly extend the time of system development. Users are expecting more support because they are more familiar with the possibilities. They want quality systems.

- There is always a gap between the need for programmers and their availability. This is natural, because programming is a technical job that requires training and experience. A pickup team cannot be used to program complex systems. Users know that quality programmers produce quality systems, but that there is a shortage of them. The obvious answer is to use CASE methodologies with trained people.

- System development groups are spending most of their time on maintenance work simply because there is a very large portfolio of systems in most organizations, and these systems are regularly in need of enhancement, enlargement, or correction. Maintenance programmers can seldom redesign systems and make them more efficient. They can only patch up existing systems and try to make them meet the new specifications. Quality *improvement* is difficult to accomplish in operating applications. It is better to start spending more resources in building better quality into the new systems that are developed.

The modern demand for quality application systems is principally in the area of on-line, responsive systems that perform specific functions for users on demand. Such systems are notorious for their use of computer cycles. Rapid response times are demanded; yet complex functions are requested that make such response times difficult. This demand cannot be met by any group of analysts and programmers using 4GLs. It is technically complex, and can only be met by experienced developers who know which languages are appropriate in given situations. Thus, professionals must be quite familiar with the capabilities and capacities of programming systems. It has become well publicized in recent years that all fourth-generation languages are not equal, and that few of them can match the operational efficiency of some third-generation systems if they are both handled by experienced programmers. The system overhead in 4GLs reduces the development effort, but frequently adds machine cycles in actual operation. This is a most important factor in systems quality that can only be realistically handled by experienced personnel.

The demand for quality application systems can only be realistically met by a quality staff that concentrates on specific aspects of system development. The majority of system analysts and programmers are working with older systems, enhancing and improving them. They cannot be expected to be on top of the most recent system development advances. A specific group can be most helpful in specializing in rapid system development where the quality of the final application is always of critical importance.

The CASE group must be responsible for ensuring the quality of the application systems that are produced. One problem with assembling a group of highly experienced personnel is that they are frequently overconfident of their ability to rapidly produce systems that readily meet the requirements set forth originally by the users. Quality management is a recognized function that must be considered in CASE. Quality assurance, quality control, audit, and security control are all interrelated staff functions that should be incorporated into the planning for the ADC if useful applications are to be delivered. It is simply a matter of fitting in the necessary checkpoints, even with high-priority, rush projects, and cooperating with the particular staff groups. Figure 57 shows how these groups work in distinct functional areas with the common goals of supporting acceptable application development.

Quality assurance (QA) can be described as a planned integration of all the actions necessary to provide adequate confidence that programs, data, procedures, and services conform to the specifications that were established and the technical requirements of operation, and that the application achieves satisfactory performance.

For a more detailed discussion of quality management, and of organizing and operating a quality assurance function, see the FTP Technical Library manual, *Quality Assurance: Organization, Management, and Implementation.* The successful quality management program focuses on quality as a strategy to produce better products in a more timely and economical manner. The pressure

FIGURE 57. Relationships and distinctions in quality management.

Area	Quality Assurance	Quality Control	Audit	Security Control
Overall purpose	Raise consciousness of quality and expedite quality control	Examine quality of information production in specific areas	Examine adherence to procedures, compliance to rules, and integrity of operations	Control and protect the assets of the organization.
Overall view	Pragmatic	Specific	Analytic	Control
Quality objectives	Determine measurable objectives	Work with specific objectives	Review established objectives	Security and control objectives
Organizational need	To gain uniform attention to quality	To control operation in particular areas	To meet legal requirements and be assured of financial control	To protect assets adequately
Interest in causes of problems	Fundamental	Peripheral	Fundamental	Security problems only
Interception of the information path	At end of each development phase and in operations	At specific production points	At areas suspected of possibly causing problems	Security risk areas

FIGURE 57. (Cont.)

Area	Quality Assurance	Quality Control	Audit	Security Control
Quality standards and procedures	Develop and provide direction	Use established standards and procedures	Review	Install for protection against loss
Quality control methodology	Develop and provide direction	Use	Recommend	Use for protection against loss
Audit controls	Recommend	Report on operation	Authenticate and recommend	Analyze in risk areas
Structured development and coding standards	Develop standards and train in use	Use	Review and recommend	Review in risk areas
Use of test and analysis tools	Recommend and co-operate in use	Use as assigned	Use independently when deemed useful	Occasional use for analysis
Amount of information reviewed	Large samples in suspect areas	Sufficient statistical samples in assigned areas	Sufficient statistical samples in assigned areas	Outline data, with samples in suspect areas

Area	Quality Assurance	Quality Control	Audit	Security Control
Statistics on production	Gather in suspected problem areas	Gather at specific control points	Request and analyze	Review aberrations
Period of checking	Before-the-fact	Immediately after-the-fact	Traditionally after-the-fact	During the actual operation
Level of personnel	Experienced systems personnel	Junior systems and clerical personnel	Accountants and trained systems personnel	Trained specialists
Technical view of personnel	General technical level	Detailed technical level	Financial with sufficient technical training	General technical level
Training	Provide	Receive	Recommend	Provide

on application appears as a time demand, but that is always directly combined with an equal quality demand. Quality management uses measuring, modeling, and metrics to keep development projects on the user-defined track.

Important elements of a quality management program are:

- Providing education and training on techniques and methods which inject into, and verify the quality of, the information system throughout its life cycle.

- Providing guidelines, standards, and policies that clearly outline the level of quality desired.

- Investigating new techniques that are applicable to the operating environment, and including them in the program.

- Providing a mechanism to check, review, and report on the actual state of quality being achieved.

- Providing a system of communicating program results—in effect advertising successes and converting failures into lessons learned.

- Providing a consulting service on quality in information systems to the corporation as a whole.

- Providing a mechanism to mediate disputes concerning quality: between end users and the development and production staff, between different end-user groups, and between different development and production staff groups.

The primary purpose of the quality management function is to foster a uniformly high level of quality EDP systems developed, installed, and operated. This purpose is achieved by means of formal provisions which have been set up for:

1. Ensuring active and coordinated participation in considerations leading to establishment, revision, evaluation, and dissemination of standards, management guidelines, and procedures.

2. Research into definition, establishment, enhancement, and maintenance of system development methodology.

3. Consultation, review, and evaluation of large systems projects at significant milestones in their development.

4. The establishment, enhancement, and maintenance of a stable, planned environment for the implementation of changes within the operating software environment.

5. Research into definition, establishment, and maintenance of a standard, consistent, and well-defined testing methodology for computer systems.
6. The implementation and maintenance of an automated project control system that facilitates project planning and accounting.

Quality management is now recognized as an accepted function in information services management. The present understanding of quality management, and realization of its profitability, developed with experience and the increasing complexity of supplying the required information services. The need has long been apparent, and has been met in a variety of ways by the traditional audit and control procedures. The following outlines the present-day relationships and distinctions between the four information areas that may overlap in their functions: quality assurance, quality control, audit, and security control.

Quality assurance is a staff function in information services that analyzes, develops, and implements control and review systems in all areas of information analysis and production. Its staff does not usually perform the full quality review work itself, but develops methodologies and oversees them. It should raise the corporate consciousness of quality information products. It requires cooperation from the application developers.

Quality control is usually a line function in information services, particularly in the production areas, that is responsible for the routine accomplishment of all prescribed quality tests and analyses, and the reporting of the results. It requires action from the application developers.

Audit is a staff function that may be in the information services department, in the financial department, or external to the organization. It is responsible for reviewing the adherence to procedures, the compliance to rules, and the integrity of the operations completely independently of the other information services groups. A prime concern is the quality of the information products.

Security control is usually a staff function in information services, the main purpose of which is to control and protect the assets of the organization and which, in doing so, may become involved with various aspects of the quality of the information products.

FIGURE 58. Evaluation of CASE systems personnel training considerations.

Item No.	Item	Software Package		
1.	Does the CASE software package require special training of personnel: a. For using the system? b. For operating the system? c. For systems programming and maintenance?			
2.	Does the supplier offer training programs: a. For users? b. For operators? c. For systems programmers? d. For maintenance and enhancement programmers?			
3.	Are these training programs available: a. On site, at the customer's location? b. At vendor offices?			
4.	How are these training programs priced?			
5.	How much training is provided with the purchase of the package?			
6.	Does the vendor supply adequate printed material with the training courses?			
7.	Does the vendor offer public courses on a periodic basis?			
8.	Does the vendor offer study material on video or audio tape with associated texts?			
9.	What is the estimated training period for the package for: a. Systems analysts and programmers? b. User management? c. Systems programmers responsible for maintenance? d. The use of the self-study video or audio tapes?			

These four functions often have the same end in mind, and may overlap in their areas of concern for the management of quality in the organization. As noted, Figure 57 summarizes a number of the differences and similarities between them. They operate in distinct functional areas despite the fact that they frequently have common goals and examine the same information areas.

In general, the quality control and security control staffs are "doers" in their specific areas, and their aims must be incorporated in the application development work. The quality assurance staff are planners and overseers, while the audit staff are reviewers.

5.8 TRAINING CONSIDERATIONS

The use of CASE requires substantial training. There is less training required for an individual CASE tool than there is for a full CASE environment, of course, so there will be a need to make a selection from a wide range of education and training needs. Experienced systems analysts will be looking for advanced courses that explain the operating details of the CASE tools. Managers will be looking for quick courses that give them an overview of the concepts.

Nine possible types of training are briefly discussed. These include: orientation sessions, demonstrations, classroom instruction, person-to-person instruction, computer-based training, video instruction, self-teaching books, vendor training, and commercially available training.

A new CASE tool or integrated system nearly always introduces new methods and procedures. At the least, the controls will be different from those previously used, and the naming of the data, variables, and reports will be new to the professional personnel. Analysts will have to radically change their mode of operation, with many of their previous tasks being automated. The many problems inherent in such a change must be reviewed in advance, with their solutions incorporated into planned training programs.

Many analysts and programmers will take a positive view of CASE, and think of the new opportunities opening up and the chance to learn the new CASE methods. Other personnel may initially be quite wary of CASE, and have real concerns about the effects on their own environment, their job activities, and even their jobs themselves. Such normal and reasonable concerns about the introduction of a new philosophy of developing systems must be met with answers in a training environment.

With the acquisition of a major CASE tool or environment, there will always be concerns in the selection of the approaches based on the degree of change they will introduce, and how all the levels of the organization can be trained to accept and use the new methods. The concerns will include:

- How the special training for the CASE system will be handled.
- The availability of the training programs offered by the vendor.
- The variety of training methods that can be used.
- The time and effort required to accomplish the needed training.

Figure 58 covers some of the specific problems that will arise when the new CASE systems, methods, and procedures are introduced into the organization.

Figure 59 reviews the status of the training that has been received, or is planned, for all levels of personnel in your organization. Before the implementation of CASE is attempted, all possible training classes should be reviewed, a training program should be planned for at least a year, and all interested personnel should be given the opportunity to participate in appropriate training classes.

Types of Training to Consider

Training should always have a specific CASE development project in mind. The types of training to consider must be limited to those courses and methods that will increase productivity and satisfy the requirements of the project.

Figure 60 reduces the great variety and gradation of training possibilities to a few areas. Always remember that any of these kinds of training can be handled by:

- Information services training staff
- Other corporate training staff

FIGURE 59. Implementation of CASE software packages training requirements.

Item No.	Item	Software Package		
1.	Have the following received appropriate training for full use of the CASE system: a. User management? b. User technical personnel? c. User supervisors? d. Data control clerks? e. Terminal operators? f. Computer operators? g. Systems programmers? h. Systems analysts? i. Internal audit personnel? j. Quality assurance personnel?			
2.	Are sufficient training materials on hand for about six months of start-up and operation?			
3.	Have necessary vendor training classes been reserved for the next year?			
4.	Has the vendor supplied the training outlined in the contract?			
5.	Was the vendor's training satisfactory and sufficient?			
6.	If the vendor's training was not satisfactory, have plans been made for improved training classes?			
7.	Are training materials on the system, such as manuals and audio-visuals, available in the information services library?			
8.	Have all concerned technical personnel been alerted to the existence of the system, and given an opportunity to receive training in it, or appropriate training materials?			
9.	Have the organization's training personnel had an opportunity to comment on the training materials supplied by the vendor?			

FIGURE 60. Possible kinds of training.

	CONCEPTUAL (General Computer Understanding)	**HANDS-ON** (Specific Technical Subject)
Orientation sessions	X	
Demonstrations		X
Classroom instruction	X	X
Person-to-person instruction	X	X
Computer-based training	X	X
Video instruction	X	X
Self-teaching books	X	X
Vendor training	X	
Commercially available training	X	X

- Hardware or software product vendors
- External associations and training companies

The variety of possibilities is extensive, and a number of approaches must be tried to stay within average budgets.

Conceptual Training.

Conceptual training is a necessity. It is good for an intro-duction, simply to get everyone using the same language and understanding the approved standards, policies, and procedures. Users developing applications will be interested in more advanced computer concepts, particularly in the database area. Specialists from the information services department should handle these.

Hands-on Training.

Hands-on training in specific technical subjects will be most important. Most of it should be done using the selected equipment and software as much as possible. The payoff is in the hands-on training. The only purpose of the conceptual training is to teach end users a common language so that you can explain the use of the hardware or software product. The hands-on training is designed to get people started with the products so they can go off on their own and use them.

Within each of these broad approaches to training, there are nine specific kinds of training listed in Figure 60. These are as follows.

Orientation Sessions.

Orientation sessions should be limited to one or two hours, usually as a classroom presentation, with time for many questions. A one-hour presentation can be a stand-up lecture. Longer presentations should include a video tape and a brief demonstration of selected products. The lecturer must acquire the capability of determining where the class is in understanding, and proceed from there to the next level. There is no set of facts that must be learned in an orientation lecture. It is simply an opportunity to present a number of concepts and to get the end users to understand the new terminology that will face them. They should leave knowing what specific technical training should be their next step.

Demonstrations.

Demonstrations can be handled by:

- Information services consultants showing the solutions to problems.
- End users helping others in their departments.
- Vendors displaying their wares and making sales.
- Information services personnel trying new technical solutions.
- Any staff person helping visitors to understand what is happening.

There should be no demonstration without hands-on use of the product by everyone in the group who wants to try it. System training demonstrations are not "gee whiz" technical displays. They are "this-is-how-you-can-do-it-yourself" demonstrations. This is a most important point, and must be considered in the planning of demonstrations. Sufficient time must be allotted for people to sit down at the consoles and get the feel of the equipment and the likely output. They must be encouraged to feel comfortable testing the keys.

Demonstrations, by nature, should not be conceptual. Teach the understanding of concepts in the classroom. Demonstrations should center on specific technical products, which can be stated as examples of the possibilities.

Classroom Instruction.

Stand-up classroom teaching methods are traditional, and are probably the most commonly used training approach today. Despite the existence of more exotic and individualized methods of training, the great majority of courses consists of assembling people in a room and giving them a set lecture. This has the advantage of rapid, mass throughput, but there are some disadvantages. Some of the problem areas are:

- *Scheduling of classes:* Rooms are usually limited and in demand. The classroom time, the instructor, and the students must all be coordinated and scheduled to be together at the same time. This has problems. It takes time for the training manager to assemble requests from a variety of students and assign an instructor and a classroom.

- *Assembling qualified instructors:* The possibilities of payout to the users attending computer classes is great. They must not be lost at the first introduction by inadequate instruction. Instructors should be selected for their teaching ability above their technical understanding. A good teacher can learn sufficient concepts and facts ahead of the class, and make the session effective.

- *Costs of instruction:* Classroom instruction is not inexpensive, particularly when the costs of all the students' time are considered. Classroom training should be planned, with estimates of the costs of the classrooms, the instructors, the students' expenses, and the materials. If management approves the costs, make every effort to supply the benefits effectively.

- *Limitations of classroom training:* Classroom training is inherently passive. Many students do not follow a complex, verbal line of reasoning, and start thinking of more pressing subjects during the session. Classroom training should thus be a brief introduction. The more quickly the people can get their hands on actual products, the better. Continually relate the concepts being presented to the possible, later solutions of the particular problems you know the students wish to solve.

Person-to-Person Instruction.

Individual, or small group, instruction is obviously the quickest and most effective way of geting people trained sufficiently to work on their own. Unfortunately, it is also the most expensive approach to training. Schedule a broad set of classes, and try to get most people to funnel through them for introductory material and new concepts. Encourage whole groups of people from the same departments to then go off on their own and start using the products, helping each other learn, and having departmental training sessions on their own. Then use all opportunities of the whole training staff, between classes and between consulting calls, to help people with specific problems. Individualized training, as hardware and software products are passed to an individual and brought up to operational use, are very efficient sessions. They should be attended by a few people who work together. Always accept any request for person-to-person instruction if it is at all possible to staff and schedule.

Computer-Based Training.

Computer-based training (CBT) is considered the wave of the future. It will be possible for everyone to achieve computer literacy through the use of computer-based software programs. In present practice it is most useful but quite limited. It has two main limitations. One is that the user has to be fairly familiar with the use of the terminal, and comfortable with it, before getting any value from CBT. The other is that it is a developing art. Some courses that are available are excellent. Others are poorly written and ineffective.

CBT is a particularly effective means of meeting the demand for instruction in fourth-generation languages. By the time they are approached, the end user will have some familiarity with the microcomputer, and will be able to move through the course smoothly at the desired speed. CBT is less effective in conceptual courses and introductory material, however, because it follows a rigid sequence, and is seldom adapted to specific situations. CBT is most useful in the software area because it is doing what needs to be learned, and the user starts getting the feel of the software immediately.

CBT has some specific advantages. It is easily transportable to other locations, where it can be used at the convenience of the user. This clearly saves time and money. Also, CBT is self-paced, and users can adapt it somewhat to their own specific requirements. This has its limits. A third, important advantage of CBT is that it is frequently supplied by a vendor specific to a software package. This makes it an ideal method of training for those applications where the CBT package is proven.

CBT training in data retrieval, data manipulation, and fourth-generation languages should be limited to the basics that are needed to get started, to retrieve information, to edit data, and to write reports. The advanced features and options should be learned by most users in actual practice and experimentation. CBT then becomes very cost-effective. Complex packages can be introduced without preparing trainers for them. Analysts can start rapidly on specific packages for their own needs. If CBT is limited to those who are already computer literate, one session of the training program should be enough to get them started doing useful work.

Video Instruction.

Instructional courses on tape for presentation on a video display screen are particularly useful for teaching concepts to individuals or small groups. The video display machines can be set up in a small classroom, or taken on a cart to an individual office. A variety of tapes can be made available, and they can be scheduled for several different groups in a day if a person is available to see that the tapes are properly rewound and in good order. Video presentations are attention-holding, and are paced for a fixed period.

Some video instruction comes in multimedia packages, with

texts, worksheets, and screen examples. These can be useful if only a few people are to be trained, but they are not as effective as having a stand-up teacher direct the same multimedia group of aids. Some video teaching can be interesting, and can include techniques for holding attention. Technical video is the same as the attention-holding commercial video, however, and is a completely passive process. It may penetrate into the minds of users, or it may just leave an impression.

Self-Teaching Books.

Books and manuals that step through a subject at the student's own pace, with examples, worksheets, and answer responses, have a definite place in the information services library. They allow training to be sent to remote users. They are low cost, and can be distributed at the end user's convenience. They can be reviewed rapidly as to content and approach. They can be taken home for indefinite periods. Their disadvantages are that their answers are fixed and simplistic, and they are hard to modify.

Many analysts are sufficiently motivated to handle self-teaching books effectively, and have schedules so tight that the books offer their only means of taking a course. They can be read during lunchtime, while commuting, or at any available moment. They can be referred to as the user steps through an actual problem on the microcomputer.

Product Vendor Training.

Specific training courses in the products that vendors sell are frequently offered at low cost to customers. These may use any of the types of training outlined above. They vary tremendously, however, from excellent to mere sales pitches. The preferred use of vendor training is to train your own trainers. Most vendors are prepared to give a few people in-depth courses in the use of the products they sell. They will show how best to demonstrate the products, and they will describe where you can find technical information in their manuals. No major product should be acquired without asking the vendors to give a few sessions of training to the training staff itself.

Commercially Available Training.

All the varieties of training listed above are available commercially through product vendors, training companies, associations, and individuals—at a price. Acquiring training capabilities from outside is a reasonable approach, and the price may not be higher than providing it from the inside. The outside vendors can work with efficient delivery of their service and multiple customers. They have the great advantage of bringing to the training sessions the experiences that they have picked up in varied situations. Their materials are preprepared, and they can work on tight schedules. They tend to lend an air of authority and urgency to their presentations. Many organizations use outside consultants to handle their training load. It can be efficient, and the cost is defined.

5.9 SECURITY CONSIDERATIONS

When new groupings of individuals are developing application systems, they are frequently unaware of the details of the security policies that have long been followed by systems development. It is important that they be given information about the security concerns and control methods of the organization. If necessary, part of the training for the introduction of CASE methods should include training in security methods that are applicable. Since CASE introduces some new approaches, new security policies may be indicated. Since CASE has highly automated transformations of the data and processes, the systems themselves can offer considerable help in enforcing security rules.

If new applications are being built in user departments, the issue of the security of their data and the use of corporate data must be addressed. If the data used are wholly within a single department, that department will be able to make most of the decisions relative to security control, but must always be aware of controls that are mandated by corporate. If the application uses corporate data, and has access to central data files, whatever security controls the corporation deems necessary must be applied. The general security considerations will not be detailed here, but the security of the data will be emphasized, as CASE systems center on data. The general considerations are available in many texts and manuals.

There are a number of considerations relative to general physical security, personnel security, systems and software security, computer operations security, and data communications security that should be brought to the attention of the CASE team. The general physical security considerations will include having adequate physical security measures in place around the computer room, and having adequate control and protection for the building around it. Protection will include management of the inventories, access control, fire protection, smoke and water protection, environmental controls, and electrical power supply backup.

Personnel controls are generally administrative controls, including the establishment of an organization with position descriptions, plus policies and procedures related to security. Standards should be set, and performance should be measured. Attention should be paid to personnel selection, testing, and training.

Systems and software security considerations include adequate control in all phases of the system development life cycle for CASE, and formal programs of management involvement and control. Data management controls must be adequate to maintain the integrity of the data, and will be discussed further in the following section. Systems and programming documentation must be protected.

Computer operations security and control start with adequate instructions to the operators, and a set of standards, procedures, and documentation prepared and in place. Data controls should be maintained throughout the processing cycle. Backup and recovery procedures must be established, documented, and controlled. Operating supplies must be appropriately controlled.

Data communications is a particularly vulnerable security area, and will be further discussed. Most end-user applications today are communications oriented, and the capability of various people accessing files must be examined. It is a particularly critical area for an organization concerned about the possibilities of theft of assets or services, intrusion with intent to defraud, or the infliction of disastrous damage. Security measures must be taken at several levels.

Data Network Security

There are particular security problems related to on-line, telecommunications, and real-time systems that have long been understood by information services, and must be reevaluated when departmental applications are brought on-line in a network. This is particularly necessary when there is direct access to the mainframe computer. All levels of security measures should be reviewed from the point of view of retaining management control over vital and important information. This is not a matter of the technical and engineering review of the information network. It is simply a matter of retaining the necessary control over the data in the organization.

The security problems in the use of data are based on common law and common sense. It is easy to break into many networks when microcomputers and terminals are provided. It is also easy to determine if break-ins have occurred. The idea of "hacking," or simply breaking into data files for the sake of the accomplishment and to see if there is anything interesting there, has become commonplace. In many cases it may pose a threat to the organization, however. Some actions commonly taken by computer users are simply against the common law. Therefore, those responsible for maintaining the data files must use common sense, and make it difficult for others to destroy, change, or manipulate data for personal satisfaction or profit.

There are a number of particular aspects of security of data that should be analyzed by the end user or appropriate security personnel. The importance of these aspects will be individual to each organization, but they all should be considered. They are:

- *Use of proprietary software:* Most software used in business is proprietary; it has a copyright protection. This protection is difficult to enforce, but, at times, the owners may get proof of violations. It is important to advertise the software package copyrights, and to do no illegal copying. This problem is difficult to control except through explicit publication of the laws involved and reliance on the ethics of the employees.

- *Respect for privacy:* The privacy laws and rules are realistically required to prevent individuals from being hurt. Not only must data with private information be controlled, but the concept of the misuse of private data must be publicized.

- *Diskette management:* Users frequently do not have a sense of the importance of the information that they have assembled on their easily transportable diskettes. In most organizations, diskettes simply lie around on desk tops. Aspects of diskette management should be part of the initial training of all end users.

- *Communications security:* The problems of security in a communications network are complex, and controls are frequently breached, both inadvertently and intentionally. All end users who communicate sensitive data should be alerted to the weaknesses involved. In some cases, when security is particularly important, the use of encryption systems should be considered.

- *Disaster backup and recovery:* End users frequently become highly dependent upon the data files that they have created and stored in their microcomputers. They must be alerted to the real possibilities that a local disaster—fire, theft, or electronic problems—can destroy their files. The simple actions to take in order to provide backup and recovery in the event of a disaster should be explained to them.

Data communications is frequently the most critical area for an organization concerned about possibilities of theft of assets or services, intrusion with intent to defraud, or the inflicting of disastrous damage. For this reason, the security measures to be taken should be at all levels: from locks and guards to systems and program measures.

The sources of information needed to review data communications security include:

- Configuration of the data communications network.
- Communications hardware: list and details.
- Communications software: list and details.
- Usage of the data communications network, such as:

    –origination and destination locations

    –frequency and times of calls

    –average and peak data rates

- Applications for which data communications facilities are used.
- Public services used for communication.
- Reports on reliability experience.
- Security measures that have been taken.

The following checklist, Figure 61, is provided as an introduction to many of the aspects of security analysis of network systems. It can be used as a screening review of the security measures in place or being considered. It helps indicate normal practice under good control. Negative responses do not necessarily indicate a security problem. They simply indicate areas that should be investigated further.

Controlling Database Activities

The introduction of a database management system has a stabilizing effect on the database. It provides a central access point to the data, and all requests for and changes in the data are performed by the system. This degree of control facilitates the management of data and promotes integrity and privacy. In addition, the improved integrity promotes more intensive use of the data and increases its value as an asset to the organization.

The numerous features of a database management system are provided to the user through a common interface. A common data definition approach allows multiple users to have simultaneous access to the same database, and the system provides all of its capabilities to each database defined. The database management system thus facilitates the interaction among people, machines, and data.

The goal of database integrity has a pervasive effect on the database administration functions. Although integrity protection is never completely achieveable (neither the technology nor the resources are available), there are several integrity controls that can be invoked by the database administrator to achieve an effective level of integrity. These controls range from the preventive measures of data definition control through the assurance measures of backup and recovery. Examples of some of the most prominent procedures that a database administrator uses to achieve database control include the following:

- *Control over the data definition* ensures that the data conforms to its definition and that conformance is maintained through the life of the data.
- *Access control* protects the data from access by unauthorized persons or for unauthorized purposes. Some form of restricted ac-

Item No.	Item	Yes	No	N/A	Comments
1.	Is there a configuration chart showing: a. Location of micros and terminals? b. Number of lines? c. Types of lines? d. Location of modems? e. Types of modems (by manufacturer/model)? f. Distance of lines? g. Branches off the main lines? h. Locally developed software?				
2.	Is there a written procedure for what to do in case of an emergency for: a. The lines? b. The modems? c. The micros and terminals?				
3.	Are there personnel trained in emergency procedures in the user departments?				
4.	Are lines switchable in case one or more of them are down: a. Automatically? b. Manually?				
5.	Has the scattering and loss of source documents been discussed with the auditors, and has consideration been given to audit trails?				
6.	Are the telecommunications systems critical enough to warrant the use of a multiprocessor environment?				
7.	Are specific micros designated "security" computers?				
8.	Do the "security" computers never operate in the unattended mode?				
9.	Is secure teleprocessed information transmitted on leased or dedicated lines?				

Item No.	Item	Yes	No	N/A	Comments
10.	If secure teleprocessed information is on dial-up lines, are checks made on access to it?				
11.	Are identification codes, passwords, or key words used, including terminal ID and operator ID?				
12.	Are these codes changed frequently?				
13.	Is there documented control of these codes, or other security features in the teleprocessing system?				
14.	Is access to the system restricted to certain levels of employees?				
15.	Are there locks on the security computers when not in use?				
16.	Can master files be updated only from selected microcomputers?				
17.	Is sufficient audit trail material retained in sensitive programs?				
18.	Is sufficient data retained to ensure that nothing is lost during outages?				
19.	Can individual records be reconstructed if they are accidentally lost in sensitive programs?				
20.	Is there computer response to check the input in systems that update files?				
21.	Are all communication junction and terminal boxes locked?				

Item No.	Item	Yes	No	N/A	Comments
22.	Are the junction and terminal boxes included in the periodic security survey?				
23.	Are all security lines within buildings secured by conduit?				
24.	Are the building entrance points for communication lines checked periodically for "illegal" breaks?				
25.	Is the system wiring run clear of known sources of noise (e.g., rectifiers, medical equipment, heavy construction equipment, generators, etc.)?				
26.	Are all lines tested periodically to ascertain that they are good?				
27.	Are all lines tested periodically to ascertain that they are not tapped?				
28.	Are signal strength tests performed on the lines routinely?				
29.	Are there written backup procedures at all user sites?				
30.	Are the backup procedures periodically tested?				
31.	Has consideration been given to T/P on a backup machine if the data center goes down?				
32.	Have the programs been tested on both the primary and backup computer?				
33.	Is vital master information duplicated (e.g., routing lists, etc.)?				

Item No.	Item	Response			
		Yes	No	N/A	Comments

34.	Which of the following techniques are utilized to guard against illegal access to storage or data files:
	    a. Table look-up?
	    b. Special labeling?
	    c. Passwords?
	    d. Program structure?
	    e. Complete memory lockout?				

35.	Is message release not possible without the message being complete?				
36.	Are updates to master files or other critical files controlled?				
37.	Are there programmed checks on the updating of files?				

cess is usually required for both privacy and integrity assurance. A regulatory mechanism is required in the database management system so that the database administrator can manage access control.

- *An audit trail* should be maintained by the database administrator to demonstrate that the confidentiality of the data has been maintained. Access is controlled by the same access control mechanism, and its incidence can be controlled by a clear separation of the testing and operational environments of the database.

- *Update control* assures that the user has the appropriate authorization to change data values. There are two levels of concern in update control: data addition and data modification and deletion. In many situations, the need to monitor the modifications and deletions to the database is greater than the need to monitor the additions.

- *Concurrency control* provides database integrity by controlling the concurrent programs which perform the update function. Typically, systems employ some form of lockout mechanism at the file or record level in the database to aid the database administrator in this function.

Database technology introduces new activities into an organization that must be considered for any user application. These activities include the database administration function. As activities and job functions change, so do the risks. While there are many advantages to database technology, there are also risks associated with the use of that technology.

The database is not a single file but, rather, a group of files intertwined into a single organizational structure. This new method of storing data poses the following new or increased risks:

- *Inaccurate or incomplete data entered into the database:* This is a usage risk, meaning that if inaccurate or incomplete data is entered by a single individual into the database, multiple users will rely on that data and thus may make improper business decisions.

- *Data not entered on a timely basis:* The failure to enter data on a timely basis may not be known to other users who rely on the timeliness of that data to make business decisions and thus may make improper decisions.

- *Integrity errors not detected:* The integrity of the database may be lost, but that fact may not be known to the users of the database.

- *Program changes incorrectly performed:* If the programs that process data in a database are incorrect, they may cause errors to occur within the database.

- *Cause of problems unknown:* Failure to provide adequate documentation or problem definition may cause the investigators of that problem to be unable to identify the cause.

- *Broken pointers/chains:* The interconnection between data elements in the subschema may be broken, which results in users not being able to recall from the database the needed data.

- *Parts of database lost during reorganizations:* The reorganization process may fail to include all of the parts in the reorganized database.

Database technology reduces or eliminates some of the risks associated with nondatabase technology. Some of the risks eliminated include the following:

- Redundancy between data in two or more application systems.

- Inconsistency of data between two or more application systems.

- Ability of anyone reading the computer file to view every record and data item on the file.

- Ability of a dedicated application to manipulate data within that application (is eliminated if the database administrator assumes responsibility for the integrity of data within the database).

- Improper decisions made due to untimely or incomplete data (assumes that data within the database is more timely and complete than dedicated applications).

- Lost opportunity due to inability to develop applications on a timely basis (assumes systems analysts and programmers adequately trained in database technology to utilize it effectively in application development).

To minimize the impact of these new and increased risks, new methods of control will be required, and the CASE users must learn about them. Selection and implementation of the appropriate controls ensure both the continued integrity of the database and the achievement of the stated database objectives.

5.10 *DISASTER RECOVERY PLANNING CONSIDERATIONS*

Disaster recovery plans, or contingency action plans, are created to reduce the detrimental consequences of unexpected and undesirable events of any magnitude. The objectives of such plans are to make sufficient agreed-upon preparations, and to design and implement a sufficient set of agreed-upon procedures for responding to any type of disaster in the organization. The purpose of these procedures is to minimize the effect of a disaster upon the operations of the organization. This is an important consideration in CASE work.

Disaster recovery planning is an action to take steps in advance to ensure the continuity of critical business operations if specific capabilities are lost to the organization, such as manufacturing, accounting, or data processing facilities. Procedures must be developed to minimize the effect of disastrous interruptions upon the operations of the organization. The emphasis should be on safeguarding the personnel and the vital assets of the organization, and on ensuring the continued availability of critical services. The objectives of such planning are to make sufficient agreed-upon preparations and to design and implement a sufficient set of agreed-upon procedures for responding to any type of disaster in the organization.

The goals of such contingency planning are to develop the detailed advance plans and arrangements necessary to ensure continuity of the critical functions of the organization. The detailed plans should cover all aspects of the total or partial cessation of any critical operation, such as the destruction of a physical facility or a computer database, in the event of a disaster. Such planning should include the procedures and the availability of equipment and personnel for both automated and manual operations.

The preparations and procedures should be well understood by the staff. The plan should specify the responsibilities to be handled both before and after a disaster event, and document them in a manual distributed to and used by all supervisory personnel. It should define the basic approach, state the assumptions and priorities, and point up areas of particular concern.

In the event of a disaster in any part of the organization, or in facilities critical to its operations, the plan must be workable for activation on short notice. It must encompass all phases of the migration to, and operation at, the backup sites, should that prove necessary. Sections of the plan must be usable for responses to minor emergencies. After initial acceptance of the plan by management, it is important to schedule complete or partial "disaster drills" to activate and test the backup capabilities.

A "disaster" can be considered any security event that can cause a significant disruption in critical operational capability for a period of time that affects the operations of the organization. For maintenance services, a disaster could be an overnight storm. For on-line data processing operations, a disaster could be a few minutes of interruption for any reason. A disaster thus means any situation which leaves a necessary facility in a nonoperative state. A disaster recovery plan is a prepared means for ensuring the timely and orderly restoration of the organization's operating capabilities. It may be called a contingency plan or an emergency management plan.

Emergency procedures to recover from a disaster are written for the most probable occurrence of a serious security event. Security events of lesser magnitude can then be handled at the appropriate level, as a subset of the recovery procedures.

Need for a Disaster Recovery Plan

Disasters of various magnitudes occur frequently in business organizations. Fires, floods, thefts, intentional damage, and other problems are remarkably common. Security measures are employed to prevent or detect such occurrences, and to maintain the smooth operation of the business. Security measures may fail, however, with damaging results to the organization's operations. Disaster recovery plans are, therefore, required to reduce the consequences of the loss of any necessary resources or capabilities to an acceptable level. Such plans are not merely planned responses to major catastrophes; they are created to reduce the detrimental consequences of unexpected or undesirable events of any magnitude.

The greatest probability is, in fact, that the damaging occurrences will be less than catastrophic, and may be confined to smaller areas of the operations. The size and scope of a disaster and its effect on critical operations are often not directly related, however. For example, a relatively small fire in the computer communications area could be quite catastrophic to the overall operations, while the loss of some offices and terminals in a completely destroyed building could be recovered rapidly. Many business operations and the data processing operations are so interconnected that there is need for a disaster recovery plan that covers both the whole operation and any individual parts of it.

Every organization must look at what the consequences of loss of specific critical operations, such as their data processing facilities, could be and then consider their exposure to such events. It is simply good business practice to examine the possibilities of disaster and to estimate the exposure of the business in specific areas. There are three areas of exposure that should be reviewed:

- Financial loss
- Legal responsibility
- Business service interruption

Financial loss: Since most financial operations are now automated, one of the most critical areas of possible disaster loss is the information services operational area. Because of the efficiency, accuracy, speed, and control of data processing methods, organizations are becoming more and more dependent on their information services in normal business operations. The regular, daily operations of large numbers of companies are now completely dependent upon the information flowing from the EDP area. Manufacturing systems, sales and reservation systems, inventory systems, and financial systems, among many others, can no longer revert to manual operations on short notice. An organization's lifeblood information can rapidly dry up if the computer systems break down. This can cause great financial loss to a company and could even destroy its business if proper disaster planning has not been done.

Disaster recovery planning is an action to help prevent financial loss by taking steps in advance to ensure the continuity of critical business processes and information if specific capabilities, such as the computer operations, are lost. It has been estimated that most businesses could survive without EDP for one shift, and probably even one day. By the time three days or a week had passed, however, many businesses would be getting into serious cash flow problems. Within a month, without information services output, most businesses would have serious problems of survival. Few modern companies could remain in business today after three months of EDP loss. Many organizations are highly dependent upon their on-line computer operations to maintain their cash flow.

Business service interruption: The problem of business service interruption does not only include the financial loss discussed above. It can also be deleterious to future relationships with clients. It can affect the public image of the organization for a considerable time. If an organization's business services are abruptly interrupted, for reasons not readily perceived by customers, the long-term effect could be devastating and far more costly than modest preparations for disaster recovery.

If the service is based on a contract with the government, it could well be a contractual requirement that reasonable precautions be planned and taken to maintain the continuity of the service.

It is simply good business practice to make contingency preparations to reduce the consequences of any security event. Management must be confident that their capabilities for day-to-day operation can be depended upon.

Legal responsibility: Management has a legal responsibility to protect the organization's employees, corporate resources, and vital documents. The common interpretation of the Foreign Corrupt Practices Act of 1977 has been that officers of a company are personally responsible if there have not been adequate preparations to meet these legal requirements.

It is also clear that officers of a company, who have not taken the necessary precautions to minimize the effects of a possible disaster, are exposing themselves to the possibility of a legal suit in the event of a disaster striking that causes losses that could have been reduced appreciably.

The Necessary Elements of a Disaster Recovery Plan

The many facets of a disaster recovery plan may be approached individually or as a single project. The completed plan will normally consist of multiple documents, generated at different times by different study groups. Each organization will have its own particular areas of concern and emphasis. Parts of the plan will be descriptive, while other parts will be action steps in the event of an emergency. The major part of typical data processing disaster recovery plans will be the detailed and complex systems programs that must be generated to prepare backup computers for running the operational programs. However, there are six necessary elements for any disaster recovery plan for any operation. They are:

- A risk assessment study and evaluation of the existing security precautions.
- A comprehensive and detailed emergency preparedness and recovery plan.
- Initial response procedures in the event of a disaster.
- Personnel assignments for both preparation and emergency action.
- Preparation of backup resources in the event of a disaster.
- Plan for full recovery of operational capabilities.

Risk Assessment and Security Evaluation.

A risk assessment is essentially a management review of the exposure of the organization to any risks that would appear to be probable, or even possible. There are detailed methods of analyzing the exposure of the organization to risks from the points of view of both probability of occurrence and possible resultant financial loss. Such detailed analyses are time consuming and expensive, however. Most managers will be able to assess their risks by comparing their operations to those where known disasters have occurred, and by making a reasonable judgment as to the value of a disaster recovery plan. They will know the importance of maintaining continuing operations in particular areas of their organization. Any reasonable assessment of their own situation will indicate that some level of disaster recovery planning is absolutely essential.

Although a detailed analytical risk assessment may not be necessary, it is most important to evaluate the security of the organization in detail. This must be done by knowledgeable persons who understand what is to be protected and what methods of protection are feasible and reasonable. The fundamental base for any disaster recovery program is to put a security program in place that will minimize the possibility of the occurrence of a disaster. An initial security evaluation can help indicate to management where problem areas may exist, and how the overall costs of the program may be reduced with a good possibility of safe coverage.

There are many actions that can be taken to prevent "security events" or disasters, to contain the scope of the damage if they occur, and to facilitate rapid recovery of the operations. Security preparations will not be discussed in detail in this report, but it will be assumed that adequate security measures have been taken previously. This is the basis of an effective disaster recovery plan.

Detailed Disaster Recovery Plan.

The results of all activities in disaster recovery planning should be brought together in a comprehensive and detailed emergency preparedness and recovery plan. This plan should cover all elements of the operations, considered from the standpoint of contingency plans and disaster recovery. It should be a plan of action in the event of a disaster that has been tested, at least in its component parts. Each area of it should be reviewed and approved by the manager who has the responsibility for that area. The document should be agreed upon, and generally accepted, throughout the organization.

The preparation of the detailed disaster recovery plan will only be possible with the cooperation and help of all affected groups in the organization. It cannot be developed by a central team and superimposed upon others without considerable consultation and general agreement. Parts of it will be completely technical and understandable in detail only by the specific group involved with those operations. Others need only receive assurance that such plans will interface acceptably with their own plans. Some parts of the plan will represent legal or financial requirements and it will be absolutely necessary to maintain them under strict control.

All parts of the detailed disaster recovery plan should be prepared, tested, maintained, and reviewed under management control and coordination. Preparation of such a plan is usually a costly and time-consuming project, and it should be handled as a controlled project with routine reporting of its progress to management.

Initial Response Procedures.

At the time of any type of disaster, it is of great benefit to have available to those involved a clearly written, succinct set of operational instructions that outline what steps should be taken immediately, as well as soon thereafter. This set of initial response procedures should be known and understood by responsible management personnel as well as duty operational personnel. They must be documented for rapid and ready access. They must be straightforward to follow if a security event triggers the need for disaster recovery response. All personnel who may be involved should be given training in the initial response procedures and in the actions that they will be expected to take.

The initial response procedures will normally be bound in a relatively small, but easily recognizable volume. They should be given reasonably wide distribution, be readily accessible, and be referred to sufficiently by management to indicate their importance.

Personnel Assignments.

Separate personnel assignments must be made for both the preparation of the disaster recovery plan and the actions to be taken at the time of an emergency. The preparation of a plan will normally have a responsible coordinator. This should be a staff person who has to work across many departmental lines. It is thus necessary that higher management prepare all participating groups for the cooperation that will be necessary. The project must be viewed as an overall organizational project, and both technical and representational participation must be considered mandatory.

Management must also take action to assign specific personnel to positions of responsibility in the event of a disaster, and to give them adequate instructions and training in their assignments. This will be discussed in more detail later in this report.

Preparation of Backup Resources.

Backup resources that will be needed in the event of a disaster must be planned in detail, prepared for use, and tested. These resources will vary from duplicated information stored in safe places, to agreements on possible emergency office assignments, to contracting for disaster recovery backup facilities. These will be discussed in this report. No disaster recovery plan is in place until all necessary backup resources have been dealt with.

Plan for Full Recovery.

The actual emergency disaster recovery plan should always be considered as a temporary expedient. Any organization will want to pass through the backup state and return to normal operation. Thus an essential ingredient of a disaster recovery plan is the section that outlines recovery at the original or alternate site after the disaster has been resolved. The steps to be taken to move from a recovery operation to a permanent site operation are as detailed as the disaster response steps. On the other hand, there will be much less time pressure in the final recovery work, and it will usually be possible to move systematically with tight management control.

Management Involvement

It is obvious that management interest, involvement, and approval are necessary ingredients of any disaster recovery plan that is to be successful. An organization has much at stake if a disaster should occur, and senior management participation in disaster recovery planning should be readily attainable.

A good disaster recovery plan is tailored to your organization.

It is documented and understood, has been approved by all concerned management, and is regularly tested and updated. It need not be complex and costly to put together and maintain. It should be easy to live with during normal operations.

From the management viewpoint, the purpose of a disaster recovery plan is to prepare in advance to ensure the continuity of the business, and of the business information, if critical capabilities are lost. Thus disaster recovery planning, particularly as it is being initiated, is a management rather than a technical issue. It deals with the realities of people, organizational relationships, and special interests. Disaster recovery actions are highly prioritized, and many normal operations are neglected during the period of a disaster. The technical issues will be complex, but management must take the lead and continually assess the technical considerations involved as to their utility.

Figure 62 is a brief checklist that can be used to determine whether your organization has an adequate plan at present. If too many answers are "No," you should work through this report and plan to create an effective disaster recovery plan that is both practical and legally sufficient. This brief checklist is oriented to information processing, since that is one of the more sensitive areas that may be affected by a disaster. Similar general questions should be applied to any other critical area of the organization.

Management must realize that EDP professionals agree there are no secure computers. Many computer operations have fine methods for security in place, and management can be assured that the best possible actions have been taken, but there are always people, electronic failures, and natural disasters that can suddenly disrupt the operations. Management must realistically look at:

- Legal obligations
- Cash flow maintenance
- Customer services
- Competitive advantages
- Production and distribution decisions
- Logistics and operations control
- Purchasing functions and vendor relationships
- Ongoing project control

Item No.	Item	Response		
		Yes	No	Needs Review
1.	Is your disaster recovery plan tailored to your organization?			
2.	Is your plan well documented and understood by the supervisors?			
3.	Has your plan been reviewed by senior management and approved by all responsible managers?			
4.	Are the procedures clear and simple enough for use during an emergency?			
5.	Does your plan include recovery capability details for: a. Data files? b. Computer Hardware? c. Operating system software? d. Application programs? e. Other resources?			
6.	Does your plan cover both individual actions in response to a disaster, and the protection of personnel?			
7.	Are the procedures and responsibilities defined clearly by individual or position?			
8.	Is your plan orderly and up to date?			
9.	Has the plan been tested?			
10.	Has the plan been retested at least annually?			
11.	Do you think your disaster recovery plan is adequate and workable?			

- Branch or agency communications
- Personnel and union relations
- Shareholder and public relations

Management must assess the importance of information and other services to these facets of the business, and then decide the type of effort that should be put into disaster backup of the various critical functions.

Even if contingency plans are documented, kept up to date, disseminated, and tested, and personnel are well trained, there may still be unanticipated or unfamiliar situations that require an emergency response in a difficult time frame. Recognizing this, management should require that personnel who are responsible for security in general, and contingency planning in particular, maintain an awareness of accidents, disasters, emergencies, etc., that have afflicted automated systems in other organizations, in order to minimize the possibility of similar events occurring at their facilities.

One of the better sources of such information is the National Fire Protection Association, Batterymarch Park, Quincy, MA 12269, Telephone: (617) 770-3300. Their statistical department in the Fire Analysis division has developed a set of abstracts describing computer-related fires. They have recorded 200 incidents since 1975. This number is probably low, however, because many organizations suppress such information. These abstracts are available for $55. The importance of this information is that the majority of security incidents of major proportions involve fires. Of course, in addition to the fires, there are many more incidents involving floods, wind damage, and bombings. The technical literature has described some of these.

Management should also recognize that in some situations personnel will not have time to stop and read the procedures. Even well-trained personnel who have been active in periodic testing of contingency planning procedures cannot be expected to memorize all of them. Although it is obvious that more frequent testing will improve employee familiarity with the plan and readiness to handle emergency situations, it is also evident that additional costs will be incurred. One of the major cost–benefit considerations in contingency planning is balancing adequacy of testing against the cost.

CHAPTER **6**

How to Evaluate and Select CASE Products

Overview

*T*he systematic selection of CASE tools and methodologies helps greatly in optimizing their benefits to the organization. Aids are given in selecting and acquiring the most acceptable CASE software packages, based on the determined requirements. The use of checklists for such purposes has proven especially valuable. CASE software varies widely, but there are a number of specific CASE considerations that are listed in checklist format. A comprehensive, proven, and useful checklist is provided for aid in the selection of CASE tools.

Some of the advantages of using software packages for CASE work are outlined. The CASE software acquisition decision process is reviewed.

The relationship of the analysts to software vendors is discussed, and the principal types of software package characteristics to be reviewed are noted. A checklist of the general software package considerations to be reviewed is provided, which may be sufficient for smaller CASE packages.

A number of detailed, proven checklists are supplied for the evaluation of software packages in eight related management and technical areas. The information from these checklists can be used in determining whether packages meet your requirements, and

335

in comparing packages in a documented, objective way. The use of metrics in software package comparison is described in detail, and their value is discussed.

6.1 THE SYSTEMATIC SELECTION OF SOFTWARE

The objective of a systematic selection of CASE tools and methodologies is to optimize their benefits to the organization. This is the same objective as in the acquisition of any other type of software package. Careful selection to acquire the most acceptable application is important, as it has an effect on the usefulness, interoperability, connectivity, ease of learning, and ease of use of the software package.

Select and acquire the most acceptable CASE software packages, based on the determined requirements and following organizational policies and procedures. The proven technique is to follow a planned, evolutionary implementation of selected CASE software packages, testing them extensively, and learning about their use. In the initial stages of CASE experimentation, it is usually best to start with a limited subset of CASE applications. Target these at specific pilot projects that have a high probability of success. These should be profitable and readily accomplished projects. The staff must devote sufficient time to the projects to ensure a good probability of success. The final choice could be a complete CASE environment, such as the Information Engineering Facility, or it could simply be a portfolio of tested CASE tools that can be interconnected through the database.

The early testers and users of CASE tools should be reasonable expert analysts so that they can make an experienced judgment on the use of the tools, and can then teach others how to use the tools selected. There should not be too many alternative tools acquired. A relatively stable portfolio of CASE tools allows the technical staff to build up their expertise with a few packages, and thereby increase their own productivity.

The more selective and better suited the CASE applications portfolio is, the more valuable it will be to the organization. The imposition of standards for a limited portfolio is a useful service.

Requirements Definition

It is a common and dangerous mistake to think that the initial planning and requirements definition phases can be shortened by the purchase of CASE application packages. Although such packages are frequently supplied with a list of the requirements which they satisfy, and although these requirements may look similar to the specified needs, there must still be a careful definition of what functions the CASE package must accomplish before any decision to acquire it can reasonably be made. It is not a small job to determine the requirements for CASE tools, because there is a wide variety of functions to obtain, from small systems to large systems and networking, and from new systems to the reengineering of the old COBOL portfolio of applications. If the job is done well, there may be a list of hundreds of requirements over the full range of life-cycle support. On the other hand, if the job is done well and objective requirements are known, the list of dozens of possible vendors can always be rapidly cut down to three or four, which can then be put through an evaluation and selection process.

In establishing requirements, all the areas that CASE should support in the reasonable future should be addressed. Do not limit the analysis to a specific major project, or specific pilot projects. Emphasize what the package can handle, rather than how it does the work. You are looking for a product, not a mode of operation. There are two sets of requirements to be developed:

- *Necessary* package characteristics, which are usually at a higher level, defining the direction and mode of operation. There are usually less than six such characteristics. They are the requirements that are used for a first-pass "screening" of products, and that will cut down the field to a very few candidates for a detailed product review.

- *Desirable* package characteristics, defining all the detailed system requirements that can be thought of, but may not be absolutely necessary. These can be used for detailed product evaluations. As will be seen in the subsequent checklists in this section, they are best grouped by category, such as:

  –Architecture or hardware requirements

–Database considerations

–Project management considerations

The statement of the requirements should be precise. When you are dealing with packages for a specific subject—CASE—any or all of the questions should be considered for rewording so that they apply directly to the CASE situation.

The statement of the requirements should include the "must nots" and undesirable package characteristics, as well as the "musts" and desirable characteristics. Be careful of the checklist wordings, however, so that no one is confused with a mixture of desirable and undesirable responses, both checked in the Yes column. Reword the "must not" questions so that the reader sees that it is correct not to have that characteristic.

The subject of weighting factors is discussed in Section 6.7, "Use of Metrics in Software Package Comparison." Be careful with them, because they are not real numbers. In weighting factors, one analyst's 2 can easily be another analyst's 6. Read the section on the use of metrics in software comparison. Metrics can be very useful, but should be handled carefully. The comparison is not a popular TV poll, but a technical analysis.

The Systematic Selection of Software

In brief, the process involved in the systematic selection of software includes:

1. Establish the *functional requirements* of the CASE software desired.

2. Search the literature and other sources for possible software candidates.

3. Use the appropriate checklists in this section to review possible software packages against the requirements that have been agreed upon. The analysts involved should go over the checklists, and agree upon which to use and which questions to use. Possibly additional questions should be added that are specific to the organization, or considered important in the selection process. Handle the checklist usage systematically, and keep all answers for comparison and for the record.

4. Screen the available CASE products that appear to most nearly meet the agreed criteria against the *necessary requirements* that have been developed.

5. Evaluate the few remaining CASE products against the detailed *desirable requirements* that have been developed. Use simple metrics if desired.

6. Select a few CASE products for *demonstrations*, vendor visits, and *hands-on trial.* Use common test data that fit the requirements.

7. Have a relatively small "CASE Tool Selection Team" use the tools, review the checklist analyses, and talk to the vendors; then recommend a selection. Rely more on consensus than on the metrics scoring.

8. Have the full CASE team and involved managers consider the results of the analyses and selection, including:

   - The *cost* to purchase and implement the package
   - The *time* to learn and implement the package
   - The experience and strength of the *vendor*
   - The *risks* associated with each product alternative

9. Prepare a *recommendation* to present to responsible management, reporting all the analyses as an appendix to the recommendation.

Gap Analysis

The systematic selection of CASE software is seldom for a single product or for the "final" solution. It is usually a stepwise process in which early tools are tested, an integrated tool set is installed, and then other tools are added. The analysts who are reviewing the selection must perform a gap analysis to determine how far the management of the organization wants to move in the test phase, the installation phase, and in subsequent development. It is an analysis of the real gap in capability, technical knowledge, training, possible coordination between departments, and budget limitations. A gap analysis determines how wide the gap is:

- Can it be crossed with the acquisition of one or more systems?
- Should interim products be acquired as "stepping stones"?

- Is there a product that can be implemented incrementally, to move in the desired strategic direction?
- Is it necessary to also select "fall-back" products?

A gap analysis also determines how difficult the gap is to cross:

- Can sufficient people be trained to use CASE in the planned time?
- Can interim products provide any immediate benefits?

6.2   THE SELECTION OF CASE TOOLS AND METHODOLOGIES

CASE software is widely varied. It covers simple CASE tools as well as complex CASE environments. All the regular questions need to be asked about CASE tools, such as usability, controls, languages, modifiability, expandibility, cost, vendor stability, cost, etc., that are asked about all software packages, plus a number of specific questions that are directly related to CASE work. Figure 63 gives a representative list of CASE-specific questions. It should be carefully reviewed before it is used to be sure the questions are applicable to the CASE work to be done. After this CASE-specific list, this section moves into considerable, helpful detail in the analysis and selection of any software product, including CASE products, support products, and application packages.

Figure 63 has a number of detailed questions. Some are more important than others. The most desirable features to be looked for in CASE products, will, of course, depend upon the environment in which the products will be used. There are certain features, however, that are generally considered to be most important in CASE products. These are:

- *Support for the entire application development life cycle*, which will include the automatic generation of most of the executable code from graphical specifications. Some products support only low-level code generation functions, such as the generation of the COBOL data division. For most efficient development and best performance, the front end of the CASE tool should be tightly integrated with an automatic COBOL generator.

FIGURE 63. The selection of CASE tools.

Item No.	Item	Response			
		Yes	No	N/A	Comments
	General and Management Considerations				
1.	Has the vendor had several years of experience in developing CASE products?				
2.	Is the vendor moving towards an open architecture with the ability to share file formats with other CASE tools?				
3.	Does the tool interface with other CASE tools that are being considered?				
4.	Can the tool generate programs that span a range of hardware systems?				
5.	Does the CASE tool contain or permit the capability of separating design, analysis, development, and testing responsibilities?				
6.	Does the CASE tool interface with the project management system that is used?				
7.	Will the vendor modify the CASE tool at the screen level to satisfy your requirements?				
8.	Does the CASE tool integrate with a relational DBMS or information repository system?				
9.	Does the vendor have useful plans for extending the functionality of the CASE tool?				
10.	Does the CASE tool, or integrated set of CASE tools, provide full coverege of the application development life cycle?				

FIGURE 63. (Cont.)

Item No.	Item	Yes	No	N/A	Comments
	CASE Planning Features				
11.	Does the CASE planning module interface with the corporate strategic planning model representation with comprehensive capabilities?				
12.	Does the CASE planning module interface readily with the business unit and information services planning systems?				
13.	Does the system have, or interface with, a requirements definition prototyping system?				
	CASE Hardware Environment				
14.	Does the tool run on an IBM PS/s with OS/2?				
15.	Does the tool run on an IBM PC/XT or PC/AT, or fully compatible machine, in a PC-DOS environment?				
16.	Does the tool run on an IBM Series/370 mainframe computer?				
17.	Does the tool run on a DEC VAX or microVAX computer				
18.	Does the tool run on engineering workstations, such as Apollo, Sun, or IBM RT PC super micros?				
	Range of CASE Life Cycle Coverage				
19.	Is the tool applicable to the *analysis phase* of the development life cycle, including feasibility analysis and requirements analysis?				
20.	Is the tool applicable to the *design phase* of the development life cycle, including both preliminary design and detailed design?				

FIGURE 63. (Cont.)

Item No.	Item	Response			
		Yes	No	N/A	Comments
21.	Is the tool applicable to the *construction phase* of the development life cycle, including procedural logic, coding, and unit testing?				
22.	Is the tool applicable to the *installation phase* of the development life cycle, including integrated testing, production testing, and system installation?				
23.	Is the tool applicable to the *maintenance phase* of the development life cycle, including changing of the specifications, systems reengineering, retesting, and reinstallation?				
24.	Does the tool support the requirements of a *project team,* including: a. A department-level repository? b. Consolidation of all specifications c. Global analysis of the consolidated specifications? d. Project management support? e. Change management support? f. Security and disaster recovery features?				
	Components of the CASE Tool				
25.	**Diagramming:** Does the CASE tool provide a set of diagramming facilities that allow the analysts to define the system in graphical form?				
26.	**Local Repository:** Is the application stored in a PC repository in both graphical and abstract forms?				
27.	Is the repository a knowledge base for all management and control information about the application as well as the graphs and data?				

FIGURE 63. (Cont.)

Item No.	Item	Yes	No	N/A	Comments
		Response			
28.	**Central repository:** Is there a central mainframe repository that is shared by all analysts working on the same project?				
29.	**Design analyzer:** Does the tool set contain a design analyzer that detects errors such as inconsistencies and incompleteness at all levels				
30.	**Code generator:** Does the tool set generate 100 percent of the code automatically from the graphical specifications?				
31.	**Expert system rules:** Does the tool use a knowledge base that contains the expert system rules?				
	CASE Analysis and Design Features				
32.	Can the CASE tool generate physical design specifications from logical design specifications?				
33.	Does it generate design specification reports automatically?				
34.	Does the tool have the facilities for maintaining the design as well as maintaining the systems?				
35.	Does the tool interface with the corporate DBMS in a way that design and development specifications can be entered and maintained?				
36.	Are the design and development specifications transmitted in such a way that they are reusable by other systems?				

FIGURE 63. (Cont.)

Item No.	Item	Yes	No	N/A	Comments
37.	Do the automatic development and code generation features of the CASE tool provide for calling for existing routines and for customization of the generic code to fit custom specifications?				
38.	Can the CASE tool read procedure and source libraries and create development specifications for existing systems that were not developed under CASE?				
39.	Can the graphical features of the CASE tool explode design diagrams and dictionary specifications to a reasonable depth?				
	CASE Diagrams Supported				
40.	Does the CASE tool support the creation and manipulation of the following diagrams? a. Entity-relationship diagrams? b. Data structure diagrams? c. Process dependency diagrams? d. Process action diagrams? e. Dialog flow diagrams? f. Procedure action diagrams? g. Other diagrams that may be required?				
	Methodologies Supported				
41.	Is the product an *information engineering* methodology, from business models to the application systems?				

FIGURE 63. (Cont.)

Item No.	Item	Yes	No	N/A	Comments
42.	Does the tool support the diagramming specifications using the *Yourdon* and *DeMarco* structured methodology?				
43.	Does the tool support the diagramming specifications using the *Gane* and *Sarson* structured methodology?				
44.	Does the tool support the structured diagrams using the *Jackson* structured methodology?				
45.	Does the tool support other structured methodologies that may be required?				
	Screens and Graphics				
46.	Does the tool provide *screen designer* or *painter* that is easy to learn, and generates screen panels, menu dialogs, and report formats?				
47.	Does the system display graphics in *color?*				
48.	Does the system support a *mouse* device?				
49.	Does the system permit the display of multiple graphics *windows* on the screen?				
50.	Can each window be used to display a different view of the specifications?				
51.	Can the CASE tool execute with *windowing?*				

FIGURE 63. (Cont.)

Item No.	Item	Yes	No	N/A	Comments
	Other CASE Tool Considerations				
52.	Does the CASE tool use an integrated *relational DBMS* to manipulate data entities in the central repository?				
53.	Does the CASE tool incorporate a high-level *fourth-generation language?*				
54.	Does the CASE tool integrate well with a *Local Area Network?*				
55.	Does the CASE tool provide on-line interfaces to enter and modify *dictionary definitions?*				
56.	Does the CASE tool provide for automatic logging of design changes?				
57.	Does the CASE environment provide for version and generation contol?				
58.	Does the CASE tool automatically generate design, operations, and user *documentation?*				
59.	Does the CASE tool have *word processing* capabilities?				
60.	Does the CASE tool make use of *expert systems?*				
61.	Does the CASE tool capture physical usage information?				
62.	Does the CASE tool provide for production system simulation?				

- *Use of an information repository* to store both the forms of the diagrams and the meaning of the diagrams in abstract form. The specifications should be convertible automatically from one consistent graphical view to another. The repository should provide an information system about the data, control the physical use of the data, and systematically gather all requirements and changes.

- *Support for at least a basic set of diagramming techniques* that represent the software system in software engineering. The minimum should be entity-relationship diagrams, process decomposition diagrams, process dependency diagrams, data flow diagrams, and process action diagrams. It must include rigorous completeness and consistency checking, and should be based on a formal information model. The product should allow flexible conversion from one graphical format to another.

- *Availability of most of the product components* shown in Figure 41, "Typical Components of CASE Products." If it is simply a front-end CASE product, of course, only the applicable components should be sought.

- *Availability of the product on the workstation to be used*, whether this be the IBM PS/2 or a DEC MicroVAX.

- *Networking capability permitting the interconnection of multiple workstations*, and facilitating access to corporate mainframe databases.

- *Central mainframe information repository* shared by all in the network, with version control, project management facilities, global consistency and completeness checking, security and disaster recovery controls, and so on.

- *Open software architecture*, including MS-DOS compatibility, to make available the many MS-DOS compatible support programs that are available in the workstation environment.

- *Compatibility with any widely used software facilities* that are available in the particular environment, including the database management systems (frequently DB2), utilities, application generators, and COBOL generators.

- *Support for a rigorous, structured methodology* that integrates planning, specification, design, and coding.

- *Possible support for recent methodologies* that may be adopted.

- *Support for prototyping tools* that integrate well with the other systems using a well-structured, high-level procedural language.

- *Use of a well-defined life-cycle process* so that all follow the same process, and improvements in development can be measured.

- *Useful human factoring*, including the elimination of complex command mnemonics, intuitive system operation, on-line diagnostic and HELP facilities, and subsecond response to on-line interaction.

General and Management Considerations

It is important that a vendor have CASE experience unless you wish to enter into a package development agreement over time. Also, the present trend is towards an open architecture philosophy for CASE because of the many different tools and levels of tools. Moving deeper into the use of CASE, there must be a smooth way of integrating a variety of tools across the whole development cycle. When CASE manufacturers have hierarchical integration agreements with other manufacturers for exclusive architectures, the products may be completely acceptable, but the future choices of tools will be limited to those particular manufacturers. There should be effective interfaces to a wide variety of CASE design and programming tools over a full methodology, with a single, comprehensive, shared dictionary.

Another important aspect of the generality of CASE tools is the ability to generate programs across the range of computers, from mini to micro to large central computers. Since much of the development work will probably be on microcomputers, this feature is critical today.

The use of CASE tools needs to be managed. They should contain or permit the capability of separating analysis, design, development, and testing job responsibilities for effective management of the overall project. The larger tools may contain project management features that produce reports on the progress of the effort. Any CASE tools should readily interface to the more common project management systems so that they can be tracked in the overall system.

Another aspect of CASE tools to be considered is whether they can be customized or modified to fit your existing standards and procedures relative to screen design. There may be a need to add or delete menu options, or modify the style of the data entry screens.

Of great importance is the ability of the CASE tool to integrate with a relational DBMS or specific information repository system. They are fundamental in supplying tool integration capabilities, and are almost a necessity for sharing information and reusable code across the CASE development functions.

The vendor's plans to extend the functionality of the CASE tool is of great importance because of the rapid movement in the CASE field. Look first for the key, required capabilities and features. If the CASE tool is good, it may then be worth acquiring if the vendor has realistic plans for future development of the tool.

Case tools should be readily integrated into coverage of the full application development life cycle, and include capabilities of interfacing with corporate strategic planning at the beginning, review and audit at the end, and management control over the whole cycle, such as interfaces with audit tools.

CASE Planning Features

The fundamental CASE planning feature is the capability of ready interface with the corporate strategic planning model and system. Also important is the capability of providing information to the business unit operational planning system, and the same for information services.

Requirements definition prototyping is a powerful tool for CASE work, which may be part of the integrated CASE tool, or may be a separate tool that can interface with the CASE tool. Prototyping is preferably handled during the analysis and design phase, but in some tools it is added into the development phase. Most prototyping is for requirements definition, even down to the screen level. Aspects of screen design, for example, may be left to the development phase.

CASE Hardware Environment

If the hardware in the CASE environment has already been selected, then only one of these responses will be acceptable. Some organizations run CASE on departmental computers, however, or are setting up a CASE operation relatively independent of the central computer operation. In either approach, there are always a number of compatible terminals and specialized workstations to be considered.

Range of CASE Life-Cycle Coverage

These questions simply point up the fact that a CASE tool set with a variety of tools will have some programs useful in a variety of the life-cycle phases. It is worth noting these facts, and determining whether the full development life cycle is being covered with a variety of tools or not.

Components of the CASE Tool

The subject of components of CASE tools was covered in Chapter 4. These questions again point to the need for categorizing the CASE tools and being sure where they fit in the CASE effort. It is worth distinguishing and clearly understanding the functions of the information repository that will be on the PC or workstation, and the functions that will be on the central computer. The repository should be a knowledge base for the application, rather than just a data dictionary.

CASE Analysis and Design Features

The trend in CASE tools is for the systems to automatically generate physical design specifications from logical design specifications. There is direct conversion of the logical design diagrams into the physical graphical displays. In any event, the tool should generate design specification reports automatically to document the system. It is at this point that some CASE tools have the capability of finding and noting flaws in the design.

The CASE designs should be maintained automatically as the systems are being maintained. Individuals tools may not have the capability, but integrated systems should have an interface between the CASE design and development systems so that modifications to design specifications that are entered and passed through to the development phase will be retained as information that can be reported. Design modules will be in the DBMS and will be recoverable and usable just as system modules are. This will be a much stronger interface between design and development, with the possibility of passing information both ways.

Most systems will depend upon the corporate DBMS environment. It is helpful to be able to enter the design and development specifications in the corporate database, and to be able to use the design and development specifications of applications that are there. These design and development specifications should be transmitted in such a way that they are reusable by other systems. Just as reusable code is one of the key advantages of CASE systems, so also should reusable design be available as a productivity and quality advantage. Design sharing is an important concept for group development work, which should be supported by the tool for larger development efforts.

The automatic development and code generation of the CASE environment should be readily able to call for existing routines for reuse, and also should provide for customization of such routines and other generic code to fit the specific requirements of the system to be generated.

To aid in maintaining existing systems, the systems can be fully reengineered, or the CASE tool can possibly read procedure and source libraries and produce CASE specifications for components of the existing system. This can be of great help in the maintenance of systems that were not developed under CASE. Look for several different levels of reverse engineering in different CASE tools.

Most CASE tools are based on graphical methodologies for the system design. The graphical diagrams, and their representative elements within the dictionary, should be able to be exploded to lower, more specific levels.

CASE Diagrams Supported

CASE diagrams are discussed in Section 4. These questions are simply a checklist that should be adapted to contain the set of CASE diagramming tools that is required in a particular environment.

Methodologies Supported

These questions are of interest only to those systems analysts who are concerned that specific methodologies may offer advantages in their situation. Most organizations will probably accept the methodology offered in a CASE tool if that tool appears to be the best from other viewpoints.

Screens and Graphics

These are critical concerns if there are particular needs expressed in the requirements, because the screens and graphics are the fundamental interface with the system and the analyst or end user. The facilities on the screens must definitely be discussed with user representatives before selections are made.

Other CASE Tool Features

The automatic logging of design changes is of considerable importance for larger CASE efforts when a number of people are involved in the design work and there is some turnover of personnel. It is necessary to leave a trail of the design changes so that it can be followed back if necessary, and so it can be checked against the specifications. This feature should be extended so that it provides for version and generation control of the CASE-developed systems.

Other CASE Tool Considerations

These considerations have been relegated to the end of the checklist only because of their miscellaneous nature. These questions should be carefully reviewed, as any of the points noted may be important in the selection of a CASE tool.

Windowing is useful in CASE work in that it allows for multiple portions of the design to be displayed simultaneously. This aids in the explosion of the design.

Design documentation is automatically entered into the dictionary by most CASE tools. It should be available in a form that can be printed out for operations and user documentation from the dictionary for documentation manuals. Also, the tool should have the capability of analyzing the documentation for completeness and consistency. This comes from the nature of the methodological rules. The analysis should be able to detect where the design dictionary entries are incomplete through the rules of structured methodology.

CASE tools should contain word processing capabilities because of the automatic generation of the documentation. It should be possible to produce the documentation in a printable form immediately. Tools with the best word processing capabilities have effective interfaces with well-tested word processing systems.

In automated design, automated development, and automated documentation, there are many choices that must be made. Simple choices can be made automatically by the program. Many choices can be made manually, by displaying the choice on a screen. The most effective way of making choices both automatically and knowledgeably is by the inclusion of expert system rules in the CASE tool. Clearly, future CASE environments will make much use of expert systems. Some tools use expert systems today. It takes time to build up a large set of expert system rules that will truly be able to make many of the development decisions automatically over a wide range of problems.

The capture of physical usage information is another function of CASE tools that has been started, but is expected to be expanded considerably in the future. It is of great help in planning and management.

There are a number of other functions of CASE tools that are being offered simply, or experimentally, but that will soon become standard, desired functions. Among these are:

- Production system simulation
- Technology selection and modeling
- User specification

6.3 THE ADVANTAGES OF USING SOFTWARE PACKAGES FOR CASE

CASE systems are the culmination of many years of system development efforts, and their structure and design are understood by many. Some companies have preferred to design and develop their own CASE tools. Other companies have systems staffs that are already too busy, and so have preferred to purchase their CASE tools, selecting a variety of software packages that are on the market. The choice is individual. This section reviews a number of considerations in making the choice.

Commercial software packages are usually different from internally developed software in that they are defined within tight boundaries that have been specified by the developer or vendor. They should also not be in a continuing process of uncontrolled change. In the classical systems development life cycle, internal software products should be produced as neat, finished packages in the same way as the purchased packages, but this is seldom the case. Software packages have a number of distinct characteristics, each of which will offer advantages in certain cases but may not meet requirements in other cases. Some of these characteristics and advantages are:

a. *Standard products:* To gain cost advantages in the competitive market, software packages must be designed to meet average requirements and then standardized.

Features	– Use of standard languages.
	– Developed for commonly used computers
	– Modular construction
Disadvantages	– Software packages are frequently not an exact fit to the business procedures or requirements of an organization.
Advantages	– Software packages are far cheaper to buy and install than the internally developed systems.

b. *Generality of specifications:* The developers of software packages want the largest possible market for their product. They therefore try to generalize specifications to industry-wide requirements and reject unique specifications for individual situations. This is related to the "standard product" concept at the program specification level.

Features	– Specifications are designed for specific industries or functional groups.
Disadvantages	– Certain language, hardware, or technical specifications may not be met in individual cases.
Advantages	– More groups will have contributed and the specifications will more likely meet the future needs of the users.

c. *Rapid installation:* The lengthy development time of many systems frequently leads to their obsolescence during the development period. User personnel and user requirements change as the systems people are developing a predefined product. On the other hand, some software packages are rapidly available off the shelf, particularly for smaller applications, and can be used immediately.

Features	– Packages have detailed documentation and instructions.
Disadvantages	– Costly systems may be installed rapidly that do not truly meet the user's requirements. This can be prevented by adequate initial requirements analysis conducted in a professional manner, and by following the procedures outlined in this book.
Advantages	– The system quickly begins meeting user needs and aiding organizational profitability.
	– The user becomes involved in a running system while there is still keen interest, and existing personnel are used.

d. *Maintenance by suppliers:* Maintenance costs of systems are frequently greater than development costs over the long term. The maintenance of programs, including minor extensions of the code and machine changes, becomes an important consideration if the vendor can guarantee maintenance.

Features	– Periodic maintenance is described in contracts.
	– Maintenance areas are discussed and published in advance.
	– User groups request priorities for changes, although they may not get their exact wishes.
Disadvantages	– Maintenance schedules are controlled by the vendor.
	– Maintenance priorities are decided by a diverse group of users.
Advantages	– High maintenance costs are also shared by the full user group.
	– Other users may find and correct problems before they become apparent to an individual user.

e. *Reduced personnel requirements:*

Features	– Fewer organizational personnel are required for the development and installation of purchased packages.

	— Fewer programmers are normally required for ongoing maintenance.
Disadvantages	— Internal systems personnel usually do not have a detailed understanding of the required system when problems arise.
Advantages	— Sharply reduced budget required for technical personnel.
	— Systems analysts tend to become more oriented to user satisfaction and less to technical detail.

f. *Professional research and development:* It is in the vendor's interest to make a packaged system as professional as possible with the latest innovations and techniques. It is also in the vendor's interest to keep on the leading edge of system techniques. This requires a dedicated, highly paid staff, particularly in advanced areas like database management and larger applications, such as on-line order entry and machine tool control.

Features	— Larger software firms have experienced professional development staffs as they prosper.
	— Smaller software firms frequently have new ideas.
Disadvantages	— The best professional expertise is developed more and more outside the user's organization.
Advantages	— Newer systems and ideas and state-of-the-art developments become available to organizations without an increase in staff.

g. *Introduction of new concepts:* The finding, testing, and developing of new concepts in software package design and use is expedited by a growing market that attracts entrepreneurs. New concepts are diligently developed to gain marketing advantage.

Features	— Software firms are on the leading edge of thinking in the field.
	— Packages are developed and marketed to gain competitive advantage.
Disadvantages	— Users have less of a competitive edge if they have packages with the same concepts as their competitors.
	— New developments depend upon the overall market rather than an individual need.

Advantages — Users can increase their profitability of operation by applying the new concepts.

— Highly technical systems are subject to great disaster exposure. Some industries, such as banking, have found that there is a great advantage in sharing similar high-technology systems so that they can cooperate in computer operations in the event of a disaster, such as fire, disrupting their computer systems.

On balance, software packages provide far more advantages to users than disadvantages. The only exception may be when a user's concepts and requirements are in advance of the field and give them a strong competitive advantage. Users with many specific requirements sometimes feel that packages are useless to them. This objection is met in the industry today by the use of multiple-module packages, which are adaptable to a wide range of special requirements by systems integrators.

6.4 THE CASE SOFTWARE ACQUISITION DECISION PROCESS

The acquisition decision process for CASE software is the same as the process for any other type of software. It should be done in a planned, systematic, controlled, and documented manner. All too often, expensive software packages are purchased by simple word-of-mouth from someone else, or because of a single, well-prepared sales pitch by a vendor. There is too much money involved, and too much riding on the success of CASE projects, to acquire CASE software informally. There are reasonable and proven steps to take to profitably acquire software packages. Following these steps is inexpensive, while not following them can be very costly in the long run.

When CASE software packages are acquired or developed, they will be a critical element in the development of application systems that may have strategic impact on the organization. There is much to be gained by following the outline given in Figure 64. The sequence of some of the actions can vary, but all the actions listed should be accomplished for any key CASE system. The reports and decisions that are listed are all needed, in roughly the order shown, if the project is to be under management and financial control, and if it is to be auditable. Figure 64 is essentially a further development of the first three steps in the "Purchased Applications" section of Figure 26, "Variations in the System Development Life Cycle." Note that the purchase of software is parallel to, but different from, the CASE system development life cycle.

This chapter contains checklists and worksheets for all the critical comparisons that are required. The checklists are grouped by subject areas, and are not necessarily handled sequentially. In some cases, the more general checklists may be quite sufficient, while for more expensive and complex systems, all the checklists can be used. For smaller, approved tools, less financial analysis may be needed, while for large CASE environments, considerably more analysis may be required.

It was noted in Chapter 3 that the life cycles for the purchase and development of software are fairly similar. In fact, the most frequent cause of failure or difficulty with purchased software packages is to neglect the standard SDLC approach and assume that certain steps, such as the requirements definition, can be handled informally. Such omissions can be the source of serious errors in the selection process, and can cause overruns or failures. No software package should be acquired until the user has first formally determined the functional requirements of the proposed system and developed the equivalent of a general systems design for the overall system. There are far too many variations of CASE tools, systems, and environments on the market to make any reasonable decision before you know what you want after reading the literature.

It should be clear that the CASE software decision process does not simply consist of whether to "make or buy," and which package to select. A new software development environment is being contemplated. The CASE software decision process should be an ongoing, connected chain of analyses, reports, and decisions. As shown in Figure 26, it is part of, and rooted in:

- The portfolio analysis, based on information services objectives.
- Corporate strategic initiatives, and the priorities established in the strategic applications plan.

FIGURE 64. The CASE software decision process.

The Software Life Cycle	Actions	Reports & Decisions
1. Planning & initiation	a. Develop and obtain approval for CASE objectives	- Information services objectives for CASE
	b. Identify general CASE requirements	
	c. Develop concepts and ideas	
	d. Prepare strategic applications plan	- Strategic applications plan
	e. Set priorities based on costs, benefits, and management desires	- Management approval
	f. Determine specific objectives for the year	- Annual plan
	g. Make preliminary requirements analysis	
	h. Analyze system feasibility	- Feasibility analysis
	i. Review alternatives	
	j. Recommend specific types of CASE	
	k. Develop a list of CASE software vendors	
	l. Inventory any possible packages and maintain an information file	
2. Requirements definition	a. Appoint CASE analysis team	

The Software Life Cycle	Actions	Reports & Decisions
2. Requirements definition (Cont'd)	b. Define the CASE requirements c. Define the system and data requirements d. Define the operations requirements e. Note the alternatives f. Design the overall system g. Establish cost justification h. Prepare requirements definition i. Obtain necessary approvals j. Establish project priorities k. Start project management system l. Establish categories of the requirements by priority or weight factors m. Start search for usable CASE packages n. Refine list of vendors o. Start "make-versus-buy" analysis p. Improve cost benefit analysis q. Establish schedule and budget	- Requirements definition report - System design review - Management approval - Project management system report - Progress reports - Schedule and budget

FIGURE 64. (Cont.)

The Software Life Cycle	Actions	Reports & Decisions

3. Package evaluation and selection	a. Assemble project team
	b. Issue request for proposal (RFP) or request for quotation (RFQ)
	c. Search for usable CASE packages
	d. Evaluate vendors
	e. Evaluate and compare packages
	  - Check references
	  - Visit operating sites
	  - Benchmark, if possible
	f. Determine hardware and software requirements
	g. Have presentations and review sessions with vendors
	h. Select most suitable CASE packages
	i. Prepare a selection report summarizing:
	  - Advantages and disadvantages
	  - Vendor selection
	  - Costs and benefits
	  - Installation plan and dates
	  - Recommend approval
		- RFP or RFQ
		
		- Progress reports
		
		- Package selection
		- Package selection report

The Software Life Cycle	Actions	Reports & Decisions
3. Package evaluation and selection (Cont'd)	j. Obtain approval	- Management approval
	k. Plan and design modifications	- Detailed specifications of modifications
	l. Negotiate contract	
	m. Acquire the most acceptable packages	- Contract with vendor
	n. Modify and install the packages	
	o. Test the systems	
	p. Evaluate the acceptance criteria	- Acceptance report
	q. Accept the CASE packages	- System documentation
	r. Install in the operational environment	
	s. Convert the system and train the staff	
	t. Review the system's operation and control	- Audit report: post installation

- The business priorities of the users to be served.
- The types of CASE projects that are being selected and planned.
- The functional requirements definition report.

There are other sources of information that detail the full, stepwise process of software package selection, including the preparation of reports to management and the relationship with the vendors. The heart of the process, however, is in the use of the checklists in this chapter. The use of checklists in the evaluation of any software package can be most helpful:

- To ensure that personnel of different levels of experience will all have a similar proven base of information from which to work.
- To apply some objective criteria to the comparison of different packages.
- To maintain a record of the items and the issues that were considered in the evaluation of various packages.

Careful analysis of the results of each checklist in its specific area will provide the analyst with a most valuable comparison tool. The information from these checklists can aid in determining whether the CASE packages considered meet the functional requirements that have been specified and are reasonable to consider in your own operational environment. The conclusions from these checklists can then be combined with the analysis of systems costs, the legal considerations, and any overriding management considerations to reach a conclusion about to the preferable package acquisition in an objective, documented way.

6.5 GENERAL CONSIDERATIONS IN SOFTWARE PACKAGE SELECTION

Software systems do not stand alone and unchanged. On the one hand, they are always interrelated with other operating systems and the computer complex. On the other hand, they are always changed and further developed as the business of the organization changes. In addition, they are always simply elements in a larger computational system that includes the users and customers, the clerks handling data, and the governmental environment. Software systems can truly be thought of as "packages" imbedded in much larger operational systems.

Because software systems do not stand alone and unchanged, they cannot be thought of as objective entities that are completely defined in the vendor's literature. Certainly, there must be as much objectivity as possible in determining whether the software package fits the defined functional requirements of the user. On the other hand, there are also a number of subjective considerations to discuss before a selection is decided upon.

The checklists in this book cover many of the objective considerations and a number of the subjective considerations. Analysis, meetings, reviews, and discussions must take place in addition to filling out and analyzing the checklists. Figure 65 is an overall view of the "bigger picture." It lists a number of software package characteristics that may be independent of the technical requirements and considerations. This list should be reviewed and kept in mind during sales presentations and discussions. Note that all these characteristics can be subjectively discussed in a review of the package with other users. It could be used as a checklist for such a review.

Vendors can talk factually about a number of these characteristics, but not all of them. Certainly, the points should be raised in vendor discussions or should be looked for in studying the vendor materials.

Frequently, packages may be observed in use at other installations. This can be most helpful if the operational aspects of the package are critical. Much less frequently can a package be tested on your computer or with your data. The problems of assembling the job control language and the data file can be great. In some cases, however, it is a necessity to test the package in operation to determine whether it could fulfill the requirements. These are rare cases, and the large cost must be considered and negotiated. Many vendors will give demonstrations and minor tests, but few can afford to give full tests of systems. If a package is given a test, the most important information that is obtained is the efficiency of the operation. This can be critical.

Figure 65 is a useful checklist to keep in mind for vendor presentations, as well as when talking to other users who have been given as references. All of the questions can be asked, al-

FIGURE 65. Software package characteristics to be reviewed.

Characteristics Of The Software Package	Review With Other Users	Discuss With Vendor	Analyze Vendor's Material	Test The Package
Ease of installation	X	X	X	X
Ease of use	X			X
Documentation	X	X	X	X
Efficiency of operation	X			X
Enhancement capability	X	X	X	
Maintainability	X			
Maintenance agreement	X	X	X	
Overall satisfaction of users	X			
Reliability	X			
Source program language and availability	X	X	X	
Training courses and material	X	X	X	X
Update frequency	X	X	X	
User group cooperation	X			X
Vendor's technical support	X	X	X	
Warranty	X	X	X	

though it must always be kept in mind that a meeting with a vendor is a sales meeting, and the best possible appearance is always presented.

Vendor Presentations

Presentation and review sessions with vendors are noted as an essential step in Figure 64. These sessions are:

- The fastest way to get questions answered.
- The best method of handling the qualitative review of the vendor.
- A good way to estimate vendor capability and support.

If there are several candidates to consider, it is preferable, from the purchaser's point of view, to schedule all the vendor presentations almost back to back. The same questions can be asked while the comparative answers are still fresh in your mind. If one vendor compares the product with other packages, some aspects of the comparison can be quickly checked. Sales literature can be laid out side by side and compared as to key specifications. Vendors comparisons can be discussed, and the list of possibilities can rapidly be reduced to three or four, or even less.

It is only reasonable from a business point of view to have multiple presentations at a site of your choosing if the package being considered is large and worth the vendor's investment of time and expense. In addition, the presentations should be handled efficiently and on schedule. The purchaser should also take the responsibility of seeing that all interested parties attend the presentations so that they are not wasted. From the purchaser's point of view, of course, the vendor's willingness to put on a presentation at your convenience may well be an indication of the vendor's willingness to rapidly come and help with an installed package that is having problems. From the vendor's point of view, a sales presentation in series with a number of competitors is only worthwhile if there is a real chance of winning the contract and a direct loss of money if the purchasers have already essentially made up their minds as to the outcome.

Vendors are most likely to cooperate with multiple presentations if:

- A detailed description of the *functional requirements* is available.
- A statement of the key considerations is given.
- There is a published schedule of the presentations.
- It is stated when decisions will be made.
- It is clear whether further presentations may be required.

Overview of Considerations

This book contains a number of checklists for considering all facets of software package selection and installation. Figure 66 is essentially a summary of many of the checklists that follow. For smaller software packages that do not interface with many other systems, Figure 66 may be sufficient as a checklist. It brings out most of the critical points to be considered.

6.6 CHECKLISTS FOR THE EVALUATION OF SOFTWARE PACKAGES

This section contains checklists for eight related management and technical areas to aid in the routine examination of vendor offerings each time a software package acquisition is considered. The checklists have several purposes:

- They can aid in determining whether all the functional requirements are met in a particular software package.

- They can be used for a functional comparison of two or more packages.

- They can ensure that analysts with different levels of experience will all have a similar, proven base of information from which to compare vendor packages.

- They allow the application of objective criteria to the comparison of different packages.

- They provide a record of the items and issues that were considered in the evaluation of various packages.

The detailed evaluation and the use of metrics in software comparison is described in the next section.

The following checklists are the key to enhancing the user's capability in the consideration and selection of a software package. Careful analysis of each checklist in its specific area will provide the user with a most valuable tool. The areas of consideratiom covered are:

Figure 67 – *General Considerations* (including the hardware environment, the software environment, package use and experience, and performance criteria)

FIGURE 66. General software package considerations.

Item No.	Item	Software Package		
1.	**Functional Requirements** a. Does the package meet the functional requirements that have been defined? b. What is the additional cost of meeting the requirements? c. Are satisfactory performance criteria stated?			
2.	**Software Package Costs** a. Cost of basic package? b. Cost of additional features? c. Cost of required modifications? d. Cost for use at two or more locations? e. Vendor's annual service and maintenance fees? f. Cost of participation in users' group? g. Cost of periodic purchase of updated versions? h. Installation cost? i. Training cost? j. Cost for manuals, forms, documentation, etc.? k. Cost for required vendor assistance? l. Computer time and data input cost for installation?			
3.	**Compatibility of the Software Package** a. Does the package operate on the existing computer hardware configuration? b. What is the additional cost of required hardware configuration changes? c. Does the package operate in the existing software environment? d. What is the additional cost of changing the software environment? e. Are the files and records compatible with the existing data management system? f. What is the cost of converting the files and records to be compatible?			

FIGURE 66. (Cont.)

Item No.	Item	Software Package		
4.	**Ease of Use of the Package** a. Is the package programmed in a language familiar to your staff? b. Is the package clearly described in its documentation? c. Are the job control language statements supplied for your perating system? d. Can the job control language statements be modified readily? e. Is the documentation of modifications handled by an automatic system? f. Is the user documentation adequate? g. Is the user training time reasonably short? h. Is the system programmer training time reasonable? i. Is the system protable among your computers?			
5.	**Vendor Capabilities** a. Is the vendor financially stable? b. How many years has the vendor been in business? c. Is the package documentation adequate? d. Are reference materials supplied for training? e. Does the vendor have a software development staff? f. Does the vendor have a package maintenance support staff? g. Does the vendor have a training staff?			
6.	**Package Experience and Stability** a. How many actual package users are there? b. How many years has the package been used by customers? c. Have contacted users been satisfied with the packages? d. Does the package rate well in surveys? e. Does the package contain current technological features?			

FIGURE 66. (Cont.)

Item No.	Item	Software Package		
7.	**Technical Features** a. Is the system design adequate? b. Was the package designed to make best use of the current level of the operating system? c. Was the package designed to make best use of the network communications features available? d. Is the input user friendly? e. Is the input adequately edited and controlled? f. Is the file structure compatible with your current systems? g. Is file integrity adequately maintained? h. Are there fail-safe and recovery features included? i. Are the output reports adequate and controlled? j. Are the reports in formats desired by the users? k. Are efficient sorting and file processing programs included? l. Are there adequate inquiry and report generation facilities?			

Figure 68 — *Technical Considerations* (including system features, input requirements, file structure, file integrity, fail-safe and recovery, on-line system features, and output reports)

Figure 69 — *Installation and Operation Considerations*

Figure 70 — *Modification and Maintenance Considerations*

Figure 71 — *Vendor Capabilities* (including vendor stability, vendor experience, vendor support, modification and installation, vendor training, and package user groups)

Figure 72 — *Personnel Training Considerations*

Figure 73 — *Audit and Control Considerations* (including general audit considerations, input controls, processing controls, data file controls, output controls, teleprocessing controls, and audit trail controls)

Figure 74 — *Standards and Documentation Considerations*

The information from these checklists can aid in determining whether the packages considered meet the functional requirements that have been specified and are reasonable to consider in your own operational environment. The conclusions from these checklists can be combined with the analysis of systems costs, the legal considerations, and any overriding management considerations to reach a conclusion as to the preferable package acquisition in a documented, objective way.

Each of these self-appraisal checklists is organized in such a manner that the prospective purchaser of a package can select the elements deemed most important, copy the most useful pages for the review and analysis, and follow the evaluation procedure. One of the results will be a package of working papers in the analysis that will be readily reviewed by others or audited.

The purchase or lease of a software package represents not only a considerable financial commitment but also an operational commitment to a relatively rigid procedure. It therefore behooves the purchaser to use the self-appraisal checklists carefully before reaching a decision. They can go a long way to see that the users' desires and the functional requirements are met. A package acquisition decision should never be made on price alone but also on all critical considerations. Many an EDP group has lived for years with package difficulties because they did not analyze their choice of package in a sufficiently objective manner.

General Considerations in the Evaluation of Packages

This checklist, Figure 67, is a guideline that can be used as an initial screening in the general evaluation of software packages. It touches on a number of characteristics that should be considered before further analysis. Most organizations will also have additional questions at this time to see that the packages meet the specific needs of their organization.

Hardware Environment considers:

- Whether the package can be realistically run on your computers.
- The degree to which the package may need to be modified before it will operate on your equipment and meet the users' functional requirements.
- The effect the package will have on other services provided.

Software Environment considers:

- The extent to which higher-level languages are used in the software package, and whether the language will be compatible with your organization's operation.
- The ease of installation under your operating system.
- The ease of modifying the package.

Package Use and Experience considers:

- The origin of the package, whether it was designed originally as a general package or whether it is tailored from an older system.
- The number and type of locations in which the package has been operational.
- The possibility of references from other users, and visits to their sites to discuss their experiences with the package.

Performance Criteria considers:

- The expected amount of processing time and resources required.
- The CPU processing overhead generated by the software, particularly for operating systems packages.

FIGURE 67. Evaluation of software packages: general considerations.

Item No.	Item	Software Package		
	Hardware Environment			
1.	On what computers can the package be used?			
2.	What is the minimum configuration necessary for the object computer on which it will be used? (List critical configuration constraints)			
3.	Will modification be necessary to run under the anticipated hardware environment?			
4.	Can the package be run efficiently on the object computer?			
5.	Will modification of the package be necessary to obtain efficient and effective operation?			
6.	Will the package markedly affect other user services when it is run?			
	Software Environment			
7.	In what language(s) is the package written?			
8.	Is this a standard, maintained language in your operation?			
9.	If it is not a standard language for you, has the impact of another language been considered?			
10.	Is source code available to the user? a. Does it come with the package acquisition? b. Is it available for extra payment? (If so, how much?) c. Is it accessible for making modifications? d. Is it accessible for audit review purposes?			

FIGURE 67. (Cont.)

Item No.	Item	Software Package		
11.	If source code is not available to the user, is it clear and acceptable how modifications and corrections can be made?			
12.	Are the operating system language instructions (JCL) available for your environment with the package?			
13.	Will the package run without modification in your operating system environment?			
14.	Can the package be updated to the next release level of your operating system without rewrite?			
15.	Does the package require special optional features from the operating system? (List)			
16.	Will the package readily fit in your job accounting system (such as SMF and a report writer) for the management review of the operation?			
	Package Use and Experience			
17.	In what year was the package first developed?			
18.	In how many different locations has the package been operational for: a. More than one year? b. Less than one year?			
19.	Is a user list available for reference concerning: a. Package performance? b. Ease of installation and modification? c. Vendor support?			
20.	Can the vendor arrange a visit to one or two sites where the package has been operational?			

FIGURE 67. (Cont.)

Item No.	Item	Software Package		
21.	Can the site visits include: a. Demonstration of operation? b. Review of output reports and the satisfaction of users with them? c. Size of the files and throughput volume? d. Experiences with software problems? e. Experience with vendor support? **Performance Criteria**			
22.	Does the package generate a summary of its performance or activities			
23.	Are standard test data or procedures available to ensure accurate testing and processing?			
24.	Are there acceptance test criteria defined that cover? a. Functions of the package? b. Efficiency of operation of the package? c. Interaction with other systems?			
25.	Is there an agreed-upon schedule for delivery and installation of the package?			
26.	Has the expected amount of processing time and resource usage been analyzed and reviewed with other users?			

- The information available for acceptance and management of the package.
- An estimate of the probable schedule of delivery and installation.

Technical Considerations

This checklist, Figure 68, covers areas that need the analysis and recommendation of systems programmers, systems analysts, and programmers. Points are covered that can only be properly reviewed by those familiar with the technical details of your systems and environment.

Any functional requirements definition of a computer-oriented system will list a great many system characteristics, features, and details that are of considerable importance for the integration of the new system into the existing operating environment, and for its ongoing control and maintenance. This checklist is fairly comprehensive, but it cannot be all-inclusive for all situations. The items themselves should, therefore, be reviewed as to criticality by technical personnel before the checklist is used to aid the analysis of package programs.

System Features includes:

- The generality of the system design and its overall flexibility.
- The general format and usability.

Input Requirements includes:

- Whether the handling of the input is satisfactory.
- Whether the input forms and controls are satisfactory.

File Structures include:

- The general efficiency of the file design.
- The compatibility of the file design with other operating system files.

File Integrity includes:

- The controls embedded into the programs and file design.
- The management and auditability of the records in the files.

FIGURE 68. Evaluation of software packages: technical considerations.

Item No.	Item	Software Package		
	System Features			
1.	Is the package modular with: a. Clearly defined programs and routines? b. Optional features that can be used or eliminated? c. Variations to cut overhead if required? d. Tailoring allowed through screens? e. Driving parameters clearly available?			
2.	Can the system be used by average systems analysts?			
3.	Is the package sufficiently general to handle other uses that were not originally specified?			
4.	Does the system print out clear error messages?			
5.	Is there good documentation of all error messages?			
6.	Does the system have clear and acceptable headings on all reports?			
7.	Are there useful system options readily available?			
8.	Are the CRT screens acceptable as supplied?			
	Input Requirements			
9.	Is input data easily obtained from: a. Other automated systems? b. Direct input from CRT screens?			
10.	Does the input interface readily with other CASE systems being run?			

FIGURE 68. (Cont.)

Item No.	Item	Software Package		
11.	Are control and reporting procedures available for controlling all input that is processed?			
12.	Are controls available to restart corrected input?			
13.	Are the input screens and documentation satisfactory?			
14.	Are the input controls satisfactory to the auditors?			
	File Structures			
15.	Are the file sturctures compatible with the files of existing, related systems?			
16.	Are detailed files layouts available for each file?			
17.	Are clear explanations provided for the contents of each field?			
18.	Do the files have sufficient expansion capabilities including: a. Ability to change or add fields to the records? b. Ability to change file definition programming?			
19.	Are the data fields organized so that their physical order agrees with their use or importance?			
20.	Are the record sizes, key structures, and other elements relatively independent of the equipment?			

FIGURE 68. (Cont.)

Item No.	Item	Software Package		
21.	Are the systems file structures consistent in physical structure and programming-level definition?			
22.	Are the file structures easily understood and logical?			
	File Integrity			
23.	Do the files contain sufficient audit trails including? a. Data and type of last record change? b. Logging of old/new records? c. Usage counts? d. Other?			
24.	Is the accuracy and completeness of a file verified each time it is processed?			
25.	Are control records required at the end of each file?			
26.	Are records analyzed for the validity of each important field of data prior to processing?			
27.	Does the package test for the existence and reasonableness of identifying numbers, such as account numbers, serial numbers, and code numbers?			
28.	Does the package automatically check to determine if all required external controls are properly set?			
	Fail-Safe and Recovery			
29.	Can the system tolerate errors and difficulties at the terminals and continue operating?			
30.	Can the system save the data needed for recovery if there is: a. Destruction of a data file? b. Power failure? c. Entry of improper or faulty data? d. Intrusion by an unauthorized user?			

FIGURE 68. (Cont.)

Item No.	Item	Software Package		
31.	Are there connections at fault points to test for the proper operation of the system?			
32.	Does the system have default options that: a. Reject entry to erroneous or illogical data? b. Log the errors? c. Transfer control to data entry points?			
33.	Are terminal operators prevented from stopping, disrupting, or destroying the systems operation by the system?			
34.	If additional fail-safe and recovery capabilities are required, can they be installed at a reasonable price?			
	On-Line System Features			
35.	Is the systems start-up satisfactory, including date, time, operator identification, control numbers, security control, etc.?			
36.	Are there clear, brief, well-documented instructions to guide the operator through the system?			
37.	Are there adequate screen menus to guide the operator in choosing programs?			
38.	Are error messages well formatted, clear, and well documented?			
39.	Are error correction options and instructions satisfactory?			
40.	Are single-key action commands used sufficiently to speed the interaction of the operator?			

FIGURE 68. (Cont.)

Item No.	Item	Software Package		
41.	Do the restart procedures have: a. A clear statement of the restore sequence? b. A test to identify the last-accepted data values? c. Requirements to reenter lost data?			
42.	Is there a reasonable data override process for the entry of exceptions?			
43.	Can the operator select report formats, call up data, and view sample reports?			
44.	Can the operator readily control the printing and reprinting capability of the output reports?			
45.	Are there reasonable inquiry routines to view selected files and data?			
46.	Does the software allow an easy exit from the action process when the operator has completed data entry or is signing off?			
47.	Do the end-of-day procedures give complete and logical commands and supply proper audit logs?			
	Output Reports			
48.	Do the output reports have reasonable content and layout?			
49.	Are the output reports readily usable by the users?			
50.	Can the output reports be modified to satisfy user requirements?			

FIGURE 68. (Cont.)

Item No.	Item	Software Package		
51.	Are there options and choices built into the system allowing changes in: a. Report headings? b. Control numbers and identifications? c. Field sizes? d. Sort selections? e. Choice of levels of detail? f. Choice of reports? g. Statements of error messages? h. Line counts and page breaks? i. Printed distribution list?			
52.	Does the system include an inquiry and reporting capability?			
53.	Does the system include a report generator?			
	Ease-of-Use Features			
54.	Is the program menu-driven? (an organized list of options on the screen from which the user can make a selection)			
55.	Does the menu have pictures, or icons?			
56.	Are the commands that drive the system: a. Single-key functions? (best) b. Multiple-key functions?			
57.	Are there satisfactory on-screen HELP messages?			
58.	Can the HELP messages be turned off if desired?			
59.	Is *status information* displayed on the screen for reference?			
60.	Is there a standard assumption of common pitch, margins, and tabs that are set by default?			

FIGURE 68. (Cont.)

Item No.	Item	Software Package		
61.	Is there a *register line* that shows margins, tabs, and decimal tabs graphically?			
62.	Are there *resettable format controls* available?			
63.	Are *document line numbers* displayed if desired?			
64.	Are *special screen effects* such as highlighting and blinking available?			
65.	Are there *forgiveness interrupts* for any command that would markedly change the file?			
66.	Are there simple, nondestructive EXIT methods?			
67.	Are there simple, nondestructive GO BACK methods to review the steps that have been taken?			
68.	Are there clear *ready prompting* messages to inform the operator that another task may be entered?			
69.	Is there *fixed screen data entry* available, where each data name and item stays on the screen until a section of the data entry is complete?			
70.	Are numbers accepted from the numeric pad?			
71.	Is there a message that anticipates an approaching *disk filled* condition?			
72.	Is the user's manual organized for ready usage, with troubleshooting suggestions?			
73.	Is there a self-teaching program available for rapid introduction to the program?			

Fail-Safe and Recovery includes:

- Tolerance of the system towards errors and problems that may arise.
- The control of terminals and the existence of default options.

On-Line System Feature includes:

- The unique requirements of on-line, real-time system operation.
- The procedures and controls available for managing terminal data entry.

Output Reports includes:

- Whether the output report formats meet the requirements specified by the users.
- The options and choices built into the system that may be desirable.

Ease-of-Use Features includes:

- Simplicity of use and smooth operation.
- Ease and rapidity of learning the system.
- Good CRT screens and a variety of HELP features.

Installation and Operation Considerations

This checklist, Figure 69, covers the critical area of getting the package system installed and bringing it up to full operation. Some of the questions refer to contractual agreements that are desirable, and others refer to good practice in installing a system.

The importance of these concerns may vary with the degree to which the purchaser depends upon the vendor's assistance in the installation. Many of the questions may appear to be answered by the contractual terms, but should be checked out with existing users of the package.

Some of the areas of concern are:

- The vendor's responsibilities in the installation of the system, both in the contract and in informal agreements.

FIGURE 69. Evaluation of software packages: installation and operation considerations.

Item No.	Item	Software Package		
1.	Are the vendor's and purchaser's installation responsibilities clearly defined?			
2.	Are the installation's specifications defined precisely enough?			
3.	Are the acceptance criteria for the package clearly defined?			
4.	Can the vendor produce a detailed installation and conversion manual with usable checklists?			
5.	Will the vendor supply an experienced person to aid in the installation			
6.	Will the vendor supply aid in the systems programming implementation?			
7.	Can the package be installed in the operating system environment without major changes?			
8.	If operating system changes are required, can the vendor supply the necessary aid?			
9.	Will the operation of the system require extensive training for the computer operators and system programmers?			
10.	Can the vendor provide these training services?			
11.	Can the vendor provide sample operating standards and procedures that can be adapted and used?			
12.	Are the vendor personnel near enough to respond rapidly when problems arise in installation or operation?			
13.	Has the level of the vendor's aid in installation and operation support been checked with two or more references who have the package operational?			

FIGURE 69 (Cont.)

Item No.	Item	Software Package		
14.	Does the system documentation conform to the installation's documentation standards?			
15.	Do the system operating procedures conform to the installation's operating standards?			
16.	Will the system operate under your installed database without major modifications?			
17.	Are the system performance criteria for acceptance clearly stated?			
18.	Is there a good set of test data available: a. From the vendor to test the system as it was offered? b. From the user to test whether the system meets the operating specifications?			

- What the vendor will supply in terms of documentation, aids, and services.
- What is practical in terms of installing and testing the system, preferably in parallel.
- What needs to be changed to bring the system into the software and hardware environment.
- A clear definition of both vendor and purchaser responsibilities.
- The criteria for accepting delivery of the package.

Modification and Maintenance Considerations

This checklist, Figure 70, aids in the analysis of the problems that may arise and the support that should be expected from the vendor. Some packages are well tested and can be installed as they are received. Other packages require much modification to meet the user specifications and constantly require maintenance and upgrading to meet changing demands.

The section on Modification aids in the analysis of the extent of the modifications anticipated, and the supplier's involvement in these modifications. In some packages, the major cost and effort is in preparing and testing the modifications. If there are no modifications to be made to any of the packages considered, then these questions can be omitted. If there are modifications to be made, some of the key points are:

- Whether the modifications are clearly understood and are necessary for system operation.
- Definition of the modifications necessary for the smooth functioning of a specific package.
- The participation of skilled personnel in defining and producing the modifications.
- The familiarity of the purchaser with the details of the specific package.
- The possibility of revising certain of the user's procedures so that only minor modifications are required. This is particularly feasible when moving from manual to on-line systems.

The section on Maintenance aids in the consideration of the problem that may arise even before a package is considered se-

FIGURE 70. Evaluation of software packages: modification and maintenance considerations.

Item No.	Item	Software Package		
	Modification			
1.	To function effectively, does the package require modifications that are: a. Minor? b. Major?			
2.	Can the package be installed, at least temporarily, without modifications?			
3.	Have the modifications specifications been defined in sufficient detail?			
4.	Can the vendor supply technical personnel, experienced in the package, to help define the modifications?			
5.	Do you have any personnel sufficiently familiar with the package to specify modifications properly?			
6.	Can the users change any of their administrative procedures to more closely correspond with the existing software package procedures, so that any modifications are few and minor?			
7.	Has the vendor priced all modifications based on the specifications?			
8.	Are the system requirements defined through parameters and tables, making certain modifications easy to accomplish?			
9.	Will the package vendor agree to correct without charge any errors that are introduced into the package as a result of modifications that are: a. Vendor-performed, minor modifications? b. Vendor-performed, major modifications? c. Purchaser-performed, minor modifications? d. Purchaser-performed, major modifications?			

FIGURE 70 (Cont.)

Item No.	Item	Software Package		
10.	Will the vendor agree to correct without charge any errors that are detected in the basic package even though the package has been modified?			
11.	Is it possible and practical to change the equipment configuration to avoid modifications?			
12.	Does your staff have the capability to perform the required modifications within a reasonable time?			
13.	Does the vendor's staff have the capability to perform the required modifications within a reasonable time?			
14.	Has the vendor discussed whether other customers have made similar modifications that may be available rapidly?			
	Maintenance			
15.	Are new releases of the package issued on a regular basis?			
16.	Are these new releases: a. Automatically available to all purchasers? b. Part of a maintenance program? c. Necessary to install to keep standard support?			
17.	Is the package updated when new features of the operating system are released?			
18.	If the user makes changes to the system: a. Is maintenance automatically terminated? b. Is maintenance to the base system continued?			

FIGURE 70. (Cont.)

Item No.	Item	Software Package		
19.	Does the vendor correct errors in a reasonable time that are: a. Critical? b. Noncritical?			
20.	Are customers advised of outstanding problems that other users have discovered?			
21.	Are customers promptly advised of all fixes?			
22.	Can system dumps be sent to the vendor for review?			
23.	If a system dump, or details of an error, are sent to the vendor: a. What turnaround time is expected? b. What is the cost? c. How are these factors controlled?			
24.	Does the vendor supply telephone contact for answering technical questions?			
25.	Is on-site maintenance available? a. Promptly, when necessary? b. At reasonable time-and-materials cost?			
26.	Does the vendor prefer to handle system errors: a. Only if the user proves the error exists? b. Only on receipt of a dump? c. With an on-site discussion if desired?			
27.	Can the vendor's maintenance support be provided promptly?			
28.	Have references affirmed that the vendor gives good maintenance support?			

riously. The potential need for maintenance and the procedure by which it will be handled is an important point in the evaluation of alternative packages.

System software packages should have definite, specific maintenance and upgrade programs, since they are usually dependent upon the operating system, which will change periodically. This fact is beyond the power of the user to control as the technology changes. Changes within the operating system, passed down by the hardware supplier, will usually result in the need to change system software packages. Such changes will frequently require major effort.

It is reasonable to assume that there will be a need for future maintenance of any package, be it system software, utility, or application. Some of the areas of concern are, therefore:

- The details of the vendor's agreement to maintain all phases of the package after installation.
- The vendor's plans for introducing new versions of the package to be compatible with new versions of the hardware and operating systems.
- The likelihood of, and the probable corrective response time for, latent errors resulting from limited operational experience and new modifications.
- The vendor's plans for providing changes that reflect user experience and legislative action.
- The precise definition of maintenance specifications.

Consideration of Vendor Capabilities

This checklist, Figure 71, covers critical areas of vendor experience and support that can be of fundamental importance in the acquisition of complex or technically advanced packages.

The importance of these vendor capabilities and characteristics varies widely. It depends upon the capabilities and practices of the organization considering the acquisition of the package. Some organizations have very little technical capability and find themselves entirely dependent upon the supplier. To these, the vendor characteristics are of great importance. At the other extreme are those organizations with technical capabilities superior

FIGURE 71. Evaluation of software packages: vendor capabilities.

Item No.	Item	Software Package		
	Vendor Stability			
1.	How long has the vendor been in business?			
2.	Does the vendor have a satisfactory financial position for support of the package?			
3.	Does the vendor have specific staff to handle: a. Administrative and legal requirements? b. Ongoing package development? c. Customer support? d. Sales inquiries? e. Problem, or "hot line," inquiries?			
4.	Does the vendor have future commitments towards ongoing development and upgrading of the package?			
5.	Will the package remain "state of the art" rather than for a specific, pre-defined environment?			
6.	Will the vendor supply a corporate annual report or a certified financial statement?			
	Vendor Experience			
7.	Is the vendor the original developer of the package?			
8.	If the vendor is not the original developer: a. Does the vendor have technical support from the developer? b. Does the vendor have a staff trained in this particular package?			
9.	Is the vendor experienced with your hardware?			
10.	Was the package originally written for your hardware?			
11.	Can the vendor supply the training that is necessary?			

FIGURE 71 (Cont.)

Item No.	Item	Software Package		
	Vendor Support			
12.	Does the vendor have a maintenance staff?			
13.	Is the maintenance automatically terminated if the user makes modifications to the system?			
14.	Is the maintenance automatically terminated when the vendor moves to a new release level and the user does not?			
15.	Does the vendor advise users of: a. Outstanding problems with the system? b. Fixes, modifications, and improvements?			
16.	Does the vendor correct errors discovered by the user including: a. Critical errors? Turnaround time _______ b. Noncritical errors? Turnaround time _______			
17.	Is the package updated when new features of the operating system are issued?			
18.	Can system dumps be sent to the vendor for aid in determining problem areas?			
19.	If a system dump is sent to the vendor: a. What is the cost? b. What is the turnaround time? c. How are these factors controlled?			
20.	Is maintenance available on the customer's site?			
21.	What is the cost for on-site maintenance: a. For each on-site call? b. For yearly maintenance? c. Other?			
22.	Does the vendor provide telephone contact with knowledgeable persons for answering technical questions?			

FIGURE 71 (Cont.)

Item No.	Item	Software Package		
	Modification and Installation			
23.	Will the vendor perform minor modifications to the programs before acceptance?			
24.	Will the vendor perform major modifications to the programs before acceptance?			
25.	Are the modifications defined and documented before being priced?			
26.	Will the modifications automatically become part of the standard package, with the maintenance assumed by the vendor?			
27.	Will the vendor support an installation that has had the package modified by a customer?			
28.	Will the installation of the package: a. Be directed by the vendor? b. Include demonstration with user data? c. Be included in the package cost?			
29.	Will the vendor be involved in the conversion effort: a. For file conversion? b. For data preparation? c. In preparing procedures and standards?			
30.	Will vendor personnel be on-site during the installation of the system?			
	Vendor Training			
31.	Does the vendor offer training programs: a. During installation? b. For both users and technical personnel? c. As self-study courses on video or audio tape? d. As public courses on a periodic basis? Frequency _____________			
32.	Are courses provided at the users location?			

FIGURE 71 (Cont.)

Item No.	Item	Software Package		
33.	Do the courses cost extra?			
34.	What is the estimated training period for: a. Users? b. Systems programmers who will be responsible for the operation of the package? c. The self-study material, such as video or audio tapes?			
	Package User Groups			
35.	Does the vendor support and encourage a package user group?			
36.	How frequently does it meet?			
37.	Is there an interchange of printed material and reports?			
38.	Does the vendor share helpful hints from one installation to another?			
39.	Are user group suggestions sometimes included in package modifications and enhancements?			
40.	Do the users listed as references feel that the user group is valuable and helpful?			

to the developer and vendor of the system and that are wholly independent. Even they, however, may become locked into the vendor's core code and development of enhancements. The buyer must be assured that problems in the vendor's organization do not affect the system's operation and useful life.

Operating system software packages, such as database management systems and on-line monitors, have a high level of sophistication and will always require significant support from the vendor even though the user may have a well-qualified and experienced staff. The viability of the vendor and the availability of source code become critical issues.

Vendor Stability considers:

- Whether the vendor can reasonably be expected to remain in the business and support its customers.
- Whether the package will remain state of the art and be further developed over the years.

Vendor Experience considers:

- Whether the package was developed by the vendor.
- Whether the vendor can realistically support your organization.

Vendor Support considers:

- The technical staff of the vendor.
- The relationships with the vendor and other users that can be expected to aid your organization.
- The possible hidden costs of fixing problems and changes.

Modification and Installation considers:

- What can be expected from the vendor in handling desired modifications.
- The contractual involvement of the vendor in installing and converting the system and making it operational.

Vendor Training considers:

- The types of training programs that are available, both as part of the contract and for an extra charge.
- The tools offered by the vendor to give independence to the user.

Package User Groups considers:

- The possibilities of getting a useful interchange about the operation of the package system and improvements to it.
- The availability of references to all aspects of the package system.

Personnel Training Considerations

This checklist, Figure 72, covers some of the specific operational problems that will arise when new systems, methods, and procedures are introduced into the organization.

The larger problem of selection and employment of personnel for specific areas is not considered here, because it is usually not dependent upon the selection of any particular software package. It will be a major problem if the operational system is moved from manual to on-line, but that problem is inherent in the overall organizational and technological change. It is a new environmental direction that must be taken.

The principal areas of concern relative to personnel in the selection of a software package are the degree of change it will introduce, and how all the levels of an organization can be trained to accept and use the new methods. The concerns will include:

- How the special training for the system will be handled.
- The availability of the training programs offered by the vendor.
- The variety of training methods that can be used.
- The time and effort required to accomplish the needed training.

Audit and Control Considerations

This checklist, Figure 73, outlines some of the principal areas that should be reviewed for any CASE package to be used for

FIGURE 72. Evaluation of software packages: personnel training considerations.

Item No.	Item	Software Package		
1.	Does the package require special training of personnel: a. For using the system? b. For operating the system? c. For systems programming and maintenance?			
2.	Does the supplier offer training programs: a. For users? b. For operators? c. For systems programmers? d. For maintenance and enhancement programmers?			
3.	Are these training programs available: a. On-site, at the customer's location? b. At vendor offices?			
4.	How are these training programs priced?			
5.	How much training is provided with the purchase of the package?			
6.	Does the vendor supply adequate printed material with the training courses?			
7.	Does the vendor offer public courses on a periodic basis?			
8.	Does the vendor offer study material on video or audio tape with associated texts?			
9.	What is the estimated training period for the package for: a. Users? b. Operators? c. Systems programmers responsible for maintenance? d. The use of the self-study video or audio tapes?			

FIGURE 73. Evaluation of software packages: audit and control considerations.

Item No.	Item	Software Package		
	General Audit Considerations			
1.	Will the software vendor update the package if hardware or other systems change, necessitating an update of this system?			
2.	Have provisions been made to have programs modified, if necessary, for new versions of the operating system?			
3.	Is adequate backup available if the operational version of the system is destroyed?			
4.	Does the vendor provide adequate documentation with the software package?			
5.	Is there a formal procedure to determine which security and control features are included in the generated version?			
6.	Can the use of the system be monitored and reviewed by a supervisor?			
	Input Controls			
7.	Are all transactions properly recorded at the point of origin?			
8.	Can the proper authorization of transactions be determined?			
9.	Are there proper controls on the complete and accurate conversion of source information into machine acceptable form?			
10.	Can recorded data be processed in a timely manner?			
11.	Are there controls to ensure that all data recorded enter the computer for processing?			
12.	Are there controls to ensure that all data received by the computer are accurate and complete?			

FIGURE 73 (Cont.)

Item No.	Item	Software Package		
	Processing Controls			
13.	Are there controls to detect the loss of data or the nonprocessing of data?			
14.	Are there controls to ensure the complete and accurate processing of data through the application system?			
15.	Are there controls to ensure that the arithmetic functions have been performed correctly?			
16.	Are there controls to ensure that all transactions are posted to the proper records?			
17.	Are there controls to ensure that all transactions are recorded in the proper accounting period?			
18.	Are there controls to ensure that all transactions have been properly authorized?			
19.	Are there controls to ensure that the organization's procedures and processing rules have been fairly performed?			
	Data File Controls			
20.	Are there controls to ensure that the data in the file are accurate and complete?			
21.	Are there means to provide both external and internal identification as to what data are on the file?			
22.	Is there information provided as to when the file was created or modified?			
23.	Is there information provided as to how long the file should be retained, in what format, and where?			
24.	Is there information provided as to who has accessed the file, and for what purpose?			
25.	Are there safeguards provided, such as passwords or authorized terminals, to protect the file from unauthorized access?			

FIGURE 73 (Cont.)

Item No.	Item	Software Package		
	Output Controls			
26.	Are there controls to ensure that the processed data do no include any unauthorized alterations?			
27.	Are there controls to ensure that the data contained in output reports are complete and accurate?			
28.	Are there controls to ensure that the data contained in output reports are reasonable?			
29.	Are there controls to ensure that all errors detected by the system have been corrected?			
30.	Can the processing system reasonably transmit reports in a timely manner to the group for which the output was intended?			
	Teleprocessing Controls			
31.	Do the transmitted messages include sufficient identification, including message number, terminal, date, and transaction type?			
32.	Are positive checks built into transmitted data, such as self-checking numbers, to validate that the entered data are correct?			
33.	Is feedback of the message reception provided to the sender including a check on the content received?			
34.	Are logs maintained to ensure that lost or garbled messages can be recreated?			
35.	Is access to a specific record limited to one transaction at a time, to prohibit concurrent updating of a record?			
36.	Is there assurance that only authorized individuals have access to the system and the data in the system by the use of techniques such as passwords, locks, or cryptography?			

FIGURE 73 (Cont.)

Item No.	Item	Software Package		
	Audit Trail Controls			
37.	Is information provided for user personnel to make corrections to erroneous transactions?			
38.	Is information provided to show users of the system why specific results were obtained?			
39.	Are controls and information provided to ensure that conformance with governmental regulations is maintained?			
40.	Is information retained to permit reconstruction of transactions to prove the accuracy and completeness of the processing?			

developing applications in accounting, financial, and other areas requiring tight control.

The audit and control considerations in this checklist can be considered a minimum set of items to review.

General Audit Considerations includes:

* The vendor's responsibility in correcting and updating the system.
* The documentation and backup of the system.
* The procedures for selecting and including control features.

Input Controls includes:

* The authorization and handling of transactions.
* The efficiency and the control of data input.

Processing Controls includes:

* The completeness and accuracy of the data processing.
* The assurance that the organization's procedures and processing rules are fairly performed.

Data File Controls includes:

* The control of the accuracy and completeness of the data in the system files.
* The existence of safeguards on the access, use, and alteration of data in the files.

Output Controls includes:

* The assurance that all the intended output is transmitted to the authorized user.
* The control of errors in the output phase.

Teleprocessing Controls includes:

* The control of the accurate acceptance, transmission, and receipt of teleprocessed data.

- The assurance that only authorized individuals have access to the system.

Audit Trail Controls includes:

- The preparation of information about the use of the system and the corrections to entries.
- The existence of information to permit reconstruction of transactions for audit purposes.

Standards and Documentation Considerations

This checklist, Figure 74, describes some areas that may be critical to the long-term success of the use of the CASE tool and the application development, and that should be reviewed. Standards and documentation are often considered as administrative problems and are given little attention. However, they are fundamental to the smooth operation of the system in the operational and maintenance phase. The lifetime cost of a system can be greatly increased if the standards are weakly enforced and the documentation is inadequate.

Some of the areas that should be reviewed are:

- The conformity of the package to existing standards and procedures in the organization.
- The detail and accuracy of the standards and procedures prepared by the vendor.
- Whether the vendor's documentation includes all the information that will surely be required by the user over the lifetime of the system.
- The clarity, accuracy, and usability of the documentation material.

6.7 USE OF METRICS IN SOFTWARE PACKAGE COMPARISON

If the project team assembled to search for a CASE software package and make a selection is not large, and the packages being considered are quite different, then a reasonable technical analysis

FIGURE 74. Evaluation of software packages: standards and documentation considerations.

Item No.	Item	Software Package		
1.	Does the package conform to existing standards and procedures within the organization?			
2.	If the package does not conform to existing standards: a. Can it be modified to conform easily? b. Can the standards be changed? c. Are the users satisfied with the standards and procedures offered?			
3.	Does the vendor describe the standards and procedures in sufficient detail to establish conformity and make documentation easy?			
4.	Does the package conform to your standards of the programming language used at the current release level?			
5.	Does the vendor provide standard documentation?			
6.	Does the vendor's documentation include: a. Narrative description of the program? b. Equipment configuration required? c. Logic flow charts? d. Run time estimates for each program? e. Record and file layouts with detailed data element definitions? f. Count of source instructions and estimate of machine operations to be executed? g. Core and disk requirements? h. Special processing techniques or data handling requirements? i. Program maintenance requirements and technical support available? j. Operating and support personnel requirements? k. Training required and suggested schedules? l. Expandability of programs? m. Definition of all audit tests and edits in the system?			

FIGURE 74. (Cont.)

Item No.	Item	Software Package		
7.	Does the documentation match the current version of the system and your hardware?			
8.	Is the documentation easily referenced?			
9.	Does it provide enough information to allow modification of the package if necessary?			
10.	Is the documentation aimed at both user and EDP personnel?			
11.	Would the documentation, as supplied, be adequate as training text?			
12.	Does the terminal operator documentation have clear representations of the screens, with straightforward and clear text?			
13.	Will new documentation accompany new releases of the package?			
14.	Are publication notices offered regularly that reflect changes in the documentation?			

of the alternatives and a few discussions will result in a clear decision as to which package to select. On the other hand, in many cases of software selection:

- Six or more on the project team are from different groups.
- Two or more departments in the organization are interested in the outcome.
- Two or three packages are quite similar in quality, but differ in detail.
- The packages are large, complex, and interrelated.
- Outside consultants may be involved in the selection.

If any of these conditions exist, it is simply not enough to "get a good feel" for the packages. It is best to state the variables involved as objectively as possible and to apply some sort of measuring scale—that is, use a metrics approach. Discussions will then tend to center on specific numbers assigned to definable points. The final outcome will arise from the sum of all the smaller agreements that were made.

A metrics approach cannot be undertaken without:

- Considerable initial discussion of the software package characteristics under review.
- Agreement on what characteristics are necessary and what are merely desirable.
- Discussion of the weighting factors being employed and a willingness to rework them until most participants are satisfied with the scale.
- An understanding that the numbers that fall out are only comparisons on a relative scale and cannot be extended to expected costs, for example.

If the project team all agree that a metrics approach is the best way to assign values and solve disputes, it will be an efficient and economical way to compare alternatives. It tends to bring people to the more important points and to center the discussions on issues that matter.

Figure 75 is one of the better types of form sheets that can

FIGURE 75. Weighted comparison of software packages.

Necessary package characteristics	Weighting Factor	Vendor/Package		Vendor/Package		Vendor/Package	
		Rating	Score	Rating	Score	Rating	Score
	*	**		**		**	
User requirements (3 or Less)							
Computer/operating system/language compatibility							
Is package acceptable or not acceptable							

* Weight on a scale of 1 to 10

** Rate on a scale of 1 to 5

Score = (rating) x (weighting factor)

FIGURE 75. (Cont.)

Desirable package characteristics			
Total Score			

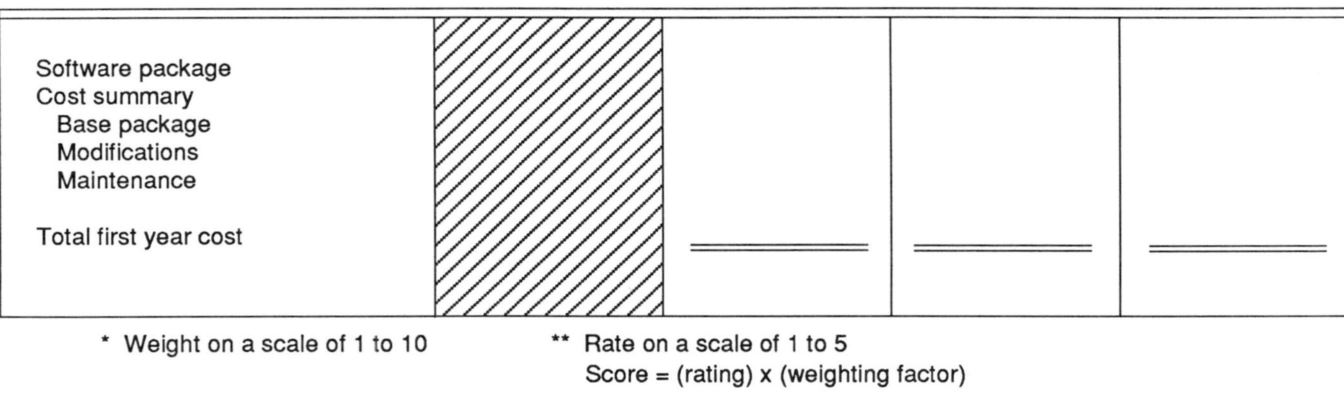

* Weight on a scale of 1 to 10

** Rate on a scale of 1 to 5
Score = (rating) x (weighting factor)

be used in a metrics approach. The steps to be followed and the use of the form sheet are as follows:

- *Preparing the Comparison Worksheet*

    a. Gather the project team and discuss the characteristics of the software package under consideration.

    b. List all the characteristics that come up in the discussion, and place them in an approximate order of importance.

    c. Decide which three, or fewer, of the characteristics are absolutely *necessary* to have in the package. These will normally be the key specified user requirements.

    d. Decide what level of computer/operating system/software language compatibility is *necessary*. Note that sometimes compatibility can be obtained at extra cost, if it is not currently available.

    e. Decide which four to twelve of the characteristics of the software package are clearly *desirable* and should enter into the analysis.

    f. Reject the other characteristics that were listed in Step b, but not until the team compares their importance individually against the characteristics already chosen. Do not hesitate to change the list several times as the discussion proceeds, but the chairperson must get decisions made on these characteristics.

    g. List the selected characteristics on Figure 28 in an order of importance or an order that makes sense technically or operationally.

    h. Assign *weighting* factors on a scale of 1 to 10 for the characteristics. The assigned numbers may be duplicated, and all numbers from 1 to 10 need not be used. Most of the necessary characteristics should have weighting factors close to 10. The other factors will vary according to the feelings of the team. Characteristics will vary greatly in importance, and there should be some low weighting factors in the list.

- *Applying Package Ratings*

    i. Have smaller groups, or the whole team, study the alternative packages and assign ratings for each package for each of the characteristics.

j. Use a scale of 1 to 5 for the ratings. These are arbitrary, and in no sense are they "real" numbers. That is, they cannot be used for extensive arithmetic or manipulation because they do not follow the laws of mathematics. One person's 2 may be another person's 4. A scale of 1 to 5 is fairly easily controlled as follows:

> 5—Excellent or completely acceptable
> 4—Good or acceptable
> 3—Average or passable
> 2—Below Average or barely meets requirements
> 1—Poor or requires modification

A scale of 1 to 10 cannot be controlled between different groups of people or even within one group at different times. The gradations of the numbers become meaningless.

k. In all cases, when several packages are being considered, give only one package a rating of 5. Select the best package for that particular characteristic and declare it the winner. The ratings for the other packages need not be unique, such as 5, 4, 3, 2, however, because trying to line up all packages for all characteristics can be quite difficult and time consuming. The team should simply give the other packages ratings according to their feelings about the approximate position they would have on the arbitrary scale of 5 to 1. Thus, they would seldom be rated 5, 4, 3, but would more likely be rated 5, 4, 2 or 5, 2, 1, or 5, 3, 3.

- *Developing the Scores*

l. Multiply each rating by its weighting factor, and enter in the score column. That is:

Score = (Rating) × (Weighting Factor)

m. Sum all the scores in each column, both the necessary and the desirable characteristics scores, and enter in the total score spaces.

- *Software Package Cost Summary*

n. Summarize the cost information obtained from the worksheets in Chapter 7, and enter comparative costs for the base package, any required modifications to the package, and the maintenance costs for the first year. This will give a rough, comparative figure to aid in the screening of the packages.

- *Determining "Go/No Go"*

    o. Review the ratings for the necessary package characteristics. If any of these characteristics have ratings of 2 or 1 (below average or poor) or if any of the necessary characteristics are not met by the package, write "Not Acceptable" in the column. If all the necessary characteristics are met and the ratings are reasonable, write "Acceptable" in the column.

    p. Determine whether modification or payment for extra features could make the package acceptable.

    q. If the package cannot be made acceptable, mark it as such, and remove it from further consideration.

- *Review of the Ratings, Score, and Cost*

    r. Reproduce the worksheet, and give it to all members of the project team.

    s. Have the project team review the validity of the scoring, and make a recommendation to accept the package with the highest score if there are no extenuating circumstances.

    t. If extenuating circumstances or other considerations are brought up to affect the outcome of the score, state them objectively.

    u. Repeat the weighted comparison of the packages that are acceptable, introducing other considerations that have been brought into the discussion.

Package Selection Report

When the project team has made a decision on the acquisition of a software package, possibly using this metrics approach, a package selection report should be written and distributed to interested management for concurrence and approval. The package selection report should contain a summary of:

- Advantages and disadvantages of the selected package.
- The vendor selection and the reasons for the selection, possibly including the weighted comparison worksheet covering the packages in the final selection decision.
- The costs and benefits of the particular package recommended.

- The installation plan with dates of key milestones.
- A recommendation for approval of the report by management.

Example of the Weighted Comparison

Figure 76 gives the types of entries and numbers that may possibly appear in such a selection. In this example, three vendors are designated C, Y, and Z. Descriptions of their packages should be attached.

Vendor Y's package received reasonable ratings on the User Requirements. In fact, it was the best package for "Reports produced." It only received a rating of 1 for Computer compatibility, however, and this rating made it "not acceptable." If the package is attractive, discussions with the vendor may show that it can be made compatible at a certain cost. If there is any interest in the package, this avenue should be explored further, and then another weighted comparison made in which that rating would be better, but the cost of the package would be higher.

On the "Total Score," the Vendor X package was higher. Note, however, that the difference between Vendor X and Vendor Z on the total score is less than 5 percent. This is not a significant difference in rating schemes with assumed numbers such as this. The difference should be greater than 10 percent ordinarily to show a significant difference. On the other hand, the Vendor X package is nearly 10 percent less expensive than the Vendor Z package. The combination of the better score and the lower cost make it very reasonable to select Vendor X in this case.

If the cost differential had been the other way around, further study would be required to distinguish between the packages. In the example shown, however, the selection would probably still go to Vendor X because of its higher ratings in the very significant "Necessary User Requirements."

The Use of the Metrics Approach

It should be clear that, when using the metrics approach in such a manner, the result does not necessarily fall out automatically and finally. Frequently, there is still much discussion needed.

FIGURE 76. Weighted comparison of software packages (example).

Necessary package characteristics	Weighting Factor	Vendor/X		Vendor/Y		Vendor/Z	
		Rating	Score	Rating	Score	Rating	Score
	*	**		**		**	
User requirements (3 or Less)							
Examples:							
Functions Handled	10	5	50	3	30	3	30
Reports Produced	8	4	32	5	40	3	24
Computer/operating system/language compatibility	10	4	40	1	10	5	50
Is package acceptable or not acceptable		Acceptable		Not acceptable unless modified		Acceptable	

* Weight on a scale of 1 to 10

** Rate on a scale of 1 to 5
Score = (rating) x (weighting factor)

Desirable package characteristics						
Examples						
Vendor support & service	5	4	20	2	10	5	25
Ease of modifying system	8	5	40	2	16	3	24
System expandability	8	5	40	3	24	2	16
System reliability	7	3	21	5	35	4	28
User opinions	4	3	12	2	8	5	20
Desired requirements:							
- Input devices	8	4	32	2	16	5	40
- Inquiry capability	3	5	15	1	3	3	9
- Report generation	3	2	6	3	9	5	15
Ease of conversion	5	5	25	2	10	4	20
Audit & control features	7	3	21	5	35	3	21
Security features	6	2	12	4	24	5	30
Total Score			366		270		352

FIGURE 76. (Cont.)

Software package cost summary			
Base package	$65,000	$35,000	$58,000
Modifications	15,000	30,000	28,000
Maintenance	5,000	13,000	7,000
Total first year cost	$85,000	$68,000	$93,000

* Weight on a scale of 1 to 10

** Rate on a scale of 1 to 5

Score = (rating) x (weighting factor)

On the other hand, the value of such an approach is great when there are several parties involved in the selection, all with different objectives in mind. This approach gives a clear description of how the packages were rated, for what reasons, and how the selection decision was reached. At any later time, others can pick up on the same discussion and know what principal points were considered, and why certain packages were rejected and others were considered most possible. In one sense, this approach leaves a clear "audit trail" of the route taken in the decision process of the project team and states their thinking objectively.

Despite some of its problems, the metrics approach to package selection is undoubtedly the superior method of reaching a final decision objectively and of documenting the decision clearly and succinctly.

CHAPTER **7**

Experiences with CASE Tools

Overview

*T*his section consists of a number of experiences with CASE tools and toolsets as reported by companies using CASE on strategic problems. The experiences have been summarized, and some notes about the CASE products used have been supplied.

• Section 7.1   Experiences With CASE Tool Selection and With Excelerator at AT&T.

CASE is a strategic decision. It is critical to establish accurate and complete requirements for your particular business based upon the way that you develop systems. With CASE, you must have a trained analyst and designer who can deal with the users, find out what the real business requirements are, and deliver the right solution.

Based upon the above premise, the evaluation and selection of CASE tools at AT&T are discussed. The CASE tool must fit within a defined strategic direction. High-level requirements and detailed tasks for product evaluation must be established. For AT&T, the major high-level requirements included: extensive use of expert systems, reverse engineering, automatic logging of design changes, design sharing, and version and generation control. The evaluation of the many potential products required that the field be narrowed and the finalists be rigorously exercised.

The results of these efforts lead to the selection of Excelerator as an interim solution, and of the Bachman Methodology as the best fit for their long-term solution. Information about Excelerator is supplied.

- Section 7.2   Selection of the Bachman Methodology by AT&T
Information about the Bachman Methodology is supplied.

- Section 7.3   The Motorola MIS CASE Program

The objective of the CASE program at Motorola is to develop an environment where the business analyst employs automated tools to create rigorous system specifications that drive application generator products to build systems based upon relational data structures. The result will be to deliver systems that are characterized by accurate definition and execution to user requirements, zero defects in the software, and rapidly modifiable system components. The MIS productivity improvement program is described, together with the portfolio of tools and procedures, and the hardware/software investment level.

The effect of CASE tools on the software life cycle is noted. Motorola's experience has been that there are CASE tools available that can significantly improve productivity, but they require a good methodology, the integration of products, and employee involvement with an expectation of success. The price is high, but so are the paybacks.

- Section 7.4   Changing the Application Life Cycle at The Hartford

The adoption of a CASE environment at The Hartford has had significant implications from the people and the management points of view. Their traditional system life cycle was widely used, was capable of supporting large project teams, and was successful in delivering computer applications. It was comfortable, but it was not data focused. It did not allow applications to be engineered from standard blocks or objects. Yet, the new application engineering methodology requires a major shift in the way that people work. The responsibilities of the customers and of data processing have become blurred; therefore, strong team interaction and commitment are required. Elapsed time is compressed. Extensive training is necessary.

To encourage the required changes, the Hartford has scrapped the traditional "systems analyst" and "programmer" job titles and replaced them with: facilitator, modeler, prototyper, designer, and project leader. There are three levels for each of these jobs: apprentice, journeyman, and master. The title of an individual is based upon experience and training.

To illustrate these changes, four projects are examined and a glimpse into the future is provided. The results of these different efforts demonstrate that productivity improvements of up to 300 percent can be delivered. The management challenge is to take advantage of the evolution in CASE that encourages change while achieving tool stability.

- Section 7.5   The Information Engineering Facility at Texas Instruments

Texas Instruments looked at CASE as a CAD/CAM for information systems, and set eight objectives for CASE development, which are listed. They met their objectives by developing and using the Information Engineering Facility (IEF), based on James Martin's Information Engineering Framework. Their concepts of Integrated CASE and the CASE Systems Factory are noted. The Information Engineering Facility is outlined.

- Section 7.6   Expert Systems in CASE and the Use of AION at Texas Instruments

The use of AI requires techniques to be learned, products to be selected, and a new mind set for systems analysts. TI developed short-term and long-term goals for their Artificial Intelligence Laboratory, and adopted a complex "technology transfer mission," with the aim of spearheading assimilation of AI tools and techniques into TI's MIS group. They have cooperatively developed a number of expert system projects, some of which are briefly described. TI selected the AION Development System (ADS) for their requirements. They are imbedding expert systems into CASE development efforts.

- Section 7.7   Experience With Implementing Systems Using IEF at Amoco

An information engineering methodology is a rigorous, data-driven methodology that uses a set of interrelated, formal techniques to build and maintain information systems for an enterprise. It has been Amoco's experience that the success of this engineering approach is dependent upon implementing seven formal stages for development and upon having a tool set that will support this methodology.

This section discusses the experiences of Amoco with implementing such a methodology and their experiences with one such tool set, the Information Engineering Facility from Texas Instruments, Inc. The paper is focused on a portion of those experiences, namely:

- Generation of code using the Information Engineering Facility.

- Methodology weaknesses as experienced by the author.

- Organizational and cultural issues.

While code generation is in the early stages and is, therefore, subject to some of the ususal limitations encountered by early adapters, it has proven to be a successful approach to reducing the effort of developing code that works. The organizational and cultural issues are by far the most difficult. They involve the commitment of senior management, the management of expectations to maintain a realistic set of objectives, the acceptance of a large up-front investment in training and in the costs of the associated technology.

7.1—EXPERIENCES WITH CASE TOOL SELECTION AND WITH EXCELERATOR AT AT&T

NOTE: This section is taken from a presentation by Mary Jane Monks, manager of analysis and design strategies for AT&T. She clearly describes their process for the selection of CASE tools.

AT&T has experimented with CASE tools, and has made an extensive, systematic analysis for the CASE tools that best meet their requirements. As a result of their analysis, the product selections made were:

- As an interim solution, Excelerator and Problem Statement Language (PSL), with and without the graphics front end. They also selected several other "point" products.
- As a long-term solution, *Bachman Information Systems* was selected.

Information about Excelerator is supplied in this section.

AT&T did an in-house prototype of a CASE tool in 1984 because there was nothing on the market that met their needs. AT&T was moving into an area of corporate data administration, integration, and database sharing. Thus, an in-house prototype was built and shared with about 40 or 50 different people—data analysts, database administration, and data administrators—on a corporate, departmental, or functional area perspective.

The conservative benefit estimates given by the users of the prototype reflected a 10 to 50 percent productivity gain, based on the tools used today. The 50 percent improvement was based on using paper and pencil, white boards, or flip charts. At the lower end of the scale, some people were using products aimed specifically at doing the data portion of the methodology.

The estimates were even higher for quality gains because the idea of a corporate view and enterprise-wide logical data model was in the prototype. People could browse through, download portions of their work effort, and then merge changes into the corporate view. When it came time to estimate the cost to build it, the amounts were phenomenal—up to $15 million for the data analysis tool alone. AT&T did not want to spend that much money. The requirements for the rest of the product were considered and the estimate was at least double the cost of the data analysis portion. With prices like that, it was time to do another industry search.

AT&T developed a set of more than 500 detailed requirements, which were grouped into categories,—resulting in two sets of requirements. One was a high-level strategic set used to make the first few passes through the products available on the market. The second set were at a detailed level where they concentrated on what to implement (not how to implement)—or what must the CASE tool provide?

AT&T wanted a full-range of life-cycle support. Every step of the life cycle, from stategic planning through maintenance and retirement of the system, needed to be supported. They also wanted it to include project management, corporate data administration, and corporate architecting of information systems. There were more than 100 products on the market; but most were ruled out rapidly. This left about 40 products on which they did a more detailed evaluation. Again, a majority of those products were ruled out. About 10 were left, and these vendors were asked to present their products. Four products were selected for hands-on evaluation in the lab. They were: Excelerator, Information Engineering Facility, Information Engineering Workbench, and Bachman Information Systems.

Once the hands-on evaluations were completed, the selections were made. Bachman Information Systems were selected for long-term strategic direction. It was a big leap ahead. However, it was not available in its entirety yet, so interim selections also had to be made. Excelerator was selected because AT&T has a large embedded base of Excelerator users. More than 100 copies reside in-house, and many users share the copies. Another part of the company has a heavily embedded base of Problem Statement Language (PSL) analyzers. Some use the front-end graphics tools for PSL, and some do not. PSL is pre-CASE, but those systems that were already using it could not be forced to use another CASE tool. Other short-term products were selected as appropriate. They are still looking at application generators, code generators, and analysis and design tools that they use because they have software that supports Joint Application Design (JAD) from a documentation standpoint.

The Nature of CASE Decisions

CASE decisions are strategic because:

- There is a significant investment.
- The future of the development environment is being set.
- There is a major cultural change.

A significant amount of money is spent on hardware, software, communications linkages, and training. The future of the development environment is being set in terms of the methodologies, tools, and workstation configurations that will be used, as well as the management processes by which the environment will be managed. It is a major cultural change because skills, job functions, and types of applications that were initially divested into separate operating arms are being brought back together under one AT&T concept. The human–machine interaction also makes the cultural change a major strategy.

AT&T has not dealt one on one with a PC in the development world. Most of the time, the users are dealing with TSO for development; they are not mouse-oriented. When it came time to look at the advisory features, it was important that a team of people write the wording for the advisory messages. It had to be very depersonalized, no "I think. . . ."

As with any strategic decision, the key is knowing where the company is today and where it wants to be in five years. The business plan for developing, operating, maintaining, and supporting business information systems is important.

The strategic plan must be developed. Make sure that the listed requirements are future requirements; they cannot be limited to today's development environment. Look at the future in terms of development environments and supporting architectures. Will development be on the mainframe? Will it move down to the PC level or to the workstation level? What are the supporting architectures that need to be put in place?

A gap analysis needs to be done between where the company wants to be at the end of the five-year planning period and where it is today in terms of the methodology used, the user skills, the development environments, and the operating environments that have to be supported in the future.

The embedded system base has to be considered in terms of the investment in that base and what the replacement plans were. AT&T has many major applications that are not going to be touched for the next 5 or 10 years. Those applications were done in the early 1980s, and they are not going to be rewritten. Something is needed that will allow maintenance of those systems in a shifting business environment.

Based on the gap analysis, strategies were developed that looked at the priorities where CASE support was wanted. Was it primarily in the area of code generation, maintenance, or analysis and design? For AT&T, it was analysis and design. The analysts had no tools other than documentation repositories to support them. Whether a single or a multiple solution was needed had to be determined. Because of the gap, AT&T needed a multiple solution. It needed a long-term strategy with interim steps to move toward that strategy. We developed a tactical/action plan that called for the establishment of a project team. The nucleus of that project team was from our own staff. The project team is made up of people from the actual development organization. It will seed those organizations with the CASE vision of the future. There was feeling that the staff role would become stale. A year or two in a staff role puts the person out of touch with what is going on it the front lines of development. Make sure that these areas are covered.

AT&T had to develop a business case. The quality improvements anticipated for CASE were enough to sell the tools to management. Thus, it is necessary to get management to buy in. We have received high-level support all the way up within AT&T. It is also important to secure developer buy-in. If the developers are not happy using that tool, it is going to be easy for them to unconsciously sabotage its use.

Establishing Requirements

Nothing was being done differently to establish requirements for a CASE tool than what would have been done to analyze the requirements of a high-level business area to perform a detailed-level systems analysis. AT&T had to figure out exactly how the development community was going to support its employees, the lines of business, and the customers. The problems and opportunities needed to be discovered that were driving the CASE exploration.

Productivity improvements were necessary and the quality of delivered systems was not as high as it could have been. Many major new development efforts were coming along because of top-down pyramiding for major business functions. The opportunity exists to develop new functional systems for huge areas of business. An outdated embedded base was becoming difficult to maintain. There was a lack of standards as AT&T brought people back together following the divestiture, combining the long distance arm with the information systems arm, and network services and technologies. The lack of standards occurred because each organization had it own set of standards.

AT&T plan to gain increased productivity and quality from the introduction of CASE. They expect to gain the ability to standardize the processes, products, and documentation. Not only were the systems not transportable from one application area to another, neither were the people. They were using different techniques and different diagrammatic conventions. They were literally not speaking the same language. Also, because of the embedded base, they needed something that would ease the migration of new environments.

All of the areas where CASE was to be supported in-house had to be addressed. Every aspect of the life cycle within the operating and development environments needed to be addressed. Emphasis had to be on the "what," not the "how." Potentially good solutions could be blocked out if concentration was on how a good CASE tool should be architected rather than what it should provide. Thus, AT&T stuck to the logical side of defining the requirements and specified the "what."

Two sets of requirements were developed. (1) A very high-level set of requirements was developed for the first passes through and for setting the strategic directions. It was equivalent to a strategic planning level set of requirements. (2) Detailed requirements were developed to set up the test plans for detailed product evaluations. It was equivalent to the analysis requirements that come out in system development.

As they looked at the high-level requirements, they saw that advanced CASE tools would be needed for:

- Extensive use of expert systems
- Reverse engineering
- Automatic logging of design changes
- Design sharing
- Version and generation control

The idea behind reverse engineering was to capture the existing product, which probably does not resemble the user's original vision. An example is a user who envisions a 747 jet and a hot air balloon is delivered. They both fly, but they have entirely different characteristics. The physical system definition has to be captured and improved to bring it over to a logical system definition without cutting out communications with the user.

The ideal operating environment for CASE tools is shown in Figure 77. The integrated CASE architecture shows the workstations connected to a local area network. It shows what is on the PCs, the minicomputer, and the mainframe. The advanced capabilities needed at the high level include: full system life-cycle coverage, reverse engineering of code, the capture of physical usage information, technology selection and modeling, production system simulation, and user specification.

Establishing requirements at the detailed level requires grouping the requirements by categories such as architecture, physical database design, or project management. Do not expect the list of requirements to be set in concrete. Use them to initially go through and evaluate various vendor products because, as more

FIGURE 77. Integrated CASE architecture.

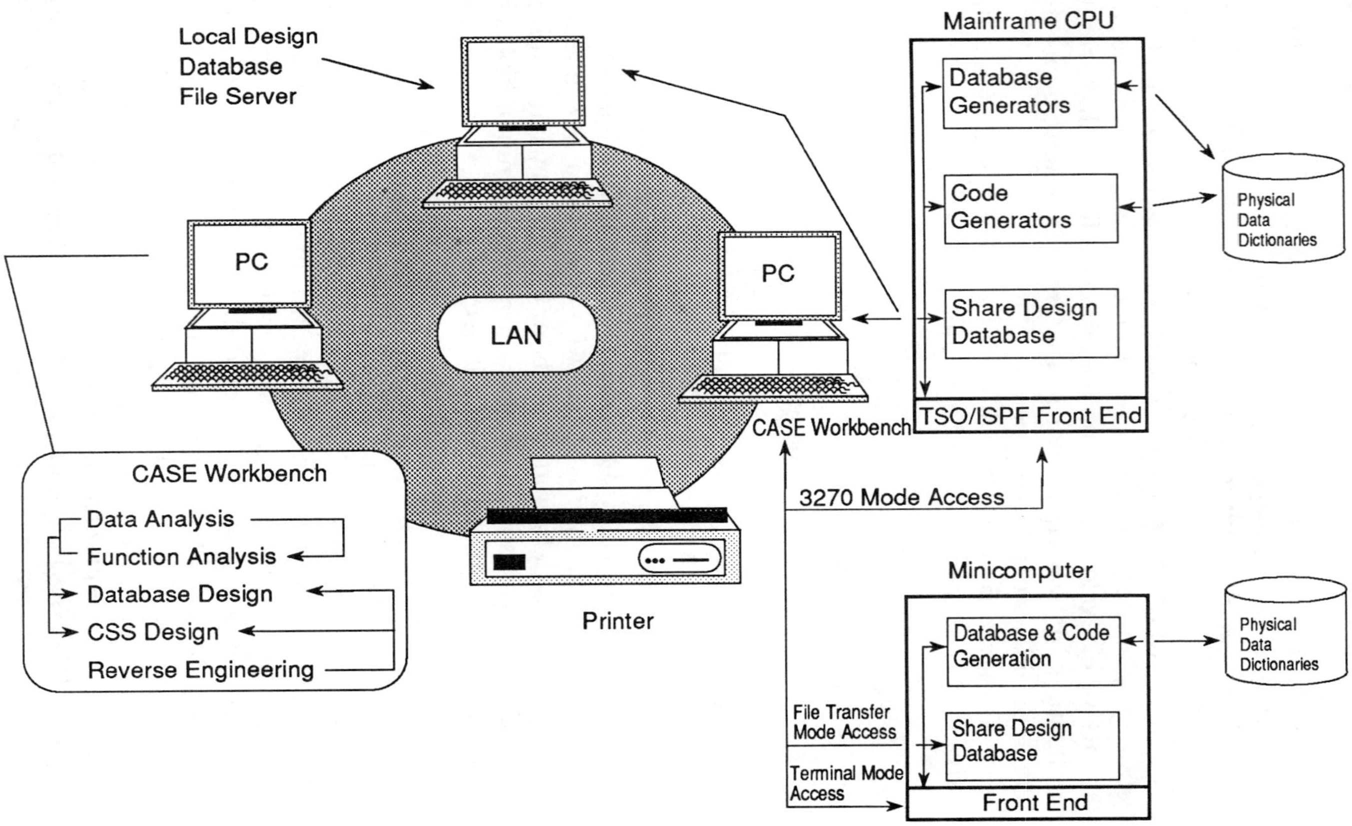

is learned through the long-term direction, more requirements and refinements are required.

It is also critical to include the "must nots" as well as the "musts." There are a number of tools on the market that try to force a bottom-up data analysis approach. This should be unacceptable, even if the tool also supports a top-down approach.

It is essential to be precise and to apply weighting factors to the individual requirements so that those requirements that are more important can be established from those that are not. Requirements do not carry equal weight. There are some that are absolute killers. If a tool could not provide a particular feature, the product was automatically eliminated.

Evaluating Products

Three steps can be applied to evaluating the products:

1. Cutting through the fog
2. Narrowing the field
3. Exercising the finalists

Cutting through the fog is also known as "cutting through the hype." There are more than 100 vendors with CASE products. A number of them are point products aimed at a particular aspect of the development life cycle and are not integrated with other tools. Many are old tools with new names. Suddenly, CASE was the latest buzzword, so things were renamed and labeled CASE even though they bore little resemblance to a full CASE tool kit. The majority of tools with front-end support for analysis and design were little more than documentation repositories for the analysts. They did not do much about validating the completeness and the consistency of the models that were being developed.

They divided CASE tools into three generations for consideration. The first generation was the minimum integrated PC-based tool sets. The second generation was a fully integrated tool set where the graphics and text were fully integrated. This was the beginning of structured specification languages for data and for function. The third generation was the real intelligence tool set that operates on an underlying expert system.

Detail work came when narrowing the field. The first pass was to make a technology scan against what was available in the market using the high-level requirements. On the second pass, AT&T used the high-level requirements again, but added more critical detailed-level requirements. This was used to narrow the scope from 40 possible products to the 10 whose vendors were invited to show them their products.

The second pass determined which products were worth the time to bring in-house for trial. The four products mentioned earlier (Excelerator, Information Engineering Facility, Information Engineering Workbench, and Bachman Information Systems) were brought in for a hands-on evaluation with their own test data. It was crucial to use their own test data because they were using data that was typical of the size of given applications and the complexity of those applications in their environment. An evaluation form was developed for each tool.

When exercising the finalists, use a two-person team. One person can operate the tool and think out loud while the other person records the comments or the individual scores. When one person does the evaluation, he has to interrupt the work flow to write down a comment. There is also an advantage in consensus scoring. There are some things that one person would rate extremely high and someone else would rate extremely low. A better score is reflected when a two-person team is used.

An example of the form developed at AT&T is shown in Figure 78. It lists each requirement by category and a weighting factor can be applied. The form was designed to indicate whether or not the requirement was in the minimum set of requirements, which simply meant, was it available in the first release or was it something they could live without for a period of time? They wanted to indicate which requirements were factual statements and which ones were judgment calls. The score was a representation of how well the product met the requirement versus the judgment call on how effective the user interface was. The availability column (AVAL) in the figure indicates the release that was available for the product or if there were no plans at all for its release. The weightings that were established were on a 10-point scale, indicating whether or not the feature was desired (lowest on the scale) or the feature was critical (highest on the scale).

FIGURE 78. Evaluation form.

Evaluation of ___________ (product name) ___________

Requirement	Wgt	Min Set	Fact Judg	Aval	Comments

1.0 Architecture
 	
  1.1 Hardware and Software operating environment
    1.1.1 No new DBMS required
    1.1.2 New TP monitor not not required at central processor
 	
  1.2 Personal workstation software operates on AT&T hardware
.
.
.
.
.
.					

COLUMN HEAD	VALUE	MEANING
WGT (weight)	2	Desired
	5	Optional
	8	Mandatory
	10	Critical
MIN SET	M	Required now
	blank	Required in future
FACT/JUDG	F	Factual finding
	J	Judgment call
AVAL	CR	Current release
	NR	Next release (within 12 months)
	ST	Strategic commitment to provide (1+ years)
	NP	No plan to provide feature

If the tool did not have a critical feature, it was eliminated. In some cases, the difference between what was desired and optional was purely a judgment call. Four codes were set up for availability: CR for currently available in the current release; NR for the next release or within 12 months from the time the evaluation was done; ST to indicate if a particular vendor had a strategic commitment to provide the particular requirement or feature; and NP to indicate when there was no plan to provide that. When a strategic plan was indicated, AT&T asked for documentation to support it.

The total score each feature could receive was based on the weighting factor, which was modified by the availability code. If a tool had 10 as its weighting factor, and it was currently available, the potential maximum score for that particular requirement would be 10. If it was not currently available, the factor would drop 50 percent or 25 percent. Based on this being the top score, they would then evaluate how well the tool met that particular feature and give it its final score for that category.

Selecting One or More Products

When there are several products to choose from, the product alternatives have to be weighed against each other. The final decision is not based solely on the numeric scores. The scores should be used as an aid. The scores should not be totaled across all the different categories. AT&T looked at a total score for a given category such as architecture, data analysis support, function analysis support, or database design for a given database management system. To total them all up would create an unfair and unrealistic depiction of a particular product's strengths and weaknesses. Other factors that had to be considered included cost, the time it would take to implement, and the "soundness" of the vendor.

The hardware and software costs for a CASE product amounted to about a quarter of the total. The hardware cost can be very expensive, if an environment does not include workstations already. If other alternatives exist to introduce the workstations into the environment, the costs may be reduced. There is an incremental cost to move up to a more advanced workstation. Depending on the solution selected, there could be an increase in central processor loads for storage and handling of shared design repositories. Software can also be expensive because it can add up quickly. Communications can add up also. Can the product support the local area networks or wide area networks? Long distance charges have to considered as well as whether or not a private line or dial-up service is needed.

The biggest costs are for people and training. In areas where people are not using a formal methodology, or where they are using entirely different kinds of methodologies, techniques, or diagrammatic conventions, extensive retraining will be required. User support is a big category, and staff may have to be added to support people as they come on-line with the CASE tools.

The risks associated with each of the products have to be determined and considered. If necessary, a "fall-back" position will have to be set up. AT&T has a fall-back position in place, although they have confidence that the vendor is going to deliver. As a result of the analysis, interim products that would move them forward toward the strategic vision had to be considered.

Planning and Managing the Introduction

Now comes the tough work—planning and managing the introduction. It is a major undertaking. AT&T has about 8,000 different developers centrally within the IMS staff and out in the lines of businesses. They have about 1,700 analysts, but they have no direct control over them. All they can do is encourage them, support them, and tell them success stories so that they will want to use the methods and the tools that are provided for them.

Planning the introduction depends on the current environment, on the tool that is selected, and on the timing of the introduction. AT&T had to consider the interim tool, the ultimate strategic tool, and an embedded base that had mechanized documentation in terms of the existing Excelerator users, existing PSL users, or other users who had picked up other tools along the way. They had major business-critical systems that were totally undocumented because the documentation had gotten lost as people moved around over the years.

The people issues associated with the introduction of the changes are critical. There should at least be a project manager with overall responsibility assigned for the tool. The project team needs to be staffed carefully, and the core team should be kept small so that everything is not run by a committee. There has to be some expertise in the methodology, hardware, software support area, and user consultation. These people skills are important when trying to introduce a drastic change into the users' environment.

Support issues have to be addressed. Who is going to be the first line of contact? Some companies have information centers, end-user computing centers, or both. The first line of contact within these organizations has to be established for the users when they have a problem with the CASE tools. They have a mixed solution. The end users' computing centers will provide some levels of support, and the staff is going to supply others.

Some of the other considerations involved in planning include: how to keep the interest up and how to keep potential users from getting tools other than those recommended. AT&T first made the decision to buy a product in 1987. After almost a year, they were getting ready to pilot the first set of applications. While waiting to start the pilot, a large amount of time was devoted to keeping interest up and, at the same time, preventing the users from going out and purchasing other tools. They have a lot of control within the organization over mainframe software, but they have very little control over something that resides on a workstation. Many of their development organizations that they support know this, and they will go out and start looking for their own tools. They are not going to force conversions from the existing tools. However, they are going to provide some conversion aids for those who elect to use them. This will create a problem, however, by going from unstructured tools to ones that have a higher degree of structure and rigor.

When planning and managing the introduction, some of the decisions will depend on the state of the selected tool. If it is a proven tool on the market, easy to get a hold of, easy to use, one approach will be required. If it is a new tool, a different strategy will be needed. AT&T decided to do staff testing before they released the tool to the pilot organization. Then they will pilot some applications. They have 14 major development centers in AT&T, and will not be able to hit all of them. By running five or six different pilots, however, they can hit five or six different locations as "seed" groups for introducing CASE into the rest of their organizations.

CASE is definitely a strategic decision. It should not be looked upon as an operational or tactical decision because mistakes made today that have led to isolated pockets of automation will continue to be made. It is critical to establish accurate and complete requirements for your particular business and for the way that you develop and support systems. Carefully evaluate the available products based upon those requirements and select the best product for your needs, not the needs of other organizations. Also, realize that the introduction is a major undertaking.

With CASE it is also critical that you still have a trained analyst and designer. They have to have a good basic foundation in the techniques and the methodologies that they are using or you will get a big mess fast. It is important for those professional people to go out and deal with the users and find out what the real business requirements are so that time and resources are not expended on building the wrong solution to a problem.

Excelerator

Excelerator is a product of Index Technology Corporation, One Main Street, Cambridge, MA 02142. It provides systems analysts with the tools required to quickly produce, modify, and verify specifications for information systems in one environment.

Excelerator automates the critical early phases of the software development life cycle—feasibility, requirements, analysis, and design. During these phases, when errors and inconsistencies can be caught and corrected before they become costly, Excelerator helps ensure the completeness, consistency, and accuracy of the design.

With Excelerator systems analysts can estimate the impact of one change on all parts of the system design, which gives them the flexibility to respond quickly to users' requests for changes and enhancements. They can consider all alternatives and then select the best design. This flexible design process reduces programming and maintenance time, and lowers costs for the entire project.

Excelerator offers a set of easy-to-use, integrated facilities that are menu and mouse driven:

Graphics.

Excelerator's Graphics facility provides a full range of capabilities for creating six types of graphs. Excelerator provides the tools and symbols to create and manipulate each type of graph:

- Data flow diagrams
- Structure charts
- Structure diagrams
- Logical data models
- Entity-Relationship data models
- Presentation graphs

Objects and flows in each graph can be "exploded" to more detailed graphs and entities. For example, the Data Model Diagram facility allows analysts to create models of data structures that include data record descriptions as well as more detailed data model diagrams. Presentation graphs are useful in capturing user requirements, and in establishing the feasibility of new or renovated systems.

Dictionary & Analysis.

Excelerator's dictionary is the heart of Excelerator and is the keystone to greater productivity. All the information about the system—including data structures, process logic, screen definitions, report layouts, and system design diagrams—can be maintained in one place. In the Dictionary facility, analysts can quickly review and update system documentation, list dictionary entries on the screen, or create or update any of the items stored in the dictionary.

The Analysis facility provides tools that verify the accuracy, completeness, and consistency of the design. Graph analysis reports, entity lists, and dictionary reports provide cross-referencing of all dictionary entities, and allow the analyst to detect and correct errors early in the design process.

Screens.

Excelerator also offers a full-function screen painting facility that allows the system designer to develop design prototypes of the system's front-end screens and user-interface menus. Field and label attributes such as reverse video, blinking, and help messages can be described and stored along with the screen descriptions in the dictionary.

Developing a screen is so quick and easy that it is possible for the actual users of the system to design their own menus and data entry screens—including help messages.

The Screen Design facility provides an effective environment for rapid production and processing of simulations of the actual screen dialogue. The system designer can work with the users to produce the most effective screen displays. By walking the users through a simulated terminal session, the designer can get immediate feedback from potential users of the system. This can be an extremely efficient way to ensure that the system meets the real needs of the users.

Reports.

The reports of a system are frequently the most time-consuming part of a system to specify. With the report design features of Excelerator, analysts can work more closely with the users of the system to develop more useful and informative reports.

The Report Design facility is similar to the screen painting facility. The system designer can use the mouse to develop the layout of the system's report—frequently with the user directing exactly how the report should look. The result is a more complete and useful report specification.

Reports can also be generated directly from the dictionary for project reviews, special user presentations, or for inclusion in the final system specification document. A complete report generation facility is available for selecting, formatting, and sorting of output fields. A special report that analyzes data flow diagrams, displaying the data elements entering and leaving each process box, is also provided, aiding the analyst in performing consistency checking.

Documentation.

Documentation is a multifunction facility that includes:

- Document Graph
- Document Production
- Word Processing

This facility allows the project manager and analysts to extract information from the dictionary and word processing files and integrate it into a final system specification document. Document Graph acts as the visual table of contents for all components (such as data flow diagrams, structure charts, data models, narratives, and the like) that you wish included in the specification document. The Document Production facility then actually produces these components. Excelerator provides an interface to PC-based word processors that allows the analyst to develop the narrative portions of the system documentation.

XLD Interface.

The Dictionary Interface facility promotes communication and coordination of many analysts on larger projects. This facility allows analysts to share data between projects as well as with host-based dictionaries. Access privileges can be set to control access to files. Audit attributes automatically monitor which analysts add or modify project elements.

Housekeeping.

Excelerator's Housekeeping facility provides a set of functions for maintaining Excelerator. It contains utilities for backing up and restoring files, changing user passwords and access privileges for the entire system and individual projects, and setting the system configuration.

The hardware support for Excelerator is standard MS-DOS personal computers with 640K, high-resolution graphics, and mouse device.

Supported machines include:

- IBM Personal System/2
- IBM PC/AT, PC/XT
- IBM 3270 PC/AT
- Compaq III
- Compaq Plus
- Compaq Portable 286
- AT&T 6300
- HP Vectra

also, 32-bit environments:

- VAXstation 2000 family
- Apollo DN3000

Customizer makes the Excelerator family of productivity tools even more effective. It helps you create a custom development environment that works the way your organization works.

With Customizer you can modify Excelerator to collect exactly the information your organization needs when designing systems. In addition, Customizer provides the ability to integrate into the design environment other facilities your developers use in the development life cycle.

When you have finished building your custom development environment, you can distribute it across the organization to systems analysts and developers already using Excelerator. These systems professionals will then have—in one tailored environment—all the facilities they need to design better systems more efficiently.

The systems they build with their customized Excelerator are structured for faster implementation; they are better documented; and they better meet end-user requirements. Also, such systems will ultimately require less maintenance.

Two key files, the System Dictionary and the System Forms Library, largely determine the behavior of Excelerator and Excelerator/RTS℠. Using Customizer's utilities, you can change these files in order to add entity types and attributes, change the menu structure, include new graph types with new graph objects, and more.

Customizer also contains facilities for integrating other software—such as project management software, custom analysis routines, and communications to the mainframe—into the Excelerator menus to work side-by-side with Excelerator's facilities.

Once you have designed the new environment, you can transfer the modified System Dictionary and Systems Form Library to all workstations currently using Excelerator Version 1.7 or later. With these new files in place, the development environment replaces standard Excelerator and becomes a design environment shared across the organization.

PC Prism

PC Prism translates business goals into systems requirements by providing an automated environment for strategic planning, enterprise modeling, and priority setting. The components of PC Prism are comprehensive, menu-driven facilities, offering step-by-step ease through the planning process. They are Prism Define, Worksheets, Reports, and Utilities.

Prism Define.

Prism Define builds your planning model by allowing you to define your categories and their relationships using your own logic and vocabulary. In this way, you have all the flexibility and adaptability needed to suit your changing requirements, concerns and business climates.

PC Prism's capacity for description and detail is virtually unlimited. You can define up to 15 categories of concern—each with up to 7 lower levels—to describe your planning model. So no matter how large or small your firm, division, or department, all your issues will fit into one planning model. This ensures that your organization shares a single, coherent view of itself and the role of information systems within it.

Worksheets.

The Worksheet Facility enables you to detail, validate, and prioritize the categories established in Prism Define. You actually build a database of information as you describe each component.

You use matrices to build and edit relationships among categories. These matrices, supported by extensive textual description, let you see key connections and related details in their proper perspective. You can then focus on the concerns that offer the highest impact on corporate objectives.

In addition, PC Prism's matrix feature has extensive sorting and clustering capabilities that open up other new possibilities. Besides revealing unnoticed connections among categories, it can also show where you can reduce duplication between systems. And, it can help you create new systems by rebundling related features and functions.

A benefit of this matrix-based planning process—which includes interviews, analysis, and verification—is better communication within your organization. According to published studies, the kind of communication eliminates the costliest errors in systems development. And, because people at all levels participate, PC Prism assures corporate-wide commitment to the action plan.

Reports.

PC Prism's extensive Report Facility creates both matrix and textual reports. In each case, PC Prism's ability to draw selectively on its database provides you with customized output.

Matrix reports display a series of matrices side by side to give you a better understanding of the interlocking relationships, and a clearer idea of the direction for your systems development. They reveal links among categories that show how a change in one area, for example, system functionality, affects other areas, such as the firm's market share.

Customized reports produce complete documentation on categories and subcategories. They provide information at various levels of detail, for more thorough, accurate, and practical analysis.

The quality and flexibility of this reporting system promote better communication throughout the organization. From the reports, top-level managers quickly see the potential impact of changes. System developers see the synergy of their various projects. In this way, PC Prism makes sure all factors and goals are clear before actual systems development begins.

Utilities.

The Utilities Facility provides effective administrative and powerful data management capabilities. It lets you:

- manage up to six scenarios
- control a network of distributed workstations
- export information directly to Excelerator
- use DOS commands within the PC Prism environment

With PC Prism, you have broad participation in your planning effort, yet maintain tight control over its framework and direction. For instance, the departments or divisions that are part of your distributed network enter information within only the categories you have established. The result is better organizational communication and commitment.

By transferring your high-level requirements directly to Excelerator, the leading software for systems analysis and software design, you can build a system that precisely matches the objectives you have defined. Before you build, you know the strategic purpose, what data are required by whom, and who is responsible at each level. This way, you significantly improve quality while you cut costs.

Excelerator's Ventura Option

The Ventura option in the Document Production Facility enhances Excelerator's documentation capabilities. Excelerator can produce output for Xerox Ventura Publisher, a desktop publishing system. When you use these two software products together, you can produce well-formatted specification documents from your Excelerator project.

The following pages were produced with Xerox Ventura Publisher. The diagrams and reports were generated by Excelerator and integrated through Ventura.

Graph Analysis.

Excelerator Graph Analysis provides a set of reports that help you to assess the status of your graphs. They apply common principles of structured design to data flow diagrams to identify omissions, redundancies, and inconsistencies.

The verification report examines the structural validity of a data flow diagram by identifying freestanding objects and illegal connections. Freestanding objects are not connected to other objects. They do not interact with the system and should be either integrated or eliminated from the diagram. Illegal connections are connections between a data store and an external entity or connections between two data stores or two external entities. These connections may indicate a conceptual problem with the diagram.

The level balancing report helps you to assess consistency between two explosion (decomposition) levels. It analyzes each process that explodes to another data flow diagram and verifies that inputs to and outputs from the process on the parent level correspond to data flows on the child or lower-level diagram.

When the verification report was run for the Clones Inventory Control System overview, a number of illegal connections were identified.

After reviewing the Excelerator verification report, the system overview data flow diagram was modified. The illegal connections were eliminated along with an external entity.

Following the modifications made to the data flow diagram, the level balancing report was run.

The level balancing report revealed several inconsistencies that were caused by the previous changes. The context data flow diagram was modified to resolve these.

7.2 SELECTION OF THE BACHMAN METHODOLOGY BY AT&T

The AT&T study group selected the Bachman Methodology for their long-term solution because of the conditions that were discussed in previous sections. There are many applications yet to be developed, and Excelerator and other CASE tools are fitted for that new development work. There is a tremendous portfolio of already developed application systems, however, which are most difficult and costly to maintain. The maintenance, enhancement, and migration of those existing applications is climbing to over 80 percent of the total systems development effort. The intent of

FIGURE 79. Clones Inc. inventory control system overview.

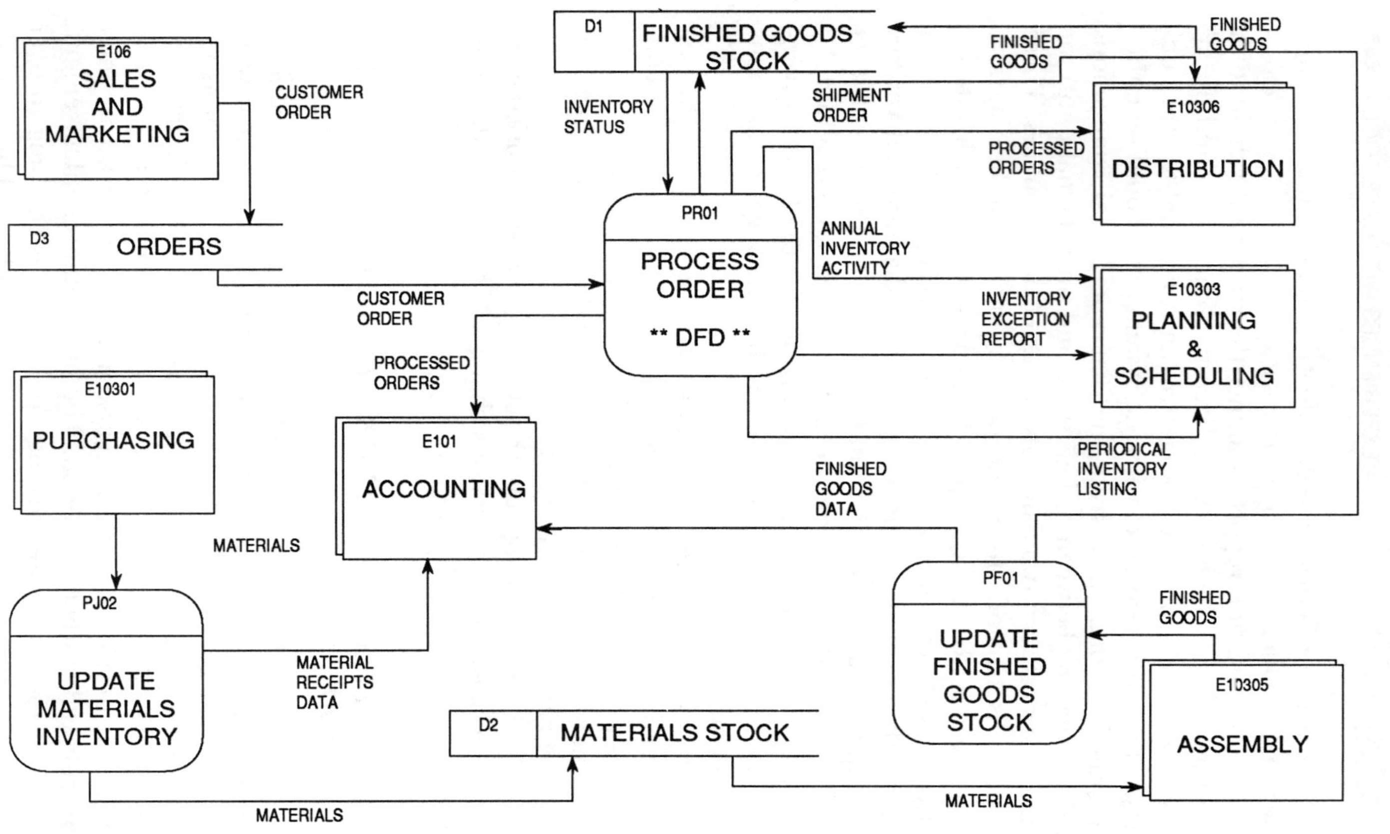

When the verification report was run for the Clones Inventory Control System overview, a number of illegal connections were identified.

FIGURE 80. Data flow diagram verification report.

```
DATE: 8-FEB-88                                                    PAGE  001
TIME: 18:15                                    EXCELERATOR
GRAPH NAME:  CLONES-INV-CTRL-SYSTEM-OVERVIEW
                                                 GRAPH FILE:  IYEAZTR.DFD


             ILLEGAL CONNECTIONS:

     ID           LABEL                        FROM / TO

     D1           CUSTOMER ORDER               EXT / DAS

     D10          MATERIALS                    DAS / EXT

     D2           FINISHED GOODS               DAS / EXT
```

FIGURE 81. Clones Inc. inventory control system overview.

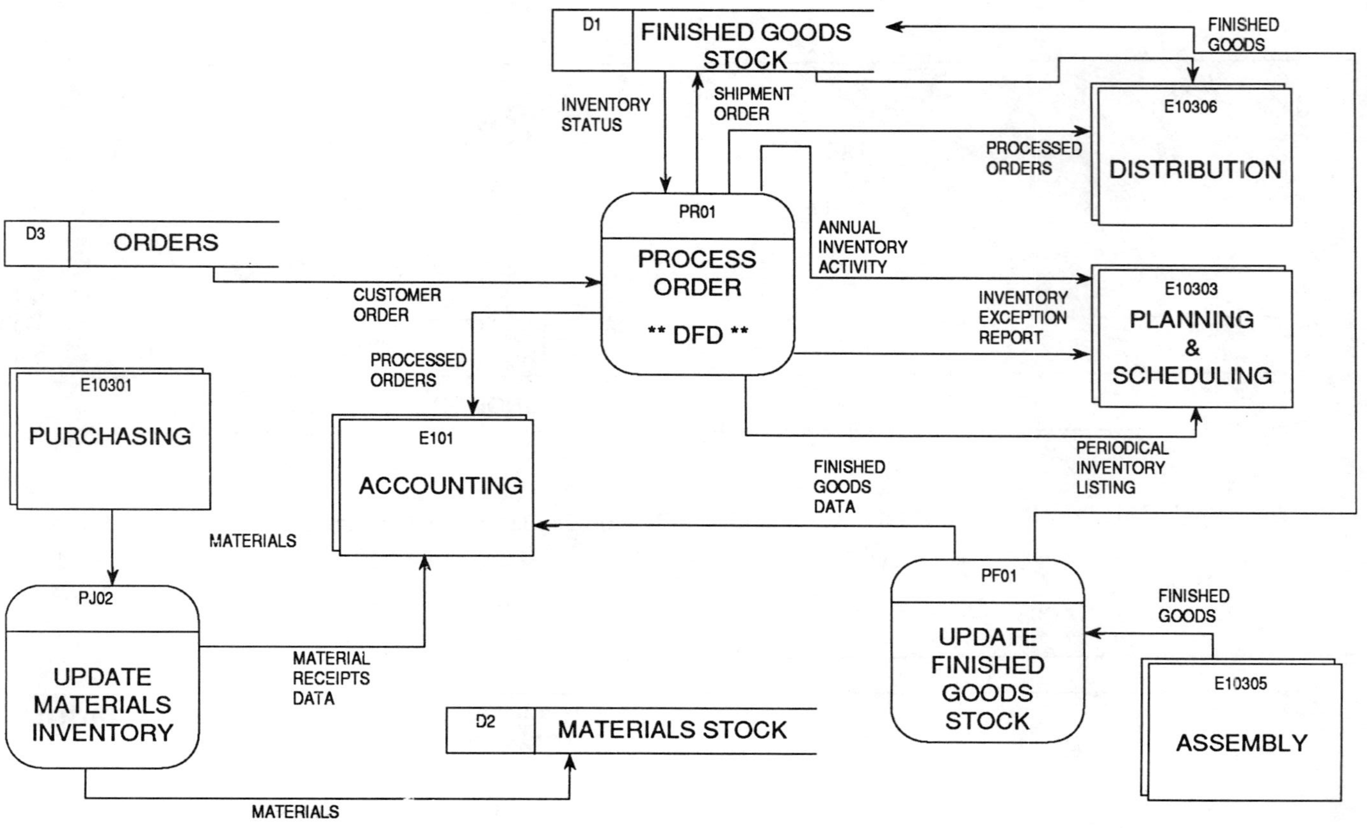

FIGURE 82. Data flow diagram level balancing.

DATE: 8-FEB-88   PAGE 001

TIME: 18:33   EXCELERATOR

GRAPH NAME: CLONES-INV-CTRL-CONTEXT-DIAGRAM   GRAPH FILE: IYHEWI0.DFD

Level Number: 0

Parent Graph Name: CLONES-INV-CTRL-CONTEXT-DIAGRAM

Entity   Prnt

Type   Dir Chld

------ ---- ---- --------Name (ID) or Error Message ----------- -------------------Label ----------------------------

Process   P 0.0   CLONES   INVENTORY CONTROL SYSTEM

Graph   C CLONES-INV-CTRL-SYSTEM-OVERVIEW

Flow   IN P D1   CUSTOMER ORDER

Record   P ORDER

   ***Error - Parent Data Flow Contents do not match any Child Flow Contents (refers to
   above item(s))

Flow   OUT P D10   MATERIALS

   ***Error - Parent Data Flow does not match any Child Flows (refers to above item(s))

Flow   OUT P D2   FINISHED GOODS

   ***Error - Parent Data Flow does not match any Child Flows (refers to above item(s))

*****END OF REPORT*****

FIGURE 83. Clones Inc. inventory control system context diagram.

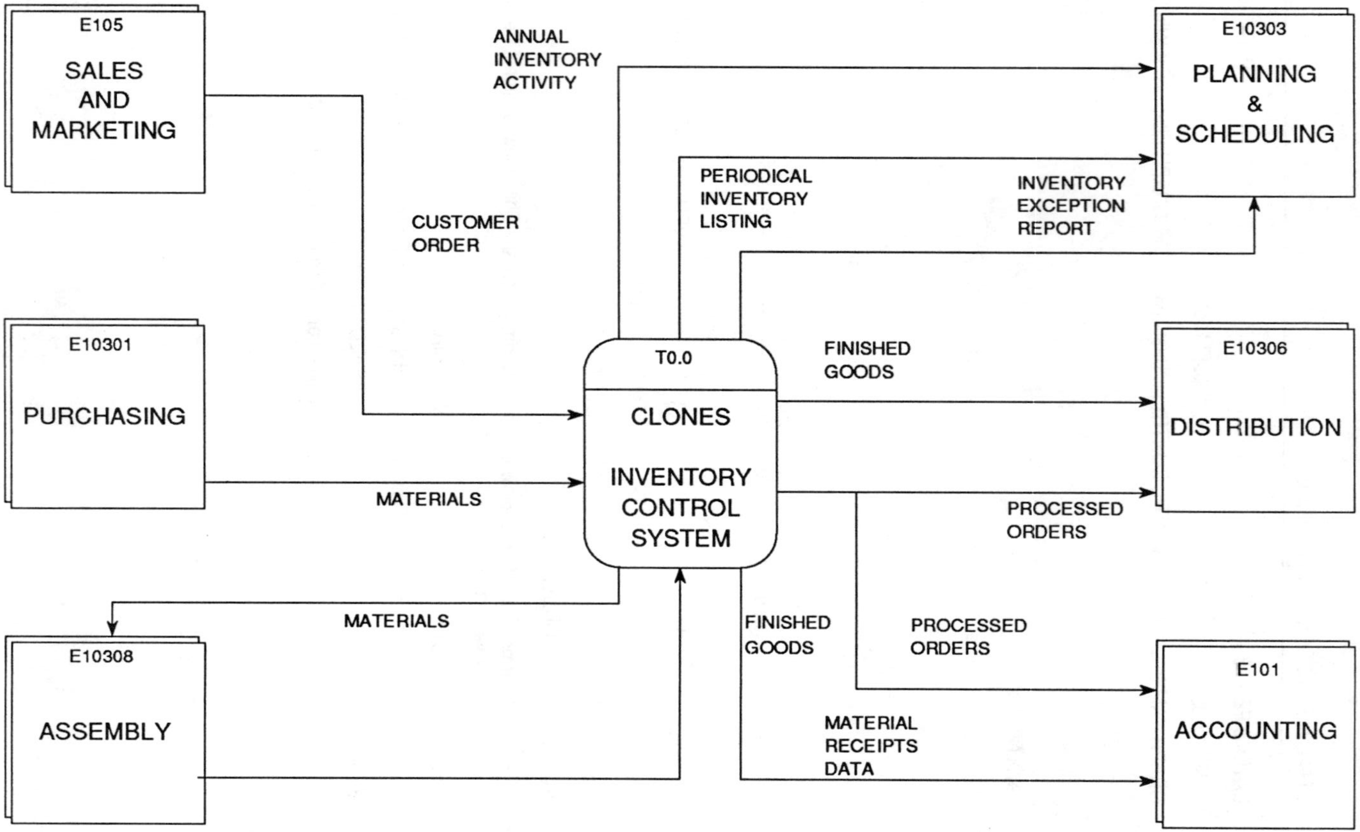

FIGURE 84. Clones Inc. inventory control system context diagram.

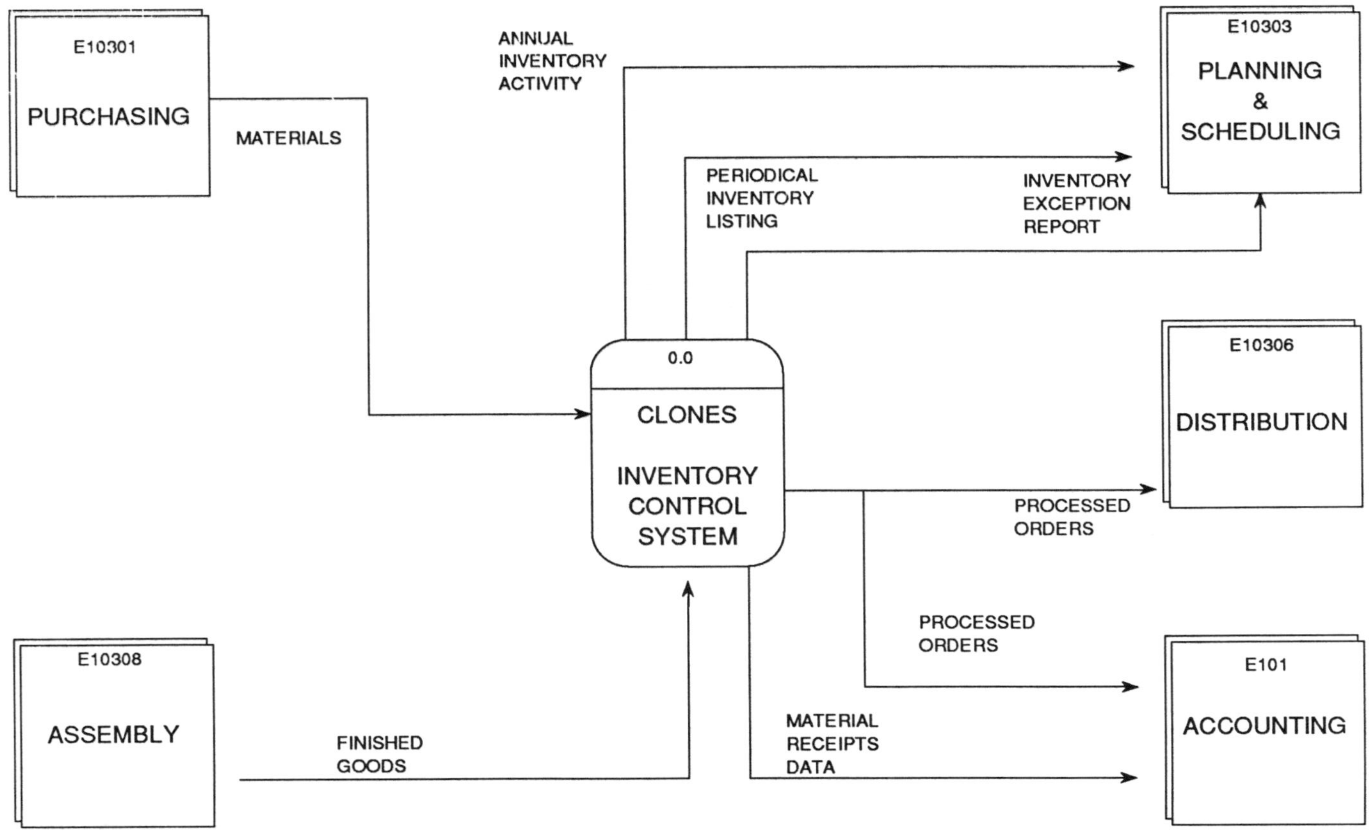

FIGURE 85. Clones Inc. inventory control system context diagram.

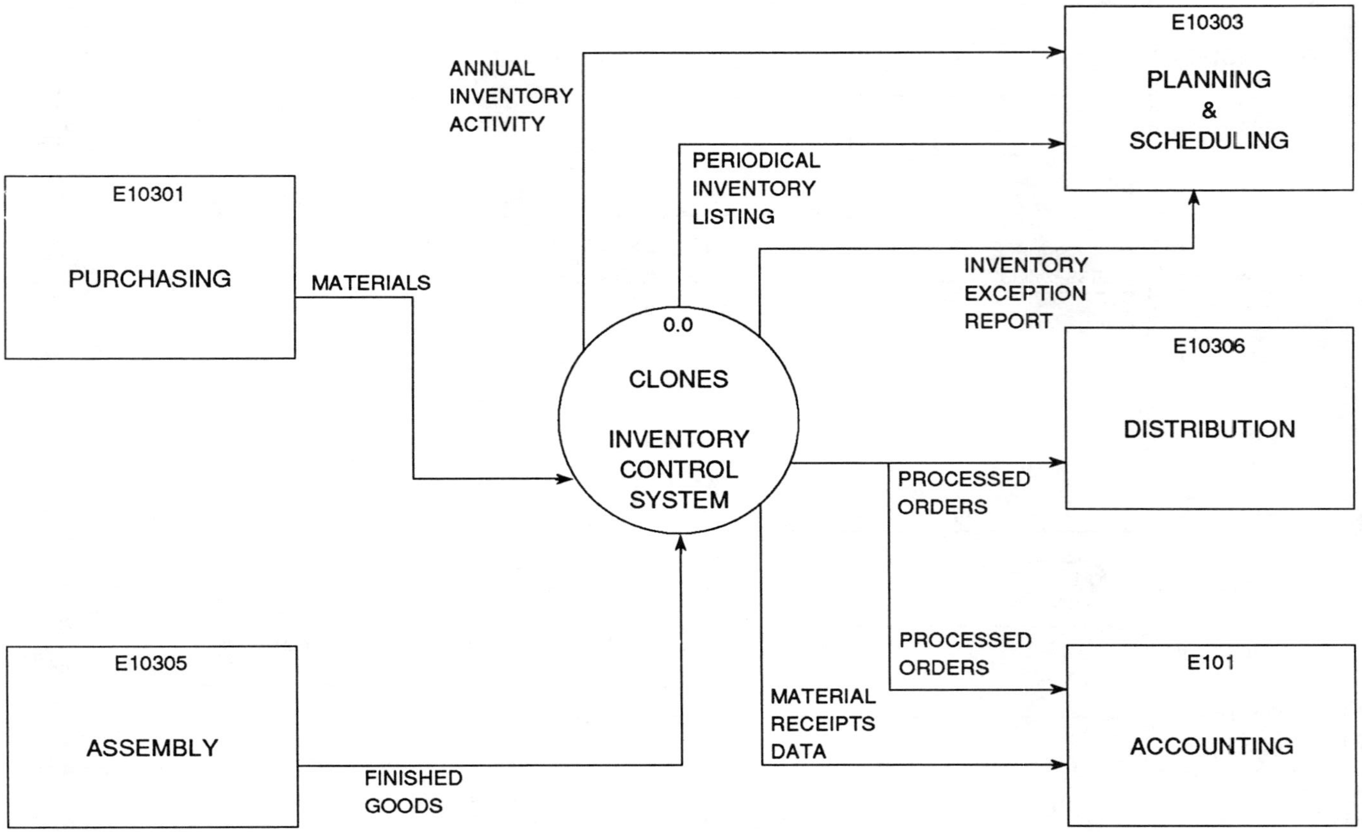

FIGURE 86. Clones Inc. inventory control system overview.

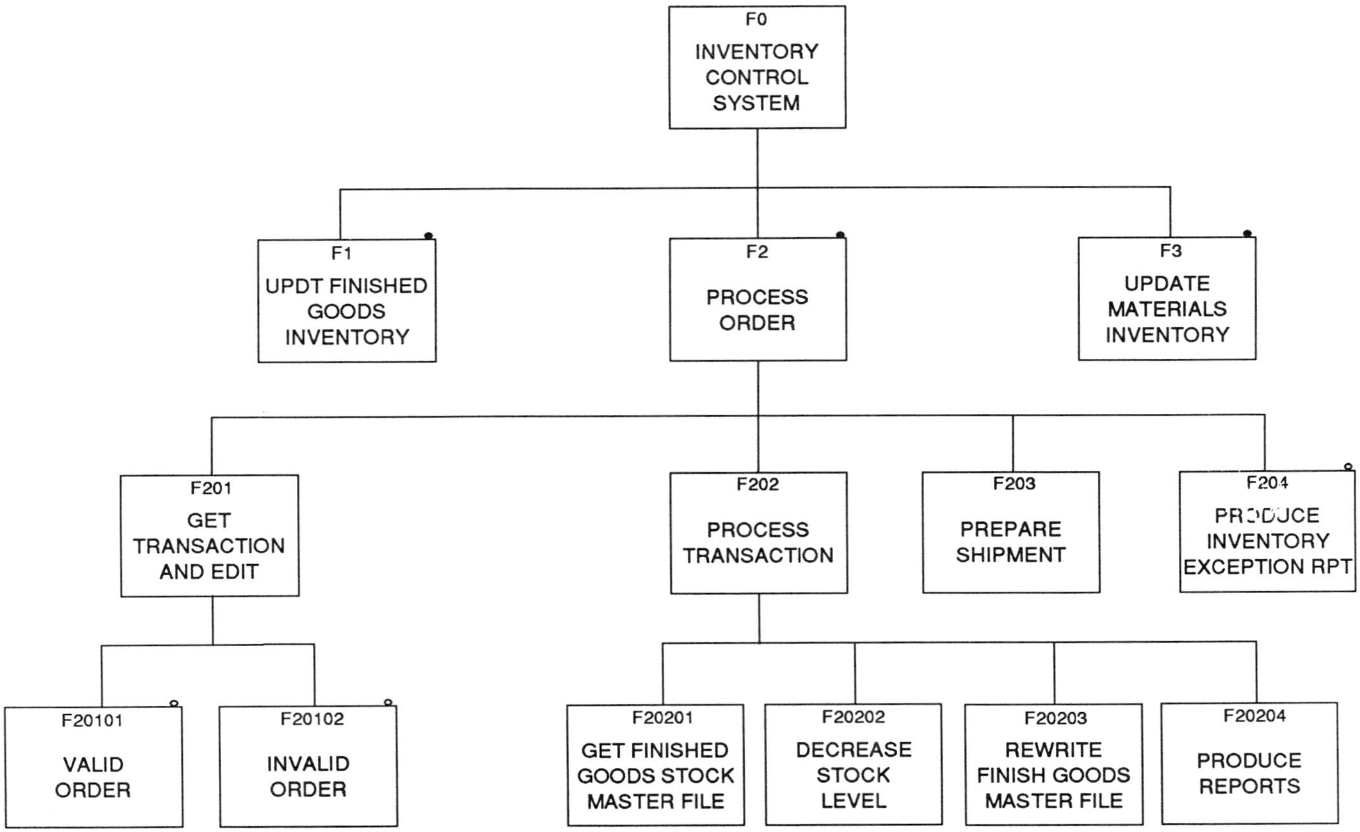

FIGURE 87. Clones Inc. inventory control system overview.

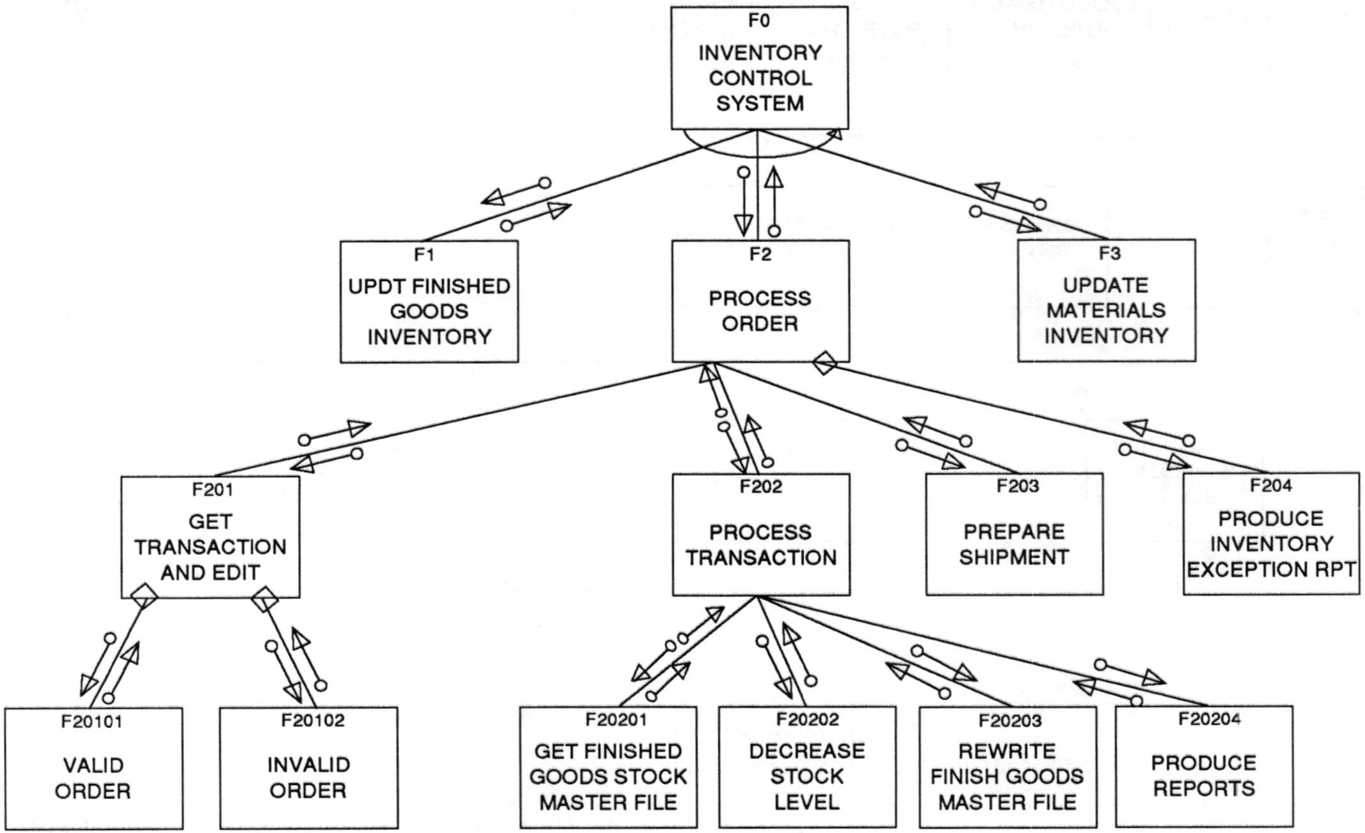

reverse engineering methodologies is to handle that large load of work.

The Bachman Methodology was developed by Bachman Information Systems, Inc., Cambridge, Massachusetts. It is designed for both reverse engineering and for new application development. That is, it is intended for both reverse engineering and forward engineering in the full development life cycle. As do many advanced CASE technologies, the Bachman Methodology includes software engineering, expert systems, MS-DOS workstations, and high-resolution graphics.

The Bachman Re-engineering Product Set

The Bachman Re-engineering Product Set includes the following features.

Re-engineering (Reverse and Forward Engineering).

Bachman products capture and analyze program source code and database descriptions for database management systems and flat files such as VSAM. The products reverse engineer the code and descriptions into implementation-independent models. These models can then be modified using the products' graphical editors and expert advisory systems. When enhancements are complete, the model is forward engineered to a physical design. Once that design has been optimized, new code or DDL is generated.

The expert advisory system in each product is derived from MIS professionals. The advisory system does validation and makes design recommendations, such as how to optimize for a specific transaction load. When it makes recommendations, it explains its reasons. The user decides whether to accept or reject the advisor's recommendations. The advisor works with the user as a copilot works with a pilot—the advisor makes recommendations and handles task when told to. The user makes the final decisions.

The Re-engineering Product Set improves the quality and consistency of enhancements, migrations, and development. And it dramatically reduces the time, drudgery, and errors of maintenance, giving MIS organizations rapid payback on their investment.

Modular Products.

The products work equally well alone or in combination. Each product supports a different job—for example, one product assists a systems analyst in most of his or her activities, another supports a DBA. Later, if an organization or individual needs support for more people or functions, additional products can be bought and simply "plugged in." The products all have an identical graphical user interface and communicate with one another automatically. All Bachman products work together as a single system and look like a single system to the user.

Bachman products treat the development cycle as a flexible set of functions that may be executed, re-executed, or partially executed as needed. Instead of forcing users to work through the cycle in a rigid sequence, Bachman/Re-engineering allows users to work where they need to, when they need to.

Figure 88 shows snapshots from five screens. The expert advisor in the Bachman/DBA (IDMS) has captured the DDL (data description language) statements for an existing mainframe database, displayed them as a Bachman diagram, and reverse engineered them into an entity-relationship diagram. The user then added and validated enhancements and chose DB2 as the new target database. The Bachman/DBA (DB2) created a DB2 relational design, worked with the user to optimize it for performance, and generated SQL DDL for DB2.

The Bachman/Re-engineering Product Set is CASE software that enables MIS organizations to use existing applications running on IBM mainframes with MVS as the foundation for new applications. The Product Set consists of integrated products that run on PC workstations with MS-DOS and interact with the user through words, diagrams, and icons. Each product advises and assists a different group of MIS professionals in the performance of their tasks, and each is named for the group it supports. Together, the products support the major jobs in an MIS organization. They communicate with each other automatically. Information flows freely between products and between team members.

Because of their reverse engineering capability, the products can be used to maintain and enhance existing applications. New development is facilitated by the fact that there is no need to start with a blank screen every time—reengineering and the products' graphical editors make old applications the real starting points for new development. The designer can begin writing a new application by editing an old one.

The Bachman/Re-engineering Product Set started becoming available in a series of product releases in early 1988. Individual products and their key features are listed below.

The Bachman/Data Analyst supports information modeling activities. It helps analysts create, edit, consolidate, normalize, and validate DBMS-independent information models. These models illustrate information requirements—they are independent of all implementation requirements.

The Bachman/Database Administrator helps database designers to analyze, design, restructure, edit, report on, redesign, optimize, and migrate existing or new databases. There will be one database administrator product for *IDMS*, one for *DB2*, one for *IMS*, and one to enhance the organization and use of *VSAM* or flat files or migrate their designs to a DBMS.

The Bachman/Systems Analyst supports function modeling activities focusing on functional description. It facilitates the creation of data flow diagrams. These diagrams are independent of the physical nature of the process. The diagrams give a clear, easy to comprehend picture of the information flows within the business.

The Bachman/Programmer Assistant supports the capture, analysis, program generation, and maintenance of business decision logic in both COBOL (the "how") and higher-level forms (the "what") and has the reverse and forward engineering capability to translate between them. Database and file manipulation statements are generated in a manner specific to the database or file system being used.

The Bachman/Information Model Library contains sample information models that business analysts can use as input to create specialized new applications for their own corporations.

The Bachman/Workstation Manager is a CASE operating environment. It runs on MS-DOS. Each product listed above can operate independently, or with other Bachman products, on a single 386-based workstation. Products are integrated, and individual users can transfer files and cooperate, through the Bachman/ Workstation Manager. It includes a personal design database so each workstation can stand alone, a common graphical user in-

FIGURE 88. Enhance, maintain, and migrate.

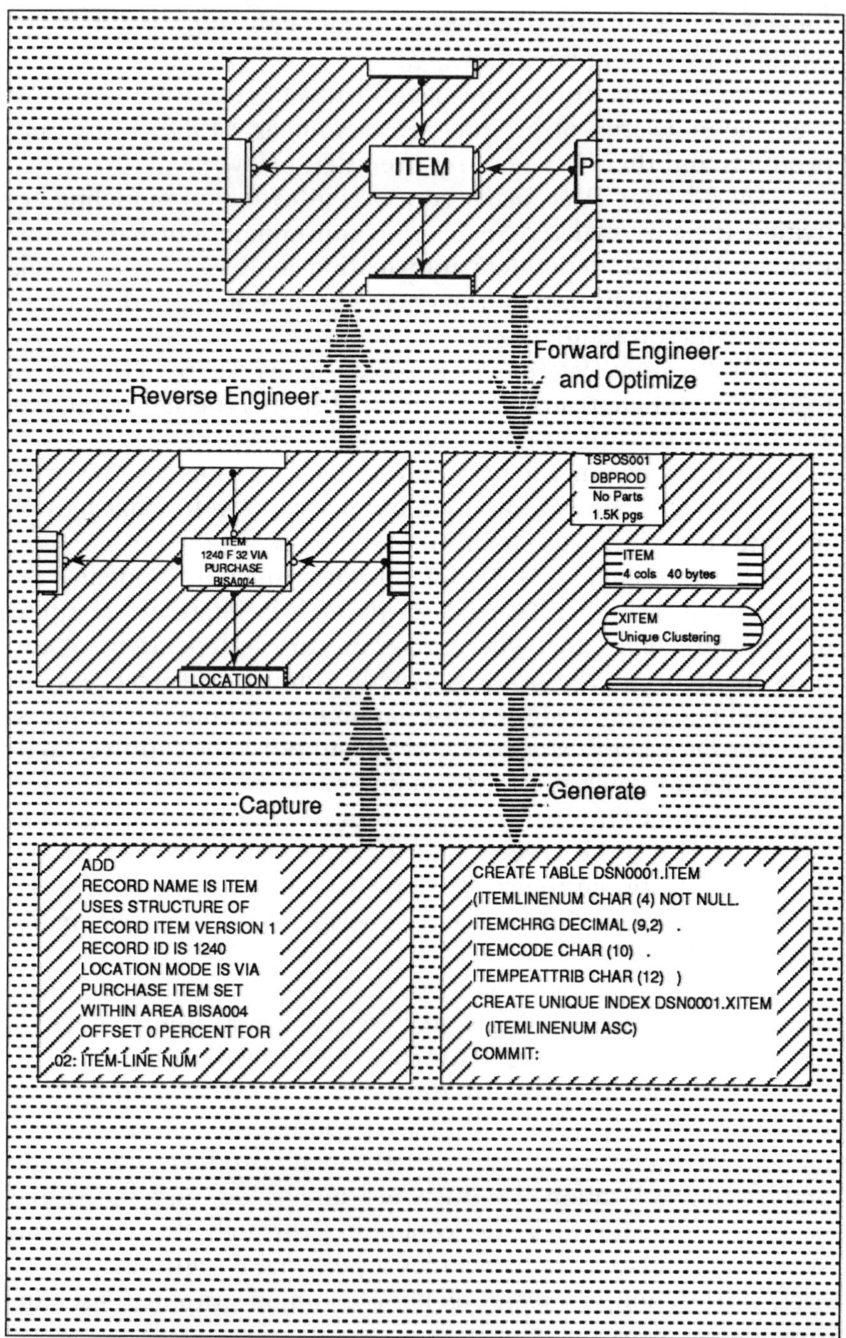

terface for all products, and a Decision Tracking System. The Decision Tracking System addresses the difficulty many organizations have keeping design information up to date and finding the reasons behind design decisions when they need them. The Decision Tracking System documents not just what decisions were made, but *why* they were made, when they were made, and who made them.

The Bachman/Shared Design Database integrates the work of many workstations on a mainframe or local area network (LAN). This product will enable team members to share designs and to review each others' work. Managers will use it for review and task management.

7.3 THE MOTOROLA MIS CASE PROGRAM

NOTE: This section is from a presentation by Les Shroyer, Director of Information Systems, Motorola Semiconductor Products Sector, Motorola, Inc. He discusses the objective of the CASE program at Motorola, the effect of CASE tools on the software life cycle, and Motorola's experience with CASE.

The CASE program at Motorola has the following objectives:

- To develop an environment where the business analyst employs automated tools to create rigorous system specifications that drive application generator products to build systems based upon relational data structures.

- Delivered systems will be characterized by accurate definition and execution to user requirements, zero-defects in the software, and rapidly modifiable system components.

- The systems development process will be responsive to the dynamic requirements of the user community, striving for a twofold to threefold improvement in developmental cycle time. A wider user base and increased business entity size will be serviced with minimal increases in developmental staff.

MIS Productivity Improvement Program

The Motorola MIS Productivity Improvement Program components are shown in Figure 89. This program was put together

FIGURE 89. MIS Productivity Improvement Program: approach.

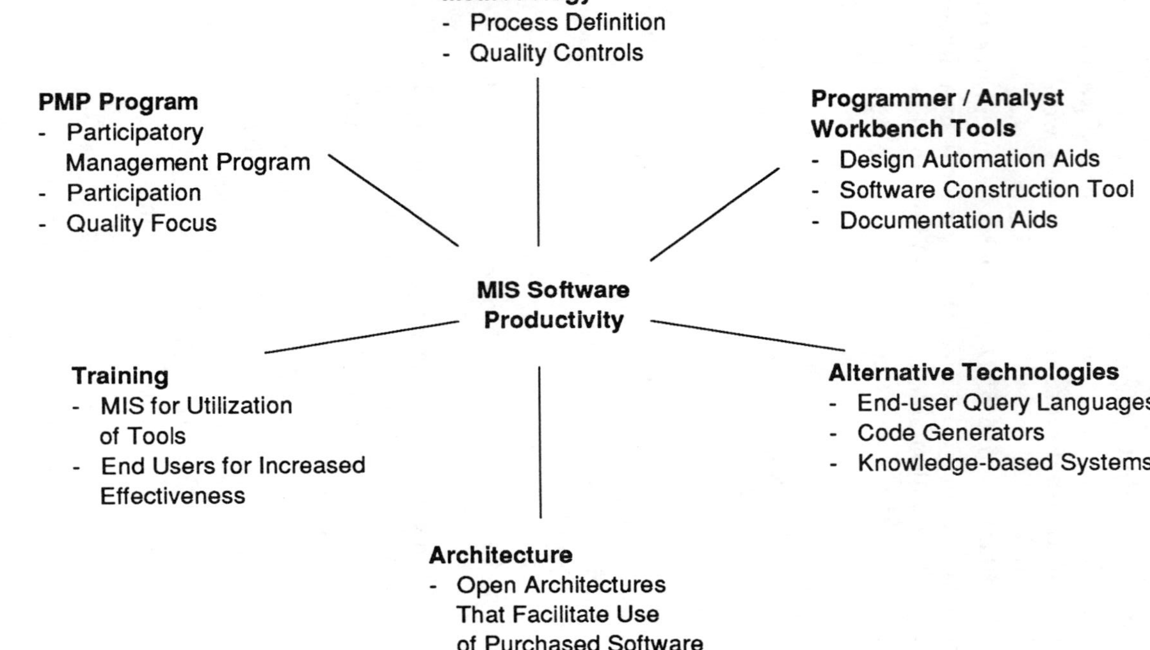

in 1986, when we started the process. We looked at what we thought were the major components of what it would take to improve MIS software activity. We were trying to address all the issues.

At the top of Figure 89 is methodology. We were like a lot of other MIS shops. We are not sloppy, but we are not rigorous about the adherence to a structured methodology. We have gone through various cycles in regards to top-down (Yourdon) structured methodologies. We had a set of books we called the rainbow manuals. Twelve volumes told you how to adhere to a software development life cycle. We issued the books to all new programmers and trained them a few times. Then they put them on the shelf above their desks where they gathered dust from that point on. We have thus been through the paper methodologies. It is a constant battle. We are really trying to break that cycle of major push, and decay of effectiveness and, over time, to define our processes better. We are looking at workbench tools, programmer analyst tools, and design aids. We will talk about some of the ones we have found that are useful for us. We are looking at alternative technologies. We are looking at such things as code generators, and we are active with a couple of leading code generator products. We are looking at the architecture and seeing that our needs become better integrated among our information systems. We are looking at being in a position where we can be system integrators, if we need to, by acquiring package software, but at the same time not falling into the trap of having 50 different commercial package systems that do not talk together or mesh well together. That is a real challenge.

Training is a very heavy component and includes the training of MIS staff and our end users for increased effectiveness. PMP is an acronym unique for Motorola. It is what the Japanese would call "quality circles." PMP stands for "participatory management program." It is our version of quality circles, involving heavy employee involvement in methods improvement activity at the grass roots level.

Figure 90 illustrates our initial goals for our MIS Productivity Improvement Program. This is what we thought we were going to achieve in terms of cycle times, penetration/utilization and cost.

We might have spent a little less than a year developing major

FIGURE 90. MIS Productivity Improvement Program: goals.

		1866	1988 - 1989
Cycle Time	– To build a major system	2 – 3 years	9 months
	– To build a subsystem	6 – 9 months	2 months
	– Produce special reports	2 – 6 weeks	1–5 days
Penetration/Utilization		System emphasis primarily – Accounting – Order Processing – Inventory control	Expanded emphasis to – Customer service – Resource planning – C I M S
Cost		Current methods imply Fractional increase in MIS census for each New function covered - Typical ratio 1 MIS exempt: 50 users	Greatly improved Software sustaining Techniques could Increase ratio to

subsystems. Today we have to get that down to a couple of months, if not hours. In fact, we are already there. It wasn't unusual for work requests to sit in a queue for six months waiting for someone to be assigned to do a couple of weeks worth of work. When we started in 1986, we didn't know if we were going to make that in the 1988–1989 time frame. Today I feel confident on all of those fronts, and we may beat several of those projections.

We are also trying for new types of systems. When we looked at our systems that were built yesterday, they were primarily accounting, order processing, and inventory control systems. Those are areas we have covered reasonably well. We have not covered things such as computer integrated manufacturing, resource planning, and some of the more exotic forms of customer service such as EDI (electronic data interchange). One of the reasons we want to lower the cycle time and boost productivity is not just to do a better job in what we are currently doing, but to cover several major areas vital to our business that we are not today covering.

Portfolio of Tools and Procedures

We now have a portfolio of tools and procedures that we are trying to make work for us. This statement, or disclaimer, should be made:

> *Reference to any software product in this presentation should not be considered an endorsement (positive or negative) of that product. All product evaluations were conducted with our specific environment in mind and may or may not be pertinent to your own situation.*

My people have been looking at the marketplace, and doing meticulous evaluations of products to determine which ones we should use. All of those people have looked at the products from the perspective of our Motorola MIS environment and how to make it work for us. We can tell you what we have done, and what we experienced from that.

We broke our task up into several components. We wanted to address the areas of design tools, project management, training tools, programmer workbenches, data dictionaries, development tools, documentation/maintenance tools, and application reporting tools. The general areas we have examined and some of the features and requirements we have considered are listed below.

Required Tools and Procedures

Design Tools

- Flow charting packages
- Data flow diagrams
- Data modeling tools
- Associated presentation graphics

Project Management

- Project planning, tracking, and reporting
- Associated presentation graphics
- Estimating

Training Tools

- Video-based
- Classroom-based
- Computer-based presentation authoring subject-specific courseware

Programmer Workbenches

- Personal computer terminals
- Off-line developement/compile/debug/test capability
- General workbench software; desktop organizers, etc.
- Micro-to-mainframe file transfer

Data Dictionaries

- Support IMS, CICS, DB2
- Support data administration
- Support code/appl. generators
- Support end-user computing

Development Tools

- Code/appl. generators/CASE/I-CASE products
- Testing/debugging packages
- Screen painters (standalone)
- Prototyping tools (standalone)

Documentation/Maintenance Tools

- Structured code analyzer
- Code restructuring tools
- Conversion tools (ALC-COBOL)
- Logic flow analyzers

Application Reporting

- File staging
- Distribution handling
- Report generation
- Graphics output

For design tools we finally settled on Excelerator from Index Technology Corporation. That is widely used in our shop now. Some of the things we look for are the flowcharting, entity-relationship diagramming capability, data flow diagrams, and so forth. We brought a number of design packages in-house, and talked to people who had been using them. We went through a formal exercise of listing what we were expecting, and then, using weighted scores, rating them on each of the features we were interested in. Finally, we made our choices. We had an evaluation team that put many hours into it.

We have settled on two project management packages for now, one of which is Microsoft Project. We are also looking at one that is part of the AGS product line, simply because we are using their product for the overall methodology controls.

In training tools, we are interested in video-based training as well as classroom training. Increasingly, we are in computer-based training, because there are more than 400 software professionals spread around the world we have to reach. Also, we want to broaden this training to users as well as MIS professionals. We are interested in offering specific training materials and providing it to the 15,000 or more users we have out there. Currently, we have selected the Phoenix product for computer-based software delivery, and we are using a large number of canned software training modules.

For hardware programmer workbenches, we have stabilized on MS-DOS compatible PC-AT clones. When we started this in 1986, our goal was to put an AT-class machine on every programmer/analyst's desk. We are carefully watching at what point we have to upgrade that to the PS/2 capability. That is driven, more than anything else, by what is required by some of the application generator tools we are trying to use. We are also piloting some products in order to move as much of the source code development as we can, down to the desktop for people who are not using application generators. We have an upstream IBM 3090 host system, and, consequently, we have to look at the library management and the testing aspect as well as the editing portion of code generation. We have been able to migrate some functions down, but not all the software development functions. Then we looked at a host of minor utilities for programmer productivity, all the way from desktop organizers to word processing packages. It turned out that one of the things we needed was just a good word processor to put on the programmers' desk because they spend a lot of time either communicating with somebody or documenting. We have tried to find a word processor that gives a good set of functionality, but doesn't overwhelm people with exotic features.

One of the areas we have started working in is data dictionaries. We have made less progress in that area and it is still an open item. We haven't yet made a selection because we are also interested in adding support to the end users for their computing problems, as well as providing a data dictionary for the programming professionals.

We have purchased a code generator package in the development tools area. It is a back-end generator for our purpose, not a front-end system. We also have Texas Instruments' Information Engineering Facility (IEF) in-house on a trial basis. Of the major code generators, we consider TI one of the top four or five. Based on our knowledge and insight, we have settled on TI's IEF products. We are looking at the reverse engineering problem as well as the forward code generating problem. Code generators are great if you are starting from scratch or if you have a clean slate; then you can develop a new application. But we own something like 7,000,000 lines of source code today that have been developed over a 15- to 20-year period. When somebody comes in and says, "I like your order processing system, but add another feature to it that is a 10 or 15 percent extension of it," it is difficult to use a code generator to do that because it has to integrate with the other 90 percent that you are not redeveloping. So we are struggling with how to mesh fourth- and fifth-generation code software products with an existing base of conventional COBOL and hierarchical databases. There are a few vendors out there aggressively chasing the reverse engineering problem of how to take the code they already have, read it in a program, decompose it, restructure it, and populate a dictionary out of that process. We are currently working with a vendor to see if we can come up with that. Peat, Marwick, Main & Company are also chasing that problem. Their Pathvu product is one of the programs that intrigued us because we can read in existing or very unstructured code, and it does diagnostics and metrics against the software and then regenerates the code in a structured fashion. We are using Pathvu for that purpose and we are also using several of the fourth-generation languages, such as NOMAD, Mark IV and Answer DB. One of our challenges now is how to port more of that type of 4GL capability down to the PCs as opposed to the mainframes.

Figure 91 illustrates where we believe some of the tools position themselves against the software life cycle. If you look at the conventional cycle, we probably started on the task before we completely had the requirements defined. We spent a huge amount of time in construction and testing, and then spent a lot of maintenance over the lifetime of the systems. That curve is exaggerated a little but not all that much. The structured methodologies will tell you to push that development curve to the left-hand side, to spend more time up front in the requirements and design, and spend less in the construction, testing, and total cost of owning

FIGURE 91. CASE tools and the software life cycle.

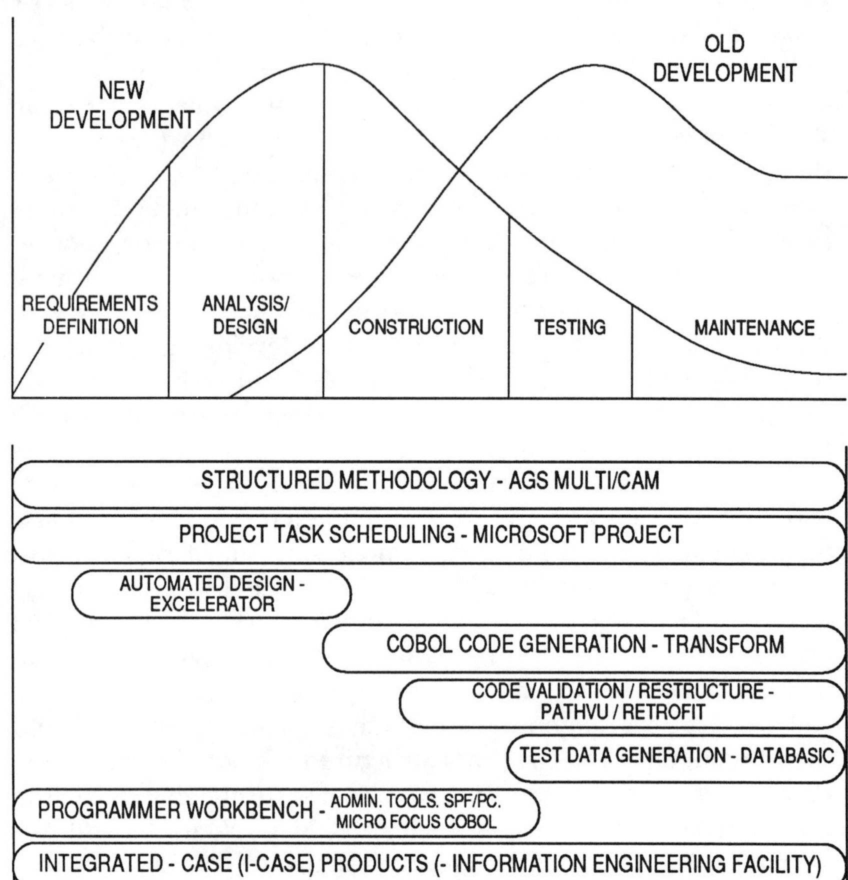

the system over its lifetime. We are trying to do that with better practical adherence to structured methodologies and better tools.

One of the methodology tools Motorola uses is AGS' MULTI/ CAM. They have been a beta test site for that product.

We are using Excelerator for some of the front-end graphics and data flow diagrams. We are using the Phoenix computer-based training to support the training exercise. In addition to putting PCs on all the programmers' desktops, we are also investing heavily in local area networks to tie all of this together.

Figure 92 illustrates our typical network environment. It is a generic model. We are using mostly Ethernet collision detection type schemes, although we have a few token rings up. We have worked to tie all those together, and are providing gateways back into our Tandem systems. Our manufacturing distribution system is run on about 120 Tandem CPUs around the world, so we have to have gateways into the Tandem environment. We also have to have gateways into the IBM 3090 environment we run on. WACC is a corporate acronym for Western Area Computer Center. That is where we have about five IBM 3090s. We are also trying to integrate the Appletalk network and the Macintoshes through servers into the same local area networks where we have the AT-class PCs.

Examples of Tool Output

We will take a quick look at some of the output of the tools. Some of it doesn't look as nice in paper versions as it does on a screen, particularly the graphics output. But we will briefly review what a menu looks like to a programmer and what we are doing with the AGS MULTI/CAM product, and then look at a few individual tools.

Almost every programmer has a PC on his desk, and it is tied in to a local area network. Programmers see a menu like the one shown in Figure 93.

It also has other items that window only. Users see a set of utilities and have access to a local mail system. We are in the process of integrating the LAN mail system with corporatewide backbone mail systems to an X.400 type protocol. There are bulletin boards and some tutorials on how to use various tools. We are moving toward the mode where we buy network versions of the tools, when available, and install them on file servers on the LANs, rather than buying individual copies for the workstations. However, not all the vendors have marketed their product in that fashion. You can get to the host connections if you want to get into our RVM environment or into IMS through items on this

FIGURE 92. LAN model.

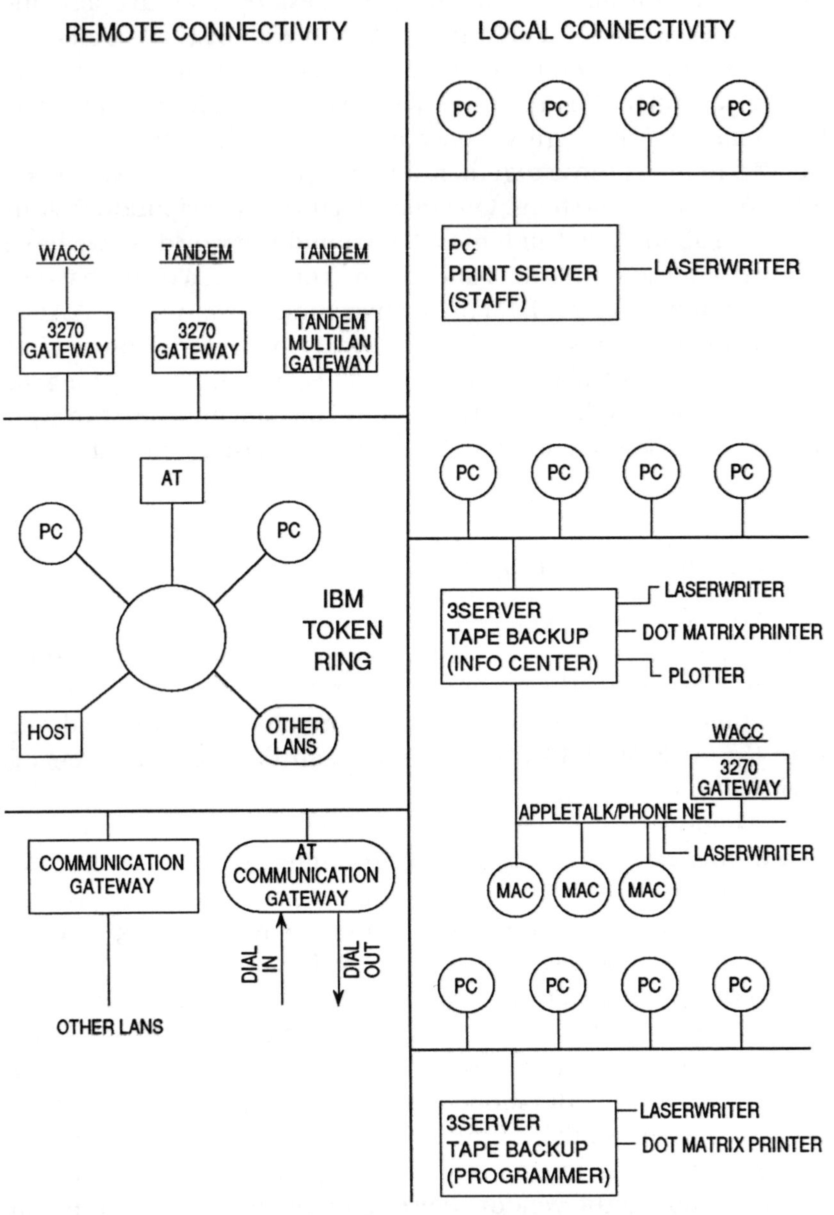

FIGURE 93. Main menu.

Main Menu

    Directories and Files
    Printer Connections
    Shared Resources
    Log Out
    A. Utilities
    B. Mail
    C. SPS MIS PC/LAN BBS
    D. Tutorials
    E. Host Connections
    F. Editors
    G. PFS Professional Write
    H. Lotus 1-2-3
    I. Right Writer

menu. They also have access to word processors, spreadsheets, and various other products.

AGS MULTI/CAM

One of the products that did not show on that menu is the AGS MULTI/CAM workstation product (Figure 94). We have about 30 pilot projects actively using this.

Figure 95 shows the elements of the MULTI/CAM main menu. The elements listed under the boxes represent submenus. For example, under the system development menu is the life-cycle menu as shown in Figure 96.

When a life-cycle option is selected from the life-cycle menu, the phase menu for that life cycle will be displayed as shown in Figure 97.

When a phase is selected from a phase menu, the task menu for that phase will be displayed. The task menu will also be displayed immediately after a management framework is selected on the systems development menu if that framework has no phases. The task menu contains all of the tasks of the selected phase or framework. An example of the task menu for the system requirements definition phase is shown in Figure 98.

FIGURE 94. MULTI/CAM.

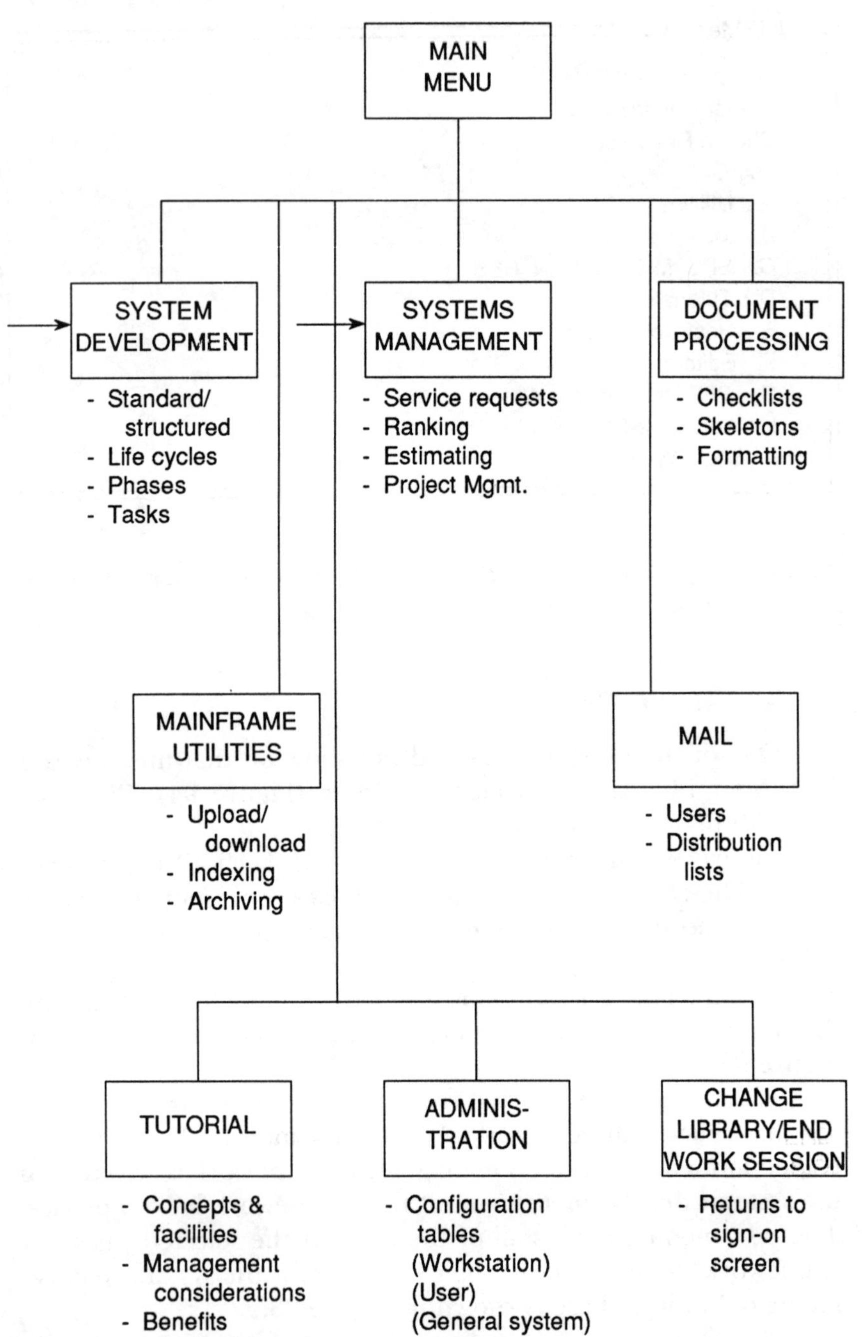

FIGURE 95. MULTI/CAM main menu.

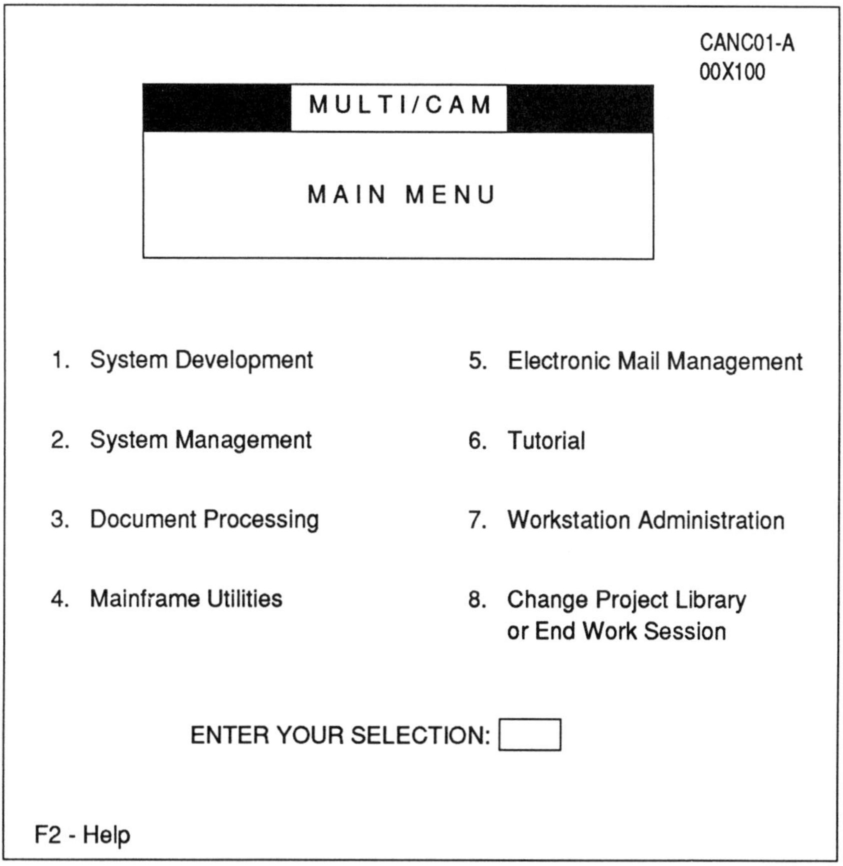

CANC01-A
00X100

MULTI/CAM

MAIN MENU

1. System Development

2. System Management

3. Document Processing

4. Mainframe Utilities

5. Electronic Mail Management

6. Tutorial

7. Workstation Administration

8. Change Project Library
   or End Work Session

ENTER YOUR SELECTION: ☐

F2 - Help

FIGURE 96. System development: life-cycle menu.

FIGURE 97. Phase menu: standard life cycle.

SDM/STRUCTURED   CANC01-E
                                                      SSX000

Function Menu

STANDARD LIFE CYCLE

1. System Requirements Definition   5. Program Development

2. System Design Alternatives   6. Testing

3. System External Specifications   7. Conversion

4. System Internal Specifications   8. Implementation

ENTER YOUR SELECTION:

F2 - Help   Esc - Previous Menu   X - Main Menu

FIGURE 98. Task menu: system requirements definition.

SDM / STRUCTURE   CANC51 - N
Phase: SRD   STR000

Task Menu

SYSTEM REQUIREMENTS DEFINITION

1. Identify Project Scope   5. Analyze the Current System

2. Establish an Index of   6. Define Requirements for the
   Collected Data   Proposed System

3. Conduct the Interviews   7. Analyze System Objectives

4. Document Current System   8. Prepare SRD Document
   (Physical Model)

9. Perform QA Reviews

ENTER YOUR SELECTION: [ ]

F2 - Help   Esc - Previous Menu   X - Main Menu

We are trying to get away from users committing all the detail to memory and to make it as tutorial and profitable as we can. We are struggling, but we have had some successes. The biggest challenge has been to take something like the AGS SDM/70 package and streamline it enough so the overhead is not burdensome on a workstation base product.

Project Task Scheduling

We have also taken a project scheduler and scheduling tools to reconcile and integrate it with the various tasks that come out of the methodology checklists. For example, Figure 99 is a Microsoft project scheduler for a distribution project. The tasks listed here relate one to one with each of the tasks inside the methodology checklists.

Application Design Graphics

In the area of application graphics, Excelerator has pervasive use throughout the industry now. It offers dataflow and entity-relationship diagramming capabilities. We have found that our programmers have readily adapted to using Excelerator because it gives them the ability to do the documentation we were always supposed to do in our procedures. Have you ever found anyone drawing dataflow and entity-relationship diagrams with a flow-chart template by manual means? It is likely those people did not last long because they probably were needed for fighting fires. We are getting a level of documentation that never existed before, and we are getting it without too much complaint out of the programmers. They are finding that it aids in bringing new people on board and in transferring information from one group of people to another.

One of my other goals is to get to the mode where, instead of having one group of people develop a system and hand it off to others for implementation, we can essentially convene world-wide project teams. An analyst in Korea, another in Austin, and someone else in Europe would electronically transmit flow diagrams and systems definitions so they could work from multiple locations. They don't have to be sitting in the same cubicle. We are starting to move in that direction.

FIGURE 99. Project scheduler.

SECTOR MANUFACTURING SYSTEMS
SPECIFICATIONS SUPPORT SYSTEM
AUTOMATIC CHANGE DETECTION

```
                                          September 1987                 October 1987
                                  31      7      14      21      28      5      12
                                  |------ |------ |------ |------ |------ |------ |------

1       SMALL PRODUCTS ANALYSIS TASKS
2   1.0 Identify the Project Scope
3   1.1 Define the Scope and Assumptions
4   1.2 Define Participating Users
5   2.0 Develop the Current Physical Model    +      +      +      +      +      +      +
6   2.1 Identify the Processes
7   2.2 Diagram the Lowest Level Processes
8   2.3 Describe the Lowest Level Processes
9   2.4 Define the Data Flows              = >
10  2.5 Define the Data Stores             >>     +      +      +      +      +      +
11  2.6 Finalize the Current Physical Model >==      >
12  3.0 Define the Current Logical Model            =
13  3.1 Define Lowest Level Logical Funct.          >=>
14  3.2 Describe the Functions                        >>
15  3.3 Define Logical Data Flows          +      +    >  >     +      +      +      +
16  3.4 Determine Functional Data Req.                  >>
17  3.5 Develop the Data Set Model                        >>
18  4.0 Develop the New Logical Model                       =
19  4.1 Identify the Logical Requirements                   >=>
20  4.2 Produce New System Logical Model   +      +      +      +    >  ==>     +      +
21  4.3 Define New Data Requirements                              >>
```

SECTOR MANUFACTURING SYSTEMS
SPECIFICATIONS SUPPORT SYSTEM
AUTOMATIC CHANGE DETECTION

			September 1987				October 1987	
			31	7	14	21	28	5	12
22	5.0	Define New Physical Requirements				>>			
23	5.1	Identify Physical Requirements				=			
24	5.2	Specify Automation Boundaries				>			
25	5.3	Establish Future Continpencies	+	+	+	+ >	+	+	+
26	6.0	Develop the New Physical Model				=			
27	6.1	Identify the New Processes				>	>		
28	6.2	Define the Output Data Flows					>		
29	6.3	Define the Input Data Flows					>		
30	6.4	Describe the Lowest Level Processes	+	+	+	+	>	+	+
31	6.5	Define the New Data Stores					>		
32	6.6	Diagram the Processes					>>		
33	8.0	Satisfy Implementation Prereq.					=		
34	8.1	Prepare Implementation Plan					>		
35	8.2	Prepare Training Plan	+	+	+	+	+ >>	+	+
36	8.3	Develop User Guide					>	=>	
37	8.4	Design Acceptance Test Criteria						>>	
38	9.0	Complete the Analysis Phase						=	
39	9.1	Prepare Design Phase Work Plans						>	
40	9.2	Prepare Analysis Document	+	+	+	+	+	+ >>	+
41	9.3	Obtain Analysis Document Approval						>	

Behind each of the boxes in a typical Excelerator diagram, you have the capability of doing some data dictionary work. You can define and describe the process for each of the process steps. You can attach textual information as to what that process is doing and what data elements it uses (Figure 100). In addition to getting graphics out of a product like Excelerator, you get validity checking as far as unresolved connections and you can get project-level dictionary information that aids the documentation process.

Excelerator is a front-end product. It is a design aid. It doesn't have a code generator, although the Index Technology people are aggressively working with several of the code generator people on that. They are working with a number of vendors to provide an import/export bridge between several products. We are following that and also looking at some of the integrated products. The one we have chosen is Texas Instruments' Information Engineering Facility. It has the capability of doing the same type of diagramming as Excelerator (Figure 101), and the capability of associating description and pseudocode with each of those boxes on the diagram for later code generation. It also can do process decomposition activities (Figure 102).

PathVu Source Code Analysis

Another example is PathVu. It is one of the products that is not comprehensive, but fits a particular niche. We can read in several million lines of COBOL source code that we have and do some analysis on the code with PathVu. Figure 103 is the output of a PathVu analysis of our manufacturing systems that ran in 125 programs with 230,000 lines of source code. It does several ratings for you. This matrix is a complexity versus a structured architecture matrix. In the top right-hand corner are a number of programs that are considered overly complex and unstructured.

In the bottom left-hand corner, are programs that are more structured, as per their guidelines, and have less complex logic in them. It can direct you to which subsegments of your existing software base would probably benefit the most from rework. You get a complete set of metrics out of that on several different counts (Figure 104). It will tell you on a module-by-module basis such

FIGURE 100. Excelerator process block description.

TYPE Process   NAME SBBS0630

    Label   EXPLODE   EXPLODES TO ONE OF:
                 PACKAGE   Data Flow Diagram
                 KITS   Structure Chart
                                Structure Diagram

Location

Process Category

Duration Value
Duration Type

Manual or Computer C

   Description
Bill or Material Processing   -   STEP 3   -   Explosion of the Package Kits

---

In many ways this step is similar to the processing in step 2 (SBBS0620). Like
step 2 this step identifies segments to be downloaded to a specified tandem. For
all of the component records it identifies as valid for download, but which do not
contain a component type, it writes out a component record for subsequent
processing. It builds distribution records to allow for the proper distribution of
segments by step 5. It is dissimilar in that instead of utilizing SPECGRUP and
BESSPROD table lookups to determine which segments are valid for download, it
uses the package kit select file created in step 2 and sorted by the sort utility.
The reason for the difference in processing is that a package kit is considered a
component of the raw stock part and the spec system does not require that the
package kit be explicitly defined as a valid part on the spec system. Therefore,
the package kit simply follows the distribution pattern of the raw stock part(s) of
which it is a component.

Modified By	MIKEF	Date Modified 870828	# Changes 6
Added By	MIKEF	Date Added 870817	
Last Project	MIPS.SPEC - RELE		
Locked By		Date Locked 0	Lock Status

FIGURE 101. Entity-relationship diagram (TI-IEF).

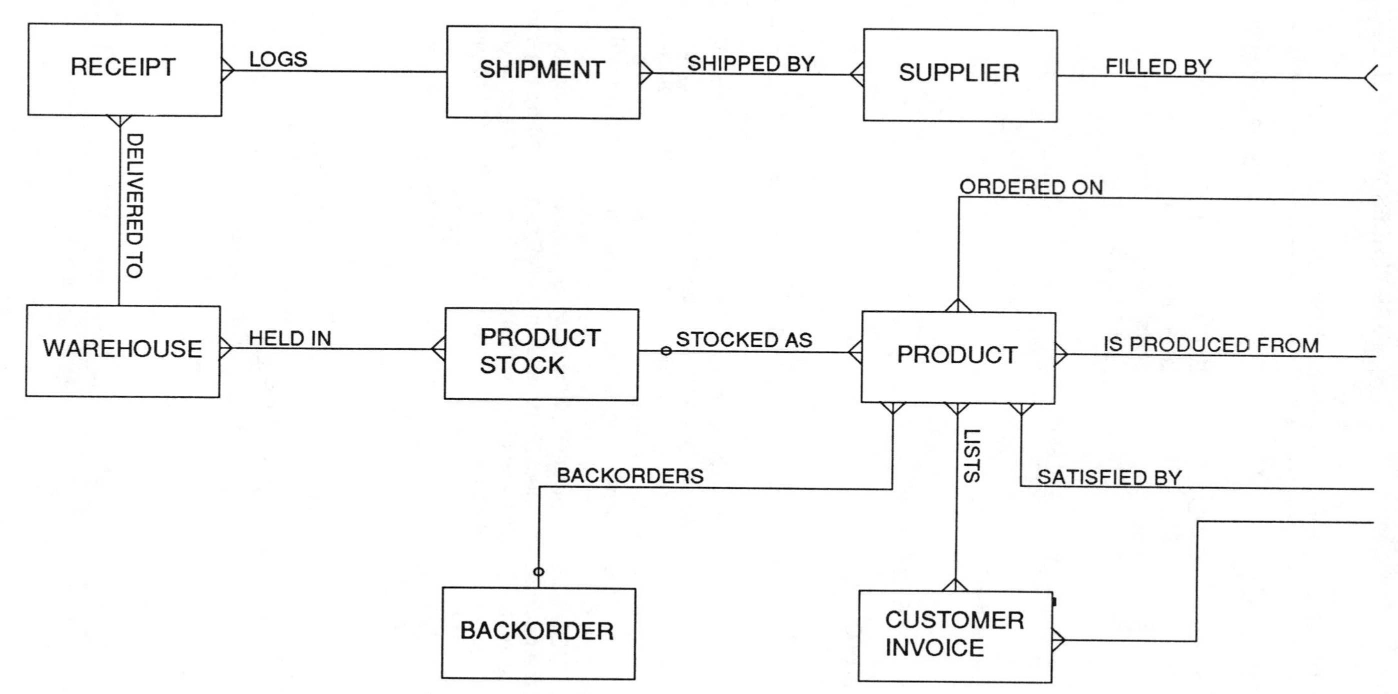

FIGURE 102. Process decomposition diagram (TI-IEF).

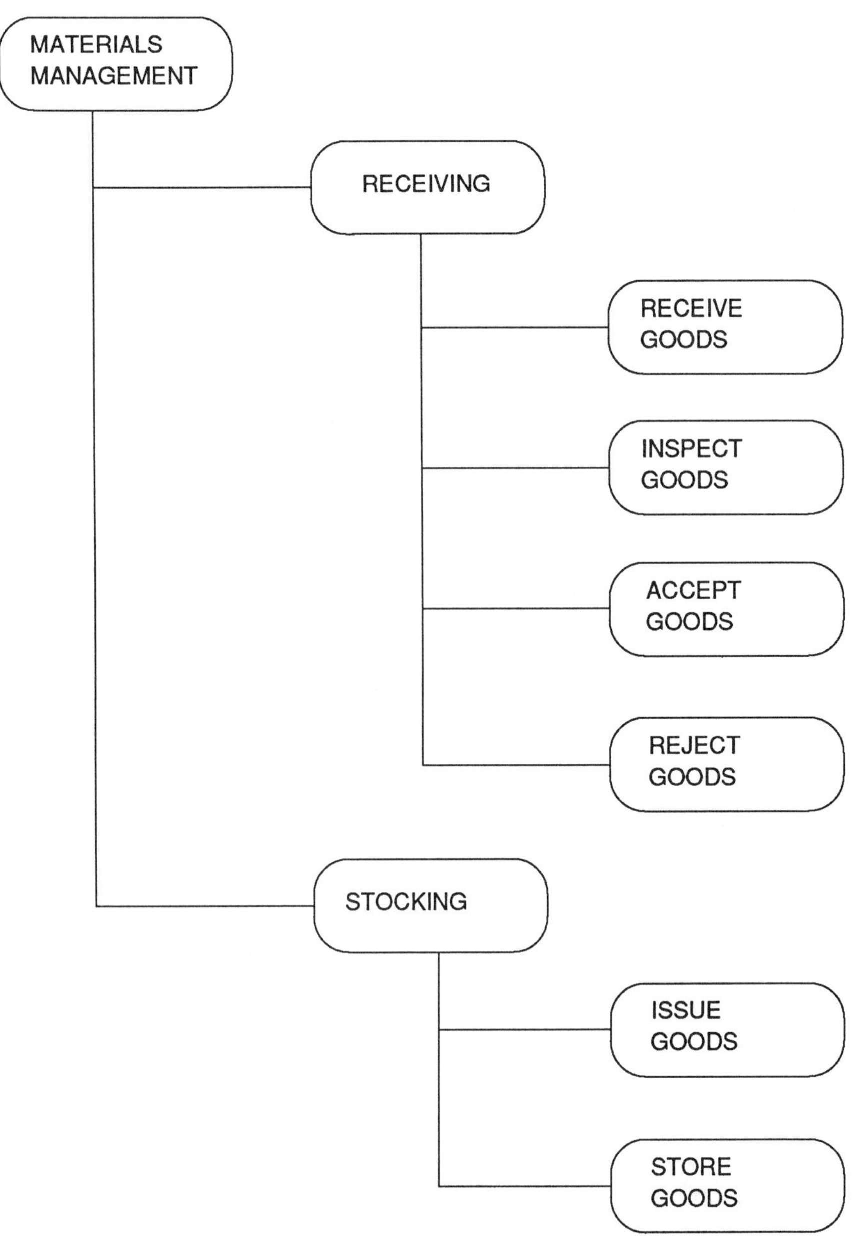

Information Engineering Facility is a trademark of Texas Instruments Incorporated.
Copyright © 1986 Texas Instruments.

FIGURE 103. PathVu sector analysis.

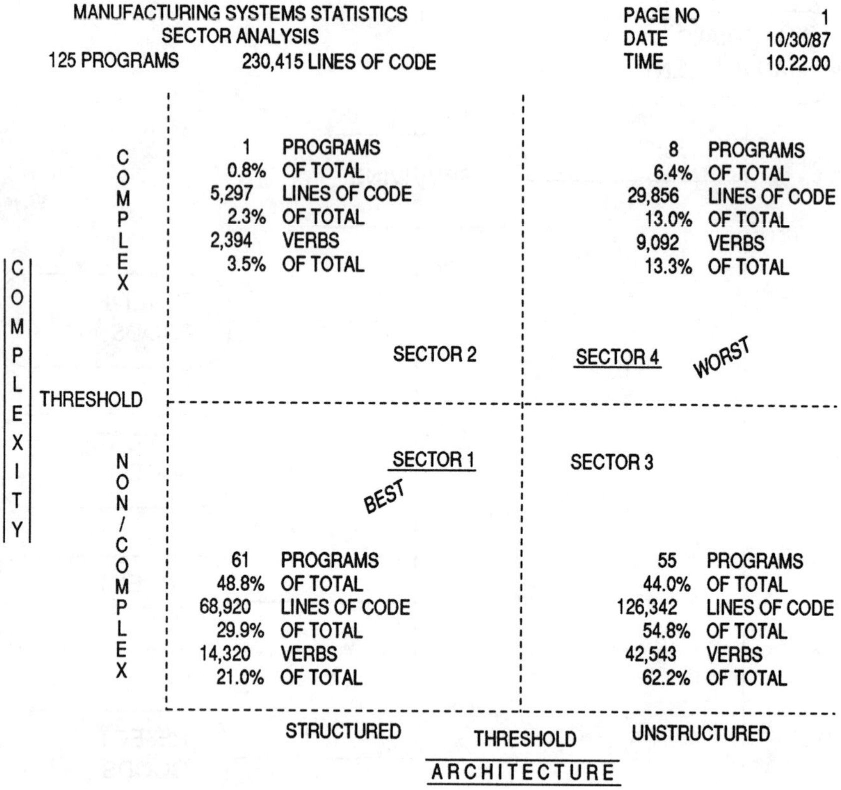

```
MANUFACTURING SYSTEMS STATISTICS              PAGE NO              1
           SECTOR ANALYSIS                    DATE          10/30/87
125 PROGRAMS          230,415 LINES OF CODE    TIME          10.22.00
```

FIGURE 104. PathVu metric analysis.

MANUFACTURING SYSTEMS STATISTICS
METRIC ANALYSIS

Most Complex · Logic Path Depth

------ PROGRAM COMPLEXITY AND ARCHITECTURE ------

		SEC	SID	ARC STR	CMP SCR	DPST LVL (NESTING)	LEVEL COMFF	PCT CTL	NUM IF	NUM LPS	PRCH (LOC)	PROC (LOC)	NUM VRBS	NUM PARA	NUM GO TO (NON-STD)	FALL THRU (NON-STD)	NUM GO TO	FALL THRU	PERF THRU	PERF PARA	PERF SECT	TERM VERB	DIAG END
1 MMRP0006	MMRP	1	T	21	55	5	1.41	31	21	0	553	212	129	19	2	1	7	9	8	0	0	1	0
2 MMRP0010	MMRP	4	T	331	278	18	3.50	45	448	5	5260	2489	1664	187	177	103	220	124	45	0	0	1	2
3 MMRP0012	MMRP	1	T	45	109	6	1.29	48	118	0	1365	515	351	44	10	5	21	22	19	0	0	1	0
4 MMRP0014	MMRP	1	T	0	54	5	1.02	37	15	0	411	150	82	12	0	0	5	6	6	0	0	1	0
5 MMRP0016	MMRP	1	T	0	54	5	1.12	33	29	0	762	341	168	30	0	0	9	14	15	0	0	1	1
6 MMRP0018	MMRP	1	T	0	112		0.92	29	7	0	271	105	59	10	0	0	2	5	5	0	0	1	0
7 MMRP0020	MMRP	4	T	514	32	47	11.47	41	171	6	4205	2233	909	154	113	146	119	146	59	0	0	1	7
8 MMRP0025	MMRP	1	T	37	40	4	0.92	39	23	0	580	283	137	19	1	2	11	10	10	0	0	1	0
9 MMRP0030	MMRP	4	T	616	679	79	25.64	43	477	46	7655	4485	2091	314	287	276	323	276	79	0	0	1	17
10 MMRP0035	MMRP	1	T	81	28	2	0.39	26	5	2	103	41	31	2	1	1	3	1	0	0	0	1	0
11 MMRP0040	MMRP	3	T	224	76	7	1.51	39	40	0	836	359	186	26	23	15	26	17	7	0	0	1	0
12 MMRP0050	MMRP	4	T	236	296	17	5.13	41	87	6	1941	733	460	76	63	32	79	41	19	0	0	1	2
13 MMRP0051	MMRP	3	T	166	69	8	1.91	31	15	4	494	232	152	25	18	9	21	13	5	0	0	1	1
14 MMRP0060	MMRP	3	T	257	234	17	4.09	42	189	15	3622	622	997	143	112	58	161	74	40	0	0	1	0
15 MMRP0090	MMRP	1	T	98	90	9	2.51	31	46	2	1220	599	316	35	19	10	37	17	11	0	0	1	1
16 MMRP0091	MMRP	1	T	55	58	3	0.59	42	8	3	272	112	45	10	0	1	4	3	4	0	0	1	1
17 MMRP0120	MMRP	1	T	69	142	2	0.48	52	15	0	249	92	46	7	5	1	5	3	2	0	0	1	2
18 MMRP0130	MMRP	1	T	0	69	4	1.00	43	11	1	329	121	72	20	0	0	6	9	10	0	0	1	1
19 MMRP0140	MMRP	3	T	123	134	12	2.35	46	152	0	2213	991	636	103	29	24	80	58	44	0	0	1	0
20 MMRP0150	MMRP	4	T	227	293	19	4.94	37	171	8	3528	1503	913	127	88	51	121	76	38	0	0	1	6
21 MMRP0160	MMRP	3	T	307	244	12	2.29	40	460	49	7858	3306	2144	290	176	113	268	164	87	0	0	1	0
22 MMRP0210	MMRP	1	T	94	56	4	0.85	39	23	6	662	222	139	25	5	5	18	13	10	0	0	1	0

Large PGM - Difficult to maintain

Trouble Spots (next page)

FIGURE 104. (Cont.)

MANUFACTURING SYSTEMS STATISTICS
METRIC ANALYSIS

PAGE NO 1
DATE 10/3087
TIME 10.23.03

PROGRAM COMPLEXITY AND ARCHITECTURE

	PROGRAM	SYS	SEC SID	ARC STR	CMP SCR	DPST LVL	LEVEL COMFF	PCT CTL	NUM IF	NUM LPS	PRCH	PROC	NUM VRBS	NUM PARA	NUM GO TO	FALL THRU	NUM GO TO	FALL THRU	PERF THRU	PERF PARA	PERF SECT	TERM VERB	DIAG END
						NESTING					---- LOC ----				- NON - STD -								
23	MMRP0220	MMRP	3 T	110	110	10	2.20	45	41	1	1096	71	228	45	1	10	22	25	19	0	0	1	0
24	MMRP0230	MMRP	3 T	239	36	2	0.45	36	7	2	352	81	42	17	1	4	4	8	4	0	0	1	0
25	MMRP0300	MMRP	1 T	96	34	3	0.60	24	10	0	326	80	83	6	6	3	9	3	1	0	0	1	0
26	MMRP0310	MMRP	3 T	290	41	3	0.71	35	5	0	185	60	26	6	2	3	3	3	1	0	0	1	1
27	MMRP0320	MMRP	3 T	142	52	5	1.37	29	16	0	365	166	89	13	2	5	4	7	5	0	0	1	1
28	MMRP0330	MMRP	3 T	136	73	7	1.73	38	29	9	762	387	182	29	13	9	31	12	8	0	0	1	0
29	MMRP0340	MMRP	3 T	128	35	3	0.81	21	13	4	462	195	100	11	3	5	7	5	2	0	0	1	1
30	MMRP0450	MMRP	3 T	150	75	6	1.33	42	23	4	614	264	137	32	8	7	21	13	10	0	0	1	1
31	MMRP0500	MMRP	1 T	66	66	5	1.19	40	30	2	948	333	161	36	4	4	16	19	16	0	0	1	0
32	MMRP0520	MMRP	3 T	146	172	2	0.49	55	14	0	286	87	55	8	10	3	14	5	2	0	0	1	0
33	MMRP0540	MMRP	3 T	118	47	4	0.94	31	28	0	551	258	170	15	16	7	21	7	3	0	0	1	0
34	MMRP0550	MMRP	4 T	124	264	5	1.20	59	13	0	356	108	61	17	2	3	10	9	7	0	0	1	0
35	MMRP0560	MMRP	3 T	146	54	6	1.22	25	33	2	1126	500	265	29	14	14	21	17	8	0	0	1	0
36	MMRP0570	MMRP	1 T	0	57	4	0.96	38	17	0	581	193	115	18	0	0	12	9	9	0	0	1	0
37	MMRP0580	MMRP	3 T	225	106	11	2.37	38	60	6	1471	644	388	66	45	28	63	34	18	0	0	1	0
38	MMRP0585	MMRP	1 T	88	67	3	0.72	46	10	0	2003	89	59	12	4	2	9	6	5	0	0	1	0
39	MMRP0586	MMRP	3 T	145	54	3	0.71	40	4	0	175	57	35	10	3	2	4	5	4	0	0	1	0
40	MMRP0650	MMRP	3 T	102	63	7	1.61	20	46	2	1027	922	478	56	3	19	15	32	22	0	0	1	0
41	MMRP0660	MMRP	3 T	134	114	10	2.52	40	130	3	1894	929	574	61	26	25	53	35	22	0	0	1	0
42	MMRP0710	MMRP	3 T	393	221	13	2.57	44	377	131	4489	3115	1725	183	205	130	314	133	26	0	0	1	1

things as the complexity score and the number and the depth of nested looping. It will give you dead code; it will tell you open areas where you violate loops by branching out of those loops. On the right-hand side, it gives you an overall score. You can be directed to the trouble spots you want to look at.

Figure 105 is an example of a particular module that points out dead code, performs range violations, runaway paths, and so forth. You get a good set of metrics. We have always had a software inspection process where the programmers have to turn their code over to a peer walkthrough before it is put into production. However, this has been a subjective exercise, although we have some documented rules as to what good code looks like. There is a peer panel looking at it and making that decision on a case-by-case basis.

With this product we are moving to a form of self-inspection where the peer panel first needs to achieve a certain score out of the metrics to validate that they are following the structured rules. Secondly, when we go in and open up old code for rework, one of the guidelines is that the score that comes out of this can't be any worse than it was before we modified the software. We are starting to use this as a way of automating that software inspection process. Figure 106 is an example of source code that is restructured when it comes back out. It will do the structuring and the indentation and put it in a form that is easier to read.

Computer-Based Training

In July 1987 we took an internal survey of who wanted to have access to which training module. Figure 107 shows the types of modules we made available to the internal MIS professionals for training. Some of these also have interest to the end users. For instance, we are putting on a tutorial on how to use corporate E-Mail systems.

Results to Date

The results of our CASE program are outlined in Figure 108. It has had a phenomenal positive impact on our morale and our attitudes, even though we were concerned initially about it

FIGURE 105. PathVu summary diagnostics.

MANUFACTURING SYSTEMS STATISTICS
SUMMARY DIAGNOSTICS

PAGE NO   1
DATE   10/30/82
TIME   10.23.03

- - - - - - - - - - - - - - - - DIAGNOSTICS - - - - - - - - - - - - - - - -

	PROGRAM	SYS	UNENTERED PROCEDURES	HIDEAWAY PATH	PEREM RANGE VIOL	LOOKING PERFORM RANGE VIOL	RECURSIVE PERFORMS	UNRESOLVED PROCEDURE EXITS	ALIENS
1	MMRP0006	MMRP	0	0	0	0	0	0	0
2	MMRP0010	MMRP	0	0	2	0	0	0	0
3	MMRP0012	MMRP	0	0	0	0	0	0	0
4	MMRP0014	MMRP	0	0	0	0	0	0	0
5	MMRP0018	MMRP	1	0	0	0	0	0	0
6	MMRP0020	MMRP	0	0	0	0	0	0	0
7	MMRP0025	MMRP	0	7	0	0	0	0	0
8	MMRP0030	MMRP	0	6	0	0	0	0	0
9	MMRP0040	MMRP	0	17	0	0	0	0	0
10	MMRP0050	MMRP	0	0	0	0	0	0	0
11	MMRP0051	MMRP	0	0	0	0	0	0	0
12	MMRP0060	MMRP	1	0	1	0	0	0	0
13	MMRP0090	MMRP	0	0	1	0	0	0	0
14	MMRP0091	MMRP	0	0	0	0	0	0	0
15	MMRP00120	MMRP	1	0	0	0	0	0	0
16	MMRP00130	MMRP	1	0	0	0	0	0	0
17	MMRP00140	MMRP	0	0	0	0	0	0	0
18	MMRP00150	MMRP	1	0	0	0	0	0	0
19	MMRP00160	MMRP	0	0	0	0	0	0	0
20	MMRP00210	MMRP	1	0	5	0	0	0	0
21	MMRP00220	MMRP	0	0	0	0	0	0	0

488

	PROGRAM	SYS	UNENTERED PROCEDURES	HIDEAWAY PATH	PEREM RANGE VIOL	LOOKING PERFORM RANGE VIOL	RECURSIVE PERFORMS	UNRESOLVED PROCEDURE EXITS	ALIENS
22	MMRP00200	MMRP	0	0	0	0	0	0	0
23	MMRP00220	MMRP	0	0	0	0	0	0	0
24	MMRP00230	MMRP	0	0	0	0	0	0	0
25	MMRP00300	MMRP	0	0	0	0	0	0	0
26	MMRP00210	MMRP	1	0	0	0	0	0	0
27	MMRP00320	MMRP	1	0	0	0	0	0	0
28	MMRP00330	MMRP	0	0	0	0	0	0	0
29	MMRP00340	MMRP	1	0	0	0	0	0	0
30	MMRP00450	MMRP	1	0	0	0	0	0	0
31	MMRP00500	MMRP	0	0	0	0	0	0	0
32	MMRP00520	MMRP	0	0	0	0	0	0	0
33	MMRP00540	MMRP	0	0	0	0	0	0	0
34	MMRP00550	MMRP	0	0	0	0	0	0	0
35	MMRP00560	MMRP	0	0	0	0	0	0	0
36	MMRP00570	MMRP	0	0	0	0	0	0	0
37	MMRP00580	MMRP	0	0	0	0	0	0	0
38	MMRP00585	MMRP	0	0	0	0	0	0	0
39	MMRP00586	MMRP	0	0	0	0	0	0	0
40	MMRP00650	MMRP	0	0	0	0	0	0	0
41	MMRP00660	MMRP	0	0	0	0	0	0	0
42	MMRP00730	MMRP	1	0	0	0	0	0	0

FIGURE 106. PathVu program analysis traces hierarchy.

PROGRAM 10 - MMRP0006   PROGRAM ANALYSIS TRACE HIERARCHY

ENTRY - MMRP0006

```
                                      1 2 3 4 5 6 7 8 9 10 11 12 13 14 15 16 17 18 19 20
      TRANSFER       TRANSFER
LINE  FROM   TO      TYPE

 1  00181  00181         ENTRY  MMRP0006
 2  00187  00188  NULL  FALL    10 - ACCEPT-CONTROL
 3  00191  00232  COND  PERF    20 - INITIAL - PROCESS
 4  00238  00239  FALL  THRU  •    20 - INITIAL - PROCESS - EXIT
 5  00395  00212  COND  GO TO  DO - NORMAL - PROCESS
 6  00219  00252        PERF  •    30 - NORMAL - PROCESS
 7  00254  00291        PERF  •  •    40 - PROCESS - 005 - REC
 8  00294  00316  COND  GO TO  •  •  •    40 - PROCESS - 005 - REC - EXIT
 9  00299  00318  COND  GO TO  •  •  •    40 - PROCESS - 005 - REC - EXIT
10  00304  00507  COND  PERF  •  •  •    70 - WRITE - 438
11  00512  00000  COND  CALL  •  •  •  •    'ISAILINK'
12  00516  00517  FALL  THRU  •  •  •  •    70 - WRITE - 438 - EXIT
13  00308  00475  COND  PERF  •  •  •    60 - UNLOAD - ARRAY
14  00484  00000        CALL  •  •  •  •    'ISAILINK'
15  00489  00490  FALL  THRU  •  •  •  •    60 - UNLOAD - ARRAY - EXIT
16  00317  00318  FALL  THRU  •  •  •    40 - PROCESS - PART - LINE - EXIT
17  00257  00347        PERF  •  •    50 - PROCESS - PART - LINE
18  00350  00381  COND  GO TO  •  •  •    50 - PROCESS - PART - LINE - EXIT
19  00357  00507  COND  PERF  •  •  •    70 - WRITE - 438 > 10
20  00365  00381  COND  GO TO  •  •  •    50 - PROCESS - PART - LINE - EXIT > 18
21  00368  00381  COND  GO TO  •  •  •    50 - PROCESS - PART - LINE - EXIT > 18
22  00380  00381  FALL  THRU  •  •  •    50 - PROCESS - PART - LINE - EXIT
23  00260  00412        PERF  •  •    55 - PROCESS - EFFECTIVITY
24  00418  00000  COND  CALL  •  •  •    'EFFECTYP'
25  00429  00534  COND  PERF  •  •  •    80 - CONVERT - TO - JULIAN
26  00540  00000  COND  CALL  •  •  •  •    'COBIJULN'
27  00548  00000  COND  CALL  •  •  •  •    'COBIJULN'
28  00551  00542  FALL  THRU  •  •  •  •    80 - CONVERT - TO - JULIAN - EXIT
29  00449  00534  COND  PERF  •  •  •    80 - CONVERT - TO - JULIAN > 25
30  00461  00464  FALL  THRU  •  •  •    55 - PROCESS - EFFECTIVITY - EXIT
31  00262  00263  FALL  THRU  •  •    30 - NORMAL - PROCESS - EFFECTIVITY - EXIT
32  00221  00222  FALL  THRU  •    80 - RETURN - CONTROL
33  00224  00000        STOP  •    GOBACK
34  00198  00507  COND  PERF    70 - WRITE - 438 > 30
35  00202  00475  COND  PERF    60 - UNLOAD - ARRAY > 13
36  00215  00222        GO TO  80 - RETURN - CONTROL
37  00224  00000        STOP  •    GOBACK
                                      1 2 3 4 5 6 7 8 9 10 11 12 13 14 15 16 17 18 19 20
```


Pathvu Version 03.07.011

FIGURE 107. CBT survey—Motorola.

Course Number	Course Description	== Responses ==		
		SPS	Other	Total
35	Project Management Concepts	30	25	55
37	Effective Decision Making	29	14	43
34	Time Management	27	17	44
39	Developing Managerial Skills	25	40	65
7	CLIST	23	3	26
33	End-User Documentation	23	6	29
9	VSAM	17	11	28
25	ANSWER/DB	16	1	17
12	SQL/QMF/DB2	15	14	29
3	JCL	14	6	20
30	Intro to the Info Center	11	1	12
31	Intro to Data Communications	11	7	18
19	UCC7 Production Scheduling	10	3	13
23	NOMAD2 for New Users	10	5	15
26	EASYTRIEVE	10		10
27	EASYTRIEVE PLUS	10	1	11
36	Basic Business Writing	10	5	15
40	Mgr's Guide: IMPLEM. COMP SYS	10	4	14
2	- ISPF	8	2	10
8	CICS	8	16	24
13	Basic CMS	8	6	14
1	Using TSO	7	4	11
5	MVS Utilities	7	4	11
15	VM / SP CMS for Programmers	7	8	15
6	COBOL Programming	6	2	8
22	PROFS	6	8	14
11	Dialog Manager	5	1	6
14	Advanced CMS	5	13	18
10	- JES2: Basic Operations	3	5	8
16	XEDIT	3	5	8
17	SQL / QMF IN SQL / DS	3	1	4
4	SORT / MERGE UTILITIES	2	2	4
20	SAS	2	8	10
21	TELL-A-GRAF	2	5	7
38	Financial Management	2	1	3
18	REXX	1	6	7
28	Computer Literacy / End Users	1		1
29	3270 Terminal Operation	1		1
32	Intro to DP for end users	1		1
2	- ISPF: Programming			0
2	- ISPF: Fundamentals			0
10	- JES2: MCO-System Management			0
10	- JES2: MCO-Job Processing			0
24	ADRS II			0
	TOTAL RESPONSES	389	260	649

FIGURE 108. Results to date.

CULTURAL
- Establishment of an environment where change is expected - not resisted
- Heightened awareness of professional methods by which information systems are developed

SYSTEMS ANALYSIS AND DESIGN
- Better definition and valuation of user requirements
- Improvement in design document turnaround time

DEVELOPMENT AND IMPLEMENTATION
- Better utilization of distributed computing resources
- Development of an estimated 14 man-months of software in 3 months using a code generator
- Elimination of manual program structure chart development
- Automation of portions of the manual program inspection process

MAINTENANCE
- Automation (and therefore updating) of critical development/operational specifications
- Better change impact analysis for systems documented using automated design tools.

going the other way. We have had a little bit of resistance, with people saying, "Why do I have to do this?" It is appreciated when you start investing in your programmers' and analysts' efforts, when you start paying attention to what their jobs really are, and where they are having difficulties. We are also tapping into some of their creativity and are getting a lot more enthusiasm about looking at methods improvement as opposed to wanting to treat software generation as a black art.

We are getting back into the metrics side of the productivity aspects. We have done some of this on faith and now it is time to start measuring what we have done, as well as trying to set an ongoing technique for quantitative assessment. We have about six or seven projects we have done with the Transform code generator. In one case, we have seen a 3-month cycle using the code generator, where we would have taken 12 to 14 months before. We think we have easily obtained 20 to 30 percent productivity improvements for the people who are higher up on the learning curve. In the long term, we are looking for two and three times that. To get there, you have to have an institutionalized methodology and the code generators in full usage. Presently, we have the code generators in heavy use in about a half-dozen particular areas. That is probably only 10 or 15 percent penetration versus what we must get over the next 18 months. Finally, we are getting better-quality maintenance and documentation out of the exercise.

Conclusion

We think there are tools out there today (Figure 109). I have been involved in either the hardware design or the software side of the business since 1961. My assessment is that, up until a couple of years ago, we had not changed the way we built software much in more than 20 years. I used to do it on a yellow tablet and hand it to a keypuncher. Today, we may do it on a TSO editor, but we still do COBOL code generation much the same way.

Up until the last couple of years, I didn't fully see the maturity of the fourth- or fifth-generation products on the level at which we could begin, on a wholesale basis, to switch over to the use of those products. I think the market out there is maturing enough so that CASE tools can do for the business applications what CAD tools have done for integrated circuit designers over the last five or six years. We are building the products in the design engineering area (68030 and other microprocessors) that could never have been produced on a paper-and-pencil basis. We are starting to see some of those same software tools become mature enough to use them on the MIS side. You still have to work the methodology. The cardinal guideline is that no tool works in an unstructured environment. Up until today, and it is changing rapidly, you have had to integrate products from various vendors. There is hope that two or three of those will shake out as major players. Those products are still coming together, however. You have to tap into your people. You can't do it from the top down. The price is relatively high. You are going to invest $10,000 to $15,000 per programmer/analyst, but if you are paying him $50,000 or $60,000 a year, with fringe benefits, that is not a bad investment. What you are going to have to invest in time is more crucial than the hardware/software investment. It is easy to afford $10,000 or $15,000 per programmer if you are just writing a check. But you may have to spend 10 to 12 weeks in training on various packages,

FIGURE 109. Summary.

- There are CASE tools available today that can significantly improve your analyst/programmer productivity and system development cycle time, **but:**
    - The tools are no better than the basic software engineering **methodology** you employ
    - You must still **integrate** the products from multiple vendors
    - The emotional and intellectual spirit of your people must be challenged such that change is **desired** and **expected** — not resisted
        - Employee involvement must be the driving force behind the program

- The **price** is high:
    - Minimum $10K per analyst/programmer for hardware and software
    - 12+ weeks training per analyst/programmer over first two years

- But so is the potential **payback:**
    - 20%+ productivity improvement after the first year
    - Potential of 2x - 3x long-term productivity improvement

and it is going to take a chunk out of their schedule. The payback is high, too. If you are not using the tools heavily, there is no reason you couldn't get a short-term increase of 20 or 30 percent. With the potential of the code generators, you can get a lot more payback than that.

7.4 CHANGING THE APPLICATION LIFE CYCLE AT THE HARTFORD

NOTE: This section is extracted from a talk given by John Crawford, Vice President and Director of Information Management at The Hartford Insurance Company, Hartford, Connecticut, as he reported on the experiences at The Hartford with the adoption of the CASE environment, and their plans for the future in application development and management.

Changing the Application Life Cycle

The Hartford is changing the application life cycle to better reflect opportunities in the CASE environment. I will not concentrate too much on tools or methodologies in this report. Instead, I will concentrate on the people and management implications of changing the life cycle.

The three categories I will outline include:

- The past — waterfall life cycle model
- The present —application engineering life cycle
- The future — the excursion map

The Past—Waterfall Life-Cycle Model

Basically, the phases in the traditional life cycle used at The Hartford were in a waterfall model. Traditional activities were defined through a feasibility study, requirements, definitions, design, programming, implementation, and post-implementation phases. The life cycle included about 300 steps and each life-cycle task had explicit deliverables associated with it for each step. The organizational responsibility, i.e., which organization was prime in preparing or building that deliverables part of the application building process, was a separate decision as to whether the applications area, the customer area, or the technical support staff of the organization was responsible.

The methodology traditionally used was a data flow diagramming approach for the requirements phase. We followed a Jackson structured design approach for detailed application design and program structure. We used a process called semantic data modeling for the data modeling, which was a seven-step process of going from a high-level business model to a normalized model for implementation. The data modelers, database, and database administration areas were responsible for all the data modeling activities. Duties within the organization were separated and compartmentalized because The Hartford is a large company. There were specialists for almost everything—data modeling, performance, security, etc. Every time a project had to be done, every one of those organizations had a role in the life-cycle activities with the waterfall model. The result was a productivity problem of getting all of the organizations to participate, cooperate, and move at a faster pace to build applications.

The tools used in the traditional life cycle included a workbench in 1982, which we called the "developer workstation." It was completely installed in 1986. It took four years to install it across the environment and is based upon a three-tier architecture, where a personal computer sits on every developer's, support person's, and manager's desk. The computer connects to a minicomputer where the project-level tools are located. The minicomputer then connects to the IBM mainframes in the data center where we port our developed applications.

We were then able to take some of the vendor tools and some of our own tools and do more integration. There are still things on the workstation for project management and benefit analyses. There are many on-line templates (where templates could be built for examples of the life-cycle deliverables) for what is expected. The life cycle is like a menu and was used to follow the work tasks that are assigned. This returned links to the tool, which was used to perform that particular task. There are standards for what a particular product should look like and there is a dictionary and a project file.

The difference between a dictionary and a project file in the workstation is one of formal specification versus informal specification. There are a lot of informal products produced in the life cycle. Informal products are those that don't go into the end application, such as a project plan. The project plan is never run in the production application. However, in a formal specification, the data element, the data schema, and so forth, drive their way into the production environment. The Hartford's concept of a workstation is to store informal products in the project file and store formal products in the dictionary.

We also have test tools and reusable libraries. Program development and testing are done at the lower level of the architecture as much as possible. It is a full office automation environment because the information management organization is also a business office. The same tools that can be applied to an environment where the benefits of office automation can be gained, can be applied to the data processing organization. Meeting scheduling, on-line calendars, electronic mail, etc., are integrated in the work station.

Human factors in the waterfall model include the following:

There are clear data processing and customer responsibilities. The corporation deals with the customer or deals with somebody who deals with the customer. There is a chain of customer interaction.

There are distinct management checkpoints. There is a review process, a formal sign-off process, and a technical or management walk-through of the product that is produced.

Project management tends to be accurate and predictable. The corporation commits the customer to the project and the time and resources required for the next phase of work. As we go through the waterfall model, there is a hard commitment on the next phase and tentative commitment on the full scope of the project, because we realize that it has to be revised as we go through the life cycle because we are learning more about the system model.

There are serial project steps. While there is some overlap, the basic concept of the 300 steps is that the activities are being done serially, at least conceptually.

How do these human factors work?

It is organizationally comfortable. Everyone understands his or her role and responsibility and knows what the deliverables are and who is going to produce them.

Over the years, the company has had wide participation in active projects using project life-cycle methodology. There have been 40 to 50 projects run each year in a development mode for the last 10 years.

The makeup of the project teams has been large. About 400 to 500 people were doing application development. It wasn't uncommon to have 25 people on a project team.

The project success rate was high. This is a conservative approach. Clearly defined steps, a methodology, customer interaction, and a workstation supporting the environment existed with as much automation as possible since 1982.

The Present—Application Engineering Life Cycle

Why change the life cycle? The concept of an application engineering life cycle is aimed at a more tightly coupled or integrated life cycle using CASE technology. The Hartford finished most of the transaction processing in the environment. The mainframe systems are primarily IMS based, and they automate most of the insurance functions. There are few transactions that can be added to the insurance environment that aren't already automated. That environment is basically maintenance.

The new world opportunities are in the area of the professional support functions, which is distributed processing. Many efforts go into systems that now reflect professional work flow by front-ending the IMS transaction processing systems with the things necessary to automate the underwriting process, the rate-setting process, and the claim adjudication process prior to creating the transactions that record the business activities.

This is what led to changing the life cycle. In the new life cycle, we allow some prototyping experimentation to replace the more traditional requirements phase of the waterfall approach. This prototyping was highly successful. However, a more aggressive stand toward prototyping was needed across the entire life cycle, not just for the requirements phase. We worked with an external consultant. Together, we create a Joint Application Design (JAD). It is called a mutually acceptable requirements specification. JAD is essentially a facilitation technique that can be applied to many different kinds of products. There are two key pieces to it: (1) What is the product the team session is trying to produce? (2) What are the facilitation techniques needed to get the people to participate in that team session to provide the input and produce the product? This was successful in the traditional environment, and we felt it could expand.

We had done a lot of research on data-driven design. The approach on the waterfall life cycle was basically a process modeling approach. The process models were done first; then the data that was going to be acted upon by those processes was defined. We went back and did it the other way around. The data needed to be defined first; then the processes that go with it had to be defined. The whole concept of object-oriented design is to encapsulate those processes with the data. When the full nature of that methodology is viewed, process logic is viewed differently. The data will define the process within the description of the data. The Hartford is not there yet, but this is the concept it is driving toward.

With these guidelines, the application engineering life cycle (AELC) can be defined. The application engineering life cycle is a concept indicating that there are things that are wanted in the new life cycle. Some of the things put in at The Hartford include:

Group Techniques—In the application engineering life cycle, group techniques are required. If group techniques are not used, then the system should not be built this way.

Customer Participation—Customer participation is mandatory. Customer participation ratios work in the new environment. In The Hartford's team session techniques, the ratios work on one to one in IEM versus customer resource participation.

Modeling Methods—New modeling methods are part of this technique.

Participant Selection—The concept is to select the best people for implementation of the new life cycle.

Specialized Training—This focuses on a prototyping approach.

Prototyping

Relational Tools—Relational tools are used for prototyping.

Forced Time Compression

Skunk Works—Skunk works try to bring creativity into the design of the applications.

Minimum Set of Products—In the new life cycle, the following question has to be answered: "What is the minimum set of products that we can produce?" The best productivity is achieved by eliminating the work step. Go back into the traditional life cycle and question the "why" of each and every activity that was required.

Concept of the New Life Cycle.

The methodology to use in the new life cycle consists of two formal requirements or formal specifications. The idea in the application engineering life cycle is to produce models of the system. The application engineering life cycle is a set of interlocking methods and techniques designed to increase application development productivity. We have gone back and looked at the methodology to simplify it and create a methodology that was linked. Objects were defined earlier in the life-cycle phase that could generate objects later at the lower level of detail. The concept is to have an entity model in place within the organization. The Hartford has an enterprise model, which it calls a business segment model because the business is large, separate, and distinct. The Hartford has four different business segments, with each having its own entity models (Figure 110).

When a project has to be defined, start with the data definition. The Hartford uses an extended relational analysis (ERA) model, which then feeds into a business thread model derived from the business function model. A physical data schema and an entity life-cycle model are then produced and are aimed at ending up with the system model (Figure 111).

Semantic data modeling produces the segment-level model. This is considered to already be in place at the time a project is started. The semantic data modeling then goes into a technique called extended relational analysis, which then feeds into the process side, called the event precedence model. It then goes into the entity structure modeling (Jackson structured design), then into a prototyping mode. At this stage, the prototyping tools used in the prototyping environment are loaded from the extended relational model.

Along with the concept of the new life cycle, graphical products and the dictionary have been expanded. A product called CADWare can be located in any traditional workstation. CADWare has rule tooling. Rule Tool allows a user to define the icons, the rules for connection between icons, and the syntax or placement of text within a graphical representation of a methodology. Rule Tool allowed us to use the same tool as we moved from the methodologies in the waterfall life cycle to the methodologies now used in the application engineering life cycle. It has now been linked into the dictionary. The dictionary is built upon a relational model and is driven by a meta-model. The meta-model provides the rules for the construction of the entities that go into the dictionary. Thus, a facility exists where we can graphically create a new methodology and load it into the dictionary. Through Rule Tool on the graphics side, and through the meta-modeling structure, we can then enforce the rules of the methodology through those tools. As The Hartford moves into the application engineering life cycle, this tool is actually brought into the team session environment and the methodology or the models are followed as we go through the participation.

The application engineering life cycle is serial in terms of the

FIGURE 110. Application engineering life cycle models.

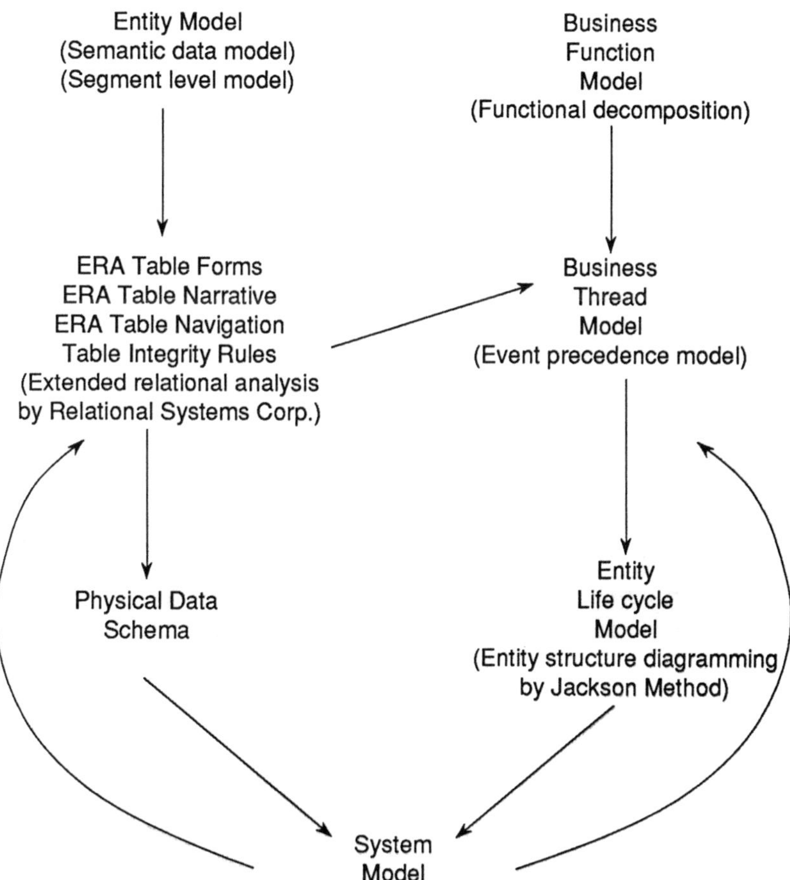

major phases (Figure 112). One of the key areas is in the project
planning phase (Phase II in the figure). It is important to scope
the application into enough subphases so that it can be operated
or built in a prototyping environment. At this point, we are concentrating on getting more comfortable with requirements engineering. The requirements engineering phase is intended to be
fully executed in either the team session environment or in the

FIGURE 111. Application engineering life cycle methods.

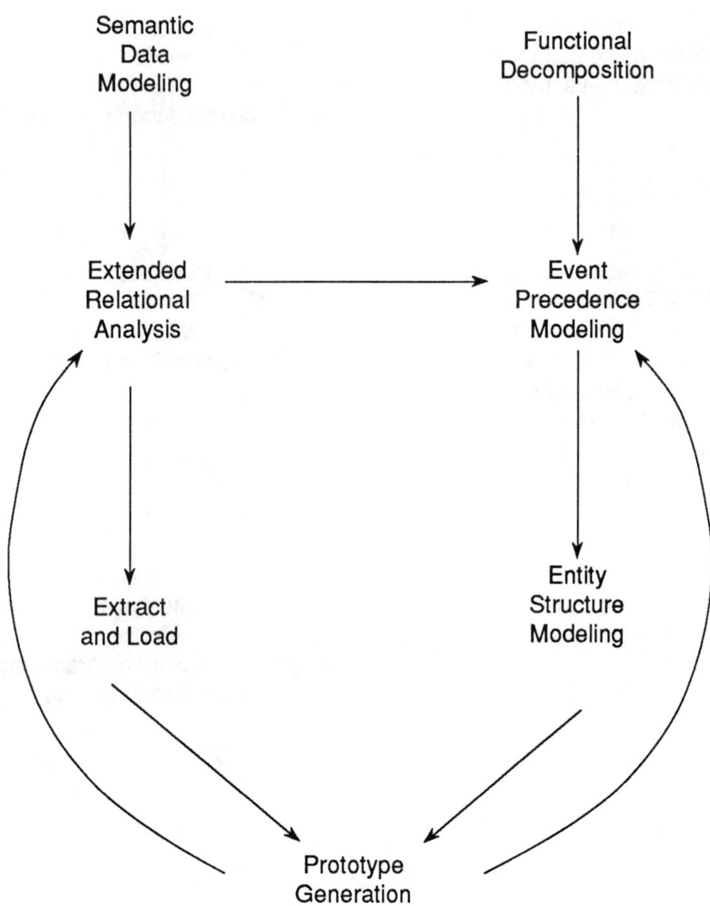

prototype mode. The steps at the bottom of Figure 112 begin with data modeling, then prototype preparation (basically the entity structure model that threads the application), prototyping, systems integration (which brings the prototype threads back together), and implementation planning.

Technically, we consider ourselves to be doing a design. We reach the same point where we would have been with detail design

FIGURE 112. Application engineering life cycle.

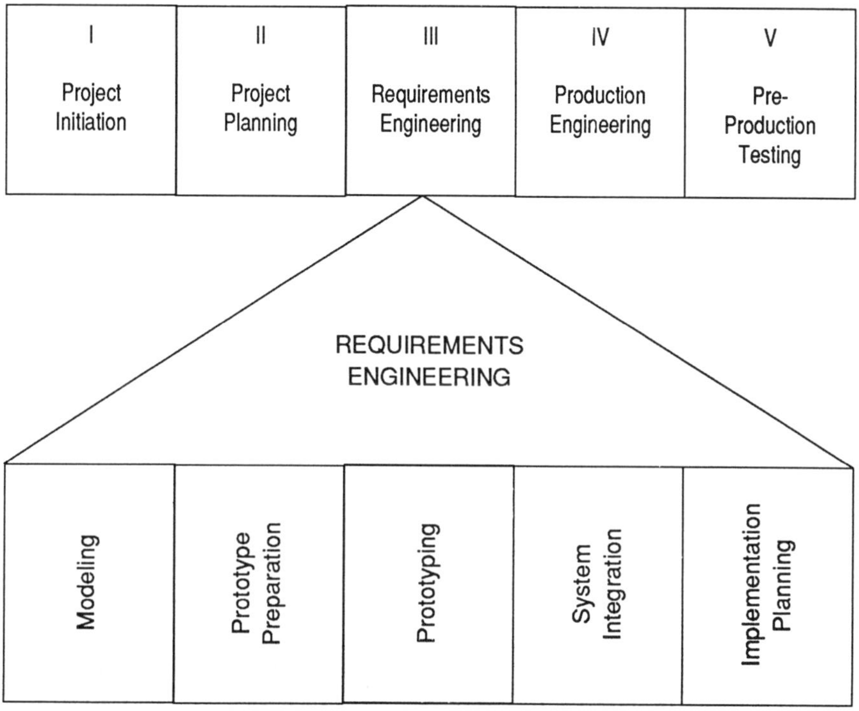

in the waterfall life cycle. When people see the results of the prototyping effort, it is a design, not a system. This is one of the hardest concepts to get across.

We commit to a sample schedule (Figure 113) with that requirements engineering phase. When a functional composition is being done, the idea is to come up with a logical subset of the application that this kind of technique can be applied to. This is a classic problem issue. Something that traditionally would have taken 3.5 years to define the requirements cannot be done in a 10-week phase. However, a class of application of that magnitude can be functionally decomposed and broken down so that the requirements engineering process can be used to prototype the model. There are some risks here because the functional decomposition and the relationship to the semantics model is the correct one.

FIGURE 113. Sample schedule.

Phase	Estimated Time	Major Outputs
Orientation	3 Days	– Problem statement, scope, objectives – Timebox scope – Expectations contract
Modeling	2 Weeks	– Relational data model – Process model
Prototype Preparation	2 Days	– Prototyping threads
Prototyping	5 Weeks	– Functional prototype of each thread
System Integration	1 Week	– Reassembled and packaged – Functional prototype
Implementation Planning	1-2 Weeks	– Recommended implementation – Environment with alternatives

10 Weeks (approx.)

The sample schedule in Figure 113 is in a fixed time frame. Another company uses a similar concept that they call Time Box. Time Box requires that it be done in 120 days. We don't do it that way. We establish in the beginning (requirements engineering preparation phase) the contract for the prototyping schedule. That is considered a time track with the customer. This can be seen from the 3 days to the 2 weeks in the figure. The customers are expected to be in the team session environment with us for that period of time.

The next step in the sample schedule is prototyping the parallel threads. The customer spends about half that time (about two and a half weeks) sitting side by side with the prototyper to define the prototype.

The next step is to go back to reassembly; then the implementation planning is back into a team session environment where the customer is directly involved.

Human Factors in Considering the Application Engineering Life Cycle.

Human factors are a major shift in the way people work.

The responsibilities of customers and data processing have now become blurred. The up-front initiation for the team session environment includes training of the information management people, which can be a 10-week training requirement. The designers of this methodology, or life cycle, hold hands with the project team. But as this is formalized throughout the organization, there is a need to make a major commitment to retrain all of the people in these kinds of techniques. That training should be 10 weeks for the information management professional and seven days for the customer. Data modeling training needs to be included in the customer training. Thus the customer gets trained in extended relational analysis and event precedent modeling, and they are shown what these products are. With the proper facilitation and guidance from the experts, the customer is the best one to define the data model.

The team sessions commitment is mandatory because of the blurred responsibilities. If team session time from a customer standpoint cannot be committed, then go back and use the traditional waterfall life cycle.

> *Time compression* has to be considered when the contract is established.
>
> *Training* is an extensive investment.
>
> *Job roles* are new (Figure 114). The Hartford now has a facilitator of job titles at three levels—apprentice, journeyman, and master. We also now have the titles of modeler, prototyper, designer, and project leader. The project leader is also the facilitator. There is a 10-week training investment to get a modeler, prototyper, or project leader to the stage of journeyman. The concept here is to have apprentice work followed by classroom training. When we do these team sessions, we have the team participants; then we back track to keep that down to a reasonable number. However, there are people observing the process, which is part of the learning experience. Then they are eventually pulled up to master. There is no title of analyst here anymore, and there is no title of programmer.

Other human factors should be considered also. One is complete dedication. We want the forced time compression to be a 150 percent effort. There should be a parallel project going on to define the reward system and expectations. If a company is going to ask its employees to make that kind of commitment, there has to be a reward system. Do they get compensatory time, a bonus, or something else? What is the employee's motivation for this kind of commitment? In the initial selection, employers are searching for people with strong interpersonal skills. The MIS community tends to attract introverted people who have trouble with good communications. The deficiencies in those interpersonal communications are brought to the forefront when they are sitting with a customer and locked in a room for 10 to 12 hours a day for two and a half weeks. The facilitator has to recognize that emotional highs and lows are going to be present.

The concept of the application life cycle points to small excellence teams. Try to run these teams with not more than four or five IS people in them.

There has to be a commitment to standards. If application generation is going to be done from these models, then, by design, the models have to be explicit. The standards for the construction of the system (the model represented) have to be an extremely explicit product. Data flow diagramming is a modeling technique,

FIGURE 114. Role development path.

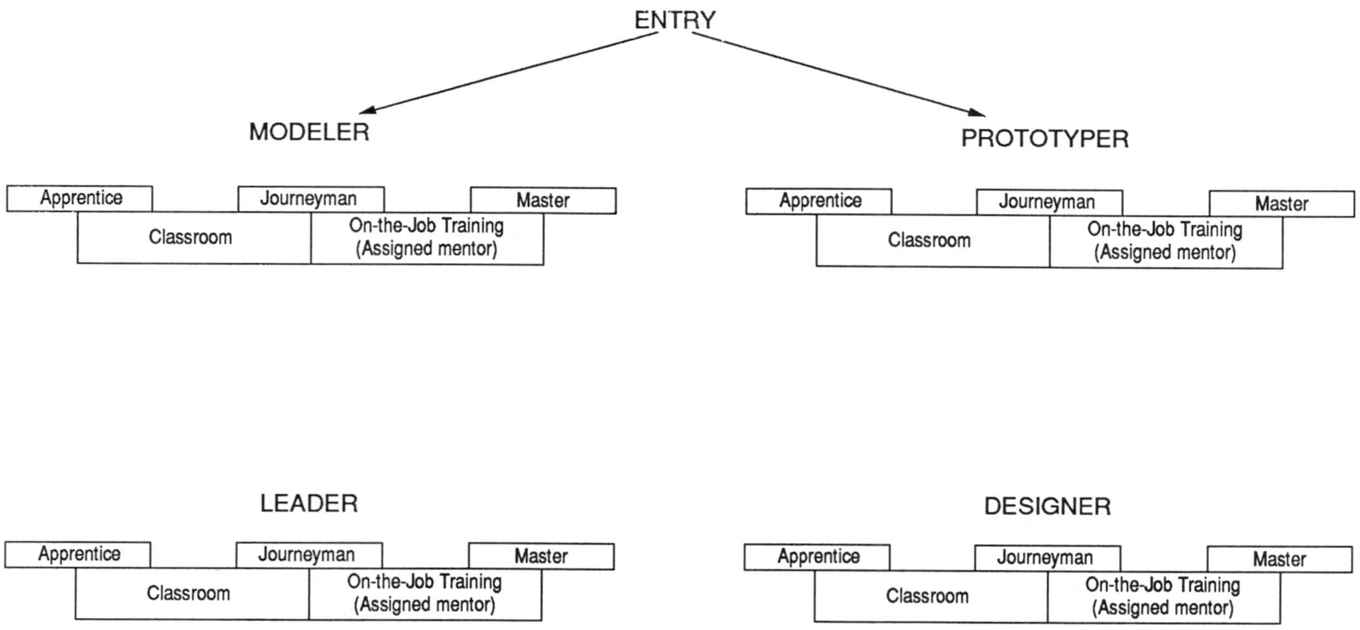

but it is not a standard (in terms of rigor) from which anything can be generated. It is a good communications vehicle. It is a good tool to model the environment and understand the business and the information flow. However, it is not a rigorous standard. Thus, it is a requirement that people understand that as the life cycle develops and evolves, there has to be one way, and one way only. There are no substitutions allowed.

There has to be limited organization participation. The best people don't have to be involved. The same expectation exists to have the sense of urgency for production implementation once the requirements engineering is completed. In the bureaucratic environment of the traditional life cycle, there is a specialist for everything. The order is signed off and the security people sign off, and then the performance people tinker with it. There is no room for all of that specialty in the application engineering life-cycle model. So it can be organizationally uncomfortable, particularly for the technical people, because we haven't been able to afford to get them involved. It requires taking some risks. If you are going to go through the production implementation, you are going to have to take some risks over what you might have done traditionally.

The management structure is also uncomfortable because, in the traditional life cycle, there were management check points, and many management walk-throughs and reviews. With the application engineering life cycle, you have to empower the people in the team to design the system. The waterfall life cycle model allowed you to go out and do the analysis, the interviews were done, the information was gathered, the requirements were documented, and then you signed off. Then you went through a design and walked the customer through the design. But it wasn't until in the back room that the processes were checked for results of a good, quality product. In the application engineering life cycle, the expectation is that the first model is not the end result because of the iteration. The customer has to be inside. People have to get accustomed to saying, "This is not my creation, this is not my ultimate answer. It is a team session iteration that is aimed at coming at the best result."

Expectations are critical. A contract with the customer has to be established. Make sure the customer understands that it is a design, not a finished product, and that it has to go through production engineering. The same goes for a tolerance concept and an improvement concept as you go through the prototyping model.

Cost/benefit has become a big issue. In the waterfall life cycle, The Hartford did a thorough cost/benefit at the design phase. This process tends to speed through the organization and leaves you scurrying to figure out how to do the cost/benefit. Currently, cost/benefit is part of implementation planning at The Hartford, but it is something that is still maturing. A good benefit, if done right, is team building between the customers and the data processing organization. The facilitation process is a key to this. At The Hartford, there are about 10 or 12 trained facilitators coming from the traditional life cycle. Those facilitators have worked closely with the outside consultants and have the people skills—how to resolve conflict in a team session, how to keep it moving, and how to keep it on target. The human factor technique is key to the process, not just a methods approach.

Four Experiences.

The following projects are four of The Hartford's experiences dealing with different people, most of which indicate a 300 percent difference in productivity.

Two of the projects in the group insurance area went through to production with excellent results. A sales order tracking process was put up for the group contract proposals. Also, a new underwriting system was put up for the risks in group insurance that are required after a customer misses the pre-signup period, according to the contract in underwriting of the individual. Both of those systems were implemented rapidly, enabling us to go through the requirements engineering phase and the production engineering phase. The Hartford's people and the customers were happy.

In another project, we went through requirements engineering. This one was with our actuarial department on the property and casualty side. However, the customer discovered that he couldn't afford the system. He found out that the scope was much different than he had expected upfront because of the iteration through the prototype. It became a data volume issue that he had not initially anticipated. The project was put on the shelf because the customer decided he couldn't afford it. The testimonial and the team in this project was about a 6 to 1 increase. It is estimated that through the same design level that traditionally it would have taken six times as long.

The last project is still being worked or reworked because, when we went through the life-cycle effort, we got to the stage where a demonstration by the sponsor and executive management was required. They looked at the prototype of the design and said, "This is awful." This was a situation where the team people were not able to come up with the management expectations for the design. So we are now going back and looping through the model again to come up with a new design. There is a lot of sensitivity on this project, because the view is, "How could you show us this failure?" It is a matter of the education process. However, if you get to that failure six times as fast, then the project is really not a failure. Even if the rework doubles the effort, you are still ahead of the game.

The quality of three of the projects was good even though one customer found out that he couldn't afford the project. Staff reaction, so far, is zero. The people in the group insurance area love us because everybody is ecstatic about the success. With 2,000 people in the organization, you have to realize that you don't do this kind of change overnight. There are a lot of people right now saying, "We need to see it happen." The people are comfortable with the ways we have been doing things, and so the staff reaction is next to sceptical or almost zero, particularly the technical staff, where the same sense of urgency has to exist when you get into that production engineering phase.

The Future—The Excursion Map

The rest of this presentation will deal with what we see in the future for the application engineering life cycle. The Hartford had developed a framework for changing its life cycle. As we look at the model for the work environment, the methodology is broken into three distinct areas:

Life-cycle management methodology
Integrated system development methodology
Quality assurance methodology

What are the expectations here? Figure 115 shows how The Hartford is defining the framework for the application engineering life cycle. We intend to work on the Customer Engineering Life Cycle (CELC) in the future, with the concept of building a life cycle for certain classes of applications that customers can completely do by themselves.

The integrated systems development environment includes the development strategy, the tool requirements, the methodology, the technology, the architectural plot form, the user environment, and the integration into our environment.

The quality assurance methodology sets up the internal verification and testing for the quality of the product.

The Hartford has several life cycles that are selectable. The life cycles are selectable based upon the initial parameters or class of the application problem that is being solved. The idea of an excursion map is to guide the developer through the necessary tasks and deliverables that go at that class of application problems (Figure 116).

Once this model is understood, you can then revert to the technical life cycle, which defines the methodology that the developers have to use and the tool structure that supports it.

There has to be a concept of systems essence. The selectable life cycle says, "Whatever path is taken, there are certain minimum requirements for systems essence to complete the formal models that are required in application generation. The techniques used to get there may be changed, but unless those objects are completed, the application cannot be generated." It is like going across the country and saying, "Take any road you want, but make sure you stop in Nashville, St. Louis, and Denver on the way." Deliverables at those steps are absolutely required and must be precisely done.

The Hartford is wrestling with the question, "What do we do with CASE as we build these new technical platforms?" The platforms of the future are not mainframe IMS. Our particular

FIGURE 115. Systems engineering framework.

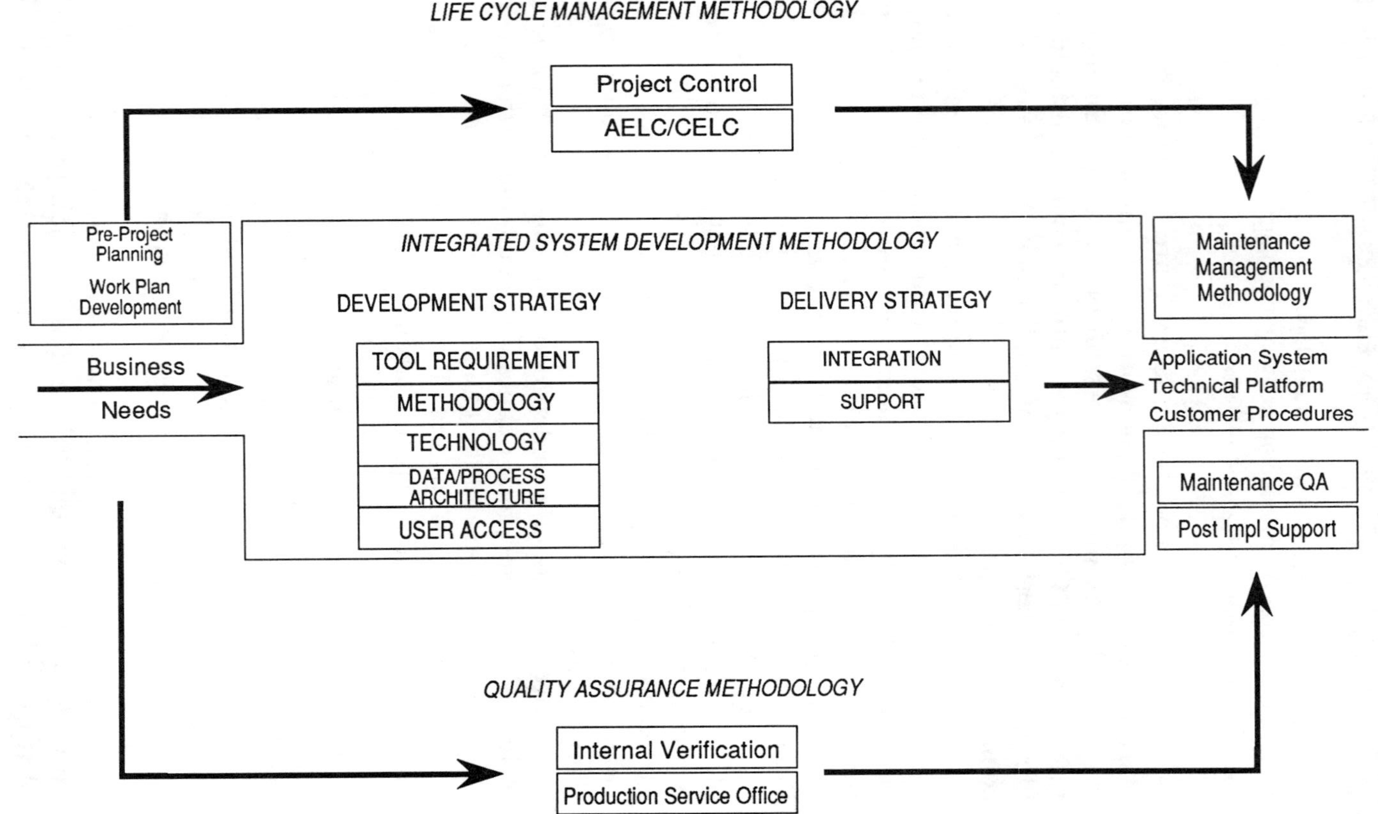

FIGURE 116. Excursion map for the application engineering life cycle.

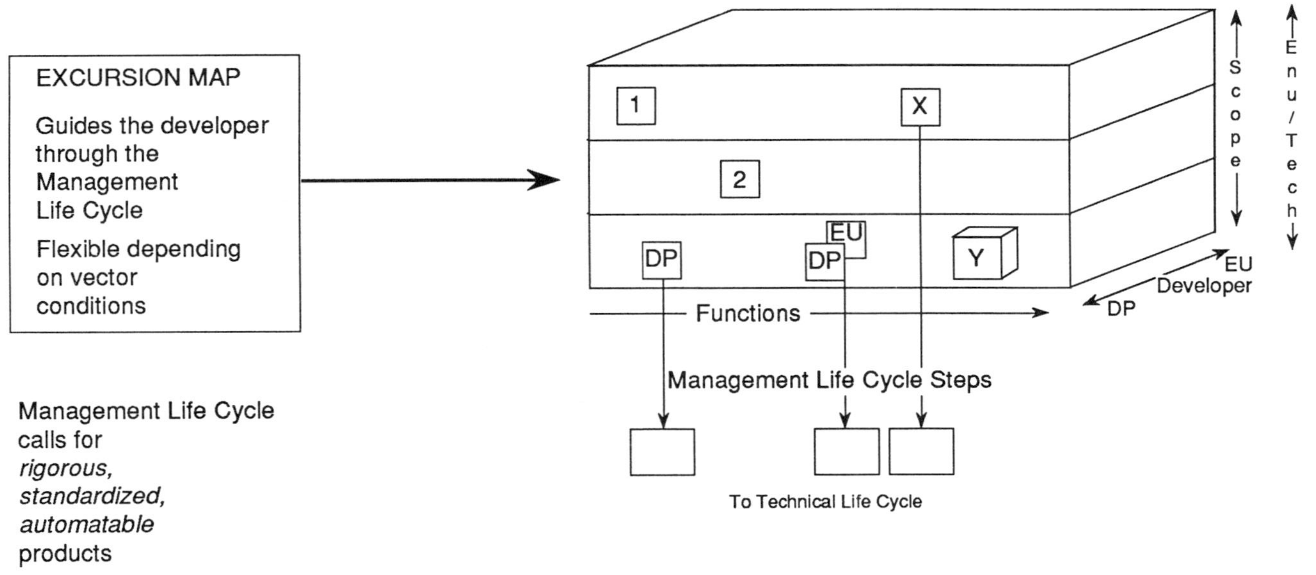

architectural model is a three-tier professional workstation to mid-range computer to mainframe. The concept is to build the application so that function and data are essentially seamless in that three-tiered architecture. Where are the CASE generation tools that allow you to build your design and then select which tier the architecture function and data reside on? What about CASE tools that support new technologies? Where do we fit in office automation objects, image objects, or voice objects? All of these have to be integrated into a new CASE environment of the future. If you look at image in particular (which we are starting to do some work on), you see that it is a data problem. Image lends itself very much to the concepts of data models and to integrating those image objects as another data type within the overall data framework.

Other Technical Aspects.

The repository, which defines the enterprise access system, is the integration "glue" that has to hold CASE together (Figure 117).

The Hartford's data modelers are coming up with a data model of the repository. Consider all of the objects in your present environment today that define the information environment. Consider all the ones in production, and consider all the design objects. Convert it into a single repository that either directly stores the object, the indexes to it, or cross references to it. No matter what the vendors come up with, the model of what we want to keep in that and how is it going to apply has to be defined.

The next concept that The Hartford is working on is called work-in-process automation. It is taking the concept of life-cycle coordination (Figure 118). Some of the objects that a life-cycle systems coordinator would do are shown in the figure. We want to automate the entire sequencing of the deliverables, and we need to focus around the expectations for deliverables in a life cycle. It shows the teams that produced the deliverable, the training necessary to use the tools, and the execution of work tasks used to produce the deliverable. Notice that the word "agents" is used. When you think about the progression of CASE and the adding of expert systems products, those products should be considered agents. They are not tools, they are agents—they are intelligent agents that are performing a particular task within the life cycle.

FIGURE 117. Integrated methodologies.

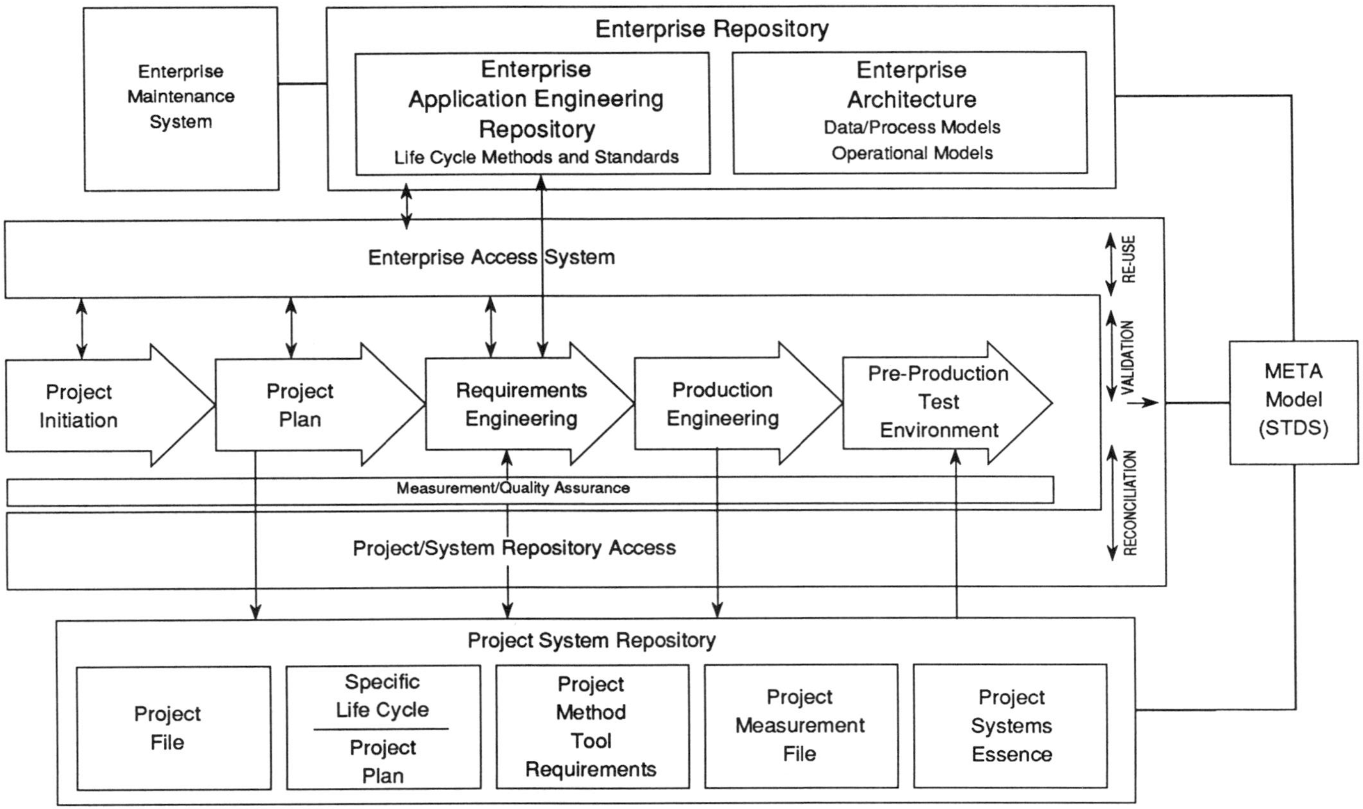

FIGURE 118. Life-cycle systems coordinator.

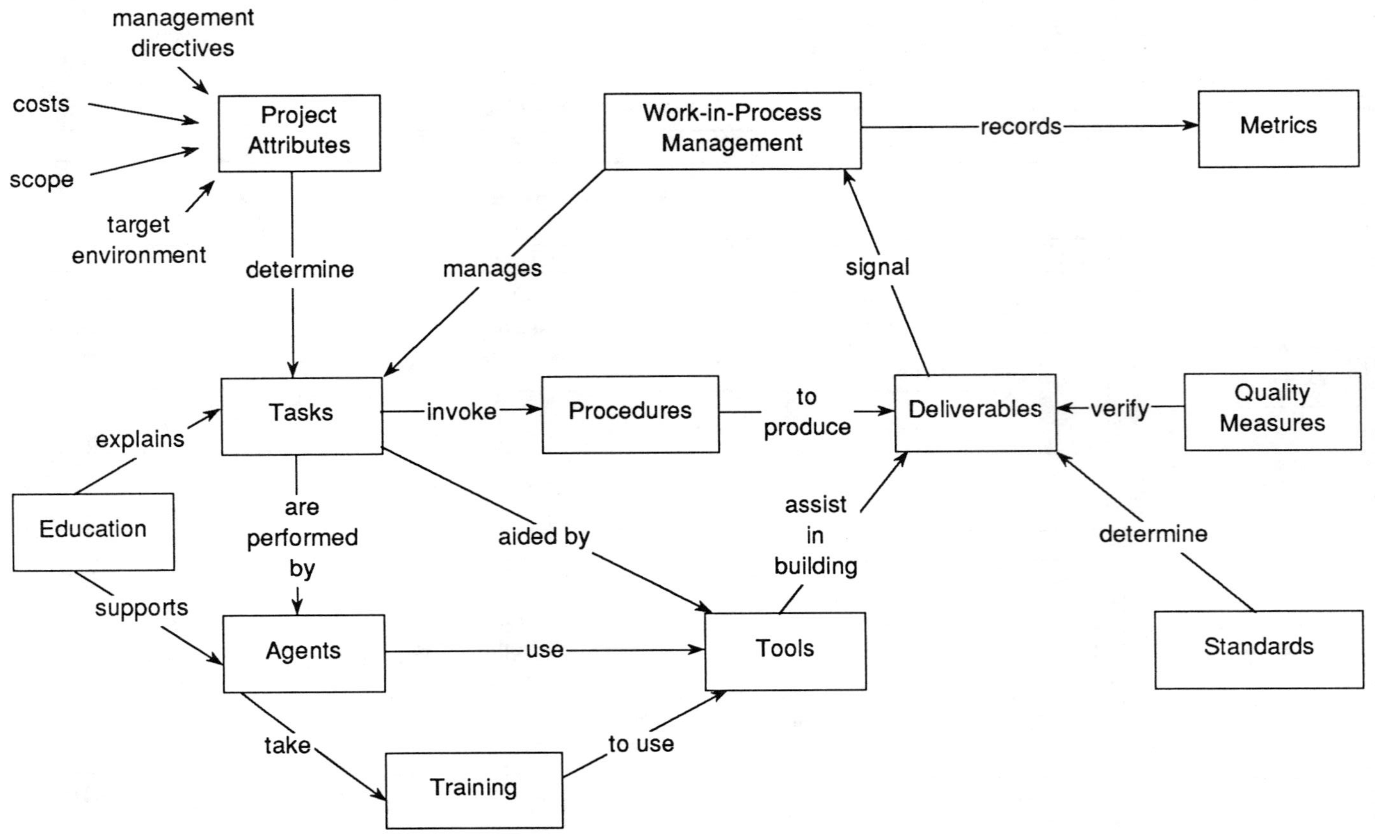

Standardized system essence was mentioned before in the context of objects and the repository. It is like searching for the Holy Grail at this point, but the definition is: a formal language that is independent of vendor and independent of tier in the architecture that allows you to keep those formal objects that are necessary to generate production systems in a particular production environment. Systems essence is what you want to do when looking at the reverse engineering problem. A standard for systems essence as an industry has to be established that all the vendors can agree on. This has to happen to have full application generation, vendor environment, and tiers of an architecture in a seamless way.

When looking at the excursion map, and as we change the environment, there are many things to consider (Figure 119). We have to worry about the life cycle itself. We have to worry about the usage support, the training and methodology, the education, and the workstation integration. We have to worry about all the layers of the environment that it has to play against—changing the tools, changing the data architecture, and changing the presentation layer. All of these are an application problem we have to be concerned with as the environment changes and as the pace changes.

The Hartford is working with a language technology for reverse engineering. So far it has been successful. The conversion cost of reverse engineering is a worry for us, but the productivity leverage is substantial.

The last management issue is the organizational absorption rate. How fast can we change the life cycle? How fast can we introduce selectable life cycles? The management discipline to enact them? The tool stability and integration? Obviously, The Hartford is going through an evolution in CASE right now. There has to be a stable platform so that these changes can be done in the real project world. On the other hand, we want to take advantage of the newest technology as it becomes available. This is a major management challenge for us in the future.

FIGURE 119. Delivery strategy integration wheel.

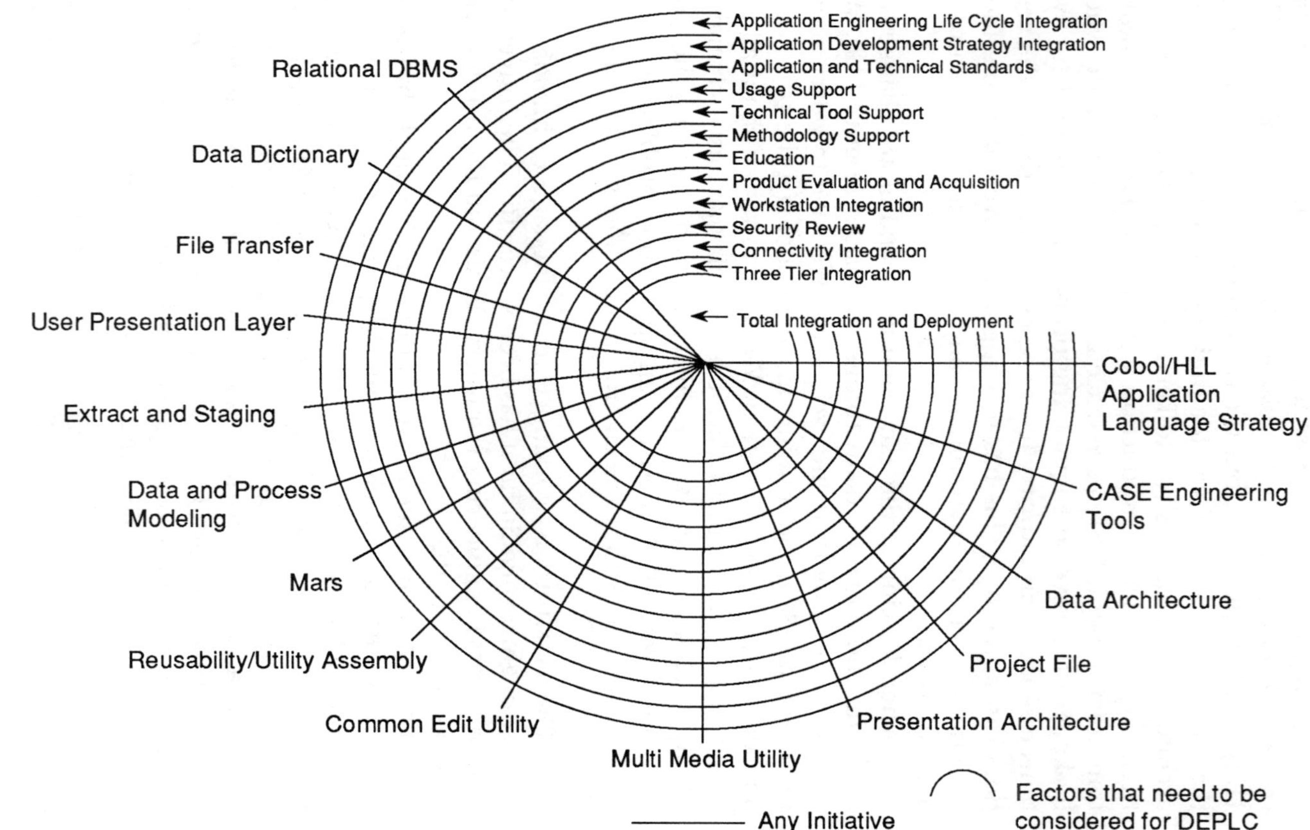

7.5 *THE INFORMATION ENGINEERING FACILITY AT TEXAS INSTRUMENTS*

Texas Instruments Incorporated had sales of $5.6 billion in 1987. It has 38 manufacturing sites in 17 countries, and employs over 78,000 people. Its principal businesses are:

- Semiconductors
- Government electronics
- Data systems
- Consumer electronics
- Materials and controls
- Industrial systems

Texas Instruments has a large information management environment, with 15 data centers around the world, 41,500 network-connected terminal devices, 27,000 intelligent workstations, and over 1,000 major information systems. They have a comprehensive and advanced distributed processing plan and data administration strategy. They have over 18,000 software developers, of whom 16,000 are in end-user computing, 1,000 are in information systems, 950 are in engineering real-time work, and 650 are in systems software work. Being an engineering company, they look on CASE as a CAD/CAM for information systems centered on an encyclopedia.

Their objectives for CASE development are:

- Obtaining the *right system*
- Handling complex *communications*
- Assuring a high *quality*
- *Data consistency* throughout the corporation
- Ability to manage *change*
- Ability to handle a heavy *maintenance* load
- Strong *documentation* capabilities
- Environmental independence

Texas Instruments was looking for the right system. Traditionally, the systems plan has never seemed to correspond to the business plan. They turned to the CASE approach because its methodology enabled:

- The continual involvement of *business management.*
- The capacity to meet their Critical Success Factors.
- The ability for systems to follow the *business strategic direction.*
- The ability of technology to be an agent of change.

In addition, CASE allows communications with diagramming standards and graphics, which are engineering tools.

Texas Instruments met their objectives by developing *The Information Engineering Facility.* It is based on their concept, shown in Figure 120, based on James Martin's ideas. The appeal of an information engineering approach was obvious to Texas Instruments. The traditional communications and diagramming standards in data processing consisted of nothing but piles of paper with no standards. Electrical engineering has had great success in the past, using symbols for such things as resistors, ground, transistors, and amplifiers, which are known across language barriers. These are used throughout the world in computer-aided engineering (CAE). It appealed to them that information engineering, using CASE methods, could have similar, universal symbols for such things as entity, relationship, process, and logic. There could then be accurate communications via graphics and diagrams for planning, analysis, and design without excess verbiage.

Meeting Their Objectives By Using the Information Engineering Facility

To meet their objective of assuring a high quality, Texas Instruments recognized the advantage of using expert systems for error checking. In 1976, Barry Boehm had reported that the cost to fix errors goes up rapidly as the development process proceeds. If the cost to fix an error is 1 during the planning phase, it rises to 10 to fix the same error during the analysis phase and 50 during the design phase. It then rises to 200 to fix the same error during the coding phase. Texas Instruments reasoned that if expert systems were used for error checking during those first three phases, then the final compilation will be much more accurate, and the final quality much better, at less cost.

FIGURE 120. Information engineering framework.

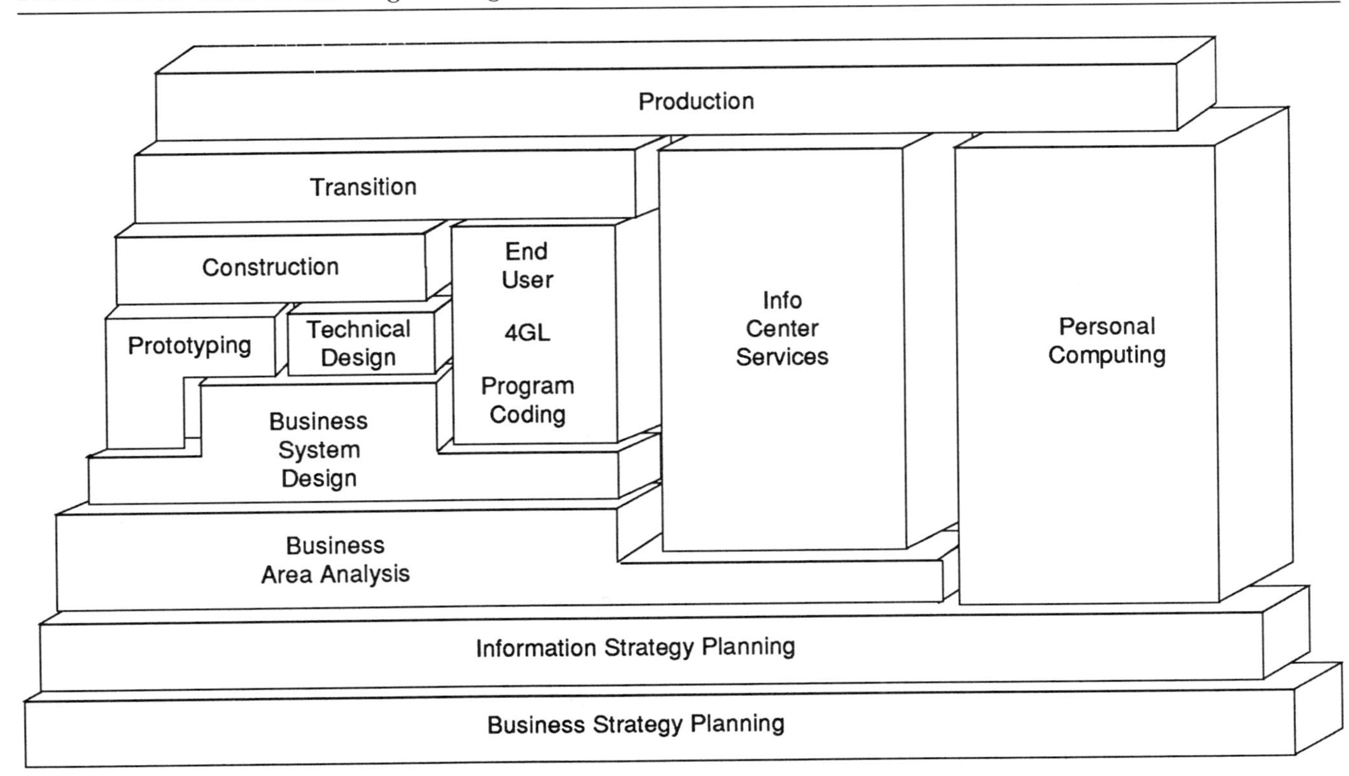

To meet their objective of data consistency, they recognized that in the traditional approach of having separate files for sales, manufacturing, and accounting, for example, the data could not be uniformly handled. The CASE approach of having a central information repository, or encyclopedia, could provide data consistency.

To meet their objective of being able to manage change, they rejected the complex paper documentation and hand-tooled code of the past. CASE offered the capability of having files of entities and their attributes that could readily be changed at a high level, with automatic generation of the necessary modified code.

To meet their objective of being able to handle a heavy maintenance load, they realized that the traditional reverse thinking of making changes in the code, then the design, then the analysis, and so on, was too time consuming. The CASE approach allowed the maintenance to occur at the high level where the diagrams describe the system, then they would be automatically passed through the encyclopedia, and the result would be a regenerated information system with consistency and accuracy.

To meet their objective of having a strong documentation capability, they determined that the accuracy of documentation fell off rapidly in traditional development work as work progressed over time. On the other hand, the automatic documentation capabilities of a CASE system would give 100 percent accuracy of documentation, covering 100 percent of the structure of the system, throughout its cycle.

Texas Instruments therefore developed an integrated CASE system, as illustrated in Figure 121, which has proved highly successful. Their concept, based on their background in manufacturing, is illustrated in Figure 122.

Figure 123 indicates the volume of CASE work that they have been involved with. Some of their experiences are listed in Figure 124.

Summary of the TI Experience with CASE

The experience that Texas Instruments has had with their CASE efforts and The Information Engineering Facility may be summarized as:

FIGURE 121. Integrated CASE.

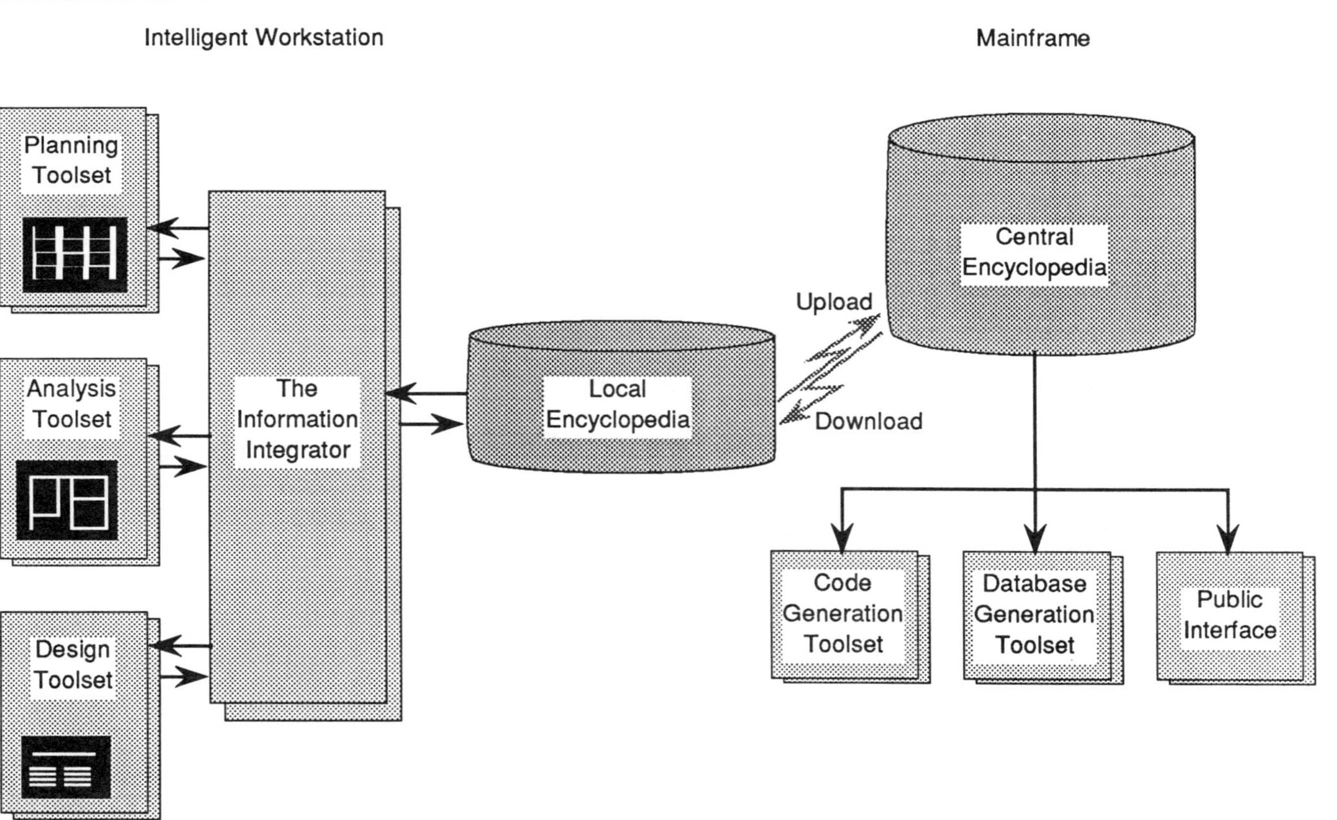

FIGURE 122. CASE Systems factory.

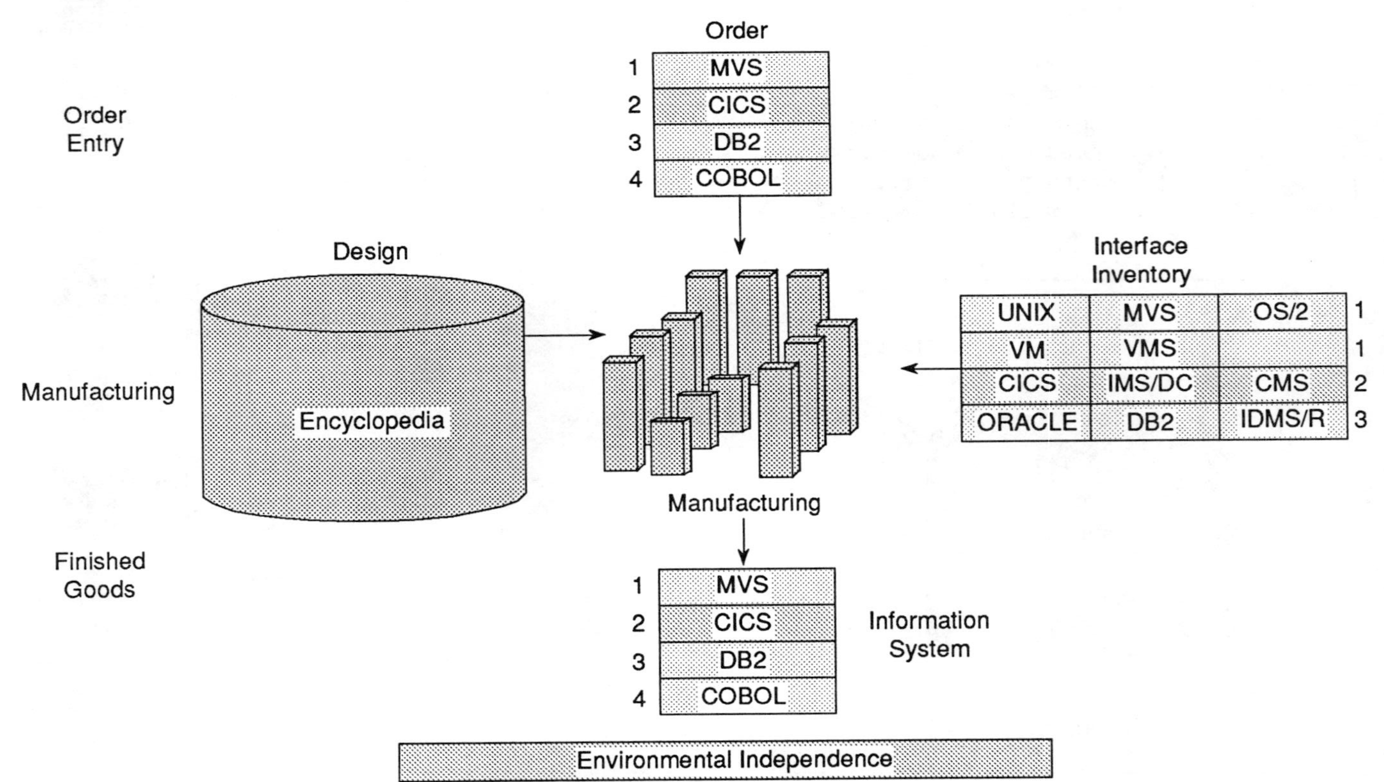

FIGURE 123. Texas Instruments Incorporated CASE fanout.

• 11 Pilot Projects	3Q85 – 2Q88
• 7 Subject - Area Databases	2Q87 – 3Q88
• Training and Consulting	ONGOING
• 23 Project Launches	1Q88 – 3Q88
• 300 People Trained	DEC 1988

- Greatly *accelerated deployment* of systems.
- Much higher systems *quality*.
- Much higher development *productivity*.
- A significant *staffing impact* upon both their information systems and their engineering/real-time groups.
- A *competitive advantage* for Texas Instruments.

The Information Engineering Facility by Texas Instruments

Texas Instruments believes that CASE offers the promise of solutions that can keep pace with a myriad of rapidly changing needs for information systems. CASE can deliver the critical benefits of quality, productivity and cycle time reduction that is mandatory in current and future system environments. The Information Engineering Facility™ (IEF)™ has been developed as a CASE solution for the systems development cycle—analysis through main-

FIGURE 124. Texas Instruments Incorporated CASE projects.

Project Name	Tables/ Databases	Trans	Lines of Code	Productivity
Library Management	10 DB2 3 DL/I	10	116K	3:1
Source Inspection	2 DB2 7 DL/I	6	44K	4:1
DSEG FAB Floor Control	20 DB2 3 DL/I	30	300K	

tenance. TI applied CAD/CAM principles to the systems process and emphasized an integrated set of tools at both mainframe and workstation levels.

The IEF Computer-Aided Software Engineering product from Texas Instruments is a fully integrated set of tools for the development of information systems—a bold alternative to traditional methods.

By automating the entire systems life cycle, IEF increases system quality and significantly reduces the time required to build and maintain systems.

IEF's distinctive features produce dramatic improvements in productivity and quality.

- Implements information engineering methodology focusing on shared data for building systems.
- Uses diagrams to represent data, processes, and their interaction.
- Creates a model from diagrams and stores its meaning in an encyclopedia.
- Performs rule-based consistency and completeness checking.
- Automates the transfer of business and systems information from stage to stage in the systems cycle.
- Allows subsets of a model to be used by multiple system developers simultaneously.
- Generates 100 percent of COBOL program code and relational data base definitions automatically.

The IEF operates in two tightly coupled environments: (1) intelligent workstation, and (2) mainframe. The combined capabilities offer ease of use, power, and a thoroughness that would be unavailable if only one environment was used.

- Workstation tools provide an easy-to-use interface with interactive color graphics, pop-up windows, and on-line help.
- Workstation-mainframe architecture allows for automatic incorporation of changes across diagrams and across business models.
- Central mainframe encyclopedia supports coordination of development.
- Public interface provides an import/export capability to support

migration, to interface with other environments, and to facilitate query reporting.

The IEF architecture contains five fully integrated tool sets, providing one comprehensive product for systems development.

- The planning tool set begins the development process with information strategy planning from a high-level, business vantage point. The business function/entity type usage matrix relates entity types to business functions, employing weighted patterns of usage. The results of the cluster analysis are used to assist in the identification of natural business systems.

- The analysis tool set focuses on correctly capturing detailed business requirements early in the development process. The Entity-Relationship Diagram records the results of entity analysis and consists of entity types, relationships, and attributes. This diagram supports data modeling and analysis. Other tools include entity hierarchy, process hierarchy, process dependency, and process action diagrams.

- The design tool set provides detailed definition of the system solution. The dialog flow diagram specifies the sequences and conditions related to procedures and procedure steps. It also specifies the contents of the data views passed between the procedures and procedure steps. Other tools include screen designer, procedure action, and data structure diagrams.

- The code generation tool set produces COBOL program code based on the system definition.

- The database generation tool set generates the system control information needed for data storage and access.

The IEF software uses diagramming tools on the intelligent workstation to create models of a business. These models are drawn with menu-driven tools using interactive color graphics, pop-up textual panels, and on-line help. Some examples of the diagramming tools in the planning, analysis, and design tool sets are:

- The business function/entity type usage matrix relates entity types to business functions, employing weighted patterns of usage. The results of the cluster analysis are used to assist in the identification of natural business systems.

- The Entity Relationship Diagram is used to record the results of entity analysis. The diagram consists of entity types, relationships, and attributes. Entity types are things of interest to the business (e.g., Product, Purchase Order, Supplier, and Warehouse). Relationships are associations between entity types (e.g., Warehouse holds Product Stock), which document the business rules. Attributes are facts about entity types. (For example, Number, Type, and Unit of Measure describe the entity type Product.)

- The entity hierarchy diagram is used in entity analysis to document entity subtypes. A subtype is a collection of entities of the same type to which a narrower definition and additional attributes and/or relationships apply. (For example, the entity Product can be divided into the subtypes of Fabricated Part and Purchased Part.) In addition, the entity hierarchy diagram may be used to view the neighborhood of an entity type. A neighborhood contains all the entity types to which the entity type selected is directly related.

- The process hierarchy diagram is used during function analysis. Its tree structure represents the decomposition of a high-level business activity (function) into more detailed tasks (processes). The order in which the subordinate activities appear shows how these activities fit into the hierarchy. The further out in the branch, the finer the detail represented. For example, the function Warehousing can be decomposed into the processes Receive Goods, Inspect Goods, and Store Goods.

- The process dependency diagram is used in function analysis to document the sequence in which business activities occur. For example, the processes Check Supplier, Check Quantity, and Check Quality must precede Report Results because these processes produce information required by the process Report Results.

- The process action diagram is used in interaction analysis to record the detailed logic of a process. This diagram enables the analyst to record the actions which are taken and the conditions under which they are taken. For example, to Receive Goods, the first entity action performed would be to READ Purchase Order, and the second entity action performed would be to READ Purchase Order Item. The second action would be taken only if the first were successful.

- The dialog flow diagram is used to specify the sequence in which procedures and procedure steps must occur, the conditions under which control is passed from one procedure or procedure step to another, whether that control is passed on a permanent or temporary basis, and the contents of the data views passed between the procedures and procedure steps. In the example, control may be passed from procedure Check Supplier to either the procedure Check Quality or Check Quantity or to the procedure step Report Results. If control is passed to either Check Quality or Check Quantity, it is returned to Check Supplier. If control is passed to Report Results, however, the transfer of control is permanent.

- The screen design diagram is used to specify the format of the data input to or output from an automated procedure or procedure step. Each screen format may be customized or developed using a template (screen skeleton) to ensure required fields are consistent across an entire system. In addition, the characteristics of each field (color, light intensity, reverse video, etc.) may be specified. For example, the Approved Suppliers by Product Number screen specifies where the Product Number (which is data required by the procedure Check Supplier) should be positioned, the domain to which it belongs, and the edit patterns which it must follow.

- The procedure action diagram is used to define the logic of a procedure, data manipulation, and the dialog management functions in sufficient detail to generate executable code. The data manipulation is specified in terms of the entity-relationship model and is independent of any database, allowing the specification to be transportable between environments.

- The data structure diagram is used during design to define how the logical data model represented by the entity-relationship diagram should be translated into a physical model containing records and fields. The diagram allows the designer to specify how entity types should be implemented as records, how attributes should be implemented as fields, how identifiers should be implemented as entry points, and how relationships should be implemented as linkages or pointers. In an example, the entity type Product would become the record Product, the attributes of Product (i.e., Number, Type, Unit of Measure) would become fields, the identifier of Product (Number) would become the entry point PRODNO, and the relationship Supplies would become the link record Supplies.

7.6 EXPERT SYSTEMS IN CASE AND THE USE OF AION AT TEXAS INSTRUMENTS

NOTE: This section is a summary of a presentation by Pam Fales, Information Systems and Services, Artificial Intelligence Laboratory, Texas Instruments Corporation, Dallas, Texas. It outlines TI's perspective on the use of expert systems in systems development, their evaluation process for expert systems, and their selection of the AION system.

The Spirit of Artificial Intelligence

Artificial Intelligence methods are being accepted rapidly and are becoming more and more available in the market. The only problem to information systems and services people is whether they are ready for artificial intelligence. It requires techniques to be learned and products to be selected. It also requires, however, a new mind set that is different from that of many experienced systems analysts. The AI mindset can be summarized as follows:

Machines excel at:

- Performing repetition
- Storing and retrieving data
- Responding quickly to stimuli
- Controlling great forces
- Crunching numbers

People excel at:

- Perceiving patterns
- Generalizing from details
- Profiting from experience
- Exercising judgment
- Processing symbols

In evaluating AI techniques and products, the TI group found a profusion of areas and possibilities to research. Some are listed in Figure 125.

FIGURE 125. AI techniques and products.

---

* AI Techniques
    - Representation production rules, frames, semantic nets
    - Searching: breadth first, best first, hill climbing
    - Matching: parsers, grammars, ATNs
    - Paradigms: declarative, object-oriented, blackboard
    - Inferencing: goal directed, data driven, constraint directed

* AI Workstations
    - Texas Instruments
    - Symbolics
    - Xerox
    - Digital Equipment
    - Sun
    - Apollo

* Tool Kits & Languages
    - KEE
    - ART
    - Personal Consultant
    - Nexpert
    - Intellect
    - Common LISP
    - Prolog
    - OPS
    - SMALLTALK
    - Objective C

There were clearly both short-term and long-term promises for the use of artificial intelligence and expert systems. The short-term promises were:

For the TI users:

* Ability to get *information* rather than data.

* Systems that are *user friendly,* not user ugly.

* Systems that are *easy to learn,* as well as *easy to use.*

For the TI Information Systems and Services organization:

* Ability to enhance the usefulness of current applications.

* Provision of capabilities for new services to be offered.

* Ability to support the computer and network operations.

* Ability to speed systems development.

The long-term promises were that the movement from data processing to the present goal of information processing to the future goal of knowledge processing would be expedited. This means that professionals who were data processors and are now system analysts and programmers will become knowledge engineers.

Technology Transfer Mission

The TI Artificial Intelligence Laboratory group recognized that they had been given a complex technology transfer mission. Through training, experimentation, and implementation, they would have to "climb the AI capability curve." This meant that starting out with little capability, they would have to initiate the AI process, learn about AI, build a staff, and build support. They would then have a period of experimentation, where tools and applications would be tested and education would be spread out through the corporation. Their mission would be to then go through a period of utilization, rapidly spreading out the technology, until a valid tool kit threshold was reached, where the methods would be accepted, many would be trained, projects would be available, and profitable results would be obtained.

The initiation phase centered on an awareness campaign. This campaign was carried out through a number of different channels:

- The Information Center
- The Education Center
- Symposiums
- Demonstrations
- Artificial intelligence newsletters

The TI Artificial Intelligence Laboratory then began a tool fanout in a planned way. This included:

- Grass roots involvement with the experimentation.
- Making it easy to get a personal consultant.
- Encouraging self study, through a variety of methods.
- Communication of successes through the newsletter and training.
- The nurturing of potential "winners" by the AI Lab staff.

Consulting support was provided in a variety of ways. The Information Systems and Services AI Lab had a small but well-trained staff and an assortment of AI products. The AI Lab sponsored projects and encouraged participation in joint development activities.

The Information Systems and Services AI Lab

The AI Lab mission was stated as:

Spearhead assimilation of AI tools and techniques into TI's MIS groups. Efforts include thorough evaluation and successful implementation of AI technology through lab sponsored projects and by working as a development partner with other MIS AI implementers.

There have been several cooperatively developed AI projects. Following are brief outlines of five of these AI systems.

- TI's *Computer Operator Advisor and Training System* (COATS) uses a combination of three AI technologies: expert systems, natural language, and speech production. It is PC based, with over 700 rules. It has had the effect of speeding operator training and reducing mainframe downtime.
- TI's *Professional Workstation Technical Support* system is for PC error message handling. It assists workstation support specialists. It has a number of standalone diagnostics possibilities. It has been fanned out to information centers, site support groups, and repair and maintenance organizations.
- TI's *Local Area Network Diagnostic* (LAND) system was devised to improve LAN troubleshooting. It is a telephone interface solution and so has a remote access requirement. It works from a TI 990 minicomputer to the users' terminals. It has improved LAN troubleshooting and speeded the training of technicians.
- TI's *Expert System Expert System* (ESES) is an expert system project advisor for new expert system ideas. It is used as an information center AI awareness tool, and telephone access is planned. The system requests details on a project idea, then rates the idea in four areas: expertise required, payoff, problem characteristics, and support needed.
- TI's *Network Order System Expert* (NORSE) is an automated data collection and verification system for order entry. It is PC based with cooperative processing. It has automated updates to an on-line database and makes automatic requests for additional data. It continuously monitors message traffic.

Selection of the AION System by TI

TI's Information Systems and Services AI Lab made an evaluation of a number of expert system tools that could be used in their CASE efforts. The evaluation involved 15 people from Information Systems & Services, Defense Systems Electronics Group, and Semiconductor Group. They selected the AION product from AION Corporation, Palo Alto, California.

The *AION Development System* (ADS) is a software environment for building inference-based data processing applications in the IBM computing environment. They found that AION significantly increases development productivity by integrating expert system technology with traditional application development technologies. Their evaluation of the AION product found that it provides:

- Embedded expert system capability within a conventional program, and behind an IMS inquiry.
- TSO/PC development and TSO/IMS/OC execution.
- Increased development productivity.
- Ease of integrating knowledge from several sources.
- Ease of modifying and maintaining knowledge bases.
- Access by large numbers of users with existing terminals.

Figure 126 and Figure 127 show the results of a survey made for TI by Harmon Associates. The AION evaluation process by TI's AI Lab took about four months, and included a number of evaluations, symposiums, interviews, and management presentations. The potential savings of using AION in their AI development projects came to well over a million dollars a year. Some of the AI systems they have since developed using the AION product and imbedded in CASE-generated systems include:

TI's *Procurement Documentation,* which is a purchasing systems enhancement for the Defense Systems Electronics Group, which is available on MF and PC environments. It is an automated form of a major procurement checklist, and accesses existing mainframe databases. It queries the user for unknowns. It is time-saving, and is used daily, and has become very important to the procurement process. There is an output analysis and checklist of documents to properly document the purchase order.

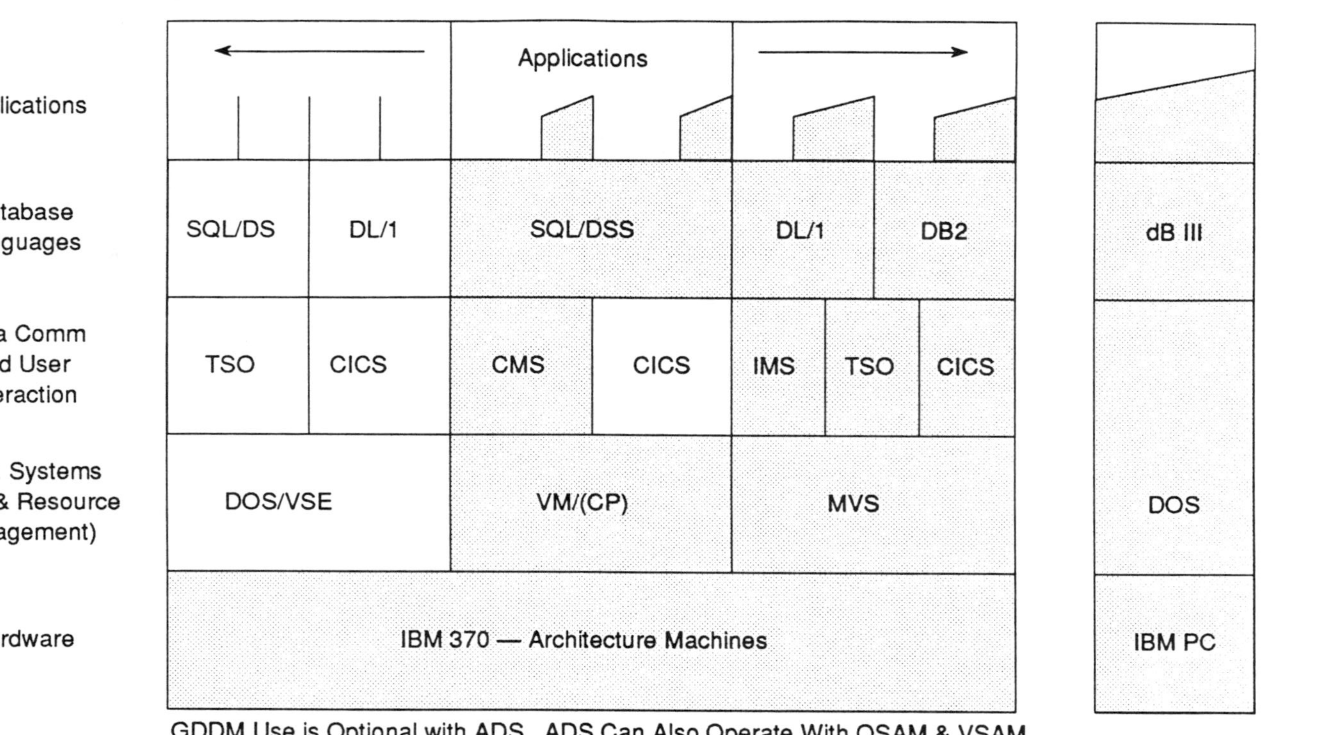

FIGURE 126. AION environments

FIGURE 127. Next closest competitor environments.

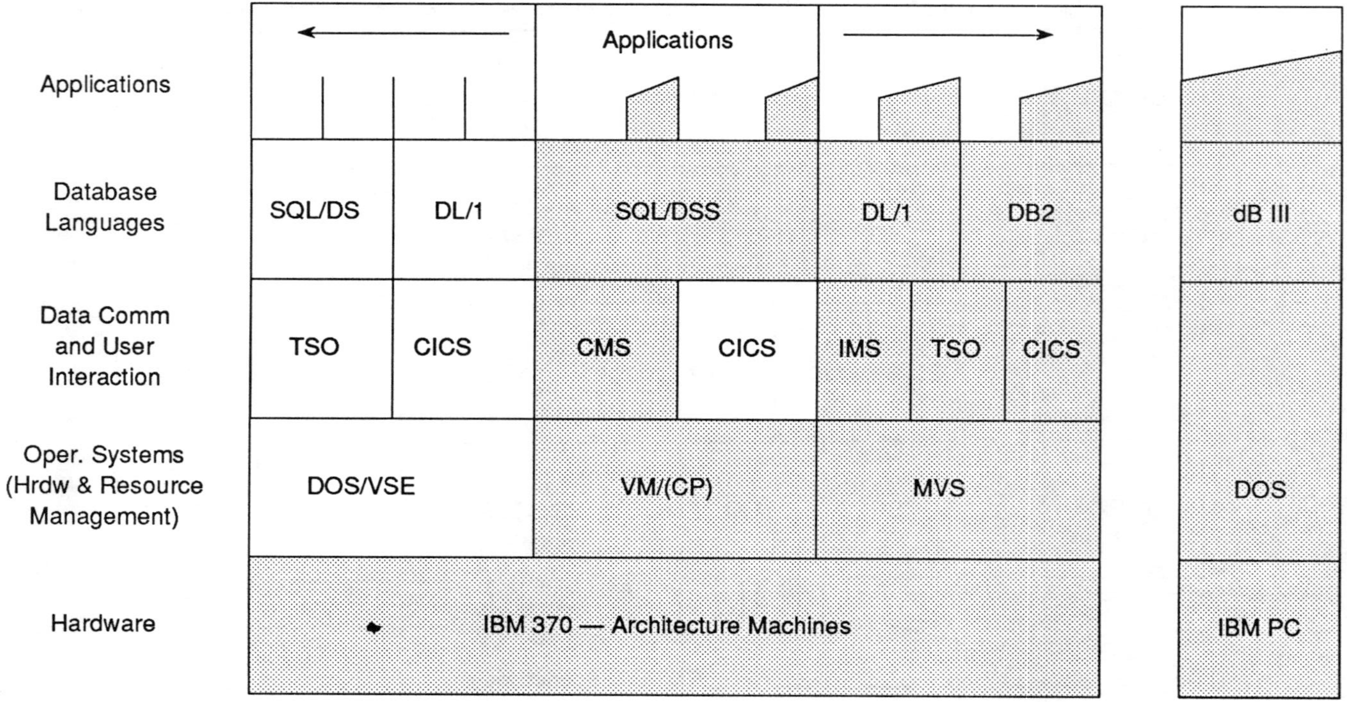

TI's *Expense Statement Generator* has proven most useful in automating expense statement preparation. It is an IMS transaction. It has reduced categorization errors and rehandling, and has reduced the load of the Cashier.

TI's *Failed Device Analysis* (FDAL) is a manufacturing process evaluation system that detects the reasons for failed devices. It is a centralized expert system that accesses a DB2 historical database. It has decreased the cycle time of failed devices by a factor of 3, and it has improved worldwide device failure analysis and reliability engineering capability.

Summary of the Use of AION

TI's AI Lab has found that the AION system is excellent for imbedding expert systems into CASE development efforts. The developer satisfaction has been very high, and they feel they have just touched the tip of the iceberg.

TI feels that AION EDS/AES is far superior to current competitor tools for their purposes.

A mainframe delivery vehicle is necessary for the integration of AI into the MIS world for CASE-developed systems. TI feels that expert systems are important and profitable right now. Waiting for more options may cause them to pass up valuable opportunities and cost savings.

7.7 EXPERIENCE WITH IMPLEMENTING SYSTEMS USING IEF AT AMOCO

NOTE: This section is part of a presentation given by Richard Frankel, Senior Systems Analyst at Amoco, concerning their experience with implementing systems using the Information Engineering Facility at Amoco.

Amoco is following the James Martin & Associates interpretation of the information engineering philosophy. Within that implementation, there may be one or more supporting tool sets. The Information Engineering Facility is one of those tool sets. Knowledge Ware tools may be considered another tool set on that branch, because they support the information engineering methodology. Different tool sets may or may not support all the phases of a methodology. The tools may or may not be integrated. The Information Engineering Facility is an integrated tool set, where each of the phases of methodology are available. There are other branches and other implementations. For example, Arthur Young has an interpretation of information engineering, but may or may not have tools supporting their own implementation. There are other tool sets that support things outside the scope of information engineering.

Defining information engineering is interesting because there is a set of methodology guides that has a number of definitions. The following is my definition.

> *Information engineering methodology is a rigorous data-driven methodology consisting of a set of interrelated formal techniques used to build and maintain information systems for a computerized enterprise.*

Note that it is a data-driven methodology; it is an integrated set of formal techniques used to create a model of the enterprise. What is normally seen in these methodologies is a three-sided or four-sided pyramid. Data is represented on one side and activities are represented on the other.

Seven Formal Stages to Information Engineering

The Information Engineering Facility supports all of the following stages: information strategy planning, business area analysis, business systems design, technical systems design, construction, transition, and production (Figure 128). What you are going to do is create a model of the business. You are going to look at the data, the activities, and the interrelationship between the data and the activities. You might not build a model of the whole enterprise. You might build multiple models depending on the desired level of integration. The methodology is a top-down approach of divide and conquer. We want to go ahead and model at the high-level parts of the business and refine them as we go along. It is a focused approach (Figure 129).

Amoco's interest in information engineering began in 1984, and the Information Services Organization did a review of systems

FIGURE 128. Information engineering stages.

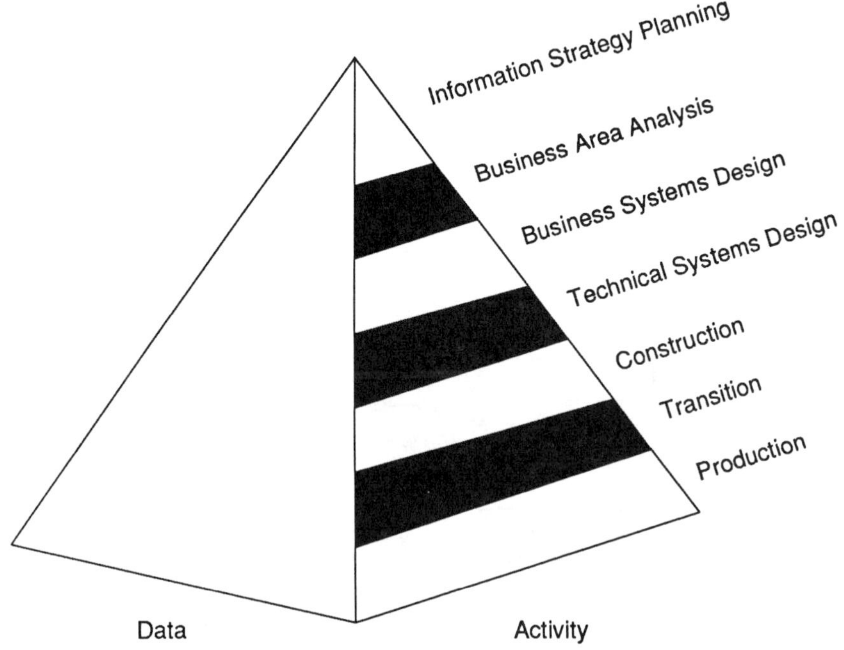

development methodologies. The review included information engineering, but it also included JAD, prototyping, and function point analysis. In 1985, the Information Engineering Facility was selected as a methodology to evaluate and, in July, Amoco signed a contract with Texas Instruments and became a Beta site. We received the software in August and began the Beta test.

In 1986, information engineering began to be used in two of our subsidiaries. Amoco Corporate continued the Beta test and initiated pilot projects. Both processes were carried out simultaneously. In 1987, information engineering expanded into the staff departments and was adopted as an approved information service department methodology. Amoco continued using the Information Engineering Facility and continued the Beta test. Today, the company has continued information engineering projects, continued use of the tool set, and continued use of the methodology.

FIGURE 129. A focused approach.

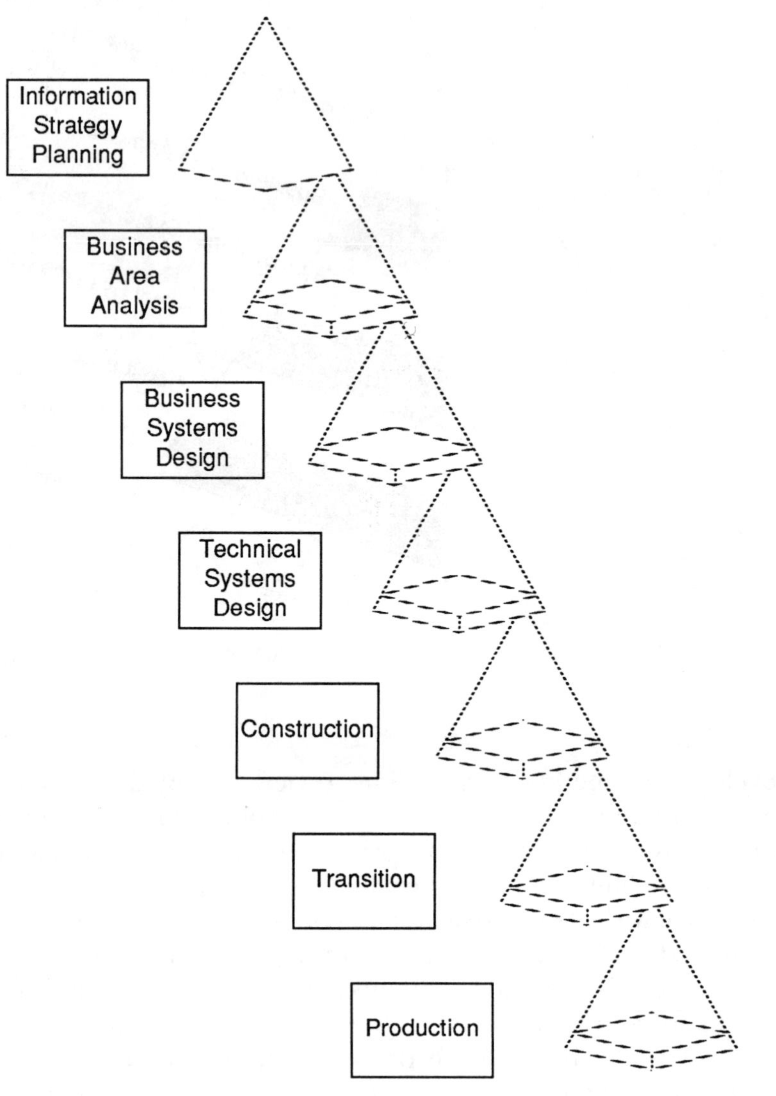

Generating Code With the Information Engineering Facility (IEF)

In terms of generating code with the IEF, one has to look at the relationships between the different diagrams and the generated code. There are many interesting things within action diagramming, and in generating and testing code using the tool set. The different diagrams that many have seen before include: entity-relationship, process hierarchy, process dependency, process action, dialog flow, screen design, procedure action, and data structure *(Figure 130)*.

Many have probably seen the entity-relationship diagram where you model the data; the process hierarchy diagram where you decompose the functions and processes within the organization; and the dependency diagram, which shows the dependencies between those processes. Each of these diagrams may or may not be used in generating code.

Some of the Diagrams That Are Used.

One is the entity relationship diagram, which goes into a data structure diagram, and is used to generate DB2 tables. It turns out that the IEF is generating code from COBOL. So the data structure in Figure 130 is a COBOL program to show the relationship between the diagrams and the generating code. However, the structure doesn't have to be COBOL. In terms of the data model created, it is involved in the segment layouts and the data access statements. One can see how that goes into the code. It is the same way with a screen designer when screens are painted. It is needed for generating a code.

Some of the Diagrams That Are Not Used.

The process dependency diagram and the process action diagram are not used for generating code; they are for documentation. So not all diagrams are used for generating code. Throughout time, the diagrams will be used more and more in terms of adding some type of artificial intelligence or knowledge-based decisions. An interesting diagram is the procedure action diagram. The

FIGURE 130. Different diagrams and the generated code.

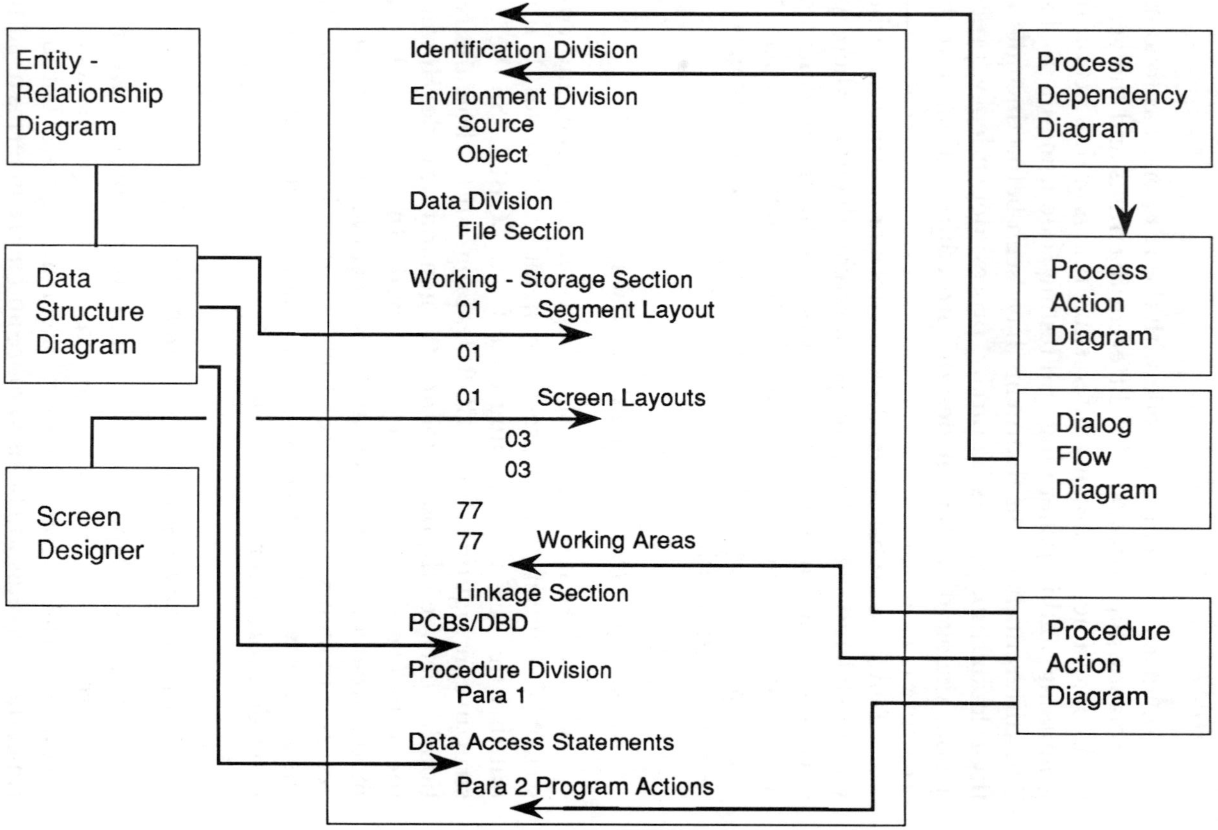

procedure action diagram describes the logic of the processor procedure. An action diagram in a business area analysis (the second level of methodology in Figure 128) describes what that process does. The next level of business system design describes how to do that process. The result of putting this logic in these action diagrams is a new programming language. Make no mistake about it—there has to be enough specified detail to generate code. Within the IEF, that is a new programming language (Figure 131).

Those are not *E*s in Figure 131. They represent the structure of the action diagrams. When creating the action diagram, the IEF will display the structure. Below the *E*s is the entity-relationship diagram. Only data described in the data model can be used in the action diagrams. The picture on the right of Figure 131 indicates that it is driven by a mouse and a keyboard.

The IEF provides syntax guides for additional things in the action diagrams. When building a statement, the IEF will make sure that you don't put something in there that should not be in there. If you are going to do an IF statement, then following that IF, there are certain things that can be put in there. Fortunately, the IEF won't force this, because it is context sensitive. For example, if you want to set a value for an attribute, it must be within CREATE or UPDATE so it knows where you are within the action diagram. It provides good guidance.

One of the problems in using the IEF for action diagramming is that view matching is tedious. All the information that is needed in an action diagram (Figure 131) must be identified to that action diagram. This is time consuming. The information needed for an action diagram must be described and view matching must be performed on it. The information that is passed between action diagrams and the information on screens must be matched. Stereotypical transactions (or stereotypical processing) should provide some relief in that area.

In terms of copying and editing, because of the view matching, it is not something you are going to do. If you ask a COBOL programmer to create a new program, he will look for an old program that matches it, copy it, edit it, and then globally change something. A user will not do that using the IEF. It slows down the process, and it includes an additional level of rigor. It is making

FIGURE 131. Action diagramming using the IEF.

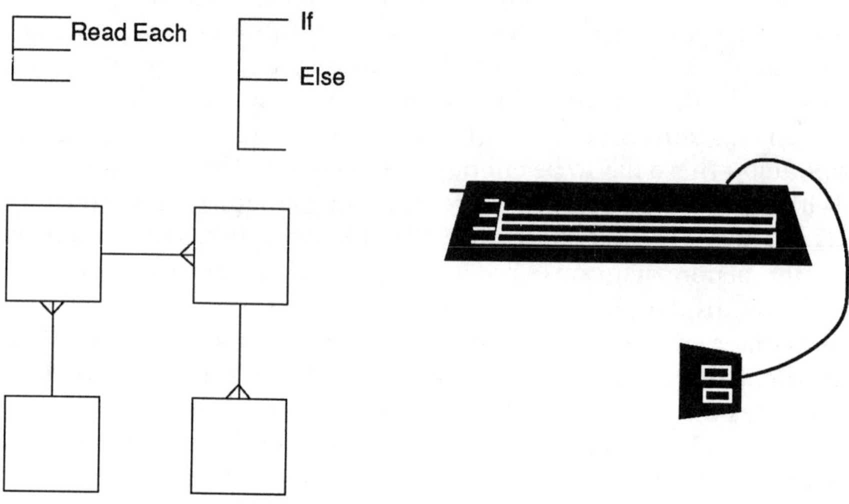

you create things and do things according to the IEF. Do not do the copying and editing; it is too tedious.

Additionally, the richness of the language is limited. It is a new language with no string manipulation. String manipulation is something you may want, and, eventually, that language will become richer. The last thing about action diagramming is, good programming practices should not be forgotten. It provides a way of programming, so don't forget all the things learned through the years.

Generating code using the IEF has extensive features that are detailed in Figure 132. Within the IEF there is a testing environment that is not working for us, so all of our testing has been done on IMS/DC by looking at both the screens and then looking at what has been created or deleted from the tables. The good news is that the code appears to be working and executing as it was intended. Once you have an understanding of the action diagrams, it seems to do what you want. When it doesn't do what you want, go to the action diagrams. The integrity of the model system should remain intact. If you go ahead and make that change to the COBOL source code, will you go back and make that change to the action diagrams? Make changes only to the action diagrams.

FIGURE 132. Generating code using the Information Engineering Facility.

Generating DB2 databases and tables

Generating code

Testing the generated code

Generating DB2 Databases and Tables

SQL, DDL, and IDCAMS (JCL) created from data structure diagram

Still must:

    Allocate VSAM disk space

    Consider security issues

    Adhere to corporate standards

    Work within corporate guidelines

Generating Code

VS COBOL II source with embedded SQL calls creates MFS, MFS Bypass or Non-BMS source

Still must:

    Allocate and specify libraries

    Specify load module packaging

    Identify screen and program names

    Copy load modules to transaction monitor libraries

Foreground versus background execution

Testing the Generated Code

Does IMS/DC and/or CICS talk with DB2?

IMS/DC testing experience

BTS testing experience

IEF mainframe testing environment

Testing the Generated Code

Generated code appears to be executing as intended

Looking at the action diagrams

Looking at the generated code

Software fix distribution

If you are going to make a change in your data structure diagram to add a field, go back into the entity relationship diagram. The model at Amoco has always been a big issue, so I suggest looking at the action diagrams when you have a problem. That should be the first place to look.

There is an interesting point about making modifications. I am suggesting that you make changes to the action diagrams, but what are you testing? You are testing the generated code. There are times when you look at the generated code if there are problems with the code generator, or if there are problems while generating code. That is rare, but on occasion you will proceed and look at the COBOL source code.

Methodology Weaknesses

We have found a number of what I call "methodology weaknesses." The following statements represent three weaknesses in the methodology:

- Identification of elementary processes is difficult.
- Lower-level issues impact higher-level methodology stages.
- Methodology is not complete at the business systems design level or below.

The identification of elementary processes is difficult. At the business area analysis level, the lowest-level elementary process has to be identified. People working on these business area analyses have a difficult time identifying what an elementary process is. There are several definitions, mainly within the methodology, and there are certainly several different interpretations. This is important because this is what the writing action diagrams are in generating code. If you are too high in terms of what an elementary process is, your action diagram will get long and, therefore, hard to maintain. If it is too small, then you leave too many of these things out—it is difficult.

Lower-level issues do impact higher-level methodology stages. When I am at a business area analysis, technical issues should not impact any of my decisions. It turns out that people are thinking about technical issues in the backs of their minds. They may be asking technical questions, and the methodology is that this should not be done. But, in reality, people do ask technical questions. That is a methodology weakness.

The methodology is not complete at the business systems design level or below. As an example, there is a task called process-to-procedure mapping. There are not enough guidelines within the methodology to say how these processes should be mapped into procedures. It is weak in terms of providing enough guidelines. For example, when I do data modeling, there is a definition for an "entity type." I know what an entity type is because I can say, "Does it meet definition?" When it comes to process-to-procedure mapping, there is a lot of flexibility and there are not enough guidelines. I am not saying that you should have one way of doing things where you impose a set of standards, but there have to be more guidelines within the methodology. You bring some baggage, and the methodology doesn't describe it.

Organizational and Cultural Issues

Methodology must be accepted by senior management. It must be sold to the client. It must be accepted.

Management expectations must be carefully managed. It is obvious that there is a lot of hype surrounding CASE and information engineering, and if those expectations are not managed, management is going to be disappointed. It is too easy to get these expectations out there, and they are not all going to come true. You have to manage the management expectations.

There is a long learning curve with information engineering.

There is a large up-front investment, which has to be dealt with in terms of short-term objectives and the reduced cost of implementing and maintaining systems.

Everything costs more. It is certainly more expensive to get married than to just pay the cost of the license. Experience shows that information engineering projects take longer. The projects take longer than the methodology suggests. They take longer than the consultants suggest. Also, the deliverables from projects are not always executable systems. You may have reports, diagrams, and plans—but it is not an executable system.

It is not easy to get people to share data—especially the

corporation's data. There is a hesitancy to share data, which has been a problem for a long time. Clients do not want to share their data. They feel they have paid for this data and are afraid to lose control of it. This is not new, but with a data-drive methodology, it is a consideration. Although you have this methodology, you still have to convince people that it is worthwhile to share the data.

In terms of the CASE product, there is productivity in the introduction of the IEF into an organization. In terms of productivity, there is a fast development time and a low development cost. Those are short-term issues. However, it is important to consider longer-term issues, such as lower maintenance cost and quality.

There is a learning curve for introducing an IEF to an organization. There should be some type of support organization, and members within that support organization should have expertise or knowledge in the complete IEF tool. They don't need to have complete methodology understanding. You have the tool set and the methodology. If you are not going to follow the methodology, then that is not an issue. As expertise grows throughout an organization, you may not need the support organization; its need will diminish.

Texas Instruments provides a well-written methodology guide for documentation on the IEF. There are also reference manuals available on the market. Although they are not where they should be, installation guides are getting better.

There is a lot to be learned about training. An IEF needs generalists and specialists. The IEF should develop some expertise in all phases of the methodology throughout the whole organization, and it should develop corresponding expertise in the tool set. The curriculum must encompass all phases of the tool set and training should be tool-set specific, because there is information strategy planning, business area analysis, and business systems design tools. It should be specific to the tool that is needed. I can be taught either internally or externally, depending on preference and the organization's structure. If there is no training department, then it will be done externally. If the company has a training department, it may be worthwhile to do it internally. It is important to have a flexible schedule. You need the training at the proper point in the project. You can't teach people business area analysis and then, two months later, expect them to go into business area analysis. It needs to be tied to the project. Training also needs to be supplemented by other support organizations, such as consultants. There is always some additional training that will be needed.

Consultants are expensive. The good news is that the need should diminish. When deciding on a consultant, you should select the firm and the consultants within the firm carefully. Consultants within the firm have varying levels of experience and expertise. This is common across all consultants. There are good consultants and bad ones. Each of the stages of the methodology requires a different set of skills. There may be a consultant who is wonderful for business area analysis. But when it comes to business systems design or information strategy planning, is he or she going to be good? The choice is critical for developing the internal expertise.

Client participation and commitment are mandatory in managing individual projects. It is especially necessary at the information strategy planning and business area analysis levels of the methodology. As you go down to lower levels of the methodology, the client need and participation in the project team diminish, but they are important. The duration depends on many factors—the scope of the project, the number of people on the project team, the complexity of the area or thing being modeled, and the level of detail. A steering committee should monitor and provide direction for the team. It is important for the project leader to have an understanding of the methodology. It is difficult to lead an information engineering project without having an understanding of what is to be achieved. There is no automated support for project management within the IEF. However, project management is at least aided by the use of information engineering because there is a set of tasks and deliverables. That helps the project leader, even though it is not automated. Successful projects have team member dedication. People have to be 80 to 100 percent dedicated—50 percent doesn't work. Project members working on information strategy planning or business area analysis level of methodology should be dedicated 100 percent of their time.

The objective with information engineering is to provide more information throughout the organization (Figure 133). That curve has to be shifted to the right, if the IEF has the strategic, tactical,

FIGURE 133. Information availability.

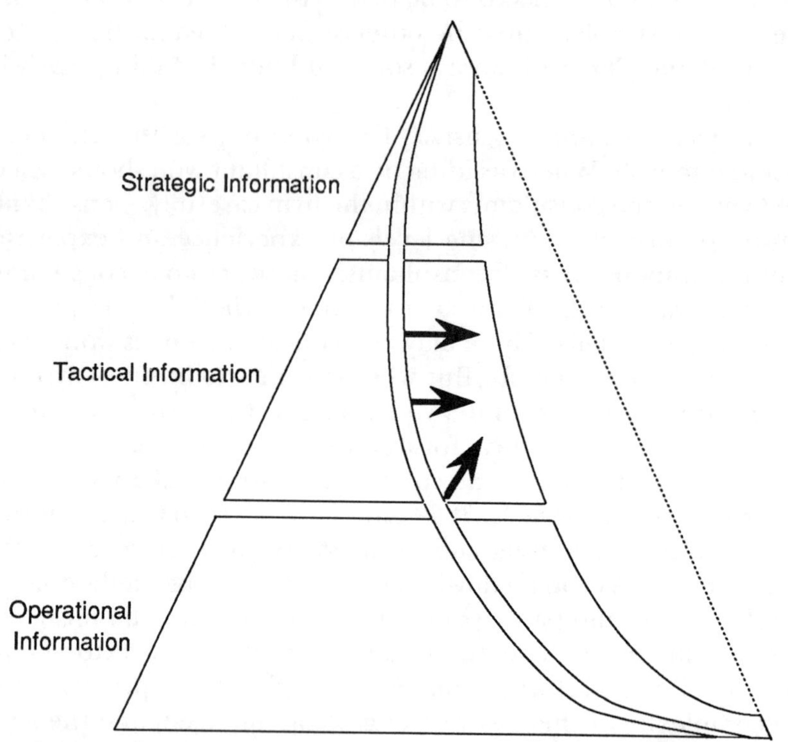

and operational information. It is assumed that the IEF provides all of the information at the operational level, less at the tactical level, and even less at the strategic level. The curve has to be shifted to provide more information. That leads to developing a corporate data model.

In theory, a company starts with one information strategy plan. It does top-down analysis. It follows the methodology word for word. In business areas, borders are not clearly defined. The reality is that there is a lot of information strategy planning done for an organization. The IEF may not want to integrate the data up to a high level of the methodology. Amoco is a large organization, and it is difficult to do one information strategy plan for all of it. So there is a lot of information strategy planning. Within that, there is other information strategy planning that gets initiated.

The business area borders are fuzzy and it creates an overlap. There are people who come in at the business area analysis level and the business system design level, which creates somewhat of a tradeoff. If you start with particular business area analyses and just do those business area analyses across the organization, how does that information get integrated into a higher level? It is difficult. The question becomes, how to create a corporate data model? Amoco's answer is a group called *Development Coordination.* The group's primary objective is to take the results of these projects and integrate them together. Some of their other objectives are to develop standards and guidelines. In addition, they integrate new and existing practices.

Each organization has implemented information engineering differently. One company may not do all the tasks; another company may do additional tasks; and another company may do them in different ways. So each company is going to have its own implementation of information engineering, resulting in many different approaches.

A company can't follow the methodology blindly; it needs to tailor the methodology to the organization. However, be careful not to allow the company to drift too far from the methodology, because it may not achieve the benefits it expects or the methodologies that were promised.

Keep in mind the following three statements about managing the implementation of information engineering into an organization:

- Qualify and quantify the methodology expectations.
- Document the implementation approach.
- Identify who is responsible for the implementation.

Qualify and quantify the methodology expectations. Know why the information engineering is being brought in; why the tool sets are being brought in; what the expectations are; how they are going to be measured; and over what period of time these benefits will occur. Manage the implementation as you would any other project. In terms of implementation approach issues, consider these questions: What are your expectations from a pilot project? Do you staff it with the best person or the average person? What do you want to achieve from a pilot project? How are other projects going to be initiated? Do you take people from pilot projects and put them on additional projects? What impact is it going to have on personnel? Are people encouraged to take risks? What support organizations are needed to implement the methodology? Document the approach to the implementations and identify somebody responsible for it. A person or project team should be given sole responsibility for that implementation. They should also be given the ability to change the implementation approach.

The lessons that have been learned are:

- Data-driven methodology takes a long time to implement.
- Client commitment must be established, especially for the information strategy planning and business area analysis levels.
- The methodology and the IEF are tightly coupled.
- The methodology is more difficult to master than the tool set.
- You must organize to provide methodology and tool set support.
- New team members must have a project leader who is competent.
- You can't tell how deep a puddle is until you step in it.

APPENDIX

A.1 COMPARISON OF PRODUCT FUNCTIONS

A variety of CASE products are listed in Figure 134. They are divided according to the area of the system development life cycle they support. These five areas of CASE product support are:

- *Products supporting requirements definition* and structured engineering. These have structured diagramming techniques, such as Yourdon-DeMarco, Gene-Sarson, or Jackson approaches, and support at least the three basic structured engineering diagramming types: data flow, control flow, and entity-relationship.

- *Products supporting analysis and design aids* for structured development.

- *Products that generate application code*, principally COBOL generators.

- *Products that support a full software engineering life cycle*, from planning to code generation, and including an information repository to maintain enterprise models, data models, and process models.

- *Products that generate provably correct specifications*.

Grouping products in a manner similar to this helps to compare and evaluate the many available CASE products on the mar-

553

FIGURE 134. Selected CASE products.

Products Supporting Requirements Definition

ANALYST TOOLKIT	Yourdon Software
AUTO/ASYST	ASYST Technologies
Design	Adpac Corporation
DesignAid	Nastec Corporation
Design Graphics System	CADWARE Group
Excelerator	Index Technology Corp.
The Manager	MSP
TIP	Technology Info. Products

Products Supporting Analysis and Design Aids

Appl. System Development Env.	Digital Equipment Corporation
Data Resources Leverage	D. Appleton Company
Design Machine	Ken Orr & Associates
DESIGN/1, METHOD/1	Arthur Andersen
ER-Modeler Package	Peter Chen & Associates
IDMS/Architect	Cullinet Software, Inc.
InfoModel	Info-Model, Inc.
Intelligent Assistant	Leading Software Technologies
MAESTRO	Softlab Systems, Inc.
MULTI-PRO	Cap Gemini Software Products
NETRON/CAP	Netron
PRIDE-ISEM	M. Bryce & Associates
ProKit Analyst	McDonnell Douglas ISG
ProMod	ProMod, Inc.
PSL/PSA Structured Architect	Meta Systems
Structured Analysis Tool	Tektronix
TEAMWORK	Cadre Technologies
vsDesigner	Visual Software

Products that Generate Application Code

APS	Sage Systems, Inc.
GAMMA	KnowledgeWare, Inc.
PACBASE	CGI Systems, Inc.
TELON	Pansophic Systems, Inc.
TRANSFORM	Transform Logic Corporation

Products that Support a Full Software Engineering Life Cycle

CorVision	Cortex Corporation
Information Engineering Facility	Texas Instruments
Information Engineering Workbench	KnowledgeWare, Inc.

Products that Generate Provably Correct Specifications

USE.IT	Higher Order Software, Inc.

ket. Comparison of products should be based upon the particular area of functionality. One organization may prefer to obtain a product that supports the full software engineering life cycle, or information engineering life cycle. Another organization may prefer to put together a tool set of CASE products, each with its particular strength in a given area. If there are tradeoffs to be made between CASE product offerings, they should be made within a framework of a planned CASE environment and the particular CASE functions that are considered to be most valuable to the organization.

Planning the CASE environment and obtaining management support and commitment are the first necessary elements to develop an effective CASE environment. After that has been accomplished, then the functionality of CASE products can be compared against the perceived requirements and against competing products.

Some comments about each of the above categories follows.

Products Supporting Requirements Definition and Structured Engineering

There are a great many CASE products for requirements definition, and they support a number of different forms of structured engineering methodologies. These tools use different theoretical bases, and support the early analysis and design phases of the CASE life cycle. Most of the vendors listed are offering more than the requirements definition tools, however, and some are committed to develop their products to support other CASE phases up to an interface with code generators.

These CASE tools may contain structured techniques that support one or more of the structured methodologies that have been advanced over the years, such as the methodologies of Yourdon-DeMarco, Gene-Sarson, Warnier-Orr, Nassi-Shneiderman, Michael Jackson, and Constantine. They include the following:

- Entity-relationship diagrams
- Process decomposition diagrams
- Proces dependency diagrams
- Data flow diagrams

- Data structure diagrams
- Process action diagrams

They may be used in business system design, design modeling, process modeling, or data modeling. Most of the tools in this category started for specific functions, then have been developed to cover more of the CASE life cycle. Some information about representative tools is given here, but it should not be taken as the present state. The field is moving rapidly, and most of the tools on the market are being enhanced regularly. For example, Excelerator, from Index Technology, started intitially as a computer-aided diagramming tool, but now has an automated information repository and supports automatic design analysis and checking functions.

CASE tools that support structured engineering are most useful to organizations that do not want the formal and complex structure of a full information engineering methodology. The training period is relatively short, and a number of different tools can be tested in an experimental way. Various groups in the organization may use different tools. They offer an excellent way to start CASE development work at a lower budget, and to train as the work proceeds. A number of corporations have successfully pieced together a few selected CASE tools. They have obtained much of the available value from the use of CASE, yet have retained considerable flexibility in their systems methods.

Products That Provide Analysis and Design Aids

There is another group of CASE products that provides analysis and design aids for structured development, but does not support all of the basic types of structured diagrams that are needed to represent a software system, such as entity-relationship diagrams, decomposition diagrams, and data flow diagrams. These tools support selected diagram types. They automatically enforce the rigorous procedures of specific methodologies, maintain an integrated design repository, ensure the consistency of the database, and generate system documentation automatically.

Some of the products that provide analysis and design aids include Design Machine from Ken Orr & Associates, DESIGN/1 from Arthur Andersen, the ER-Modeler Package from Peter Chen & Associates, ProKit Analyst from McDonnell Douglas, ProMod from ProMod, Inc., PSL/PSA from Meta Systems, and Teamwork from Cadre Technologies, Inc.

Products That Generate Application Code

The system components of COBOL application code generators include a data dictionary, librarian, documentation manager, and application code generator. They usually incorporate an interactive screen menu interface for specifying design-level information, such as edit criteria, screen layouts, database descriptions, data access, and control procedures. Some constructs cannot be specified by using such design facilities, and must be written in custom COBOL code.

COBOL code generators are complex, and are designed for use by professional programmers. They usually do not have user-friendly interfaces or support the degree of integrated functionality or database management capability provided by application generators that are fully integrated into CASE development systems. The vendors of COBOL application generators are constantly improving their products, however, and are extending them back to the CASE design phase to integrate them with other CASE systems. More CASE products are coming on the market with approaches to generalized interfaces to code generators, such as the available COBOL code generators. CASE structured engineering and structured development tools that integrate with a COBOL generator essentially start supporting the entire CASE life-cycle process, and become competitive with the information engineering packages.

In addition, modern COBOL generators are generating code that is competitive in run-time efficiency to hand-generated COBOL code. This, obviously, will greatly increase programmer productivity. It also allows a continuing commitment to COBOL, to support the vast library of COBOL programs that many organizations currently have.

Some of the COBOL code generators on the market include APS from Sage Systems, GAMMA from KnowledgeWare, PAC-BASE from CGI Systems, Inc., TELON from Pansophic Systems, Inc., and TRANSFORM from Transform Logic Corporation.

Products That Support a Full Software Engineering Life Cycle

These products support all the functionality that the above products support, from planning to code generation, and include an information repository to maintain enterprise models, data models, and process models. They are usually called information engineering products. Information engineering is an accepted term for a life-cycle process that is based on a top-down view of the organization's business and data processing strategies.

Information engineering products are necessarily a set of tightly integrated, formal techniques in which business system design models, design models, process models, and data models are assembled in a comprehensive information repository that may be called an *encyclopedia*. The models are used in a step-wise, tightly defined life-cycle process to develop and maintain software systems.

Because information engineering methodologies are highly integrated throughout the full CASE process, they can provide an organization-wide set of automated disciplines that can be interlinked. They can help to ensure that the strategic demands of the organization are satisfied in the strategic applications that are developed. All interfaces within the CASE process are seamless because of the automation of the tools. A common information repository ensures that all process and data definitions are consistent.

The major functional areas of information engineering are: information strategy planning, business area analysis, system design, and construction. The functions and diagrams that are included are:

- *Information strategy planning.* In this step, the organization's goals and Critical Success Factors are collected in the information repository, or encyclopedia. An overview of the entity-relationship model is created. Data subjects are addressed. Some of the outputs of this step are:

  –Enterprise model

  –Organization chart

  –Hierarchy of goals and critical success factors

–Decomposition of functions

–Function dependency diagram

–Matrices showing relationships among planning information

- *Business area analysis.* In this step, the processes are determined that are required to provide information for specific business areas. The interrelationship of the processes and the data that are needed are determined. Fully normalized data models are produced for each business area. Some of the outputs of this step are:

–Fully normalized data models

–Entity-relationship model

–Process decomposition diagram

–Process dependency model

–Process/entity matrix

–Process life cycle diagram

- *System design.* In this step, selected processes to be implemented are specified by direct end-user involvement, data flow analysis, and formal procedures. Systems are designed using the fully normalized data model. Working prototypes of the application are produced to demonstrate the sequences of screens, reports, menus, decision trees, and procedural logic. Some of the outputs of this step are:

–Data structure diagram

–Data descriptions

–Data navigation diagram

–Data flow diagram

–Action diagram

–Decision tree

–Dialog design

–Screen layouts

–Report layouts

–Prototype systems

- *System construction.* In this step, the application system is constructed using a variety of code generators, fourth-generation languages, and decision support tools. The whole process has attempted to accumulate sufficient details of the specifications so that the system can be built automatically from consistent, computable specifications. Some of the outputs of this step are:

−Program view of data

−Data descriptions

−Action diagram with code

−Fourth-generation language code

−Prototype application systems

The information engineering approach is the most powerful and comprehensive set of CASE tools available. It is excellent for building strategic systems on demand. It requires considerable management commitment and high expenditures of money and time in training, however. It necessitates that the staff adopt a completely new view of systems development. The entire system development process must be completely integrated under a rigid set of procedures.

Some of the diagram types that typically are supported by information engineering systems include:

* Decomposition
* Data flow
* Dependency
* Action
* Data analysis
* Data structure
* Entity-relationship
* Data navigation
* Decision trees and tables
* State transition
* Dialog design

The most comprehensive information engineering systems on the market include Information Engineering Facility (IEF) from Texas Instruments, Inc., and Information Engineering Workbench (IEW) from KnowledgeWare, Inc. Other information engineering systems available include CorVision and APPLICATION FAC-

TORY from Cortex Corporation, which is in the DEC VAX VMS environment.

Products That Generate Provably Correct Specifications

One of the goals of the CASE approach is to prove the logical correctness and completeness of the system specifications. The design analyzer component of CASE tools provides this proof. The most common techniques used in CASE products to validate the specifications are:

- Program logic, used in many CASE products.
- Expert systems heuristics, and associated rules of inference, which have successfully been used by KnowledgeWare in the Information Engineering Workbench, and are being used by more CASE products in more areas.
- Mathematical algorithms, which were pioneered in the USE.IT product from Higher Order Software, Inc.

The HOS techniques use a type of tree structure with mathematical properties that can be proven to be logically correct. Applications that can be specified in the tree structure can be tested for mathematical correctness.

The approach of the HOS concept is significant because it has proven that any application that can be specified following certain rules can be tested mathematically for logical correctness and consistency. Those specifications that have been proven to be logically correct may then be converted automatically into program code.

Product Functionality

Figure 135 provides a rough assessment of the capabilities of a number of CASE products. Products should not be selected from this matrix, but it should be used to note the possible functionality of a number of well-known CASE products. Products should be selected by:

- Reviewing the desirable features of CASE products, noted in Chapter 4.

FIGURE 135. CASE product functionality matrix.

	Hardware					Life Cycle Coverage					Components						Graphics			Diagrams Supported					Integrated Functions						Methodologies				
	IBM PC/XT, AT	VAX Mate, VAXstation	Apollo, Sun, IBM RT CP	DEC VAX	IBM mainframe	Analysis	Design	Construction	Installation	Maintenance	Diagramming Tools	PC Respository	Mainframe Repository	Design Analyzer	Code Generator	Expert System Rules	Color	Mouse	Windows	Data Flow Diagrams	Decomposition Diagrams	Data Model Diagrams	Data Navigation	Action Diagrams	Screen/Report Painting	Dictionary Definitions	Data Base Mgmt. System	Prototyping Tools	Procedural Language	Networking Capability	Information Engineering	Yourdon-DeMarco	Gane-Sarson	Jackson	Others
Adpac	•	•	•	•	X	X	X	•	•	X	X	•	X	X	•	•	•	•	•	X	X	X	X	•	•	X	•	•	X	•	•	X	X	X	X
Arthur Andersen	X	•	•	•	•	X	X	•	•	•	X	X	X	X	•	•	X	X	•	•	X	X	•	•	X	•	X	X	•	X	•	X	•	•	X
ASYST Technologies	X	•	•	•	•	X	X	•	•	X	X	X	•	X	•	•	•	•	•	X	X	X	X	•	X	X	•	•	•	•	X	X	X	X	X
Cadre Technologies	•	X	X	X	•	X	X	X	X	X	X	X	X	X	•	•	X	X	X	X	X	•	•	•	X	X	X	•	•	X	X	X	•	•	X
The CADWARE Group	X	X	X	•	•	X	X	•	•	•	X	X	X	X	•	•	X	X	X	X	X	X	•	•	X	X	•	X	•	X	•	X	X	•	X
Cap Gemini	X	•	•	•	X	X	X	•	•	•	X	X	X	•	•	•	•	•	X	X	•	•	•	•	X	X	•	•	•	X	•	X	X	•	•
CGI Systems	X	•	•	•	X	X	X	X	X	X	X	X	X	•	X	•	•	•	X	•	•	•	•	•	X	X	X	•	•	X	•	X	•	•	X
Chen & Associates	X	•	•	•	X	X	X	•	•	•	X	X	X	X	•	•	X	X	•	X	•	X	•	•	•	X	•	•	•	•	•	•	•	•	X
Computer Command	X	•	X	X	X	•	•	X	•	X	•	•	X	X	X	•	•	•	X	•	•	•	•	•	X	X	•	X	•	•	•	•	•	•	X
Cortez Corporation	X	X	•	X	•	X	X	X	X	X	X	X	X	X	X	•	X	X	X	X	•	X	X	X	X	X	X	X	X	X	X	X	•	•	•
Cullinet	X	•	•	•	•	X	X	X	•	•	X	X	X	X	X	•	X	X	•	X	•	X	•	X	X	X	X	X	X	•	•	X	X	•	•
D. Appleton Co.	•	•	•	X	X	X	X	•	•	•	X	•	X	X	X	X	•	•	•	X	•	X	X	•	•	X	X	X	•	•	•	X	•	•	X
DEC	•	X	•	•	•	X	X	X	X	X	X	•	X	•	X	•	•	X	X	X	•	•	X	•	•	•	•	X	•	X	•	•	•	•	•
Dialogic Systems	•	•	•	•	X	•	•	X	X	X	•	•	X	•	•	•	•	•	X	•	•	•	X	•	•	•	X	•	•	•	•	•	•	•	•
Hewlett-Packard	•	X	X	X	•	X	X	X	X	X	X	X	X	X	•	•	X	X	X	X	X	•	•	•	•	X	X	•	•	X	•	X	•	•	X
Index Technology	X	X	•	X	•	X	X	•	•	•	X	X	X	X	•	•	•	X	•	X	X	X	•	•	X	X	•	X	•	X	•	X	X	X	X
Info-Model	X	•	•	•	•	X	X	•	•	•	X	X	•	X	•	•	X	•	X	•	•	X	•	•	•	X	•	•	•	•	X	•	•	•	•

FIGURE 135. (Cont.)

	Hardware					Life Cycle Coverage					Components						Graphics			Diagrams Supported					Integrated Functions						Methodologies				
	IBM PC/XT, AT	VAX Mate, VAXstation	Apollo, Sun, IBM RT CP	DEC VAX	IBM mainframe	Analysis	Design	Construction	Installation	Maintenance	Diagramming Tools	PC Respository	Mainframe Repository	Design Analyzer	Code Generator	Expert System Rules	Color	Mouse	Windows	Data Flow Diagrams	Decomposition Diagrams	Data Model Diagrams	Data Navigation	Action Diagrams	Screen/Report Painting	Dictionary Definitions	Data Base Mgmt. System	Prototyping Tools	Procedural Language	Networking Capability	Information Engineering	Yourdon-DeMarco	Gane-Sarson	Jackson	Others
Ken Orr Associates	X	•	•	•	•	X	X	•	•	•	X	X	•	X	•	•	•	X	X	•	X	X	•	•	X	X	X	X	X	•	•	•	•	•	X
KnowledgeWare	X	•	•	•	X	X	X	X	X	•	X	X	X	X	X	X	X	X	X	X	X	X	•	X	X	X	•	•	•	•	X	X	X	•	•
Leading SW Technologies	•	•	•	•	X	•	•	X	X	X	•	•	•	•	X	X	•	•	•	X	•	•	•	•	•	•	•	•	•	•	•	X	X	X	X
M. Bryce & Associates	•	•	•	X	X	X	X	X	X	X	•	•	•	•	•	•	•	•	•	•	•	•	•	•	•	X	•	•	•	•	•	•	•	•	X
McDonnell Douglas ISG	X	•	•	•	•	X	X	•	•	•	X	X	•	X	•	•	X	X	X	X	•	•	•	•	X	X	•	•	•	•	•	•	X	•	•
Meta Systems	X	•	X	X	X	X	X	X	X	X	X	X	X	X	•	•	•	X	X	X	X	X	X	•	X	X	X	X	X	X	•	X	X	X	X
Meta Software	X	•	X	•	•	•	X	•	•	•	X	X	•	•	•	•	•	X	•	•	•	•	•	•	•	•	•	•	•	•	•	•	•	•	•
MSP	X	•	•	•	X	X	X	X	X	X	•	•	X	X	X	X	X	X	X	X	X	X	X	•	•	•	•	•	•	X	X	X	X	X	X
Nastec Corp.	X	X	•	•	•	X	X	X	•	•	X	•	•	X	X	•	•	X	X	X	X	X	•	•	•	X	•	•	•	X	•	X	X	•	X
Netron	X	•	•	X	X	•	X	X	•	X	•	•	•	•	X	X	•	•	•	•	•	•	•	•	X	•	•	X	•	•	•	•	•	•	X
Polytron	X	•	•	X	•	•	•	X	X	X	•	X	•	•	X	•	•	•	•	•	•	•	•	•	•	•	•	•	•	X	•	•	•	•	•
ProMod, Inc.	X	•	•	X	•	X	X	X	•	•	X	X	X	X	X	•	•	X	•	X	•	X	X	•	•	X	X	X	•	•	•	X	•	•	X
Sage Software, Inc.	X	•	•	•	X	X	X	X	X	X	X	X	X	X	X	•	X	•	•	X	•	X	X	•	X	X	X	X	•	•	•	X	X	X	X
Softlab, Inc.	X	•	•	•	•	X	X	X	X	X	X	X	X	X	X	X	X	X	X	X	•	X	•	•	•	X	•	•	X	•	•	•	•	•	X
SYSCORP Intl. Co.	X	•	•	•	•	X	X	•	•	•	X	X	•	X	•	•	•	X	X	X	X	•	•	•	X	X	•	X	•	•	•	•	•	•	X
Tech. & Info. Products	X	•	•	•	X	X	X	X	•	X	X	•	X	X	X	X	X	X	X	X	X	X	X	•	•	X	X	X	•	•	X	X	X	X	X
Texas Instruments	X	•	•	•	X	X	X	X	X	X	X	X	X	X	X	X	X	X	•	X	X	X	X	X	X	X	X	X	X	X	X	•	•	•	•

FIGURE 135. (Cont.)

	Hardware					Life Cycle Coverage					Components						Graphics			Diagrams Supported					Integrated Functions						Methodologies				
	IBM PC/XT, AT	VAX Mate, VAXstation	Apollo, Sun, IBM RT CP	DEC VAX	IBM mainframe	Analysis	Design	Construction	Installation	Maintenance	Diagramming Tools	PC Respository	Mainframe Repository	Design Analyzer	Code Generator	Expert System Rules	Color	Mouse	Windows	Data Flow Diagrams	Decomposition Diagrams	Data Model Diagrams	Data Navigation	Action Diagrams	Screen/Report Painting	Dictionary Definitions	Data Base Mgmt. System	Prototyping Tools	Procedural Language	Networking Capability	Information Engineering	Yourdon-DeMarco	Gane-Sarson	Jackson	Others
Transform Logic Corp.	•	•	•	•	X	•	•	X	X	X	•	•	X	X	X	X	•	•	•	•	•	•	•	•	X	X	X	X	•	•	•	•	•	•	•
Tektronix	X	X	X	X	•	X	X	X	X	X	X	•	•	X	X	•	X	•	•	X	X	•	•	•	•	X	•	•	•	•	•	X	•	•	X
Yourdon Software	X	•	•	•	•	X	X	•	•	•	X	X	X	X	•	•	X	X	•	X	X	X	•	•	•	X	•	X	•	X	•	X	•	•	X

- Stepping through the evaluation and selection process provided in Chapter 6.

The product functionality matrix in Figure 133 is not intended to be complete. Most developers of CASE products are continually improving their products and adding new functionality. Any of them may now be superior to the amount of functionality shown in the figure. This book is a "how-to" book, not a current description of available products. The figure is simply presented as a guide to the search for the product that meets your particular specifications.